An Introduction to
Physical Methods of
Treatment in Psychiatry

Chapter on the Treatment of Epilepsy

ERIC WEST
M.B.(London), M.R.C.P., M.R.C.Psych.

Consulting Psychiatrist, Belmont Hospital, Sutton, Surrey

Chapter on Diet, Vitamins and Endocrines

JOHN POLLITT
M.D.(London), F.R.C.P., F.R.C.Psych.

*Physician in Psychological Medicine and Lecturer
in the Medical School, St Thomas's Hospital, London*

*Chapter on Drug Treatment in Childhood
and Early Adolescence*

EVA FROMMER
M.B.(London), M.R.C.Psych.

*Psychiatrist in Charge of the Child Psychiatric Clinic,
St Thomas's Hospital, London*

An Introduction to Physical Methods of Treatment in Psychiatry

WILLIAM SARGANT

M.A., M.B.(Cantab.), F.R.C.P., F.R.C.Psych.

*Physician in Charge of the Department of Psychological Medicine and
Lecturer in the Medical School, St Thomas's Hospital, London.
Formerly Physician, Maudsley Hospital, London*

ELIOT SLATER

M.A., M.D.(Cantab.), F.R.C.P., F.R.C.Psych.

*Formerly Physician in Psychological Medicine, National Hospital, Queen
Square, London. Physician, Maudsley Hospital, London*

assisted by

DESMOND KELLY

M.D.(London), M.R.C.P., M.R.C.Psych.

Consulting Psychiatrist, St George's Hospital, London

SCIENCE HOUSE

NEW YORK

FIFTH EDITION

*Dedicated
to the Memory of
Edward Mapother*

THE observation and classification of mental disorders have been so exclusively psychological that we have not sincerely realised the fact that they illustrate the same pathological principles as other diseases, are produced in the same way, and must be investigated in the same spirit of positive research. Until this be done, I see no hope of improvement in our knowledge of them, and no use in multiplying books about them.

HENRY MAUDSLEY,
Goulstonian Lectures, 1870.

PREFACE TO THE FIFTH EDITION

In a few months now, at this time of writing, the last of us (W.S.) to retain clinical connections will be leaving his teaching hospital and National Health Service beds when he reaches the official retiring age. This is, then, the last edition of this book which we shall write. The book has been founded on personal bedside experience; and any further private practice, with much smaller numbers of beds than one controls in a hospital, will hardly provide that flow of personal treatment experience which is required for keeping our findings up to date. We hope that our collaborators, Dr Peter Dally and Dr Desmond Kelly, will be persuaded to adopt and foster a manual which has been so widely read all over the world and in many translations. We are convinced that the teaching, which is founded on varied and extensive personal clinical experience, has something very important to contribute to a field of knowledge and practice in which the contribution of scientific method must also play an increasing role.

We do not regard these two approaches as in any way in conflict; they are, indeed, complementary. One initiates; the other provides the necessary critique. In the course of one's day to day practice, vague gestalts and isolated and unexpected treatment findings emerge from the background 'noise'. These become treatment hunches and get tried out in practical application. By watching carefully what then occurs, one soon gets a very good idea of whether a new treatment idea is working out or not. One's own lengthening experience does, in fact, also provide quite good machinery for self-criticism. Nevertheless, as we all know, we may yet deceive ourselves, and be more optimistic (or pessimistic) than the observations warrant. It is just as likely that, when we have varied a treatment technique in one important respect which has been planned, other aspects of treatment have been altered too. We may then erroneously attribute to the planned variation of treatment something which has arisen from other causes. No one can apply adequate correction to his own work. So it comes that the treatment methods which are worked out in clinical practice, sometimes suggested by an advance in scientific understanding, sometimes wholly empirical, have to be checked in properly conducted experiments. These include the 'double-blind' experiments which have come so much into fashion.

In the early years of therapeutic experimentation in psychiatry, the trials carried out were often of a crude kind, in which observational data were collected by members of the team much less experienced than the clinician in charge. The observational data were, in fact, much less detailed and subtle than the observations which were stored in the memory, the conscious and pre-conscious mind of the un-trammelled clinician, working with his own patients in his own way. It was, then, far from surprising that again and again the results obtained by the latter could not be supported by the double-blind trial. The lack of confirmatory evidence, unfortunately however, was sometimes taken as disconfirmation or rebuttal. The conscientious clinician, moreover, would be very unwilling to let his patients go into a controlled therapeutic experiment, in which they would be treated as units instead of as individuals, and be given drugs and doses not chosen to suit them individually but ruthlessly standardised. It is a great pleasure, accordingly, to see that compromises between a trial and individual treatment are possible, as has been carried out lately with the investigation of the normothymic effects of the lithium ion in affective disorders (Coppen et al., 1971). There is, we believe, every reason to hope that the two processes of making pro-posals and checking with results will go forward together. The always exploring, working clinician will expect to hear the results of checks on his work; the sceptical tester will plan his experiment to allow the widest freedom for individualisation of treatment, in subjects and controls, apart from the chosen variable under test. This is in fact by far the best kind of trial, i.e. one that is conducted against a wide background of patient characteristics, rather than one that has been artificially homogenised. Let us match members of pairs, but not restrict the field of trial.

It is with a certain degree of gratification that we can look back on the historical record of all the treatment methods which have been proposed or modified in successive editions of this book. Much of what we have published has become standard practice; very little has been proved wrong. We have been able to incorporate advances as they occurred, and, indeed, we have used this book as our main channel of communication rather than articles in journals. Our worst error, so far as we are aware, was to say in early editions that the short-acting barbiturates did not have serious tendencies to habitua-tion. The changes in therapeutic methods and therapeutic results which we have also seen between the appearance of the first edition in 1944 and the present one have fulfilled what were then considered to be rather wild dreams about the possibilities and future of a physical approach to psychiatric treatment.

This book might have been almost indefinitely enlarged, if it had been expanded to an adequate reference source and a critique of work done by so many hundreds of therapeutic teams. We have preferred rather to keep the book as small as convenient, and continue to base it mainly on personal treatment experience. In the present edition much has been rewritten. There is a new chapter on prefrontal leucotomy, which is justified by the new and more accurate stereotactic technique which is now possible. With traumatic side-effects so much reduced, the potentialities of this operation have been much enlarged. A new chapter on sleep treatment combined with antidepressant drugs and ECT has also been written. By such methods we are now beginning to glimpse the possibility of a person going through even a long and distressing psychiatric illness shielded from the worst miseries, by being treated, while mainly asleep, in such a way that, at the end, recovery occurs as from a dream, in which nearly all memory of the sufferings of illness and the experiences of treatment has been lost. It is, in fact, possible that we are on the way to a psychiatric equivalent of the anaesthesia for surgery. The implications are enormous.

The chapter on the epilepsies has been rewritten by Dr Eric West, who has always remained close to intimate clinical experience in this field; and Dr Pollitt has extensively revised the chapter on diet, vitamins and endocrines. We also think it timely to ask Dr Eva Frommer to discuss recent advances in drug treatment in children and early adolescents which she has done so much to pioneer at St Thomas's Hospital. All chapters have, in fact, been brought up to date in respect of treatments used practically in teaching hospital units, such as at St Thomas's, or in ordinary open-ward psychiatric beds at Belmont hospital. We have even decided to retain the chapter on insulin coma; for several times a year, when all other methods have failed to help a patient, we have still observed recovery with insulin sopor or coma added to other more easily practised methods. Though this is a book on physical treatments, we have never tried to play down the great importance of helping in every place where help can be given, e.g. in social and psychotherapeutic ways as well as the physical ones. So psychotherapy at one end of the scale, as well as insulin coma at the other, keep their place here.

We have had a very happy time in the psychiatry we have practised and taught during the last thirty years. For the dedicated doctor, there is still no need to contemplate leaving the bedside to join the ranks of the professors or superintendents or administrators or statisticians. One cannot successfully live in two such worlds at once. The five editions of this book have showed how many real practical advances in treatment there are still to be made using a personal bedside approach. We believe that it is only by this dedication to the single individual patient that the best results can also be obtained, only if his needs are put first, only if no method is left forgotten or unused if it has chances not as yet explored. We have taken part in the beginning of a revolution in treatment and have watched the transformation of the natural history of so many mental disorders from terrible causes of chronic suffering and incapacity into much more hopeful and manageable states. We hope that those we have taught will have the optimism and endurance to get and to provide the best out of their work, and that they will always have in their psychiatric careers the same happiness we have enjoyed.

WILLIAM SARGANT.
ELIOT SLATER.

PREFACE TO THE FIRST EDITION

During the last ten years advance in the therapeutic aspects of psychiatry may be said at last to have got safely under way, and it is the singular good fortune of the authors to have spent this time, the greater part of it at the Maudsley Hospital, in active clinical work and largely unhampered by administrative duties. We have had the great privilege, under the auspices of the Rockefeller Foundation, the one of us in spending the better part of a year in close association with psychoanalytic teaching and treatment in the U.S.A., the other in studying for a similar time in the German School of constitutional psychiatry founded by Rüdin. We had the inspiration of working under the late Professor Mapother at the Maudsley, and learned from him, we believe, a balanced view in which the genetic, the somatic and the psychopathological aspects all met their due appraisement. The exigencies of war, which brought us to one of the two evacuation centres of the Maudsley Hospital, have tested the principles we have absorbed, in the hard school of work under pressure and on the largest scale. These principles, and the techniques which represent their embodiment in practice, form the subject of this book.

This is not a complete text-book on the subject. Many techniques and details of technique, with which we are not personally acquainted, have been omitted. We have no knowledge of drug withdrawal states; but there are plenty of publications on the topic. We make no mention of hydrotherapy, physical training, massage or indeed of occupational therapy. We do not doubt their efficacy in selected cases, but cannot discuss with confidence their precise indications. The chapter on the malarial treatment of general paralysis is drawn very largely from the publications of the workers at Horton, with whose experience ours is not to be compared. But in general we have tried to write about only those subjects of which we have made direct clinical study on a fair scale. Only personal experience can teach one to know when a given method of treatment holds out no hope of benefit, so that it is not given unnecessarily, to pick the appropriate treatment for the individual case, and to know just how much can be expected from it.

The book has been written primarily for the young clinician in psychiatry, for the general practitioner, and for the student, who come to psychiatry from general medicine, and properly demand some community of approach. We hope that it will also prove useful to the psychiatric nurse, on whose skill the success of treatment so greatly depends. For readers with little acquaintance with psychiatric terminology the introduction may, perhaps, prove a little difficult and could then be postponed till after reading the rest of the book. We think, however, that the reader who approaches the subject from general medicine will find its basic principles less nebulous and alien than some of our colleagues would have us believe.

We are very conscious of the book's many faults and limitations. Much that is written is in a dogmatic strain, and we have nowhere discussed controversial points at the length they would have deserved, nor adduced more than a fraction of the evidence that might have been brought for and against the views that we have stated. These views are the result of personal experience, and we have thought it best, in the interests of coherence and simplicity, to present them uncomplicated by critical discussions which would leave the average reader only confused. For other faults we can only beg the indulgence of the reader, and hope that they will inspire the criticism and comment that will enable them, perhaps, to be corrected.

Nevertheless, there should be sufficient material here to provide a basis for active treatment in the psychiatric ward of a general hospital, or in the reception and treatment wards of a mental hospital. These methods have served us well as a selected battery for the treatment of the early and recoverable cases seen at the Maudsley and at Sutton. The variety and range of methods of treatment now available will by many people be found more surprising than the vast lacunae still left uncovered by recent progress. Psychiatry is now at a critical stage in its development. The enlarging interests of general medicine have at last brought within its compass a subject which had its birth in a very different field, fathered by metaphysics on the asylum care of the insane. The fertilising influence of the new approach has only just begun to make itself felt.

We have numerous people to thank for their help, but firstly Dr Russell Fraser, to whom we owe so much for his constant collaboration in so many of the organic aspects of treatment. But we have drawn material and ideas from very many of our colleagues of the past and of the present. Among our collaborators have been Dr Robert Barbour (bromide intoxication), Dr Nellie Craske (modified insulin and amytal abreaction techniques), Dr Eric Guttmann (benzedrine), Dr Denis Hill (EEG), Dr Francis Pilkington (continuous sleep and bromide intoxication), Dr Dalton Sands (convulsion therapy), and, in America, Dr Robert Schwab of Massachusetts General Hospital (EEG and respiration problems). We particularly wish to thank Dr Aubrey Lewis and Dr Mayer-Gross for general criticism and much helpful advice, and Dr Minski for his support while at Sutton. There are numerous other colleagues and teachers with whom we have worked and who have contributed to the formulation of our views. Though we cannot shelve the responsibility of this book on them, we realise that without the inspiration of working with them and the stimulating discussion of common problems, we should not have been in a position to write it.

WILLIAM SARGANT.

THE MAUDSLEY HOSPITAL,   ELIOT SLATER.
    LONDON, 1944.

Contents

Introduction

There is no need to labour the practical value of the various physical methods of treatment in psychiatry. Although they appeared on the scene long after the earlier advances in psychotherapy, it is to them that we owe the transformation of our mental hospitals from what they were a generation ago to what they are today. It is on the basis of improvements gained by physical methods of treatment in the individual case that progress in the social field, in the treatment of patients in groups, and in the development of the therapeutic community, has become possible. It is only because we can control the graver symptoms of mental disorder and help the patient rapidly through the acute stages of a psychosis, that we are now able to throw open so many of the hospital doors and give our patients the hope of early discharge. It is through the use of these methods that community care becomes possible, that day hospitals and night hospitals become practical propositions, and that the treatment of acute psychiatric patients is everywhere shifting from the specialised psychiatric hospital to psychiatric wards in general hospitals. If we were now to give up physical methods of treatment with those suffering from acute psychoses, we can be sure that we would have to re-introduce old and hated security measures, give up general hospital units, and in fact fall back all along the line.

It is never possible to foresee the changes that scientific and technological advances will bring with them. The development of psychiatric units in general hospitals has had important consequences for the place taken by psychiatry in medical teaching, and in the attitude taken towards psychiatry, both as a scientific endeavour and as a vocation of care, by the psychiatrist's senior medical and surgical colleagues and their students. The exchange of views and information is a two-way traffic. We are certainly having some effect on our colleagues, how beneficial it is for them to say. The effect that closer contact with them is having on us is valuable and profound.

The effectiveness of methods of treatment is also tending to change the nature of our clientele. Since potentially severe psychotic states are being controlled, mainly by drugs, in their early stages, the demand they make on psychiatric facilities has been greatly reduced. These facilities, in-patient and out-patient, have become progressively more available to patients with neurotic syndromes. Such syndromes are often difficult to distinguish from mild and early psychotic states, schizophrenic or affective; and clinical work has become more subtle and demanding, as it has become more rewarding. But even more than this is required of the psychiatrist today; and he is faced in increasing numbers by patients who cannot be said to have fallen ill in any kind of way, but who are concerned with life-problems with which, as they think, he can be of help. As human relationships come more and more into his field, the work of the psychiatrist diversifies. He may, for instance, turn to the social sciences for special training or fraternal help; or he may turn back with renewed interest to psychotherapy, which not long ago seemed so helpless and now once more looks relevant.

All this is only possible because straightforward solutions are available, and very generally effective, for the simpler kinds of clinical problems. It is not now too difficult, with an understanding of a few fairly simple principles and with patient study at the bedside, to give efficient and economical treatment and to spare the patient experiences which have little chance of benefiting him. Psychiatry still lacks the clinical tradition of general medicine. In the medical wards of a general hospital there are established standards of treatment, based on a lifetime spent in bedside study by generations of physicians. To these standards innovations may be added, but below them one may not fall. In psychiatry, however, the only standards sanctified by tradition were until recently those of cautious pessimism, or of no treatment at all. While this attitude is hardly possible now, there is no general agreement on what should constitute good practical standards of treatment. Yet there is much that ranks for consideration in this light. Eighty per cent or more of involutional depressives remit with the new anti-depressant drugs and electrical treatment; and 80 per cent of schizophrenics in their first year of illness are responding to the new tranquilliser drugs combined with ECT and modified insulin treatment. The ground is laid for the development of new standards; but it is only the careful clinical study of the patients who do and who do not respond to what is now a great variety of possible treatments, which will enable us to establish them.

Recent developments are bringing psychiatry nearer to general medicine; but the gap still remains a wide one. The gulf is not so much between the two arts as between their exponents. On the one hand medical and surgical specialists may give the whole of their interest to a pathological process which they think of as proceeding in an isolated organ, and little or no regard to the emotional and psychological factors which may be influencing the course of illness and recovery. For them the affairs of the patient, and his personal relationships, his temperament and personality are esoteric matters which, if they obtrude themselves, must be referred at once to the appropriate specialist. Fortunately this tradition is on its way out. With clinical psychiatrists penetrating into the wards of the teaching hospitals, not only the students but even senior colleagues are gaining a fuller appreciation of psychosomatic relationships, and what a physical illness means to the man, as a human being, in his family and social setting.

On the other hand, psychiatrists, even those who are treating their patients mainly along physical lines, may show an equal lack of interest in the chains of cause and effect which link the physical interference on one side with the psychological results on the other. Interest in psychosomatic problems has so far been rather one-sided, devoted to the interpretation of bodily symptoms as the result of psychogenic causes, or the symbolic expression of an unconscious urge. But we are now beginning to get a better understanding of the ways in which the experiences of a man reverberate from higher areas of the brain through subcortical centres to the vegetative nervous system and the orchestration of all bodily functions; and equally how physical changes convey their messages to the centres which sustain the affects and tensions that direct our conscious attitudes and drives.

Psychologically orientated doctors are, of course, entitled to attack any problem that seems appropriate by methods of enquiry peculiar to their own discipline. Psychometric and sociological methods of attack provide avenues to great advances in knowledge. But psychiatry will remain isolated and remote from the general body of the biological sciences until it is knit firmly into general medicine in those regions where the two overlap. Until this point is reached we cannot expect to build up satisfactory rationales of treatment.

The fact that the most important methods of physical treatment are purely empirical, even if they were inspired in their initiators by theoretical notions that have little solid basis, underlines the inadequacy of theoretical knowledge to provide even a starting-point for successful therapy. The treatments themselves are no worse for that, and our understanding of psychiatric theory will give us much help in their application. This is, when the whole field is reviewed, only too familiar a circumstance in medicine. It is into the hands of the bold experimenters that success has fallen. But whereas in general medicine the discovery of an empirically successful treatment has led to an examination of its theoretical basis, this has only recently begun to make headway in psychiatry. Treatment by malaria, convulsion, and leucotomy proved their worth without any theoretical justification; and it was on theory that objections to their use were and are still sometimes raised. Gadelius, one of the assessors for the Nobel Prize, reported in his time that a man who could inflict on the general paretic malaria, in addition to the disease he already had, was in his opinion more deserving of imprisonment than a prize; and correspondingly harsh judgments on the other treatments have been made since. Theories which have no place for established clinical findings have to be remodelled or abandoned. Those who maintain that depression in middle age is caused by frustration and deprivation in infancy are required to explain how the depression can be cured by one or two non-specific convulsions. As in the past, so probably for a long time yet in the future, methods of treatment will appear that will have little sure basis in psychiatric theory, but which will justify themselves by their results. We shall, however, fail to get the best out of them if they do not cause us in turn to re-examine their theoretical consequences and implications.

The Constitutional Approach

Our understanding of aetiology in psychiatry is so primitive and incomplete that it is only here and there that we can use it directly to direct our methods of treatment. General paresis used to provide a splendid model of a mental disease, familiar to every practising psychiatrist. It exhibited its specific cause, the *Treponema pallidum*; there were evident predisposing causes, such as the time of life and the lapse of a number of years from the time of the primary infection. Precipitating causes showed up regularly, when a florid psychosis was suddenly released by an accident or an illness. Pathoplastic features could be demonstrated in the cyclothymic prepsychotic temperament of those patients whose onset took the form of a mania or a depression. Lifelong habits of mind and individual psychological experience would show traces in the content of delusional ideas, or the reaction to spouse and family. Unfortunately for the teacher (though for no one else), this model is no longer available. Our very understanding of the illness, coupled with the accidental discovery of penicillin, has led to effective treatment of the primary cause, long before it could manifest itself in gross brain pathology; general paresis has become such a rarity that it is hardly ever seen by most psychiatrists.

The example has gone; but the model is still useful. We still have our specific agents in microorganisms, as with the viral encephalitides, or poisons, as with the amphetamine psychoses. The duration of a chronic insult still shows its significance with hormonal and nutritional disorders and with long-term poisons such as alcohol. The precipitating causes which release a mental illness often owe their importance to their effect in bringing to notice a state of affairs that has been going on for some time. The fact that a man is well advanced in cerebral arteriosclerosis, for instance, may be made noticeable by a mental shock releasing a severe depression; or an attack of delirium tremens, precipitated by an accident, shows up the ruin of the physical constitution by chronic alcoholism. And everywhere, through our practice, we have to be alive to the factors which have a formative influence on the individual peculiarities of the clinical picture, such as the influence of a strongly religious upbringing on the self-reproach of the depressive, or the effect of physical factors in modifying the symptoms of a puerperal schizophrenia.

Factors which in one type of illness are of primary importance, in other types may occupy a less significant place. The head injury, which is directly responsible for the unconsciousness of concussion and for the subsequent symptoms of cerebral irritation, may be predisposing for the appearance of neurotic symptoms, may precipitate an epilepsy of which the genetic basis was inborn, or may merely colour the symptoms of an eventual compensation neurosis. Age, which we may regard as the primary cause of a senile dementia, provides a predisposition for the functional symptoms of later life, and may be the precipitating agent in an involutional melancholia; in the recurrent psychotic phases of the manic-depressive, it merely alters the tendency to mania, which may be prominent in early life, to a tendency to depression, which is seen so much more commonly later on. The constitution, which supplies the primary cause in Huntington's chorea, and probably also in schizophrenia and manic-depressive psychoses among others, in other states is of lesser significance; but it is that which lends the greater part of all that is particular to the individual case, and its secondary (pathoplastic) effects can never be ignored.

As the same agent can in different cases play a different part, so identical symptoms can arise from the operation of different agents. We are all liable to a shift of mood in the direction of depression; but while the reactive depression of the normal or mildly neurotic individual can be accounted for by depressing experiences, the depression of the true manic-depressive can appear spontaneously, derived via a physiological predisposition from the genetic make-up. We have, indeed, been made aware by the work of Angst (1966) and Perris (1966) that there are separate and distinct genetic predispositions to affective illness, a predisposition to depressive states only ('unipolar'), and a predisposition to spontaneous mood changes in both manic and depressive directions ('bipolar'). The circular course, which is so characteristic of the manic-depressive and is probably the direct result of the primary pathogenic factors themselves, in the schizophrenic, though perhaps still derived from the same agent, is now no longer a necessary and characteristic feature of the illness. In any individual case, clinical analysis will often show in striking fashion how much of the more obtrusive elements of the picture are due to secondary effects, which have completely overgrown the specific results of the pathogenic agent. This is especially frequently seen in organic syndromes, which thereby can become very puzzling. On the basis of the earliest results of cerebral arteriosclerosis, which even to the most careful clinical examination shows no certainly present direct effects, there may arise a slight shift of the personality towards a more primitive level, with an excessive lability of reaction to psychogenic stimuli; this again may then cause highly typical functional manifestations, such as crude hysterical symptoms of the conversion type. As with the progress of the disease mental impairment proceeds, the pseudo-neurotic manifestations may once more recede into the background, and the typical encephalopathic symptoms appear for the first time. The importance of the most careful clinical analysis in such cases, to avoid the possibility of disastrous mistakes in diagnosis, prognosis and treatment, hardly needs stating. When we come to the consideration of treatment, we shall wish wherever possible to direct the attack in the first place on the pathogenic agent. It will therefore be necessary to disentangle the primary and the secondary symptoms as nicely as we can, and to determine how far the latter are the result of a dynamic effect, or are only present as an accidental admixture.

Unfortunately, in the great majority of patients who come our way, we cannot single out any specific pathogenic agent. A breakdown in social adaptation has occurred, with the appearance of a variety of symptoms, and only because, as far as we can see, the patient has not been able to bear up against stresses, mainly social and psychological, which are no different in kind, though perhaps in degree, from what we all have to support. We can see no obvious relation between the kinds of stress incurred, and the nature of the symptoms. To understand the form the symptoms take we have to delve into his past history, the stresses he has undergone in earlier years, the formative influences of his youth, his childhood, even his infancy; and all this, very likely, without any great enlightenment. Ultimately we come back to the permanent core of a personal constitution, which was determined in its main tendencies by the genetic inheritance he received from his parents.

We have only recently been made aware of the extent and degree of human genetic diversity. Neel and Schull (1968) give as a minimum estimate 100,000 loci encoding for protein structure. If we make reasonable assumptions about the proportion of those loci at which there will be a substantial degree of polymorphism, we are led to the fantastic estimate that even the individual who combines all the likeliest chances will have a probability of the order of 10^{-270}. We are, indeed, each of us genetically unique (unless we have a monozygotic twin). There never was such a one before, and there will never be another such again. The message for the clinician and therapist is a plain one. We must treat each of our patients as a unique individual. General rules can apply to him only in part. We must feel our way, guided indeed by past experience, but always keeping the options open, maintaining a flexibility of approach. If one treatment does not work, we must be willing to try another; if each of two treatments produces only a partial benefit, it may be possible to do better by combining them. As treatment proceeds, and we remain alert to what the patient tells us, both by his reactions and by letting us know how he is feeling, we get a better and better idea of the manifold potentialities that have gone, in unique combination, to make him what he is. It is only by our willingness to learn from the single patient, afresh, again and again, that we can do our best for each. It is inescapable biological fact that informs us that we shall make only a botched job of our treatment, if we adopt fixed drills and conveyor-belt systems.

To recapitulate, then, the human individual begins life with a large but limited number of inherited tendencies. The genes, their physical determinants, operate harmoniously together, in their totality provide for the development of a complete human being, and each separately causes large or minute specific differences between individual and individual. None is probably without influence on the operations of any one other. These all-embracing and specific tendencies are potentialities, which may be interfered with by other factors, environmental and genetic. No one can become more intelligent than his genetic equipment allows; but injury or disease may easily make him less so. The genes exert their specific effects at different times in development, and as the child grows into the man, more and more of them become manifest, from the early definition of eye colour, for instance, to the much later determination of eventual stature. If the action of the genes is prolonged or delayed, there is so much the more latitude for environmental influences also to have an effect. As life proceeds to middle and old age, a higher and higher proportion of inherited traits will have shown themselves in this way; but there is no point in life at which one can say that all the inborn potentialities have been realised, and it is indeed probable that all of us die with possibilities both for achievement and for disease never made manifest. At some point the essential environmental stimulus has been lacking, or some opposed hereditary tendency has predominated.

The environment exerts its influence on the developing organism at all points in its career, stimulating some tendencies, inhibiting others, and implanting at the same time its own seeds of pathological change and disease. These environmental influences will themselves not be all in the same direction, and the effect of some will outweigh that of others. Some of these influences will be so far-reaching and profound, and exerted over such a length of time, that they will produce fundamental alterations in the bodily and mental constitution; it is probable that large changes in nutrition in early life can have such important effects, and possibly early psychological education also. Other influences will have their effect abruptly, like a trigger mechanism. These precipitating factors are commonly the griefs and hardships of everyday life, and do not always deserve the amount of attention that is paid them in the individual case history. Their importance varies from case to case; for while they are, as a rule, of little significance in the psychoses, they may be crucial in the treatment of a recent anxiety state.

At any one time the total potentialities of the individual cannot be completely gauged from what has been previously exhibited, though the previous record can provide the material for deductions of a high degree of probability. Inherited tendencies to involutional melancholia and to schizophrenia lie hidden through the years, to manifest themselves in due course when time and circumstance favour their appearance. The personality, which may appear to be fully developed by early middle life, can conceal within itself weak points that need only an adequate and appropriate stimulus to become manifest. This point was illustrated by the men who broke down under the severer stresses of war. These men tended to show as a group some degree of emotional immaturity, constitutional anxiety, or personalities that were otherwise feeble, fragile or unstable; but, if they had been permitted to live out their lives in peace they would have never known what it was to shake and sweat and tremble, and to be woken by nightmares night after night.

Under the most favourable environmental circumstances, heredity sets an upper limit to our powers and achievements. There are probably few so fortunate as to have attained this peak. Most people at some point have been hampered in one way or another by their environment, some very seriously. Inadequate nutrition, infection, trauma and other noxae can permanently affect physical structure; and in the same way psychological factors of an unfavourable kind can alter and pervert the development of the personality. In both cases the damage, once done, is difficult or impossible to modify. It would probably not be difficult so to educate even a naturally good-hearted child that in adult life he would regularly behave in an egoistic way, and effective re-education might be very hard by the time adult life is reached. But one may doubt whether the best directed education could make a child who was naturally thick-skinned and cold-blooded into a sensitive and warm-hearted man; and the practical aim should be to induce him to modify the actual expression of his selfish impulses. The same can be said of other psychological traits, tendencies to anxiety and worry, obsessional pedantry, hysterical demonstrations, etc. Nature lays down the potentialities; it is our task so to control the environment that they are realised as favourably as possible.

Of all the environmental factors that may interfere with normal functioning of the mind, those that operate through direct action on the brain are prepotent. In utero and in infancy sufficient destruction of the brain tissue will produce mental deficiency, which shows itself not only in intellectual defect and inability to learn, but also in abnormal traits of temperament and personality, such as feebleness of persistence and will, inadequacies of attention and self-control, emotional liability, and liability to neurotic symptoms of many kinds. In later life correspondingly gross changes in cerebral structure produce, in the intellectual field dementia, and in the emotional field irritability, aggressiveness, hypochondriasis, excessive susceptibility to fatigue, emotional instability, and greater susceptibility to psychogenic stimuli of all kinds. If these organic changes occur rapidly, there are clouding of consciousness, confusion, hallucinations, violent disturbances of affect; if they occur slowly, acute symptoms will be absent, and in their place will be seen intellectual deterioration and progressive change of personality. In addition, there will very often be specific symptoms, referable in art to the nature of the pathogenic factor, in part to its site of incidence.

These symptoms are the direct results of the pathogenic agent itself, and are, as a rule, independent of the personality of the individual and his hereditary make-up. Nevertheless, under the impact of these changes latent dispositions of the personality will show themselves more clearly. Both in acute confusional states and in chronic dementias, the suspicious man becomes openly paranoid, the cyclothymic extravert elated or depressed, the anxious man increasingly agitated. Factors which may be crucial for the fate of the patient may themselves be secondary in nature and derived as much from the underlying and permanent personality as from the degree, site and nature of the damage to the brain.

Changes that occur in the personality, either as the result of environmental interference or as the manifestation of a previously latent hereditary (or endogenous) tendency, themselves provoke further changes and adaptations on the part of the individual. Not only external, but internal stimuli can act as psychogenic precipitants of reactive manifestations. The well-preserved schizophrenic patient, faced with morbidly altered perceptions, interprets them as best he can and builds round the skeleton of a few primary delusions and hallucinations a complex structure in which the whole external world may become secondarily involved. The involutional melancholic, conscious of an overwhelming sense of guilt, searches his past for acts to which this guilt may be attached. The man who is vaguely or acutely aware of the gradual failure of his memory and intellectual powers may be in a constant state of anxiety lest he give himself away, or obstinately determined to prove to himself and to the world that he is as good a man as ever he was. The obsessional, faced with situations which provoke an intolerable anxiety, builds himself defences in the form of rituals which may become scarcely less tolerable. By a process resembling conditioning, a stimulus that has once excited a neurotic response may continue to do so long after the total situation has radically changed. The acute war neuroses exhibited this phenomenon in a simple form. In a situation of great hardship and danger, the man who had previously never given way to fear because he had never had occasion to experience it in an acute form, found himself introduced to panic. Thereafter his susceptibility was so increased that he was over-

come with fear in situations which would previously have left him unmoved, by the rumble of a train or the screech of motor-tyres, sounds
merely resembling those that he had learned to dread. These secondary reactions may be of great importance from the therapeutic point
of view, as they may be more disabling than the primary defect or disability on which they are built. The results of appropriately chosen
therapies, such as a long course of combined sleep and ECT, or
perhaps leucotomy, have shown that reactions which had become self-
perpetuating can still be broken up, if an essential element in the
central nervous mechanism is attacked.

The modes of breakdown of the human mind are few and constant.
Organic causes produce symptoms, both general and specific, which
are typical of themselves, and so loosen the integration of the personality that secondary effects are more probable. Specific endogenous
factors, alone or in a favourable environment, can initiate the symptoms that we associate with schizophrenia, cyclothymia, involutional
melancholia, obsessional neurosis. To all such changes, and to a world
full of stresses and strains, the predisposed personality can react only
along limited lines. With anxiety, hypochondriasis, depression,
hysteria, suspiciousness, excitement, anger and aggressiveness, the list
is almost complete. If the stress be severe enough, the most secure and
stable personality can show such symptoms. In the greater part of the
range of ordinary human experience such reactions are the product of
a stress situation on one side with some degree of constitutional
susceptibility on the other. Certain fear-provoking situations have a
specific preference for the production of anxiety syndromes; prolonged physical illness of a minor degree favours hypochondriasis;
the conversion symptoms of hysteria are favoured by a localised
physical lesion or organ inferiority. Yet in general the specific quality
of the reaction is determined more by the constitutional make-up than
by environmental factors, though it may have been the latter which in
a given case decided that breakdown was to occur.

These largely inborn determinants are, in fact, nearly always
recognisable in the personality, and it is very much easier to predict
the type of neurotic reaction to which a well-known personality is
liable, than the type of psychotic change he may eventually undergo.
But whether such a response occurs at all, and the extent to which it
occurs, is decided not only by the constitution, but also by the kind
and strength of the stimulus experienced, and on the individual mental
and physical (biochemical) equilibrium at the time. One man when
drunk always gets sleepy, another euphoric, a third quarrelsome; but

the quarrelsome may not be notably so when not in his cups, and in general the same stimulus is reacted to very differently when drunk and when sober. The usually stable man may be reduced to a state of deep but temporary depression by an attack of influenza, or by the loss of a dearly loved wife. The cyclothymic is plunged by the one into a depressive psychosis, by the other stimulus perhaps into a manic excitement. Worries that previously meant little may be found insupportable at the time of the menopause, and, depending on the constitution, may result in a hysterical hypochondriasis or an involutional melancholia. What is predisposition and what precipitation, which are the pathogenic and which the merely formative factors? Only a careful analysis of the past history and of the present state can provide the information we require, and so lead us to apply our therapeutic efforts at the points where they are most likely to be effective.

This short account of the pathogenesis of mental disorders is necessarily extremely sketchy and incomplete, but some such framework is necessary for the comprehension of the individual patient and the problem in treatment that he provides. Without it one cannot reach conclusions on the range of health normally obtainable, on the nature of the causative factors and the degree to which they can be eliminated, the nature of the morbid changes and the extent to which they can be halted and reversed. It is, of course, not the same thing to come to fairly firm conclusions about the causes of a condition, and to be in a position materially to influence them. This is even often true of environmental precipitants of a psychogenic kind; it is, for instance, often out of the power of the doctor or patient to remedy an intolerable home situation. It is not the same to eliminate the original cause and bring about cure; the illness once under way may continue of its own momentum, or it may set up secondary changes which conspire to its continuance and require their own specific therapy. One of the reasons for the great importance of early treatment lies in the frequency and severity of these secondary changes. They are seen in the organic psychoses in the effects of scarring of the brain and in morbid adaptations to the primary disabilities; in schizophrenia in affective dilapidation and paranoid reaction; in the neuroses in faulty habit formations and functional physical changes. In all states, continuing illness and incapacity modifies the total environmental situation, nearly always to the prejudice of the patient's chances of eventual rehabilitation, and more and more gravely with time. The accident of a prolonged absence from work or estrangement from relatives may offer insuperable problems when the clinical ones have been solved.

Towards a Rational Therapy

A rational therapy is directed to the halting of the disease process (if it exists), to the elimination of specific pathogenic factors (if they are known and accessible), to the fortifying of the bodily and mental constitution, and to the education of the patient in the way to deal with such unavoidable stresses and symptoms as will have to be met with in the future. The treatment of the individual patient will therefore be conducted along a number of different lines, several of which may be followed perhaps at the same time. The first consideration both on medical and social grounds is the urgency of treatment. Organic conditions if allowed to persist for any length of time, produce some scarring, or permanent maladaptation, from which there can never be complete recovery. The same is true of schizophrenia; and of all psychiatric states it can be said that unfavourable psychological adaptations are the more probable and the more severe the longer the condition is allowed to last. Social reasons for rapidity of treatment are not less important. It is easy to get a man back to work if he has been in hospital for only a few weeks; it is progressively more difficult if the weeks run on into months. At most hospitals this lesson has been learned; and there is a systematic policy of early discharge, even with incomplete recovery, with intensive after-care. Ever fewer now are the patients who live on in hospitals for years. With them there eventually comes a point after which it is difficult even to get them taken back into their own homes. Relatives have lost heart and interest and have adjusted their affairs to the exclusion of the patient, and the patient himself has become timid of even that degree of responsibility involved in managing his personal affairs without help.

In the choice of methods of treatment one will therefore be impelled towards those which are most rapid. An incapacitating illness which is allowed to drag on untreated for weeks and months is not only an unnecessary misery for the patient, but may be sufficient to spoil his chances for the rest of his life. Nowadays general practitioners are alert to psychiatric symptoms, and will often begin treatment themselves, with referral to a psychiatric clinic held in reserve. It is, then, rarely that we see an uncomplicated affective psychosis which is allowed to run its natural course. In the old days, spontaneous recovery within the first 12 months of onset was the rule; but those whose illness dragged on longer faced but gloomy prospects. In recent years, the long-standing depressives have been those who have failed to respond to simple methods of treatment, and had been allowed to sink into a state in which all serious effort at a cure has been suspended. With drugs and sleep and ECT one can still show how long a depression may have lasted, and yet get better; but the depression has to be recognised for what it is, perhaps under a mask of schizophrenic-like withdrawal or 'hysterical' complaint and indifference.

For early treatment, one must begin by making a diagnosis in the wider sense, by estimating the importance of endogenous factors, of the stresses in the environment, of the extent to which the picture is coloured by neurotic and psychopathic admixtures, etc. Having cleared the ground, one should not wait long before beginning active treatment, most probably in the out-patient department, at least to begin with. A rather different range of therapies comes in question, severally, for the reactive (neurotic) depressives, the endogenous depressives, and the bipolar manic-depressives. Only in those rare cases of the manic-depressive syndrome, in which the depressive phases are very regularly of the same short duration, would one be justified in withholding active treatment for a time in the expectation of spontaneous recovery.

In the case of schizophrenia treatment is still more urgent. It is indeed true that the outlook in this illness is much better than it used to be, even when the illness has been a long-standing one. Some patients who have been ill for some years are getting better now with drug and ECT combined therapies. Moreover, perhaps because of greatly improved hospital regimes one rarely sees nowadays the profound dilapidation, the hebephrenic states, which used to be the rule after many months of illness. Nevertheless, the withholding of treatment from the actute schizophrenic, to study his symptoms, to teach one's students, even to try the effects of psychotherapy and social management, is totally unjustified. The prognosis is worsened by delay and there is no reason why he should suffer, unprotected by drug therapy, the mental torture of his symptoms.

Diagnosis, of course, is not always easy in the early stages, or even later on in an insidious or anomalous case. When a patient presents himself with suggestive symptoms one should try to make up one's mind about him quite quickly. In cases of doubt, even when the illness is a mild one, a short period of in-patient observation may be worth weeks of watching in an out-patient clinic. Even the best clinicians find themselves not infrequently in a state of indecision about a patient who shows an atypical picture, and should not be ashamed to ask for the advice of their colleagues. The value of the clinical conference cannot be too strongly emphasised. In the diagnosis of schizophrenia first impressions are often more valuable than long acquaintance, and what seems obscure to one doctor who knows the patient well, may be crystal clear to another who sees him for the first time, but with all the facts in his possession.

The choice of milieu for treatment is often a matter of great difficulty. One is often reluctant to take a patient away from work which he is still carrying out with fair efficiency, particularly when the only alternative to be offered him is admission to the mental hospital. As a matter of practical experience it can be said that it is quite simple to treat patients suffering from all the major psychoses in their initial stages in special wards in general hospitals, provided they are staffed by experienced psychiatric clinicians and nurses. These facilities are now being more and more widely provided, and what we have pressed for since early editions of this book is at last coming to pass, as part of Government policy. These in-patients units in general hospitals are capable of coping with the whole variety of cases that used to go into the admission units of mental hospitals, and in addition are tapping a new clientele. Patients are appearing for treatment much earlier; and the contribution to the whole made by neuroses and personality disorders is more prominent. Furthermore, this development is helping to heal the divorce between psychiatry and general medicine, to the benefit of both.

Having once got the patient into circumstances in which he can be treated, one has to consider the priority of different lines of treatment. The first principle is to halt any irreversible change that may be taking place. Is there an irreversible process, involved in schizophrenia? Once few, and now more, doubt that there is; but we dare not carry the risk. A fortiori, the same principle holds with organic disease. One often hears the thoughtless repetition of the cliché, that one should treat the patient and not the disease. It would perhaps be truer to say that once one has treated the disease, one should not forget to treat the patient.

The reversibility or irreversibility of changes that are occurring in a patient have constantly to be held in mind in psychiatry. This is true, not only of the disease process, but also of certain methods of treatment, and where they are here involved, caution is indicated. Once the frontal lobes have been damaged by leucotomy, or a lesion made in the thalamus, any harm done can never be made good. The usefulness of these methods of treatment depends to a large extent on the small functional disability involved. Destructive changes are also caused by convulsive therapy, but, apart from prolonged courses in which many fits are given, are as a rule practically negligible. Insulin coma treatment may also produce slight destructive changes in the brain, but of still less functional effect than those seen in convulsion treatment. This may be a disadvantage as well as an advantage. A good result obtained by leucotomy in a severely anxious obsessional patient may well be permanent; there can be no guarantee of non-relapse after the treatment of schizophrenia, the convulsion treatment of depression, and even less after the psychological treatment of the neurotic.

The next principle for application in treatment is to interrupt any vicious circle that may be operating. Continuing anxiety will tend to produce loss of weight and deterioration of the general physical condition, which in its turn increases the susceptibility to anxious situations; anxiety causes insomnia, insomnia anxiety. Temporary alteration of the physical constitution by the use of insulin or sedation can start the circle of events moving in the opposite direction. These vicious circles, or vicious spirals leading ever downwards, can be seen in many patients, and often in more than one area of the patient's life. To interrupt them is a common sense task, and needs no justification by any kind of theory, diagnostic or aetiological.

The last principle that we wish to emphasise is that of therapeutic persistence. When a direct attack has been made on the primary cause of illness itself, the secondary symptoms must not be forgotten. Often the actual disability is as much or more due to them as to the more primary symptoms. Perhaps after treatment the schizophrenic patient is still somewhat inert and mildly depressed; the effect of antidepressants or a few convulsions may be tried. After recovery from his depression, the involutional depressive may still hold on to some of his old fixed beliefs, or still lack the confidence he should have; now for the first time a somewhat more energetic psychotherapeutic approach may win results. Very frequently the depressive is grossly under-weight; he will not respond to modified insulin treatment while the depression is in full blast, but will readily do so once it has been cured by other measures. The estimation of the causes of a disability may be a much more refined matter than a simple diagnosis. One may know that one patient is partially incapacitated by a past attack of schizophrenia, another by arteriosclerosis, a third by the sequelae of a head injury. Yet in the first the actual incapacity may be due not to an irreversible thought disorder, but to a functional hypothymia, in the second not to destructive changes in the brain but to a vitamin deficiency, in the third not to gross organic changes but to a fundamentally neurotic incapacity for re-adaptation to changed circumstances, which will yield to a process of re-education.

Persistence should continue until the last possibility of rehabilitation has been exhausted. Where much cannot be done, the little that is possible should not be left undone. It is an achievement won to move a patient from a disturbed to a quiet ward, to be able to grant him parole, to get him usefully employed, to get him out of the hospital back to his home for a week-end, for a month, for good. Because a patient is or has been schizophrenic, that is no reason why he should be kept in hospital indefinitely. A man may be 'mad', and yet be readily maintained in the community and even leading a useful life. Any symptoms whatever that stand in the way of a patient being moved from one stage of a disability to a lesser one should be carefully examined. More often than not a hopeful method of attack can be found.

It is by these methods and along these lines that psychiatry has made such broad advances since the first edition of this book was written. We regard it as certain that this is the way development will continue. There is no conflict between the methods of treatment we advocate and describe, and the humane approaches of social and psycho-therapy; each of them potentiates the others. Open-minded enquiry and empiricism have brought about stupendous advances in medicine and surgery in the last 50 years. It is only a sign of our infantile dependence on authority, when we tolerate the existence of rigidly dogmatic schools. If we permit the claim that there is only one treatment, whether this be psychotherapy or ECT, for every kind and condition of psychiatric illness, we set our feet on a slippery path. The step that inevitably follows is contempt for diagnosis or for any objective examination, as irrelevancies, and a religious fervour in which reason and self-criticism are submerged. Scientific progress then stops. Each of the methods of treatment described in this book has its limited values, its dangers and contra-indications. Each is only applicable to a group of patients, whose limits we have attempted to define. It is our task to seek for better definitions, as well as to seek for still other methods, and to be ready to abandon any one when another is found to serve the purpose better, to subordinate ourselves to facts and not to dogma and theory.

CHAPTER ONE

Chemical Sedation and Stimulation

In recent years chemical methods have come to occupy first place in the treatment of mental illness. This advance alone has profoundly changed the entire psychiatric scene. We have now reached the point where, by altering body chemistry, we can produce selective effects on the primary symptoms of mental illness, relieving depression in one case, suppressing hallucinations and delusional experiences in another. In all parts of the field the psychiatrist faces an entirely new set of problems. The administrator, whose patients have suddenly become so tractable, has to seize his opportunities and develop a policy of universally open doors and large schemes of rehabilitation. The theoretician, concerned with the investigation of ætiology, is shocked out of fixed habits of thought by unexpected similarities and differences in response to drugs. And the clinician whose immediate concern is the individual has to try to sort his patients into groups in terms of their reactions. He has to learn to recognise the clinical features of the patients who will be benefited by any particular drug, and to get to know its advantages and dangers. With new drugs continually appearing on the scene, with overlapping actions and applications, and under the pressure of insistent advertising, he must still keep his head and make a balanced appraisal.

In treating patients with either sedative or stimulant drugs one of the problems we have to face is that of addiction. Of course some drugs are more dangerous than others because of their tendency to induce a habit and to necessitate an ever-increasing dose. But a personal factor is also involved, especially in the less common addictions. In this country those who are addicted to cocaine, opium derivatives, pethidine and even amphetamine are usually people of abnormal and psychopathic personality. For most patients under drug treatment the risk of addiction is not very serious. Nevertheless, just as there are compulsive alcoholics whose first drink or two engenders a pathological craving for more, so there are those who, when once given barbiturates, amphetamine or tranquillisers, of their own accord rapidly increase the dose beyond control. Any drug with a euphoriant action is especially liable to this sort of misuse. Such patients are unusual, but it is important to recognise them early. A much larger proportion of neurotic patients have among their phobias one of addiction, and take less than the prescribed dose rather than more.

Another set of problems, which in practice receive little consideration, are those involved by variations in individual susceptibility. Such variations probably depend in part on genetical factors, and they have received little systematic study. Quite apart from the rare subjects who have an enormously enhanced susceptibility to some specific drug such as scoline, one has to reckon on normal quantitative variation. Even when it is calculated weight for weight, some people only need half the dose required by others for an equivalent effect. One cannot lay down rules for dealing with this situation. Nevertheless, if the principle is remembered, here and there we shall be able to do much better for our patients than if we treat them like recipes for cooking, the same amounts to be used on every occasion.

Sedation

For many years the question of how best to sedate a patient was relatively simple to decide. The barbiturates were, in general, the first choice, although older drugs such as bromides, paraldehyde and chloral still had their uses. But since 1952 the problem has become increasingly complex due to the development of a whole new range of sedatives and tranquillisers. These drugs, which by definition sedate without exerting a marked hypnotic effect, have profoundly altered the treatment of both the psychoses and sometimes the neuroses. So rapidly have these new drugs multiplied, being made available for general prescription before adequate clinical testing, that it is now virtually impossible for anyone to have first-hand experience of them all. Nor, since many of the drugs are similar in structure and activity, does this necessarily matter.

To avoid confusion we have divided sedative drugs into two main groups.

1. Those drugs which are mainly of value in treating the psychoses and controlling disturbed behaviour and have only a small place in the treatment of neuroses. These include the phenothiazine derivatives, haloperidol and lithium. With the exception of lithium, they may all cause extrapyramidal side effects.

2. Drugs that are useful in neurotic states, but are much less effective in the psychoses, except to relieve secondary symptoms. Extrapyramidal effects are never produced, however high the dosage. We

have included drugs such as meprobamate (Equanil), methamino-diazepoxide (Librium), Valium and the older sedatives like bar-biturates in this group.

GROUP 1

THE PHENOTHIAZINE DERIVATIVES

Phenothiazines were first synthesised about 80 years ago, but interest was not aroused until after the last war. It was the introduction of chlorpromazine (Largactil) into clinical psychiatry in 1952 that heralded the start of the chemical revolution that has so transformed treatment and medical attitudes in the last two decades, and during this time a very large number of different phenothiazine compounds have appeared. The majority of these differ only slightly from one another in structure and may be no more effective than chlorpromazine in controlling psychotic symptoms. The group of derivatives containing a piperazine ring in the side chain, such as trifluoperazine (Stelazine), differ much from chlorpromazine in some of their effects. We shall, therefore, for the sake of clarity, only discuss the uses and actions of chlorpromazine and trifluoperazine (Stelazine), although we recognise that other phenothiazine compounds may be just as effective or more so in individual cases. We must also deal with a group of long acting drugs like fluphenazine (Moditen) which are particularly effective when given intramuscularly.

CHLORPROMAZINE (Largactil). This was initially used as a 'stabilisateur végétatif', to bring about what Laborit called 'artificial hibernation' in surgical patients and cases of shock. In this state the patient relaxed and became indifferent to his surroundings, although remaining fully conscious, and the usual adaptive responses to stress were decreased (Laborit and Huguenard, 1951).

It was then suggested that if the theory that stress led to mental breakdown by exhausting the body's ability to adapt was correct, then chlorpromazine might be able to protect patients from such exhaustion and so be helpful in psychiatric treatment. At first it was used in combination with hypnotics and pethidine to bring about a modified form of continuous narcosis. And soon Delay and Deniker in 1952 recognised that its most effective use was in treating acute schizophrenia. Chlorpromazine combined with ECT has now mainly replaced deep insulin therapy in the treatment of this illness.

The use of chlorpromazine has had far-reaching effects on the attitudes of psychiatrists towards their patients and on the setting in which treatment is given. It has been possible to relax security arrangements; and physical restraints have been almost abolished. Patients who previously would have needed admission to a mental hospital can now be taken into the open wards of general hospitals, with the sense of freedom given by ready access to the coming and going in the corridors and in the street outside. It is particularly gratifying to be able to treat the young patients, with a sharp attack of illness and good chances of full recovery, in such a benign environment. Rohde and Sargant (1961) reviewed all the cases of schizophrenia treated in St. Thomas's Hospital in the years 1950 to 1959, and showed that treatment with chlorpromazine, together with ECT and modified insulin, resulted in better and quicker recovery than could be got with insulin coma and ECT.* Kelly and Sargant (1965) subsequently confirmed this advance. With an average stay of only six weeks, more than 80 per cent of patients were still back in the community in a two-year follow-up. Relapses were mostly in the cases in which chlorpromazine medication had not been maintained. In fact, maintenance doses of chlorpromazine must generally be continued after the patient has left hospital to prevent relapses, whatever the treatment which has been used in the early stages.

Chlorpromazine seems to bring the schizophrenic process to a rapid halt, and to lessen the chance of chronicity and deterioration of personality. Provided maintenance doses are continued after the patient has left hospital, relapse is less likely to occur than used to be the case after successful insulin coma therapy or ECT without chlorpromazine.

Chlorpromazine is especially effective in the treatment of the disturbed schizophrenic patient with florid delusions and hallucinations, still capable of showing plenty of emotional response. Large doses, 300 mg to 600 mg or more per day, quickly reduce excitement and abnormal affect and enable contact to be re-established with the patient. In recent cases symptoms may be totally and permanently relieved. In long-standing but well-preserved schizophrenics, delusions and hallucinations may still remain after treatment but are now divested of their emotional content and no longer bother the patient unduly. Provided such a patient continues to take chlorpromazine he may be able to lead a relatively normal life. Unfortunately, the drug is sometimes stopped for one reason or another, occasionally by the patient's general practitioner; and disaster falls on the patient and his

* Recent experience has shown, however, that there are still isolated cases responding to insulin sopor or coma combined with chlorpromazine and ECT.

family. We must provisionally accept the view that some patients will need to take chlorpromazine for the rest of their lives, and that in some cases it may be no more justifiable to stop the drug than it is to stop a diabetic's supply of insulin.

Chlorpromazine is less effective in dull, apathetic, deteriorated schizophrenics who have lost the ability to show emotion. Such patients may become even more inert or depressed on chlorpromazine. One should then consider adding an antidepressant such as Tryptizol (Elavil) or giving some more ECT. This is a matter of the first importance. It may happen, particularly in schizo-affective states, that when the acute attack has responded to large doses of the drug, and these large doses are continued, a phase of depression then sets in. This may be wrongly diagnosed as schizophrenic deterioration. However, if the patient is taken off the chlorpromazine and given an antidepressant and ECT, an immediate remission occurs. The whole attack may come to be seen as a manic-depressive illness with schizophrenic features. We must be very careful of not keeping our wards full of over-chlorpromazined patients as, years ago between the two wars, they were filled with patients doped down with bromides.

Once the diagnosis of schizophrenia had been made, treatment should be started without delay; 300 mg or more of chlorpromazine a day in three divided doses is given initially and increased progressively until symptoms respond, or side effects become too troublesome. Doses of up to 3000 mg a day have been reported, but we have rarely had to give more than 1200 mg a day. Seriously disturbed patients should be started on 600–800 mg a day, and some of this can be given intramuscularly if the patient refuses to co-operate.

ECT generally speeds up the remission produced by chlorpromazine. It must always be considered, though these may be good reasons for not using it. The difference between a six-weeks and a three-months illness is very great to a mentally tortured patient. Lost weight should also be restored, for physical debility may release schizophrenic symptoms and can also retard recovery. Many patients put on weight rapidly when taking chlorpromazine, but in some cases weight remains low or patients refuse to eat adequately; in such cases modified insulin can be very useful. **As a general rule, when the time comes for discharge from hospital, the patient should be back to his normal weight or better.**

Once symptoms have disappeared or come under control the dose of chlorpromazine should be progressively lowered to the minimum needed to maintain improvement. In practice this is usually between

150 and 300 mg a day, although larger doses are sometimes needed. Patients with acute and recent onset often lose all symptoms, but it is advisable for them to continue on a maintenance dose for at least one to two years. For convenience, this can be taken as a single dose at night. Even after this length of time, after stopping the drug the patient should be followed up for at least six months, and the chlorpromazine should be restarted at the first sign of any return of symptoms. Chronic schizophrenics, whose symptoms are merely kept under control by chlorpromazine, will need to continue to take it indefinitely. Tolerance does not seem to develop and there seems to be no ill effect from such long-term therapy.

As we have said, on this maintenance therapy, while showing no return of thought disorder, some schizophrenics become depressed and ECT may then be required. But many of these patients respond well to a combination of an anti-depressant drug and chlorpromazine. MAOI antidepressants should not be given alone, as they may cause the schizophrenic symptoms to flare up. However they can be used with chlorpromazine, and the tricyclics and chlorpromazine make a very valuable combination.

Chlorpromazine is also a very useful drug in other states of over-activity and agitation—mania or hypomania, organic and senile conditions, post-operative confusional and psychotic states, hyperkinetic states in subnormal and psychotic children. Up to 1000 mg a day or more may be needed in mania before symptoms begin to subside. Chlorpromazine is far less effective in depressive illness, although when combined with ECT or one of the antidepressant drugs it can be useful in relieving the agitation that is sometimes present. However, it is as well to stop or reduce the drug as soon as possible, for it may otherwise increase or prolong the depression.

Chlorpromazine is of little value in neurotic states and, in general, should not be prescribed for them. Tension symptoms and anxiety states may occasionally be helped, but the majority of patients with anxiety, anxiety-hysteria, or neurotic forms of depression tolerate the drug badly. Obsessional patients often become more depressed, with a consequent increase of their obsessional symptoms. Hysterical symptoms become more pronounced and bizarre. However, Dally and Sargant have shown that large doses of chlorpromazine combined with modified insulin are invaluable during the in-patient phase of treatment of anorexia nervosa (Dally *et al.*, 1958; Dally and Sargant, 1960). Details of this treatment are given in Chapter VIII.

Large doses of chlorpromazine are also extremely useful in dealing with drug or alcohol withdrawal symptoms, and if there is no contra-indication will often enable the drug of addiction to be completely stopped soon after admission. It must be remembered that with some drugs sudden withdrawal is likely to be dangerous, as in barbiturate addiction where it may lead to fits. Delirium tremens can sometimes be cut short or abolished if chlorpromazine is given when the first signs arise, or immediately alcohol is stopped, Heminevrin (p. 29) is even more successful. Many patients are underweight and mal-nourished, and it is of course usually necessary to combine with the chlorpromazine other forms of treatment such as modified insulin and general rehabilitation measures.

Chlorpromazine has many uses in general medicine, particularly in controlling the nausea of pregnancy, uræmia, post-irradiation sick-ness, and intractible or terminal pain.

STELAZINE (trifluoperazine). Whereas chlorpromazine has a wholly sedating effect, the piperazine side chain phenothiazines like Stelazine tend not only to sedate by reducing anxiety, but also to stimulate and increase available energy. On occasion this stimulating effect can be excessive and even cause motor restlessness and increased feelings of anxiety. Stelazine may therefore sometimes be better than chlorproma-zine in the treatment of withdrawn, apathetic or depressed schizo-phrenics. Of course, if depression is at all marked or persistent, there should be no hesitation in giving an antidepressant drug with the Stelazine and starting ECT. Involutional states of depression with hypochondriacal and paranoid delusions may respond particularly well to a combination of Stelazine and ECT; but if agitation is also present it is better to give chlorpromazine. Doses of between 10–20 mg or more of Stelazine, in two divided doses, are necessary in these psychotic states.

Because of its tendency to increase energy and drive, small doses of Stelazine, unlike chlorpromazine, are sometimes useful in treating neurotic states of anxiety and tension. Older patients seem to benefit more than younger ones; and very good results occur when Stelazine 1–2 mg t.d.s. is combined with a MAOI antidepressant in the treat-ment of exogenous depressions, where free-floating anxiety is prominent. Individual sensitivity to Stelazine, as to chlorpromazine, varies widely, and often determines the dosage given. Some schizo-phrenics can take large doses of 40 mg or more a day without notice-able effect, while hysterical patients may react severely to as little as 1 mg t.d.s.

Complications and side effects

PHENOTHIAZINE SIDE EFFECTS. Side effects are common with both chlorpromazine and Stelazine and are related not only to the dosage, but also to the personality of the patient.

In general, autonomic and endocrine effects are more frequent with chlorpromazine, while neurological complications are more likely to occur with Stelazine. Allergic or sensitivity reactions may occur with both, although obstructive jaundice has mostly so far been reported after chlorpromazine.

Autonomic and Endocrine Effects. Postural hypotension may sometimes occur and cause dizziness or unsteadiness sufficiently unpleasant to prevent adequate dosage being given. Large doses of phenothiazines, such as are given to patients with anorexia nervosa, may cause the patient to faint as soon as she stands; lying down allows the blood pressure to return quickly to a safe level. Schizophrenics, with their unreactive autonomic systems, are sometimes quite unaffected in this way by enormous doses.

A dry mouth, blurring of vision, lachrymation, facial pallor, constipation, and pyrexia may cause complaints, though these symptoms often disappear spontaneously as treatment continues. Amenorrhœa, and more rarely lactation, sometimes occurs with chlorpromazine, due to the drug's action on hypothalamic centres influencing pituitary functions. Menstruation returns to normal after stopping the drug.

Neurological Effects. Parkinsonism is common after large doses of phenothiazines. Rigidity, tremor and salivation may be marked if large doses are given uncontrolled by anti-Parkinsonian drugs. Stelazine in particular is associated with dystonic reactions. These can occur suddenly and assume very bizarre and alarming forms. This is particularly so in children, and such reactions may lead to a mistaken diagnosis of tetanus or meningitis, or be dismissed as hysterical. Individual idiosyncracy plays a part, for some patients invariably develop these symptoms, even after small doses. There may be loss of voluntary muscle control and involuntary spasms causing trismus, opisthotonous, oculogyric crises, and so on. Motor restlessness may occur also, and the patient describes this as a feeling of 'inner anxiety' or 'jitters'. Alternatively, in different regions of the body there may be muscle weakness and discomfort, joint pains and curious paræsthesiæ. These extrapyramidal effects can often be diminished or abolished by an anti-Parkinsonian drug such as Disipal (orphenadrine) 50 mg t.d.s.

It is advisable to give this or similar drugs concomitantly when large doses of phenothiazines are given.

Epileptic fits may occur when large amounts of phenothiazines are first given, or if the dosage is suddenly greatly increased.

A number of patients with anorexia nervosa, treated with 600–800 mg a day of chlorpromazine, together with modified insulin, have had fits during the first ten days of treatment. Withdrawal symptoms may occur if large doses of chlorpromazine are suddenly stopped.

Allergic or Hypersensitivity Effects. Jaundice sometimes occurs with chlorpromazine, usually within the first two months of treatment. It is an obstructive type of jaundice, associated with eosinophilia, and it is unrelated to the dosage. Nearly all such cases resolve quickly and fully when the drug is stopped. Some people claim that there is no need to stop the drug, the jaundice disappearing whether this is or is not done. We feel, on common sense grounds alone, that chlorpromazine should generally be stopped and that subsequently, after recovery, another phenothiazine should usually be given in its stead. Undoubtedly many of the cases of jaundice are really concomitant attacks of infective hepatitis. There seems to be so much less jaundice now than there was when the phenothiazines were first introduced.

Agranulocytosis is a rare complication, but should always be thought of if a patient develops a sore throat or an unexplained pyrexia. Dermatitis may occur with both chlorpromazine and Stelazine, but only if it is severe or progressive need the drug be stopped. Photosensitivity is common with chlorpromazine; and patients should always be warned of the dangers of sunshine, for severe burns may follow only a few hours of sunbathing.

Some American reports at one time stressed the supposed dangers of giving ECT to patients on chlorpromazine. We have never found any dangers in this; but if large doses are being given at the same time as ECT, the patient should be kept lying down after treatment to avoid postural hypotension and the drug should generally be stopped for three or four hours before each treatment.

Overdosage leads to drowsiness, extrapyramidal effects, and convulsions. Gastric lavage should be carried out; the patient should be kept flat, and noradrenaline should be given if persistent hypotension makes it advisable. Convulsions may be frequent, and intramuscular paraldehyde or barbiturates may be needed to control them.

FLUPHENAZINE (Moditen). It is wise to learn all there is to know about just a few drugs. Trying to acquaint oneself with many, like but not quite alike in their action, and perhaps madly switching from one to another, leads only to confusion and error. For this reason we have no mention of the many phenothiazines having a similar action to chlorpromazine and stelazine. But Moditen (fluphenazine enanthate) must be specially mentioned. It is a long-acting phenothiazine which can be injected weekly or at long intervals. Sometimes it brings about a great improvement in schizophrenic patients who have not responded very well to phenothiazines by mouth. The commonly given explanation is that orally administered drugs have failed of their effect because the patient has been taking them only irregularly. But this is not always the case. However that may be many patients who have not till then improved as much as one hoped, once the drugs have been switched, improve and stabilise in a most impressive manner.

Although the drug is injected weekly, usually the patient still has to take anti-Parkinsonian drugs daily to combat the side effects. He is the more ready to do this, since leaving them off can release very unpleasant symptoms. So it is that irregular takers of phenothiazines by mouth become regular takers of the side-effect antidotes!

The dose of Moditen given by intramuscular injection will be between 25 mg and 100 mg, once a week to begin with. The intervals may be lengthened when a remission is obtained. It seems, possible that schizophrenia is on the way to being controlled, like pernicious anaemia, by regular injections given in out-patient clinics.

Modicate (fluphenazine decoanate) can be given at longer intervals of a month or more; but we have no extensive experience with this drug.

Moditen is a valuable drug in **other** conditions than schizophrenia. Several patients with rapid manic-depressive swings have been brought under control with weekly Moditen injections. For reasons we do not understand, two cases of recurrent hysterical stupor, defying all other treatments for years, stopped having attacks when put on Moditen. Sometimes severe obsessive tension states can also be helped. In such patients Moditen should be given combined with antidepressant drugs; with combined therapy the obsessive thoughts create less tension. Moditen may also be helpful following modified leucotomy, to stabilise recovery, as well as in anorexia nervosa.

Korenyi and Whittier (1967) obtained remarkable results using Moditen in Huntington's chorea. We have ourselves observed striking improvement in patients with hysterical blepharospasm and compulsive mouth movements, when other treatments had failed; when the drug was stopped the symptoms returned.

Polypharmacy is essential in modern therapy, especially if the symptoms of schizophrenia and manic depression coexist in the one patient. Thus Moditen in the acute phase of schizophrenia may need to be combined with ECT and possibly modified insulin treatment. In manic-depressive illness, ECT and the antidepressant drugs or lithium may all have to be given with the Moditen. If one is out to test a drug it is one thing; but when treating a patient one must not be deterred from using any drug or drugs in combinations which commend themselves.

Occasionally a severe depression may supervene, with treatment by Moditen as with all phenothiazines. In our experience this is not common. But those who are giving Moditen to out-patients must remember this possible complication, and not forget a tactful enquiry at the time of giving the weekly injection. As far as possible the administration of the drug should be under medical supervision.

HALOPERIDOL (Serenace). This drug, structurally related to gamma-amino-butyric acid, is especially useful in controlling states of agitation and severe excitement. It can be a most effective drug in the treatment of mania often best used together with lithium and ECT. Psychomotor overactivity will often be brought under control within a few hours, and all symptoms abolished in four or five days. Schizophrenic excitement may also respond, but although the hallucinations and paranoid delusions of chronic schizophrenics have sometimes improved, the basic schizophrenic process is not usually helped by haloperidol. Restless and difficult behaviour in subnormals, both children and adults, is also often considerably improved.

Haloperidol sometimes has depressive side-effects. But a combination of haloperidol with an antidepressant drug may help to stabilise some cyclothymic patients who swing rapidly and frequently between mania and depression.

To control mania and other states of overactivity up to 5 mg of haloperidol has been given intravenously, and repeated six-hourly until symptoms are controlled. Oral haloperidol can then be substituted, the average daily amount being 3–12 mg, in three divided doses. Some chronic schizophrenics have received 60 mg or more a day.

Seignat (1961) obtained good results, quite unexpectedly, with haloperidol in Gille de la Tourette's syndrome. This has been confirmed by others since. Even the troublesome coprolalia seems to be influenced by the drug.

Extrapyramidal side effects are common and often limit the amount that can be given. It is therefore advisable to combine an anti-Parkinsonian drug like Disipal with haloperidol at the start of treatment.

HEMINEVRIN (chlormethiazole). This is a drug which has been in use in France for 10 years and for a lesser time in other countries. It is becoming recognized as a tranquillizer of considerable power. At present it is mostly being used to withdraw alcohol, and in the treatment of delirium tremens, a condition which can be caused by the rapid withdrawal of barbiturates and other addictive drugs as well as alcohol. In these conditions it may be a life-saver; it is sometimes forgotten how often death can result in severe withdrawal states.

Given intravenously, Heminevrin can induce very deep sleep in a matter of minutes, and it can be so used in the treatment of a psychotic emergency state; 200 to 300 ml of an 0·8 per cent solution nearly always induces sleep in the next 15 minutes. It can be given as an infusion by intravenous drip: and, so given in delirium tremens, can be continued for 48 hours during which 0·5 to 2 litres will be used. Generally, it is possible to switch over much earlier than that to oral administration.

When it is proposed to give the drug by mouth, one begins with an immediate dose of 2·0 g (four tablets); then give one tablet (0·5 g) every half-hour until sleep is induced. Doses varying between 0.5 and 2·0 g are then given at 3- to 6-hourly intervals. The tablets should be swallowed with a fair amount of water to promote absorption.

We have been very impressed by the value of this drug in delirious states, and it seems to be a definite improvement on the phenothiazines. One can, however, switch to the phenothiazines, with a lesser risk of habituation, once the delirium is over. More than once, in the middle of a continuous narcosis when the patient had become delirious, we have switched from the phenothiazines to Heminevrin, and back again later.

The uses of this drug, apart from delirious and confusional states, still wait to be fully explored. Among other actions, it seems to be an anti-epileptic.

LITHIUM CARBONATE. Although many manic states respond to haloperidol or phenothiazines, combined with ECT if necessary, this illness can still prove difficult to manage. Patients may be refractory to these drugs, or severe side effects may prevent them being given in adequate amounts. In such cases Cade (1949) showed that lithium salts may be extremely helpful in controlling symptoms.

Lithium was used widely in the last century for various medical conditions, but it has only been used in psychiatry since 1949. Rice (1956) also reviewed the literature and confirmed earlier reports of the effectiveness of lithium salts in mania.

More recently, claims have been made by Schou and his colleagues (1960) that lithium is a 'normothymic', i.e. a stabilizer that tends to flatten out manic-depressive swings; not only are manic attacks helped, but it is said that depressive attacks also are shortened, made milder or abolished (Gattozzi, 1970). This seems to be true in some cases; and if lithium is continued over months manic attacks cease, and the duration of depressive attacks gets less (Coppen, 1971). But, it seems at present, this is not so in all cases; and we do not know how to distinguish those patients whose depression is also helped from those who are only relieved when in a manic state. Part of the answer may lie in the rate of excretion of lithium. The advance of understanding in this field would have been aided much more by research into the mechanisms involved, than by the obstinate and total scepticism evinced by some critics.

For the effective control of manic attacks it seems that blood levels of around 1·2 mEq/1 may be needed; it should not be lower than 0·6 nor higher than 1·6 mEq/1. Blood lithium levels are quickly estimated on a flame photomotor, if the instrument is available.

The deaths originally reported with lithium occurred when large doses of around 3000 mg a day were being given; and some deaths have occurred on smaller doses than that. Fortunately there are unmistakable clinical signs of toxicity, especially a tremor of the hands. One of us has been using lithium for several years now, using hand tremors, thirst and diarrhoea as indicators of excessive dosage. When the drug is stopped, the excess is quickly excreted; and administration can be begun again at a lower level in a day or two. But better results may well be obtained if blood levels are followed weekly or monthly, to make sure that rapid excretion is not reducing the blood lithium to too low a level to be therapeutically effective. This may be one of the reasons why some patients are helped more than others.

As a rule 1200 mg of lithium carbonate a day rarely produces hand tremor or other upset. In acute manias the doses should be higher than that for a few days, up to 2000 mg. It seems that the more acute the mania, the more the lithium is retained, and recovery is accompanied by increased excretion. The dose of 2000 mg should not be maintained for long in the absence of blood level controls. In about a week the dose should drop to 800 to 1200 mg daily as a maintenance dosage, the level required being controlled by blood levels or at least careful watching for toxic side effects. Deaths are only likely to occur if too large a dosage is used, and if too little attention is paid to early signs of toxicity; we have had no deaths in lithium treatment in several years of use without using repeated blood levels but lowering the dose when hard tremor occurs.

Anorexia, nausea, ataxia, tinnitus and blurred vision are other side effects which should be looked out for and, if noted, should lead to stopping the drug temporarily. Still more alarming are attacks of arm hyperextension and fits. When such severe toxic symptoms appear, the blood level is generally around 2·0 mEq/1. There is no antidote, though salt (sodium chloride) may be given and general supportive measures instituted to promote rapid excretion.

In the authors' experience, the tricyclic drugs Surmontil and Tryptizol (Elavil), but not Tofranil, are also effective in the control of some manic as well as of depressive attacks. Doses of 100 to 150 mg are taken at night continuously for a year or two. Side effects are minimal. Such a dosage can be combined with low doses of the more toxic lithium given at the same time. In several patients attacks of depression have stopped or diminished in length, as well as the manic attacks, when given this treatment. In combined therapy, 400 to 1000 mg of lithium carbonate can be combined with 100 to 150 mg of the tricyclic antidepressant in the 24 hours, lithium being taken by day or night, and the tricyclic all at night.

In acute manic attacks up to 2000 mg of lithium may be given alone for a short time, or 1200 lithium and 150 mg Tryptizol or Surmontil. In addition chlorpromazine or haloperidol may be added, and also ECT. When the attack of mania is over, the tricyclic helps to prevent the depressive swing, and smaller doses of lithium can be continued. This is where blood levels help one to see just what is happening to the blood chemistry. Sometimes going on with the lithium seems to deepen the depression that often follows a manic attack; but Schou and others report that the post-manic depressions may be progressively lessened in length. Of course, ECT can be used to shorten the depression if necessary, as can the MOAI antidepressants, both the latter being given together with a continuation of lithium.

Patients with strong tendencies to swing between mania or hypomania and depression can be very difficult to stabilise. In the present state of our knowledge, it seems worth while to continue lithium and the tricyclic antidepressants in such patients, where required. Several patients have finally been stabilised by the additional use of Moditen intramuscularly.

GROUP 2

The drugs of this group, in contrast to those of the first group which we have discussed, are of little or no use in controlling psychotic symptoms, but are helpful in relieving neurotic anxiety. They do not affect autonomic centres to any degree and never cause extrapyramidal side effects. There are many of them to choose from, but we shall only mention diazepam (Valium) and methaminodiazepoxide (Librium). In previous editions we have discussed the uses of meprobamate (Equanil), but omit this here, as the two we mention are less addictive and cause fewer withdrawal symptoms. However, like all drugs relieving tension and causing some degree of euphoria they too are liable to cause habituation, especially if given in large doses.

METHAMINODIAZEPOXIDE (Librium). This drug was introduced in 1960 for the treatment of neurotic states in which anxiety is prominent. It can also be helpful with obsessional neuroses, and the control of alcoholic withdrawal symptoms.

But in recent years diagnostic classifications in the neuroses are becoming blurred, especially between anxiety states and depressions. It has been found that, in patients of adequate previous personality, the start of a depressive attack may take the form of an anxiety state. The symptoms then respond better to antidepressants, especially of the MAOI group, than to sedatives used alone. Because of the effectiveness of the new antidepressants in combating anxiety attacks as well as depressions, it is only the life-long anxiety state that is found to respond better to sedatives alone, than to sedatives and antidepressants combined. One of the great mistakes still being made by some psychiatrists and many physicians is to use Librium alone in recent anxiety states. Because so many of them have a depressive basis, the Librium used alone may increase depressive symptoms, even if some of the tension is toned down.

It is in combination with a MAOI antidepressant like Nardil or Parnate that Librium is so effective. Anxiety and phobic states, and reactive forms of depression accompanied by tension symptoms, will respond well to this combination, provided the underlying personality of the patient is adequate. Details of this combined treatment are given in the next section.

The dose of Librium used alone varies from 5 mg b.d. to as much as 50 mg a day, although so large a dose should be reduced as soon as possible to 30 mg a day or less to avoid dependence and addiction. Too large a dose will neutralise the effect of any antidepressant drugs given at the same time. It is, accordingly, most important that only a limited dosage is given when Librium is merely a part of the total treatment.

The common side effects are drowsiness and, particularly in older patients, memory upset and ataxia. Reducing the dosage will usually stop or lessen these effects. Rashes may occur. Suicidal attempts with the drug have been made, and call for the usual methods of resuscitation.

VALIUM (diazepam). This was introduced into practice some time after Librium. It is a drug with somewhat similar effects, and in pharmacological experiments has proved somewhat more potent. Again, it is better combined with the MAOI antidepressants in recent anxiety states, than when used alone. The dosage is usually from 2 to 10 mg three times a day. It has also been recommended in spastic syndromes after strokes and in disseminated sclerosis, because of its muscle-relaxant properties. It is for this reason that it is also used in obstetrics. Withdrawal symptoms occur when the drug is suddenly stopped after heavy dosage.

Intravenous Valium in phobic anxiety states. The majority of diffuse phobic anxiety states respond to combined MAOI drugs with Valium or Librium by mouth (see below). But deeply rooted single or multiple phobias may need something more. Dally found that such patients were often greatly helped by twice weekly intravenous injections of Valium; and Spears at St. Thomas's has been following up this lead with a special out-patient intravenous Valium clinic.

The patients are all kept on Parstelin alone, or Parstelin during the day and Surmontil at night, while having this treatment. Twice a week they are given intravenous Valium in doses gradually increasing from 10 mg to 40 mg. That dose is found which makes them relaxed and sleepy for half an hour on a bed provided. When they get up, and often for the next two days, their anxiety is in abeyance; and they must then tackle the phobic situations, not till then previously able to be faced even with the MAOIs. Each time after the injection more fears are tackled, and gradually deconditioning is put through by repeated practice.

Valium has a most interesting effect intravenously, which it does not seem to have when taken by mouth. Patients with phobias only helped a little by the MAOIs can tackle them effectively with additional Valium. It is interesting that the sedative effect lasts for around two days.

One possible danger is, as when methedrine was given intravenously, that the patient starts to like and then to demand weekly or twice weekly injections. Phobias should therefore be deconditioned as soon as possible, and the treatment then tapered off. However, we have found one or two patients who were able to return to work after years of phobic incapacity, who have come to depend on the injections, and present the problem of being 'conditioned' to them. Intramuscular injection may be substituted in some cases to help tail off the drug. The MOAI drugs should be continued by mouth after intravenous Valium has been stopped to maintain improvement.

BROMIDES. At one time, before the introduction of barbiturates, bromides were the sedatives most commonly prescribed. They have now been almost entirely replaced by barbiturates and the newer sedatives, though they are still occasionally given in the form of mist. pot. brom, and valerian to patients with a chronic mild tension state, particularly by general practitioners. Bromides are, indeed, preferred by some patients to all other sedatives for the effect obtained; but they have the great disadvantage of being liable to cause bromide intoxication. For this reason they should not be given to old people. Unfortunately, it is still possible to obtain some proprietary medicines containing bromide without prescription, and cases of bromism are seen from time to time.

Bromides act by replacing the chlorides in the body fluids. The rate of substitution depends on the quantity of bromide given, the fluid and chloride intake, and the renal efficiency of the patient. As the salt intake varies in different individuals, so does the amount of bromide, remaining in the body after a standard dose. The prescription of bromides without knowledge of the intake of sodium chloride is tantamount to the prescription of an indefinite amount of bromide. The amount given in a single dose may remain in the blood for over a month if no salt is taken. Bromides may therefore accumulate very readily, even on a small daily intake, and when the blood bromide level reaches a certain point symptoms of intoxication will appear.

The earliest symptoms of bromide intoxication may be excessive fatigue and sleepiness. There may be ataxia. Poor appetite, loss of weight, increasing mental dullness go on into broken sleep, delirium or stupor, with hallucinations and a panicky fear as common features. If the condition is suspected, it may be recognised by promptly withdrawing the bromides and administering salt, or by the estimation of the blood bromide level. The level at which symptoms of intoxication appear depends on personal idiosyncrasy, age, arteriosclerosis and renal efficiency. A blood bromide of 150 mg per cent may be significant in a man of 60 with arteriosclerosis, but is unlikely to be so in a fit young person. Levels of up to 350 mg per cent have been seen exceptionally without symptoms; but as a rule 250 mg per cent are sufficient to produce undesirable effects. Fatal intoxication or death from secondary heart and chest complications may occur with levels of 350 to 500 mg per cent. Treatment consists in ample sodium chloride and fluids till the blood bromide drops again to normal level.

PARALDEHYDE. A much more useful hypnotic than the bromides is paraldehyde in 5 to 10 ml doses. It acts more quickly than most other sedative drugs, and can be given by mouth, per rectum, or intramuscularly. Its chief objection is that it makes the breath smell, and so cannot be prescribed except as a hypnotic in ordinary practice. It has very little effect on the heart and is extremely safe; but after aiding sleep it often leaves a hangover and should not be given for long stretches for this reason. It is of particular value as a hypnotic, and given intramuscularly (10–15 ml) in the treatment of acute and grave psychoses involving excitement or agitation and rapid exhaustion; and it is still a standby in the treatment of status epilepticus. It is so useful for the noisy and troublesome patient that it tended to be over-used in hospitals in the past. Nowadays its place has generally been taken by the phenothiazines and other sedative drugs.

The barbiturates
The barbiturates won acceptance as routine sedatives more slowly than their deserts warranted. They are controlled in sale and distribution, so that the physician can be fairly sure that his prescription is not being over-stepped. No physical harm results from their moderate use even for fairly prolonged periods; most of them are fairly quickly eliminated, so they do not tend to accumulate as bromides do. Sudden withdrawal, if the patient has been on a heavy dose or has been taking them for a long time, is very inadvisable, because of the likelihood of producing a confusional state or one or more epileptic fits. But we have not seen any ill effect from gradual withdrawal; and if withdrawal symptoms are to be expected, they can be

avoided or damped down by large doses of chlorpromazine or Heminevrin.

The main disadvantage of the barbiturates is the ease with which they lend themselves to misuse. Because they are so effective there are large numbers of the middle-aged who have become habituated to them in small doses. They are a convenient means of suicide. And recently, as euphoriant drugs have become harder to get, some young people are starting to use them for kicks, and to dissolve and inject them intravenously. It would be a social mistake to restrict their use too strictly by order or regulation; but undoubtedly doctors should more frequently replace them by antidepressants or tranquillizers. The matter is further discussed on page 38.

PHENOBARBITONE (Luminal) is relatively slowly absorbed and is long acting. Its effect may not reach a maximum for some hours, and then continues for a number of hours longer. It is of value in the treatment of some cases of anxiety (and, of course, of epilepsy); but it is of little use as a hypnotic. It should be prescribed as a basic seda-tive, and not *pro re nata*. It may be used when a general damping down of the nervous system for long periods is required. Anxiety symptoms in hypertensives may be helped by it, although a combina-tion of Nardil and a tranquilliser is usually more effective and should be given if depression is also present. Phenobarbitone should rarely be given to depressed patients, as they invariably feel worse on this drug. It may be given to neurotics in doses of up to mg 60 to 120 a day; and it is often helpful to give it in fortnightly or three-weekly courses with intervals between. Withdrawal symptoms are much less prominent and troublesome than with the short-acting barbiturates.

SOLUBLE BARBITONE also has a comparatively slow and lasting effect, though less so than phenobarbitone. Its effect lasts about eight hours, and comes on more rapidly so that it is a very useful hypnotic. For this purpose it should be taken about three-quarters of an hour before going to bed. Some patients complain of a hangover in the morning, but this is not necessarily unpleasant and in some is felt as a slight euphoria. The best type of patient for such medication is the man who goes to sleep fairly easily, but tends to wake up in the early hours of the morning, unable to get to sleep again; or the man who sleeps throughout the night, but restlessly and disturbed by dreams and is unrefreshed in the morning. These types of insomnia are particularly frequent in depressives, for whom this drug, com-bined with specific antidepressive therapy, is very useful.

The patient who sleeps adequately when he can once get to sleep, but has great difficulty in composing himself for the night, a state of affairs seen especially in the anxiety neurotic and the obsessional, needs something with a much more rapid action, such as sodium amytal, or perhaps chloral hydrate (1 to 2 g). Barbitone should be avoided when its hangover effects are unpleasant, and this is most commonly so in the elderly and arteriosclerotic. Sometimes the effect can be so severe that during the greater part of the next day the patient is slightly confused, and may even fall about or become faulty in his habits. In those without some idiosyncrasy of this sort, the drug may be used with confidence. It must be remembered that many patients who complain that sedatives make them feel poorly in the mornings are depressives who suffer from a morning exacerbation, and wrongly blame the drugs they take. Therapy should not be half-hearted. If sleep is required enough should be given to secure it. In doses up to 600 mg it is safe enough.

SODIUM AMYLOBARBITONE (Sodium Amytal). There are a number of more rapidly acting and more quickly excreted barbiturates, of which sodium amylobarbitone will be taken as a typical example. This is the drug *par excellence* for the minor emergency. It is useful both as a sedative (mg 60 to 120) and as a hypnotic (mg 200 to 400). In the latter capacity it is the drug of choice for the patient who has difficulty in getting to sleep; and it may also be taken in the middle of the night by the patient who wakes up after sleeping well for a few hours and cannot sleep again. The neurotic who knows his limitations will keep a few capsules available, on prescription from his doctor, and take one as a prophylactic measure on going to bed after a worrying day when his head is buzzing with thoughts, and he knows he will have difficulty in getting to sleep.

Sodium amylobarbitone is also of particular value in dealing with the panicky attacks to which the phobic anxiety neurotic is liable, particularly if this is a chronic state. The man who is terrified that he will develop an acute anxiety state if he has to travel by train can secure relief by swallowing a capsule, and will very likely feel safe enough even if he knows he has one in his pocket. The neurotic who is compelled to avoid particular situations because of his fear of fear can guard himself by taking mg 60 to 120 of the drug about an hour before the situation has to be faced. The very fact that he knows that he has the relief available may save him hours of misery and persuade him to tackle his particular phobia afresh. But there is a real danger that the patient may start to increase the dose. An addiction develops quickly, with unpleasant withdrawal symptoms when one tries to cut the dose. Fortunately, as Sargant and Dally (1962) have shown, recurrent phobic attacks, particularly in patients of good personality, often do much better with a combination of Nardil and Librium or Parstelin.

Fortunately the tricyclic antidepressants, such as Surmontil or Tryptizol (Elavil), are very useful for keeping patients asleep; from 25 to 150 mg are taken at night. Tolerance develops much more rarely than with the barbiturates. A patient who is on a large dose of barbiturates should be gradually weaned off. A small dose only, say 200 mg, is given with which to get to sleep; and the tricyclic drug, in a dose up to 150 mg, will keep him comfortably asleep till morning. Often the barbiturate can be withdrawn entirely and a tricyclic substituted; though this may mean greater difficulty in getting to sleep, there will be less early morning waking.

In recent years the use of the short-acting barbiturates has grown very greatly, and certain real dangers have not always been remembered. Habituation and addiction may both occur; and then an increasing dosage leads to a vicious spiral of confusion and increasing rather than diminished tension. If doses of 200 to 600 mg of sodium amylobarbitone have been taken at night for long periods, a state of chronic tension is particularly likely to occur. As a result of the habituation the body is demanding more and more of the drug, and is not receiving it. Withdrawal under the protection of large doses of chlorpromazine or Heminevrin then becomes imperative. Also too much barbiturate neutralises the effects of any MAOI being also given.

If the drug is quickly withdrawn, anxiety will increase and confusional and psychotic symptoms may occur. Even a short period of very heavy sedation causes some adaptation, so that rapid withdrawal after continuous narcosis may also cause confusional states or epileptic fits. Withdrawal over a period of a week or more will obviate such dangers. For these reasons, however, the daily dosage in any prolonged course should be kept as small as possible. Because of the relaxing and euphorising effects of these drugs, it may easily occur that too large a daily dosage is demanded, and carelessly prescribed. One should be particularly careful about an over-liberal dosage in the case of psychopathic patients, who may abuse the benefit of the drugs and the confidence of the doctor.

Emergency uses of barbiturates

In psychiatric emergencies barbiturate sedatives can be usefully administered intravenously, and for this purpose sodium amylobarbitone or pentothal are probably the best. If adequate nursing help is available, it is certainly a much more effective method than the classical one of giving morphia and hyoscine, and is quicker and less painful than intramuscular chlorpromazine or paraldehyde. Prolonged periods of panic, or wild struggling, are often remembered by the patient when the acutest phase of the psychosis has passed off, and remain for him a nightmare which he would wish to forget. The more such episodes can be abbreviated the better both for his immediate and subsequent state; 250–500 mg of penthothal given intravenously produces unconsciousness and deep sleep immediately. The breathing space will give time for more slowly acting drugs like chlorpromazine or haloperidol to take effect, and for the nurses to get the patient settled. When he comes round the patient may still be mildly confused, euphoric and suggestible, and then susceptible to reassurance or suggestion. Sodium amylobarbitone 200 to 500 mg intravenously does not produce total unconsciousness as a rule, but may secure relative calm. In general, intravenous amytal is better for states where anxiety is the most prominent symptom, pentothal where there is excitement and aggressiveness.

Barbiturates can also be used as a prophylactic to prevent breakdown and the development of phobias in those who are exhibiting psychiatric symptoms under exceptional stress for the first time. Often the earliest sign of impending breakdown in the good previous personality is that sleep does not occur when there is both the opportunity and the desire for it. With increasing exhaustion a vicious circle of anxiety and insomnia starts. The nervous system is then open to the acquirement of a wide variety of conditioned phobias. Really heavy sedation, such as sodium amylobarbitone 200 to 600 mg, combined if necessary with chlorpromazine 100–200 mg, should procure many hours of deep sleep and break up the vicious circle before permanent damage or neurotic conditioning has occurred, especially if supplemented by other treatment that may be necessary later.

OTHER SEDATIVES

With every new edition of this book it has been necessary to provide comments about new sedatives, which have appeared from time to time and as these drugs come and go in popularity. Popularity is to some extent a matter of mere fashion; but there are differences in the quality of the effects produced and in the fields of usefulness. As has been repeatedly emphasised in these pages, it is best to get to know a very limited list of sedatives really well. Only in this way can the dosage be suited sensitively, expertly and successfully to the needs and idiosyncrasies of individual patients.

PHENERGAN (promethazine) is a useful hypnotic, and has been used to reinforce other sedatives, such as Mandrax, during a course of continuous sleep treatment. The dosage is from 25 mg to 75 mg, when used as a sedative on its own.

MANDRAX is a combination of methaqualone 250 mg with Benadryl (diphenhydramine) 25 mg. It gives a relaxing and sound sleep. It has euphoric effects, which make it popular for 'kicks', and special restrictions have been placed on it governmentally. It is very useful for sleep treatment; or methaqualone can be given by itself. At the end of treatment the withdrawal symptoms are much less severe than with the barbiturates. In treating anxiety and depressive states with early waking and difficulty in getting to sleep, Mandrax to induce sleep and Surmontil to keep the patient asleep is a good combination. One danger is that there is no antidote (apart from ordinary resuscitation measures) when an overdose is taken. But more Mandrax than short acting barbiturates are being given by us at present because withdrawal symptoms and increasing tolerance seem less marked.

MOGADON (nitrazepam) is useful for the contrary reason: it is very difficult to commit suicide with this drug. It is an effective hypnotic, and could well replace the barbiturates and Mandrax in early cases with poor sleep.

DORIDEN (glutethimide) is related to the barbiturates; it is widely used as a sedative and hypnotic. But it seems that addiction is common, and patients quickly deteriorate when this happens. It should be used only guardedly.

One word of warning should be borne in mind. When a patient has become addicted to one of the euphorising sedatives, it is no good just switching to another; that also will be abused. Because of their tendency to get addicted to sedatives, some patients can only be treated for sleep disturbances with the tricyclic antidepressants and chlorpromazine. With the sedatives, as with alcoholics, small doses simply create a craving for more.

Stimulation

The advent of the phenothiazines and other tranquillisers made a great difference to the treatment of schizophrenia, but had little effect on depressive illnesses. Numerous derivatives of amphetamine had been tried, but were not found very useful except in mild neurotic types of depression. New drugs came and went and for many years ECT remained unchallenged as the most effective means of alleviating depression.

Then in 1957 Marsilid and Tofranil were introduced into psychiatry. Very high success rates were claimed at first, and these drugs were advertised as being as good as ECT, or even better. But experience has shown that these new drugs are no substitute for ECT in serious depressive states, although they can be most useful in some milder depressions. What is so exciting, however, is that the antidepressants have turned out to be useful drugs for the patients with phobic anxiety and panic states. The differences between the treatment of anxiety states and of depression in those of adequate previous personality is becoming less and less, as we learn more about the proper use of these drugs in long term follow up. There are still disagreements about their effectiveness and the selective indications for their use; but this may reflect rather the lack of an agreed system of classification of the affective states, than fundamental differences in clinical experience.

MONOAMINE OXIDASE INHIBITORS (MAOI)

IPRONIAZID (Marsilid) was the first MAOI to be used in psychiatry. Its antidepressant activity, like that of others in the same group, is believed to be related partly to its ability to inhibit the enzyme monamine oxidase (MAO), which is intimately concerned in brain function. A number of possibly less toxic analogues, all capable of inhibiting MAO, have been developed. None of these is, unfortunately, as effective as Marsilid, but in many cases the newer compounds like Nardil (phenelzine), Marplan (isocarboxazid), and Parnate (tranylcypromine) provide a satisfactory form of treatment. Their actions and side effects are similar, and to avoid confusion we shall only describe those of Nardil and Parnate, which are typical of this group.

What worried people about Marsilid in the early days was the risk of jaundice, and this led to its being banned in the USA. But it has been used over here now for 10 years, and there has been no more jaundice than with other MAOI drugs. Some of our patients have been on it for years, including one who had had what was supposed to be Marsilid jaundice. Undoubtedly many of the early cases of supposed Marsilid jaundice were due to an undiagnosed infective hepatitis.

NARDIL (phenelzine). West and Dally (1959) and Sargant (1960) at St. Thomas's have shown that the type of depression responding best to phenelzine is the reactive, exogenous, atypical or 'hysterical' depression. Here anxiety if often the predominant feature and depression seems sometimes to be of secondary importance. These depressions were often most difficult to treat in the past. Psychotherapy frequently seemed to have no effect; electro-shock might do more harm than good; and simple sedation relieved tension but left the patient feeling more depressed.

Symptoms may vary widely, and probably depend on how severe the anxiety is and on the type of personality affected. The patient may complain of a constant, yet irrational dread of impending disaster. Or somatic symptoms such as headache, palpitations and muscle pains may come to dominate his life and fill his mind. Sometimes anxiety becomes displaced on to outside objects and situations; phobias of harming people, travelling or going out alone are common symptoms, and the picture is often very similar to that of an anxiety-hysteria. Occasionally frank hysterical conversions occur, and we have seen fugues and amnesic states that did not clear up fully until the underlying depression was recognised and treated with Nardil.

Clinically these patients may show few signs of endogenous depression. They tend to project rather than introject their feelings, and blame other people rather than themselves for their plight. Sleep disturbance takes the form more of difficulty in getting to sleep than early morning waking; in fact these patients may be sleeping heavily when it is time to get up and have the utmost difficulty in waking. Instead of feeling worse in the first half of the day and then steadily improving, they may be at their best early on and may feel dreadful later in the day. An almost constant feature for women is a marked exacerbation of symptoms a week or ten days before the period.

Sometimes symptoms have been present for years, or have run a chronic phasic course, and the patient may have come to be looked upon by his relatives or doctor as a difficult neurotic for whom little can be done. In other cases symptoms develop rapidly after some special or prolonged stress. For instance, a middle-aged woman devotedly cared for her bed-ridden mother for two years, and at the same time held a responsible job. A month after her mother's death she developed an overwhelming fear of going out alone. She had to give up her job, and over the next six months became a miserable recluse. Another woman, with an unsatisfactory marriage, drifted into an affair with one of her husband's employees. Feelings of guilt were suppressed, but somatic symptoms became increasingly prominent, and continued long after the affair had ended. Both these women recovered when treated with Nardil combined with Librium, earlier treatments having had little effect.

Although these patients may be regarded as neurotic or inadequate personalities, this is not really so. One of the characteristics of the exogenous depressions responding to Nardil is that the patients are well able to cope with their problems before they break down, and the personality before the illness is a good one. Typically, they tend to be over-conscientious, rather sensitive, highly strung people, with a lot of energy and drive. Often they seem to have over-reactive autonomic systems, which may account for some of their symptoms. They may push themselves to the limit of their capacity, and in spite of disabling symptoms, they try to carry on with their work.

Lifelong inadequate personalities, who may present with somewhat similar symptoms, are not helped much by Nardil. In fact, such patients may become more tense, and in some cases inhibitions may be lessened, releasing irresponsible or anti-social behaviour. Generally they respond better to barbiturates or Drinamyl; but there is a serious risk of addiction in this type of patient. This emphasises the importance of taking account of basic characteristics of the pre-morbid personality; and that, of course, requires a full and perceptive history. Psychiatrists who take no trouble with their histories cannot expect to distinguish the advantages of one drug over another, and may look forward to making the same mistake over and over again. Nardil is not going to help a patient who since childhood has constantly proved unable to cope with relatively minor difficulties.

Where anxiety is very marked, the effect of Nardil is considerably enhanced by combining it with a tranquillising drug. In fact it seems that this combination of drugs, properly given, is one of the most effective treatments for anxiety states in people of good personality. Phobic anxiety and somatic anxiety symptoms seem to respond well to a combination of Nardil and Librium, while free-floating anxiety sometimes responds better to Nardil combined with one of the piperazine phenothiazines such as Stelazine. Neither a tranquilliser nor Nardil given alone is nearly as effective as the combination (Sargant and Dally, 1962).

Patients with cardiac neurosis or effort syndrome, who do not respond to reassurance, do particularly well with this combination of drugs. Palpitation, hyperventilation effects and pain over the heart may convince the patient that he has heart disease and lead to a vicious spiral of mounting anxiety and autonomic over-activity. Even when true angina is present, anxiety may increase symptoms out of all proportion. Treatment with Nardil combined with Librium will usually lead to marked improvement within 10 days (Sargant and Dally, 1962). There have been claims made recently that Nardil will relieve anginal pain, supposedly by increasing coronary blood flow or raising pain threshold centrally. It seems more likely that such improvement as does occur is secondary to relief of depression and anxiety.

Fatigue is a common complaint of these patients, and many say that they wake up in the morning just as tired as when they went to bed. They feel drained of energy, dull and lacking all interest and the smallest molehill becomes a mountain. Unlike truly endogenous depressions, with these patients appetite for food and sex often remains good; they may sleep heavily both day and night; and they look well physically. Small wonder that they receive scant sympathy and understanding from others.

Psychosomatic states sometimes respond as fully as exogenous depressions to Nardil. Mucous colitis may improve rapidly and even ulcerative colitis in the early stages before permanent organic changes have occurred. So may rheumatoid arthritis and some cases of skin conditions and asthma, although changes are often more apparent to the patient than to others, and reflect merely a more cheerful mood.

In general, it is fair to assume that if a patient fails to respond *at all* to proper treatment with Nardil or Parnate he is unlikely to do so with another MAOI, with the exception of Marsilid, which still so often helps when the rest fail. However, there may be differences in the degree of response by individual patients to different MAOI drugs, so that after a *partial* response only to Nardil it may sometimes be better to change to another MAOI.

The effective dosage of Nardil varies a lot from patient to patient.

It is important to find the right dose as quickly as possible. Too small a dose will be ineffective; if it is too large, side effects may counteract its benefits. In out-patient practice it is best to start with 15 mg t.d.s. and to warn the patient of possible side effects, and tell him to reduce the dose if they become too troublesome. If, after a fortnight, there is no improvement and no troublesome side effects, the dosage can be increased to 15 mg q.d.s. With in-patients, of course, larger starting doses can be given.

One must remember that there will be a delay before symptoms begin to improve. It is rarely that improvement comes in under a week, and it may not be for a fortnight or even longer. In the true endogenous depression one may wait a month; but in atypical depressions of the type we are discussing three weeks is long enough for a trial. Once symptoms are relieved, the dose can be progressively lowered to the minimum needed to maintain improvement. The effects of a reduction in dosage, for instance a relapse into depression, also take a time to show; and one should wait seven days after reducing the dose to see whether the new dose is not too low. Since the drug seems to act upon symptoms rather than upon any fundamental process, it may have to be continued for some time until the underlying depression resolves itself. The tendency for spontaneous improvement is, of course, one of the characteristics of depressive illness. So far there is no evidence that the anti-depressive drugs hasten the onset of this natural improvement, although if given towards the end of an attack all symptoms appear to clear up rapidly. But as a rule medication will have to be continued after symptoms have been relieved, if relapse is to be prevented.

Nardil should not be stopped suddenly, for in some patients a sudden cutting off results in exacerbation or return of depressive symptoms, and other anxiety effects. It seems best to reduce and stop the drug over the course of a month or more.

In some cases of closely recurring attacks of depression, it has proved possible to abort or modify attacks by continuing therapy with a reduced dose during the recovery phase. One or two tablets a day of the drug are taken continuously, and the patient increases this to an agreed effective dose immediately he feels symptoms beginning to return. In this way the usual time lag is reduced between the start of treatment and improvement, and the depressive process has not time to deepen and establish itself. Some of our patients with recurrent depressions and anxiety states have now been having this type of treatment for 10 years, with no need to increase the dosage.

Previously no other form of treatment had influenced their attacks, and the uncertainty of never knowing when symptoms might recur had led some of these patients into a state of demoralisation.

PARNATE (tranylcypromine) and *Parstelin* (tranylcypromine 10 mg, trifluoperazine 1 mg). Parnate is a non-hydrazine MAO inhibitor. It is generally best used in a tablet combined with a small dose of Stelazine as Parstelin. The effects are similar to a combination of Nardil and Librium in one tablet. Parnate and Parstelin have the same action, and what has been written about Nardil applies equally to Parnate.

The main difference is that Parnate has a stronger and quicker action than Nardil. Patients may start to improve, if they are going to do so, in a matter of 5 to 10 days. To the previously despairing patient, whom the MAOIs so often help, the quicker the improvement the greater is the chance that he will not lose faith prematurely. But, as with Nardil, the really severe depression may not be helped, or it may still take a month for improvement to come.

Parnate or Parstelin is particularly effective in the treatment of phobic anxiety states. If the personality is adequate, the autonomic overaction—palpitation, breathlessness, heart pains, turning over of the stomach, headaches—may all not occur, or occur in diminished degree, when with the help of the drug the phobia is tackled afresh. When she finds she can go to the shops, and has done so several times, without fainting, the phobia is deconditioned. But the drug may have to be kept on for a year or two if the illness has been of long duration. Difficult patients, while being given the Parstelin, can be helped additionally by twice weekly intravenous injections of Valium (diazepam) (see p. 33).

Most of the patients who come to psychiatrists with anxiety and depressive syndromes have had the tricyclics given them by their doctors already; much of our work now consists simply in switching to the MAOIs, which are still too often neglected. But Parstelin is as ineffective as Nardil in patients who are really requiring ECT.

One of the indications that a MAOI is needed, and not a tricyclic, is when the patient reports that after deep sleep all night he is still waking tired in the morning. Patients like this, who are helped by the MAOIs, feel worse on tricyclics, especially if they are given during the day. If it is given too late in the afternoon or evening, Parstelin can affect falling asleep. It is best to give two tablets in the morning, and one after lunch or not later than tea-time.

For further uses of Nardil and Parnate, see under Combined Antidepressants (pp. 53–54).

IMIPRAMINE (Tofranil). Nardil and Parnate are less effective in cases of endogenous depression characterised by feelings of guilt and self-reproach, retardation and agitation, early morning waking, feeling worse in the morning and so on. These cases generally respond better to imipramine, especially when retardation is present.

Imipramine is very similar in structure to promazine. It was, in fact, first tried in the treatment of schizophrenia, with rather poor results, its antidepressive properties coming to light accidentally. After it was introduced in 1957 the usual excessive claims as to its efficacy were made. But experience showed that, while it was a useful drug in milder depressions, it was certainly inferior to ECT in the treatment of severe states of depression, and was sometimes liable to make agitated patients worse when given on its own. In the first clinical report on imipramine it was stated that the best responses occurred in cases of endogenous depression, showing the typical symptoms of mental and motor retardation, fatigue, hopelessness, and guilt. At St. Thomas's it was found, with a group of typical endogenous but not severe depressions, that 70 per cent of the patients responded to imipramine within 14 days, and about one-third of them responded fully. This compared with a response rate of under 40 per cent when patients of this group were treated with Nardil, and the quality of response was also less stable and satisfactory. From a study made before the introduction of the antidepressant drugs, the expected recovery rate for such a group with ECT was about 85 per cent; but at least 20 per cent of the recovered patients can be expected to relapse within two months. Kiloh and Ball (1961), in their follow-up study of imipramine-treated depression, found that because of the tendency of ECT-treated patients to relapse the percentage of success six months after treatment was just the same whether the patient had been treated with ECT or imipramine. However, the relapse rate will be reduced if the drugs and the ECT are given together, and the drugs are kept on after stopping ECT.

Manic depressive illness, provided it is not too severe, will generally respond well to imipramine; and, as with Nardil, it may be possible to modify or abort closely recurring attacks by giving a steady maintenance dose of imipramine during normal phases and increasing the dose immediately symptoms recur.

As with Nardil there is a time lag, sometimes up to three weeks or a month between the start of treatment and clinical improvement. But whereas with Nardil symptoms sometimes lift very suddenly, almost as though a switch had been turned on, with imipramine improvement is usually relatively slow and is more a gradual steady return towards normality. The patient notices that he has more energy, he feels less concerned about himself and the future seems brighter. Frequently one of the first symptoms to improve is the disturbance of sleep, and this improvement may be accompanied by vivid dreams, often a good prognostic sign.

Agitated states of depression, such as typically occur in involutional depression, should only be treated with imipramine in conjunction with a tranquilliser like chlorpromazine. And they generally need ECT as well. Imipramine given alone may lead to an increase of agitation; this may be due to lessening of retardation, but is more probably related to the delay before imipramine begins to be effective. In these cases, by damping down the agitation chlorpromazine gains time for imipramine to become effective. Once the patient starts to improve the chlorpromazine should be slowly and progressively reduced, for of its own it may tend to bring on or to increase depression.

It is a striking fact that imipramine will sometimes be of great benefit in a variety of syndromes in which good results could not easily be expected. This probably is a consequence of the ubiquity of depressive illness, and our inability to be sure of recognising the underlying depressive change when masked by other symptoms. The drug has, in fact, been found to clear up a number of rather confusing psychosomatic conditions which had failed to respond to any other treatment, and it is apparent in retrospect that these conditions were depressive equivalents.

The side effects of imipramine for the first two days are sometimes unpleasant, and the patient may even feel more tired and depressed, so it is probably wise to start out-patients on something less than the dose which is likely to be needed eventually, say 25–50 mg t.d.s., increasing progressively to 75 mg t.d.s. if necessary. There is rarely much point in going beyond this dose, except perhaps in chronic states of depression who have failed to respond to ECT. In-patients can be started on 150 mg a day, and quicker initial results may be obtained by giving this dose intramuscularly for the first four days.

Once symptoms have fully lifted the dosage should be adjusted by trial and error to a level just sufficient to prevent symptoms returning. This dose may vary from 50–150 mg a day. As with Nardil, once improvement has occurred the drug must be continued until the underlying depression has resolved. Sometimes the patient himself recognises when this has happened, but generally it is necessary to lower the dosage every two or three months in order to find this out. And imipramine should not be suddenly stopped, but be gradually tailed off.

Clinical indications for giving imipramine and ECT are similar. But it is certainly not true to say that imipramine has abolished the need for electro-shock. ECT should never be withheld in severe states of depression, nor in most cases where there is agitation. But imipramine, as well as Nardil of course, can be given concomitantly with ECT; and it appears that in some cases the total number of ECT then needed may be reduced. Apart from an additive effect, it may be that imipramine somehow sensitises a patient previously refractory to ECT. For instance, cyclical depressions at the start of an attack sometimes do not respond at all, or only partially, to ECT given at this time, although a few shocks given towards the end of the attack may have a dramatic effect. If now imipramine is given to such a patient at the beginning of a depression, he may then respond fully and promptly to ECT. But afterwards maintenance imipramine will have to be continued for long periods. There seems to be no additional risk from combining antidepressive drugs with ECT and there are many advantages; in fact it is almost routine now for us to give them to all depressed patients receiving ECT.

TRYPTIZOL (amitriptyline) and SURMONTIL (trimipramine). These two tricyclic drugs have largely superseded Tofranil (imipramine) in many depressions; the authors are now using Tofranil very little, and Tryptizol and Surmontil much more. They have more sedative action, and a large dose (mg 100 to 150) can be given at night to combat the early morning waking so typical of many severe depressions. They do not get the patient off to sleep—Mandrax or Mogadon are useful for this—but, if given together, smaller doses of these latter drugs are required to keep the patient asleep. Another advantage they have over Tofranil is that while some patients can be precipitated by Tofranil into a manic or hypomanic state, Tryptizol and Surmontil in adequate dosage (mg 75 to 150) stop or greatly reduce hypomanic swings, as well as helping the depression.

In depressive patients troubled by early morning waking as much as possible of the total dose should be given at night. As the early waking diminishes the patient is likely to start to improve. Sometimes it is found that a patient is very sensitive to Surmontil or Tryptizol, and even a small dose given during the day makes him feel tired or 'terrible' (as they so often say). This generally means that a MAOI will do much better. Worsening of symptoms by the tricyclics is one of the best clinical indications that we should be using MAOI drugs instead.

If Tryptizol or Surmontil is being used alone, half the dose can be given during the day and the rest at night; but if early waking persists the dose given at night should be increased until an optimal effect is obtained. With both drugs, the dose varies from mg 50 in 24 hours to 150 or 200 in very depressed and agitated patients. If ECT is given, the drug should be continued at night between treatments and after they are finished.

Tryptizol and Surmontil can be given at night while a MAOI is given during the day. The combining of drugs is discussed below (p. 53). The two drugs are also useful in schizo-affective states, the antidepressant being given in full dosage (up to 150 mg) at night, while the phenothiazine is given by day by mouth, or by injection weekly or monthly. Most recoverable schizophrenias have affective components, and a combination of drugs is often much more successful than using phenothiazines alone.

Tryptizol and Surmontil can also be given at night in full dosage as a means of getting patients off large doses of addictive sedatives. To prevent withdrawal symptoms, the sedatives are gradually withdrawn and the tricyclic drug is increased. The end may be reached when the patient is left with quite a small dose of sedative to get him to sleep, the rest being done by the tricyclic.

Tryptizol has rather more in the way of side-effects than Surmontil, making the latter usually the drug of choice. There are many other tricyclics; most of the new antidepressants brought out recently under a variety of names are tricyclics. For general purposes only one or two are really needed, but those should be thoroughly understood. It is no good dashing wildly to every new drug that comes along, when it has only the same basic action under a different trade name.

Complications and Side Effects

All the antidepressants, and this particularly applies to Nardil, seem to be capable of potentiating the effects of other drugs, and outpatients should be warned of what this means. In particular they should be told of the dangers of drinking too much alcohol, and should be given an explicit warning against driving under such conditions.

Side effects are common, particularly at the start of treatment, and are mostly directly related to dosage, although individual sensitivity varies.

Postural hypotension is frequent with both the MAOIs and imipramine, causing dizziness and unsteadiness. Amphetamine will sometimes help to raise blood pressure, but is not without its own danger. If hypotensive effects are severe the dosage must be reduced. Especially with the MAOIs, patients must also be warned to get up slowly and not to run up stairs—both of them actions which may bring on hypotensive symptoms. **The occurrence of hypotensive symptoms is not a contra-indication to continuing with the drug; the patient should simply be put on a smaller dose.**

A dry mouth, dirty or black tongue, and thirst are particularly common with imipramine, and may worry the patient until he is re-assured. Blurred vision and difficulty in accommodation are also frequent. Dyspepsia may take several forms, and patients may complain of a burning sensation beneath the sternum or epigastrium after imipramine in particular. Weakness and tiredness may occur at the start of treatment, and usually wear off after one or two weeks. Excessive sweating, often involving only the head or top half of the body, is particularly liable to occur with imipramine. There may be difficulty in starting micturition (also occurring with the MAOIs), or there may be frequency and sleep disturbed by nocturia. Sexual functions may be affected in a variety of ways, more often with the MAOIs than after imipramine. Men may complain of impotence; but sometimes erection occurs normally while orgasm is delayed. Which of these two effects occur seems to depend largely on the dose; a high dose usually causes impotence. This anti-orgasm effect of the MAOIs has been used for the treatment of premature ejaculation, and Bennett (1961) has reported a number of successful cases responding to them. Women may also be affected; in some libido is lost, in others it is heightened, and orgasm may be inhibited.

Dally and others at St. Thomas's have treated a number of women continuously with MAOIs from early pregnancy nearly to term with no apparent ill-effect on the mother or child; and have also tried to prevent puerperal psychosis from developing in women at risk, by giving tricyclic antidepressants before and after the confinement, during the puerperium and for a few months afterwards. The MAOIs have to be stopped a month before pregnancy to allow morphia to be used; but they can be added again to the tricyclic two or three days after the birth. No harmful effects have been reported from the use of these drugs in the way suggested.

Oedema, which is usually dependent, seems to occur mostly with the MAOIs, although slight puffiness around the ankles may be seen in patients treated with tricyclics. The oedema can be quite severe, but can usually be controlled by a diuretic such as chlorothiazide.

Muscle tremors and jerkings, epileptic fits in predisposed patients, and sometimes a reversible peripheral neuritis may occur, which may respond to large doses of pyridoxine when resulting from MAOIs. With imipramine muscle tremor may be very great, and the whole body may shake. There is often reduced need for sleep, and it is as well to warn patients of this possibility. On the other hand, one of the first noticeable effects of the drug may be that sleep returns to normal.

A most unpleasant and potentially dangerous reaction to all the MAOI is a sudden severe pounding headache. This starts at the back of the head, and may be associated with or preceded by tachycardia, dyspoena and great distress. Blood pressure rises, and a subarachnoid hæmorrhage may even occur in a few patients. The acute symptoms may last for several hours, and milder symptoms persist for some days. These attacks are due to the taking of fermented foods which contain tyramine, such as over-ripe bananas and other fruits, high game, or pâté, etc., and also Marmite and tinned fish. Cheese is the commonest offender. Small amounts of alcohol (except Chianti and fermented German beers) are safe: too much causes hypotension and interferes with the action of the antidepressants. Except in an emergency, when a small dose should be given to test sensitivity, *opiates of any sort* (pethidine, morphine, etc.) should not be given within 10 to 14 days of taking MAOIs. Anaesthetics, both general and local, are safe provided there is no opiate pre- or post-medication. Methedrine by injection can be fatal; but amphetamines **by mouth only** are safe in ordinary doses. Some nasal drops give rise to headaches and should be avoided. Ordinary pain killers of a milder type, such as aspirin, may be used as may most sedatives.

The hypertensive headache is treated by lowering the blood pressure as soon as possible. Intravenous Rogitine, if available, brings the blood pressure down quickly. Intravenous sodium amytal or chlorpromazine intramuscularly can be used. If nothing else is available sodium amytal mg 400 to 600 or chlorpromazine mg 200 can be given by mouth. Until the blood pressure has come down there is the danger of a subarachnoid hæmorrhage.

Fortunately such a grave accident is rare in relation to the number of very severe but non-fatal headaches. With reasonable precautions such headaches are exceptional. The possibility of their occurrence is not to be taken as a contra-indication, when clinical considerations suggest that a MAOI drug will be helpful.

Manic, schizophrenic and confusional states, and disturbed anti-social behaviour may arise rarely during treatment. An undiagnosed schizophrenic may suddenly start to show florid psychotic symptoms; this will be if an MAOI has been used alone, and not in combination with a tricyclic or tranquillising drug. But although one should proceed carefully in such cases, the antidepressant drugs can be very useful in treating the recurring bouts of depression to which some schizophrenics on maintenance doses of a phenothiazine drug are prone. MAOIs should generally be given with cover by phenothiazines. In cyclothymic personalities mania is liable to occur with the MAOIs and with Tofranil, but less with Tryptizol or Surmontil. The appearance of such a state should be an indication for stopping the MAOI or Tofranil, at least temporarily. Occasionally mixed manic depressive symptoms may occur, and a combination of an antidepressant drug with lithium may be effective.

A great deal of publicity has been given to the risk of jaundice with the antidepressants, particularly the MAOIs. Tofranil may also supposedly cause jaundice. Many of the jaundices reported have almost certainly been cases of infective hepatitis. It was this complication with Marsilid, which sometimes but rarely proved fatal, that caused many people to stop using it. But we have continued to use Marsilid for 10 years now, with no more jaundice than with other MAOIs. Jaundice is, indeed, very rare and more rarely fatal. We feel that the risks, slight if any, of using the MAOI, including Marsilid, must always be weighed against the amount of suffering and distress caused to patients and their families by prolonged depressive and neurotic illnesses. Psychiatric illness can be just as disabling as organic illness and carefully calculated risks are as justified in one as in the other. And Marsilid may still help patients helped by no other of these drugs.

Combined Antidepressants

Warnings are frequently given about the dangers of combining the MAOIs with other antidepressant drugs. But we have used the combination in some thousands of patients during the last 10 years without proven danger. (Gander, 1965.) The few deaths reported several years ago may well have been undiagnosed cheese reactions or have been otherwise caused*. For instance a withdrawal delirium tremens may occur if a patient comes off a large dosage of sedatives to go onto combined antidepressant treatment, and can cause death if not diagnosed as due to the withdrawal.

Side effects, such as fainting, may occur if Tofranil is combined with MAOIs, and this combination should generally be avoided. We have yet to see anything but benefit when Tryptizol or Surmontil mg 50 to 150 given *at night* are combined with a *MAOI during the day*. If the patient sleeps too deeply, the tricyclic is reduced; if the patient is giddy on standing, one reduces the MAOI. The correct dose for each patient must be that dose of the tricyclic that keeps them asleep all night, and the dose of MAOI just below the dose causing postural hypotensive faint feelings. Sometimes the tricyclics do not get the patient to sleep. Then with Tryptizol or Surmontil mg 50 to 150 at night, and two to four tablets of a MAOI during the day, a half to one tablet of Mandrax or Mogadon or a small dose of a barbiturate at night may be all that is needed.

Many depressed and anxious patients who do not fall into the clear categories of those who respond to MAOIs or tricyclics will be helped by the combined drugs. Particularly those, for instance, who suffer from fatigue and phobic anxiety during the day but also from early waking. Actually many patients who require ECT but have not responded satisfactorily show excellent results if the ECT is coupled with combined antidepressants. With a good anaesthetist, there is no risk in giving ECT under this regime, stopping the drugs only on the morning of the ECT.

Those who use this combination will find a whole group of atypical depressives and phobic states respond, who have failed to benefit when either drug has been given alone.

Amphetamine

In 1937, together with Guttman, one of us published the first large scale clinical trial of benzedrine (Guttman and Sargant, 1937) and in the first edition of this book an approximate formula for Drinamyl was suggested, later to be publicly marketed on a large scale. We can therefore talk on the basis of thirty years continued treatment experience with the amphetamines but our present views do not differ

* A recent American paper also concludes that case reports reveal 'no convincing evidence that the antidepressant combination taken in therapeutic dosage' was responsible for any deaths reported in the literature Arch. Gen. Psychiat. 1971, **24**, 509.

materially from our original ones about its important if limited value.

Amphetamine produces a general psychological stimulation, which is experienced subjectively as increased confidence, initiative, and ease in making decisions. There is also a tendency to talk more than usual. An increased feeling of restlessness that occasionally occurs may be pleasant or unpleasant according to the extent of the accompanying somatic symptoms. The physiological action of amphetamine resembles in some ways that of adrenalin. Doses of 20 mg may cause a distinct rise in blood pressure, with fluctuations of 10 to 30 mm. Vasolabile subjects tend to have dizziness, shivering feelings, palpitations, tremor, and some loss of appetite.

Because of its effect on appetite, amphetamine has been used as a weight reducer. It inhibits the movements of the stomach and so may diminish the tendency to vomiting. This effect has been exploited in its use for the treatment of sea-sickness, where its euphorising effect is also of value. Amphetamine increases alertness and counteracts any desire for sleep. But hangover effects are rare, and even after a night of poor sleep the patient may still get up feeling surprisingly fresh and active. The length of action of amphetamine is approximately eight hours.

In normal persons there is a wide range of variation in response, and individual susceptibility can only be determined by experiment. Anxiety and tension may predominate, with the result that the drug does more harm than good. However, unpleasant autonomic effects can sometimes be countered by combining a barbiturate or tranquilliser with the amphetamine; a number of commercial preparations such as Drinamyl are available.

For the normal person, the main use for amphetamine is when he wants a temporary stimulant to tide him over some hours of fatigue and stress. It has an obvious value in times of war and emergency, when a man has to hang on and remain mentally alert several hours longer than is normally possible. It was this which made it the drug of choice used by the astronauts in a recent perilous descent. It works best when used only occasionally and not as a routine. The euphorising effect wears off if the dose is too frequently repeated, but addiction may occur. After prolonged dosage a hallucinatory or paranoid confusional state may supervene, which clears up on withdrawal of the drug.

The drug has only a limited value in the treatment of the depressive patients who get as far as the psychiatrist, although in the past it has been widely used by general practitioners for their milder depressed patients. Of all depressive symptoms a minor degree of retardation is most susceptible to the beneficial effect of the drug. Accordingly a few patients, who are just hovering on the brink of invalidism and whose main incapacity is their difficulty of concentration, can be carried over for a short time with the aid of amphetamine. But here, too, the effect wears off after a week or two. Severe depressions are scarcely touched by the drug; a few days of comparative normality may be attained, but after that the patient slips back. Depressives who are not retarded but anxious are usually made worse.

In the schizophrenic amphetamine, like the MAOI, can be a dangerous drug. On occasion it will relieve the hebetude and inertia, but it may do this only to precipitate an unexpected outburst of excitement, or to provide the initiative to carry out a murderous attack inspired by the patient's delusions. Some schizophrenics have attempted suicide when under the drug, having shown no such previous tendency.

Another use of amphetamine is in the behaviour disorders of children associated with abnormalities of the electroencephalogram. Periodic and recurrent outbursts of destructiveness, aggressiveness, etc., may improve very much. The activity of the hyperkinetic child is made less disjointed and more constructive, and the span of attention is lengthened. The child seems to attain a greater sense of personal security. Conduct and behaviour become quieter, despite the stimulant effect of the drug. However, tranquillisers, antidepressants and lithium have now replaced amphetamine as better suited to many of these cases. In some adults of immature personality, who have outbursts of spontaneous aggression resembling those of childhood, the same ameliorating influence may be shown, and in these cases it is sometimes more effectively employed combined with epanutin.

Some children and adults who suffer from enuresis also derive benefit from amphetamine. These are the patients who sleep very deeply and are not aroused by the stimulus of a full bladder. A dose of amphetamine should be found by trial and error which lightens sleep to such a level that this stimulus is perceived and can be consciously reacted to. To prevent the development of tolerance, the drug should only be given at bedtime, five times in the week. Up to 15 mg or more may be required.

Both for adults and children the normal daily dose of amphetamine is 5 to 15 mg. It should be given in the morning or at lunch time, to allow its effect to wear off by the time of going to sleep.

Recently any use of this drug, for any purpose, has come under strong and not always judicious criticism. This is solely because it has been abused by the young for 'kicks'. Some groups of general practitioners have decided to stop prescribing it at all, for any patient (except the narcoleptic), to prevent its getting into the wrong hands. This is a policy of panic. Certainly it is very important to prevent abuse, and to guard against the passing of the drug on from the patient to whom it is prescribed to other hands. Certainly prescription must be restricted. Fortunately, also, the antidepressants are diminishing its sphere of usefulness. But neither these nor any other drugs provide a substitute **for the use to which it is uniquely suitable,** i.e. by normal people needing support to cope with short periods of stress; and this is one of its most important uses. Such people rarely become addicted; the numbers of normal people who have used an amphetamine during or after World War II, without harm, must be legion. Those who are helped by the drug must not be deprived of it out of the fear of spreading addiction or misuse by the young. If the psychiatrist keeps this danger in mind, he should find it possible to prescribe it when and as he thinks it will be a useful aid.

CHAPTER TWO

Convulsion Therapy

It was as long ago as 1798 that Weickhardt recommended the giving of camphor to the point of producing vertigo and epileptic fits, and other physicians followed his example. The treatment was revived by Meduna, who in 1933 recommended the intramuscular injection of a 25 per cent solution of camphor in oil to schizophrenic patients. Camphor was replaced by more efficient drugs, which could be given intravenously or which would for other reasons produce a fit more rapidly than by the older methods—cardiazol, triazol, picrotoxin. Finally, Cerletti and Bini (1938) in 1937 produced therapeutic fits by passing an electrical current through two electrodes placed on the forehead; and a comparatively safe, convenient and painless method of convulsion therapy was made available.

Since that time the treatment has gone through more than one revolution. The objections of those who had thought the treatment by chemical induction was brutal and inhumane were largely abandoned. Converts were rapidly made when it was discovered how effective the treatment was with sufferers from endogenous depression, how the risk of suicide was reduced nearly to vanishing point once effective treatment could be started, and how it was at last possible to treat patients in out-patient clinics who a few years before would have had to be admitted to a closed ward.

Then came a period when the treatment was used over-much. In some hospitals it became a routine method of keeping patients, especially schizophrenics, in an affectively flattened state, in which problems of management would be made easier, even though there was no hope of providing any permanent benefit. Courses of twice-weekly ECT would be continued at intervals through the months and years, until some patients had had numbers of treatment running into the hundreds.

With the appearance of the tranquillising drugs and the anti-depressants, this phase of over-enthusiasm also came to an end. There were even hopes that ECT might be entirely replaced by drug therapy, though no drug has yet appeared which equals it for effectiveness in a large range of patients. We are now in the stage of learning just what the indications are by the hard way, by the accumulation of experience in giving drugs and ECT, separately, serially and together, in a variety of types of illness not so easily delimited from one another. There is still much to learn, although the treatment is over 30 years old.

Indications

SCHIZOPHRENIA. Convulsion therapy was first used in the treatment of schizophrenia; but before the tranquillising drugs appeared as most powerful adjuvants, it was not a very satisfactory treatment, and compared unfavourably with insulin coma. In a large American survey (Ross and Malzberg, 1939) a thousand schizophrenics treated with metrazol (cardiazol) convulsions did not do as well as an equal number of untreated controls, and nothing like as well as an equally large series treated by the insulin method. Better figures were reported from the same source with electrically induced convulsions, but they did not compare favourably with insulin (Malzberg, 1943). Linford Rees (1949, 1952) has provided convincing demonstration of the ineffectiveness of convulsion therapy used alone.

However, in the last few years the use of convulsion therapy in schizophrenia has become much more valuable with the advent of the tranquillising drugs. These drugs appear to have the power to stabilise and maintain the temporary improvements which convulsion therapy can bring about; each seems to reinforce the other. And whereas in the old days convulsion therapy was most effective in schizophrenia when combined with insulin coma treatment, now its combination with drugs such as chlorpromazine is often sufficient, a modified form of insulin therapy also being added when it seems desirable to restore lost weight or reduce tension during treatment.

It can, in fact, be maintained that all recently ill schizophrenic patients should receive combined drug and convulsion therapy as early as possible. Some therapists prefer to use the phenothiazine drugs alone initially, adding convulsion therapy if recovery is slow. In our view this may unnecessarily delay progress, and in most cases, where there are no special contra-indications, the two treatments should be combined. For convulsion therapy can break up the abnormal patterns of behaviour and thought in this disease, enabling us to get the best out of the easier method of stabilising improvement with drugs and perhaps modified insulin instead of the old full insulin coma therapy.

Certain syndromes should certainly receive convulsion therapy in the early stages. Catatonic stupor as a rule responds rapidly if temporarily to a convulsion, but will often remain unaffected for some considerable time by the tranquillisers. The effect of the convulsion treatment used alone may be to convert the stupor into a deluded, hallucinated and excited state; and large doses of drugs such as chlorpromazine, and sometimes modified insulin, should now accompany the use of convulsion therapy in this group of cases. The hyper-acute catatonic patient with confusion, fever and leucocytosis may well die under one's hand unless treatment is immediate; and three convulsion treatments on three successive days, or even more, as a life-saving measure, accompanied by phenothiazine drugs in large doses, may produce dramatic improvement.

Apart from the acute states with confusion, the schizophrenic symptoms which benefit most from convulsion are affective ones. Where the patient is anergic, retarded, apathetic, listless or lacking in interest because of a real, even if unrecognised, state of depression, the treatment is likely to be helpful. A course of convulsion therapy accompanied by phenothiazines, and with modified insulin to reinforce physique, may also play an important part at a later stage in the illness, in circumstances in which ECT alone used to be tried, and found without effect. It might for instance be needed when the patient has got into a rut, and it is desired to apply a total physical and psychological push towards recovery.

Far too often, when phenothiazines are used alone for the treatment of schizophrenia, when the acute symptoms have subsided and the patient is being kept on a large maintenance dose, he suddenly becomes depressed again, although the schizophrenic symptoms do not return. Here ECT must be given, and not more phenothiazines but antidepressants. Not infrequent are schizo-affective illnesses, in which the schizophrenic features show up in the excited but not in the depressive phase. If such patients are kept on chlorpromazine without other help, the drug will keep them depressively ill.

It is of little service hammering away at most patients with repeated convulsions, if worthwhile benefit is not obtained after a reasonable number of treatments. However, the schizophrenic patient is more tolerant of convulsion therapy than are some depressives; and 6 to 20 ECT should be given, if there are some signs of improvement, before deciding that no more is to be obtained that way.

To summarise, when a patient is admitted in an acute recent schizophrenic state, treatment with ECT accompanied by tranquillising drugs, such as chlorpromazine in doses from 300 to 1500 mg a day, should be started immediately. In the very acute case ECT may be given three to four times in the first week, this being reduced to twice or three times a week as the conditions begin to clear and further reduced to once or twice a week later on. As treatment proceeds, the tranquillising drugs are kept on in smaller doses; and sometimes it may be advisable to give modified insulin treatment, or insulin sopors between the ECT treatments, to restore body weight and still further to reduce tension during treatment. We have seen this combined treatment bring very material help to patients for whom not much could be hoped, who have even been ill for two or three years, who have slipped somehow into the back wards of mental hospitals, with an underlying personality still relatively well preserved. The combination of tranquillisers, ECT, insulin sopor and modified narcosis (Chapter III) should probably all be tried before deciding finally to proceed to leucotomy, especially if the initial treatment has been rather half-hearted, or has involved the tranquillisers without the other adjuvants in combination.

There is no final answer to the question how many ECT to give in a full course. If the patient continues to improve, up to 20 ECT can be given, and more in exceptional cases. Far fewer than that may be required, if the tranquillisers and insulin are also being used as they should in resistant patients. ECT may also be used from time to time in the long-term maintenance therapy by tranquillisers, especially if there is a tendency to depression. One should always be on the look-out for this. Depressives of good previous personality can drift into the back wards, misdiagnosed as deteriorating schizophrenics. A change of treatment in such patients will often produce unexpected and startling recoveries.

Finally we must emphasise that some schizophrenic patients of good previous personality may recover, even after five years or more of illness when treated by a long course of modified narcosis, combined with ECT and antidepressants (Chapter III). This is a recent finding of great importance, several times confirmed.

INVOLUTIONAL DEPRESSION. From their use in schizophrenia, convulsions came to be tried in depressive states, and here their results were even more brilliant and have stood the test of time. Of all depressive syndromes those of later life react best. These states, which are of obscure ætiology, must be distinguished from the true manic-depressive psychoses. The underlying bodily and mental constitution are different. Whereas in the manic-depressive one finds most typically a pyknic habitus and a cyclothymic temperament, in the involutional depressive one finds more commonly an asthenic habitus and an obsessional type of personality. In the manic-depressive syndrome the depression may come on rapidly, even abruptly; in the involutional melancholia symptoms sometimes appear and progress very gradually and insidiously. The picture at first presented may be one that used very frequently to be called 'neurasthenia', in which the patient is chiefly conscious of a failure of interest, an inability to concentrate, and a gradually increasing incapacity for all the ordinary affairs of life. These symptoms,with an intractable insomnia and progressively deepening depression, lead to the full-blown picture of mixed agitation and retardation, with hypochondriacal preoccupations, ideas of guilt, delusions. Convulsive therapy has proved our most powerful weapon in the treatment of such states, and figures of from 70 to 80 per cent recoveries are constantly being reported. This is a great achievement, as previously these states were very refractory to treatment. The prognosis with treatment is even more favourable now that ECT can be supplemented with antidepressant drugs. Although there was a natural tendency to remit, the illness seldom ended spontaneously before six months, and often lasted one or two years or even drifted on into a chronic melancholia. In addition, the risk of death from exhaustion, intercurrent disease and suicide in the acute phase was far from negligible.

Such high recovery rates with ECT will only be obtained in the central group of involutional depressives. Patients not of a previously rigid and obsessional personality, and those who have been of a markedly hysterical or anxious make-up, do not do so well. Mood rhythm is important in selecting the most favourable patient. Early morning wakening, and increase of retardation and indecisiveness in the forenoon, are characteristic features of the depressions which react to ECT. Furthermore, there is a tendency to self-reproach, and the general lowering of vitality is shown in diminished libido.

Many patients who present themselves in late middle life with symptoms of depression are of a different kind. Their illness is based on constitutional tendencies to anxiety, or hysteria. They have difficulty in getting off to sleep at night, but do not usually wake early. They may also begin the day well and feel at their worst in the evening. These patients are not such favourable subjects for ECT, and even if this treatment gives temporary help it will often have to be supplemented by other methods. Depressed patients who suffer no disturbance of sleep often turn out to have a primarily obsessional or anxiety state, and we remember only a few who have been helped by ECT, many who have only been made more anxious. In our experience, also, those whose libido is increased rather than diminished do not generally do well. But it is this group of 'neurotic', 'hysterical' or 'atypical' depressives who do so well, if they were previously of good personality, *with the monoamine oxidase inhibitor group* of antidepressant drugs (Sargant, 1961). These drugs help many such patients, who are made worse rather than better by ECT. Yet others only finally recover when the MAOIs and tricyclics are combined.

Those who are found to be suffering from involutional depressions of the most favourable kind should have their illness attacked early. They can be readily treated in a psychiatric ward in a general hospital, and the risks of suicide are not great if treatment is prompt. If they are recognised early they can be treated in an out-patient clinic, and the necessity for admission to hospital be thereby avoided. The time factor is important. As the illness advances the physical state of the patient deteriorates. A larger number of convulsions will probably be necessary to bring about recovery. The longer the patient is away from work, the more difficult it will be to get him back to it. And finally, the sooner one begins treatment, the more months of misery the patient will be spared. This, of course, does not mean that every middle-aged patient complaining of worry, insomnia and similar symptoms should be operated on with convulsion therapy at the first interview. Nowadays up to 60 per cent of patients or more can avoid ECT if they are put on the right groups of antidepressants. It will be perhaps a month before one can tell whether the drugs will work or not; and some patients are too ill to wait this time. But when the case has been fully explored, and when it is thought that drug treatment alone will not be enough, then further time should not be wasted. A prompt beginning should be made with ECT, combined with antidepressants to reduce the total number of treatments that will otherwise be needed.

Depressions of the involutional type may occur very late in life, well into the period associated clinically with senile changes. If no organic basis in senile dementia or cerebral arteriosclerosis can be discovered, just as favourable results as in earlier years can be expected. Even severe depressions accompanying and complicating the early stages of arteriosclerotic and senile dementia respond well to convulsion treatment; and a high blood pressure or advanced age are certainly not contra-indications to treatment justifiable on other grounds. The pathological emotional lability of the organic patient must, of course, be distinguished from the true depression. But too many treatable depressives are still slipping into geriatric wards. Dullness and slowness may present the appearances of dementia, or if some dementia is there, may make it functionally much worse. Active treatment may in either case demonstrate most sastisfactorily how much of the incapacity was depressive and recoverable. With the short-acting anaesthetics and Scoline given with due precautions, patients of 80 years of age are now being treated at St. Thomas's in the out-patients' department.

Involutional depressions with marked paranoid features frequently respond very poorly to convulsion therapy alone, as a rule because the clinician has failed to recognise their paraphrenic nature. It is important to recognise this group of patients as their chances of recovery will be prejudiced by incorrect treatment. A satisfactory remission will often be obtained by a combination of antidepressants and tranquillising drugs, and especially by combining phenothiazines, by mouth or by Moditen injection, with ECT. If ECT alone is given, and sometimes even after combined treatment, the depression is lifted but the paranoid ideas become more and more fixed. A course of combined ECT and narcosis (Chapter III) may be tried; and if that fails leucotomy provides the only hope and should not be delayed to the point when disintegration of the personality is beginning to set in. If significant improvement is obtained by the combination of ECT and drugs, a maintenance of the drug found effective may have to be continued for some two years or more to prevent relapse.

MANIC-DEPRESSIVE SYNDROMES. In depressions of earlier life, particularly before the age of 40, one should be rather more cautious. The phasic changes of the manic-depressive may be very troublesome to treat. It is a more frequent event in this type of illness for a depression, relieved by convulsion therapy, to pass over into a temporary hypomania which may prove even more difficult to manage socially. Or the depression may lift, but only temporarily, and then relapse again every time that treatment is intermitted. The swings of mood of the manic-depressive may be endogenously determined, and dependent on biochemical changes that are at present beyond analysis and control; they certainly seem to be more refractory to treatment than the involutional depressions. Furthermore, the spontaneous recovery of the true manic-depressive may be awaited with much more certainty than that of the involutional patient. The point where intervention is most likely to be successful is when the depression seems to have lasted an undue length of time, as may be shown, for instance, by the records of previous attacks.

These remarks apply particularly to that type of manic-depressive who has well-marked recurrent phases. Convulsion treatment in those with the most regular recurrences may disturb the normal rhythm but do nothing to prevent it recurring.

The authors have seen many patients with recurrent depressive illnesses, who have been unsuccessfully handled through neglect of the principles of caution mentioned above. They were treated on one occasion at the end of an attack with success, and were then told to present themselves without delay for treatment when the next attack occurred. Several courses of ECT were then given with only transient benefit; and when the patient eventually emerged of his own accord at the end of his allotted span, he was labelled as having a hysterically motivated illness by the disappointed psychiatrist who had failed to recognise what he was dealing with. Some of these patients, still submerged in depression, are referred for leucotomy, when a little more patience, and a further course of ECT given at the right time, will produce the long-awaited remission.

The single severe illness, however, which is known to be manic-depressive by the pyknic cyclothymic constitution and the family history, often responds very well to treatment; and the recurrence of the phase, which may not be due for a number of years, is of little immediate moment.

With the introduction of the antidepressant drugs the treatment of the cyclothymic depressions has become considerably easier. Where the drug is not sufficient by itself, and ECT is combined with it, this can be given with more hope of success earlier in the attack than used to be possible. If the drug is continued for some six months or more afterwards, the improvement obtained with ECT will very likely be stabilised, the natural tendency to relapse being held in check. The patient must be kept on a full dose of the antidepressant until the illness cycle is obviously over. Then an earlier relapse calls clearly for more ECT. If antidepressant drugs are stopped prematurely, one does not know whether a relapse requires more drugs or more ECT, and the handling of the case is made muddled and difficult.

When we turn to consider the manic states, we find that convulsion therapy plays a much smaller part nowadays than it used to. The first line of attack will be with the phenothiazines, the tricyclics and lithium salts; and the right dosage of one or other of these, or all in combination, will often make ECT entirely unnecessary. If it is desired to try the effect of ECT as well, this may be done; in such a case many fewer treatments will be needed than in the old days before modern drug therapy was available.

Many states of acute excitement in young people, clinically closely resembling true mania, prove eventually to be schizophrenic; and it is well to be on the look-out for schizophrenic symptoms, so that the appropriate treatment is not unnecessarily delayed until progressive personality deterioration makes the diagnosis obvious.

REACTIVE DEPRESSION. In reactive depressive states considerable caution is called for diagnostically. Many persons who under environmental stress, even head injury, pass into such states, have the rigid and obsessional type of temperament which one sees in the involutional depressive. Once driven into a state of depression by force of circumstances, the patient seems unable to find his way out again. While first trying antidepressant drugs, it is well to keep the possibility of convulsion therapy in mind. If environmental causes of the depression are disposed of but the patient still remains stuck in the mire, a few therapeutic convulsions may be all that is required to break the vicious circle and start him on the road to recovery. It is in this group that early morning wakening and morning retardation can be such useful pointers to success.

It is otherwise with the reactive depression that occurs on the basis of an anxious temperament, where in the present state of practice the greatest mistakes are made. Here sleep may be normal, or of the pattern usually seen in anxiety states and hysterias. During the day the mood fluctuates and shows no constant rhythm. The patients respond in mood to changes in the environment and can be temporarily distracted from their woes by cheerful company. They have often been ill for long periods; treatment is begun with enthusiasm, and continued, with a patient who shrinks in fear from the treatment, until memory changes are unmistakable—and yet no improvement occurs. Great harm can be done in this way, and the last state of the patient may be worse than the first. Fortunately, this group of reactive, 'hysterical' or 'atypically' depressed patients, who did so badly with ECT, have been found to do well with the MAOI antidepressants, best combined with small doses of the tranquillising drugs, the tricyclics or Librium (see Chapter I). Where clinical judgment fails, the results of one or two treatments will often make clear the true nature of the illness. The depressed patient who is going to respond to ECT often feels somewhat better after a treatment, though the depression may return in a few hours; the patient whose predominant symptoms are due to anxiety feels more tense after each treatment, though the tension may subside as the hours pass.

DEPERSONALISATION. States of depersonalisation as a rule do not do well. Good results may be obtained when depersonalisation is seen in a setting of depression; but sometimes the depression lifts and the depersonalisation remains. States with an obsessional basis and a considerable degree of anxiety, in which depersonalisation is common, can be made worse by ECT. Unless the patient is obviously depressed, convulsion therapy should not be persisted with if the first few treatments do not produce some symptomatic improvement. However, some depersonalisations in a setting of depression have been seen which have needed a long course of ECT, combined with the antidepressant drugs, to bring about remission. If mild symptoms of depersonalisation come on during ECT therapy, the course may be interrupted and treatment postponed for a few days. Very likely the depersonalisation will then clear, and treatment can be resumed.

HYSTERIA. Convulsion treatment is sometimes of use in the neuroses, but in general other methods are to be preferred. Conversion hysteria may be 'cured' by a single convulsion, as by any dramatic method of treatment; but less drastic and more suitable methods are nearly always available. *Not infrequently depressive patients exhibit hysterical symptoms as a reaction to the difficulties caused by their illness.* When the depression clears the hysterical symptoms go along with them. In such a patient convulsive therapy may provide a cure for the outstanding hysterical symptoms by attacking their cause. Especially in the middle-aged woman, a hysterical superstructure may almost completely mask the underlying depression. We have met a number of patients, apparently chronic hysterics, but people who had been coping with life quite adequately before the illness began. These were patients who got better when given quite long courses of modified narcosis, ECT and antidepressants (Chapter III). In such cases the illness may have been of long duration, but what probably started as a depressive state took on a hysterical superstructure which masked the basic disturbance of function.

Hysterics are more prone than most patients to develop memory disturbances after a very few fits, and then to make them the subject of bitter complaint. This may be understood from the hysteric's liability to amnesic and other dissociation symptoms from many kinds of excitatory stimulus. It should be guarded against by the careful therapist. If ECT is going to be tried in hysteria with a possible depressive basis, one of the MAOI drugs should be tried first of all, as they often help this group. And if ECT is given it should generally be combined with these drugs to reduce to the minimum the number of treatments needed.

ANXIETY NEUROSIS. The use of convulsions in chronic anxiety neuroses is as a rule to be avoided. Where the neurosis is of recent origin and has important environmental precipitants, readjustment of the environmental set-up with or without psychotherapy and the use of sedatives, antidepressants, and possibly modified insulin treatment are much more likely to be of service. Where the neurosis is of long standing and largely constitutional no benefit from convulsions need in any case be expected. Most patients with 'anxiety neuroses' who benefit from convulsions are those who are wrongly so called, who are in fact suffering from a depressive illness in which agitation is to the fore. We have already drawn attention to the characteristic symptoms, retardation, disturbance of sleep rhythm, etc., by which these cases are generally to be recognised. An occasional patient can also be dis-covered by a favourable response to one or two trial ECT where a depressive component is suspected.

Furthermore, if a patient of excellent previous personality and no previous neurotic history suddenly and for the first time, between 30 and 55, presents what seems to be a severe anxiety state, an *under-lying depression* should always be thought of; it may very well respond to ECT and antidepressants.

OBSESSIONAL NEUROSIS. Similar principles hold for obsessional neuroses. Convulsion therapy will not produce change for the better in the obsessional personality, nor in any compulsive or phobic symptoms that may be presenting. A persistent attempt to produce effects which are not obtainable is only likely to add to the patient's difficulties. Some are oppressed by the disturbance of memory to which they are particularly sensitive; others develop feelings of de-personalisation.

But it has already been pointed out that the obsessional personality is peculiarly liable to depressive symptoms, which once they have appeared may persist for an undue length of time; and for these patients the treatment holds out considerable hope. It is not unusual to find an obsessional admixture in a true depressive psychosis, particularly in later life. A depressed woman may, for instance, com-plain that she is haunted with the fear that she may destroy her children; every time she goes to the knife-box she is seized with the idea afresh. It may then be found that in her past life and in her personality she gives evidence of an obsessional type of constitutional make-up. Such patients as these will be very suitable for treatment by convulsion, but they can hardly be called obsessionals in the stricter sense. Quite a few obsessional patients, in whom the picture is dominated by depression and tension, will also be helped by an antidepressant; and this may avoid the need for ECT, or reduce the number of treatments needed. Finally it has recently been found that quite a number of longstanding obsessionals can be helped by combining modified narcosis, antidepressant drugs and ECT, long courses of combined treatment may be needed (see Chapter III).

OTHER CONDITIONS. Up to recent times some psychiatrists appeared to believe that they needed only two weapons in their armamentarium, psychotherapy and the electric shock-box, one sure where the other fails. Thus the literature records the use of ECT in almost every imaginable psychiatric condition from G.P.I. to a stammer. It is possible to produce effects of a kind, as even the most excitable nervous system can be convulsed into temporary quietude by repeated ECT; but the patient gains nothing thereby if the symptoms immediately return and, as is often the case, are then worse than before. There is obviously one sort of special case in which even very temporary relief is of vital consequence, i.e. when the symptom is itself of temporary duration and while it lasts constitutes a serious danger. We have already mentioned the use of ECT in this way as an emergency treatment of dangerous symptoms in schizophrenia; and its use in confusional and delirious states to secure a few days of improvement, during which the patient's life may be saved by starting treatment of a specifically needed kind, is on the same level.

Other occasions in which ECT proves valuable are of a very different kind, namely, when a true depressive illness appears under the mask of other symptoms. Thus we have seen on occasion hypochondriacal states, and especially states in which the dominant symptom is pain for which no physical cause can be found, clear up with ECT, with or without modified narcosis, even after long illness. In all these patients, even though the underlying depression was so slight, even if existent at all, as to be unnoticed by the patient, yet there were marks of an affective change; these patients were usually of somewhat rigid or obsessional personality, and nearly always at the involutional period of life; the affective change in increased energy and cheerfulness after recovery with treatment was always noticeable.

It must not be thought that, because of the existence of this narrowly limited group, it is justifiable to treat psychosomatic states of all kinds with ECT. Most such conditions, when they are based on an emotional change, can be traced to long continuing anxiety and tension. They are often made worse by ECT, seldom benefited. In organic states such as the sequelae of encephalitis, head injury, Parkinsonism, etc., ECT has only temporary or no improvement to offer, and is contra-indicated, always with the proviso that the patient does not have a superadded depression. In all such states there is no evidence that ECT can provide the nervous system with such qualities as placidity or stability which it has never had or of which it has been deprived by organic disease.

In Chapter III we have shown how some resistant patients, of adequate previous personality, can be helped by modified narcosis when courses of 12 to 20 ECT are also given under the narcosis. Illnesses of many years duration sometimes remit, and these include those presenting as depressions, obsessional neuroses, schizophrenia and tension states. It is possible that many are basically depressive illnesses in which the diagnosis has not been obvious. And some depressives do seem to need very long courses of ECT to bring about remission. Under narcosis patients will tolerate these long courses when necessary. Also it seems that ECT can be more effective when combined with narcosis for reasons not yet understood (Sargant, Walter *et al.*, 1966; Walter *et al.*, 1972).

Risks and Contra-indications

It can hardly be sufficiently emphasised that convulsion therapy is a surgical treatment in psychiatry, and the general rules governing the admissibility of surgical intervention apply. While the operation should not be unnecessarily delayed, it should not be undertaken in a light-hearted spirit, and should never be employed as a mere placebo. The decision when operation is necessary requires a refined clinical sense, and the opinion of an expert in the treatment should be sought when available. When operation is decided on the patient should be examined to exclude possible dangers, the position should be explained both to him and to his relatives, and the permission of both sought. Finally, when the treatment is eventually carried out, every method should be used to minimise any special risks.

The risk of death with convulsion therapy is usually negligible. Actual figures are hard to obtain, but the rate is probably well below

1 in 1000, and is comparable with that of giving a general anaesthetic without other operative procedure. Will and others (Will and Duval, 1947) could only find 33 reported deaths from ECT in the world literature. In 1953 Maclay reported that there had been 62 deaths associated with ECT in the collective mental hospitals of England and Wales in the previous five and a half years. In no fewer than 28 of these cases muscle relaxants had been used, or some other premedication, and some had died before ECT was given (Maclay, 1953). But that was in the early days of their use; nowadays, with a good anaesthetist, the risks are minimal.

The therapist will be well advised if he obtains a thorough examination, preferably by a specialist, of elderly patients he proposes to submit to the treatment, and of others where the indication arises. An electrocardiogram is a very useful aid to decision. Death is commonest at the first treatment, and the greatest care should be exercised then. Caution is necessary, but it is possible to be over-cautious. Patients over 80 have often been successfully treated, though here muscle relaxants should always be used to diminish the severity of the fit. Senile depressions and confusional states may respond very well to ECT. Patients have also been treated with angina, recovered coronary thrombosis, and even existing heart failure (Evans, 1945). Unimportant irregularities of the heart action should not be regarded as a bar to treatment; and it is here that the opinion of a cardiologist, backed by an electrocardiogram, is of particular service. The final decision must however be taken by the psychiatrist after getting all relevant help. It is unfair to expect the cardiologist, without long experience of ECT, to be the final arbiter, and if he is, he often proves over-cautious. It has been found that as a result of treatment changes arise in the electrocardiogram, which have proved, however, not so much indicative of damage to the heart muscle as of alterations in the vagal control of the heart of a quite temporary nature. Nevertheless, where there is existing myocardial disease, one cannot expect the treatment to be of any benefit to the heart; but one need not withhold treatment simply because mild degrees of arteriosclerosis or hypertension are present provided the heart is still sound. One should, however, beware of too high a pulse pressure.

To put matters in their proper perspective we can cite personal experience at St. Thomas's, where we have always had the help of expert anaesthetists. Where we thought the treatment was essential, we have taken every kind of risk that had to be taken. In 20 years, during which thousands of ECTs have been given, we have had only one death, in a man of 84. The patients are very few indeed who have to be rejected on physical grounds when skilled anaesthesia and muscle relaxants are available.

The most frequent risk to be faced with convulsion treatment used to be that of fracture, particularly of compression fractures of the vertebral bodies. With the older method of applying no physical control during the fit they occurred very frequently—in anything up to 40 per cent of patients—but were most usually symptomless. This was so much the case that it was only after the treatment had been given for some years that their occurrence and then their frequency were discovered by routine X-ray before and after treatment. At first they were judged a serious complication, and as a definite contra-indication to the treatment being given; but this is no longer so. As has been said, they are usually symptomless, and even when they do cause some disability, this is usually limited to pain in the back which passes off after a few weeks. The usual sign, apart from routine X-ray, is a pain in the back, which may also be referred to the front of the chest. A few patients will say it is really severe; but it lessens in a few days, and gradually in succeding weeks it diminishes to an occasional twinge when heavy work has to be undertaken. Unfortunately those patients are most liable to it who are most disabled by its occurrence, i.e. muscularly well-developed manual labourers and athletes. Al-though it is not such a severe complication as has been thought in the past, it is to be taken seriously, and the right methods of bodily control or use of muscle relaxants will avoid its occurrence in all but a trifling percentage of patients. What these methods are will be described later. The possibility of a spinal or other fracture has, of course, to be taken particularly seriously where there is some bone disease, e.g. Paget's disease, and in patients who, through being long bedridden, have some decalcification of the bones. In such patients precautions should be especially rigorous.

Other fractures which used to occur during treatment were on the upper part of the humerus and femur. Dislocation of the jaw or shoulder may also occur, especially in people who have had such accidents before. Exactly the same considerations apply as to spinal fractures; they are best avoided by administering the fit under the most favourable conditions and applying suitable methods of re-straint or muscle relaxants. A different point arises when fracture occurs early in the treatment. Should it then be regarded as an abso-lute contra-indication to the continuance of treatment? The authors have never taken it as such; but the use of relaxants or other special methods is then especially applicable.

Chest complications are rare after convulsive treatment, and seem to have been commoner with cardiazol than with ECT. The occurrence both of pneumonic conditions and the lighting up of old tuberculous conditions have been reported. ECT has been used where necessary with tuberculous patients and an accompanying severe depression, with no apparent worsening of the tuberculous state; but in such cases risks have to be carefully assessed (McClellan and Schwartz, 1953; Will and Duval, 1947).

Memory disturbances are very common, especially in elderly people with hypertension. Sometimes they will take on an acute aspect and be of fairly severe degree, when the patient will be precipitated into a temporary confusional episode. This will most frequently occur when the treatment is being given in a course in a routine fashion, and sufficient notice of the individual peculiarities of the patient is not being taken. If adequate attention is paid some degree of temporary clouding of consciousness will be noted after the fit before one of these severer states occur. It is very important that such notice should be taken, especially in patients being treated in an out-patient clinic. Of course there is post-epileptic clouding in every case for a period lasting up to an hour or so, and it is only when the patient seems to have had full time to come round and is still muddled that one begins to consider the desirability of intermitting the treatments for a time.

The therapeutic aim is in every case to give the minimum number of fits which will produce the desired result. In elderly people and those suffering from arteriosclerosis these memory disturbances are likely to be of more noticeable degree and longer duration than in young people, and one should be particularly careful in their case. One should also be cautious with the man who uses a highly trained memory in the exercise of his profession. Memory disturbance is also common in neurotic subjects, another reason why convulsive treatment is generally unwise in their case. Electroencephalographic studies indicate that the effect of the convulsion is very similar to that of a mild concussion. The disturbance is in the first place functional, and if it is given time to recover no permanent impairment need necessarily be feared. Nevertheless, work with tests of intelligence, memory, etc., does indicate that some slight degree of impairment, in most cases temporary, does exist in the majority of patients shortly after the conclusion of a course of treatment, though this may need refined testing to demonstrate and may be apparent neither to relatives nor the clinician. Some slight degree of impairment may be a price worth paying for recovery from a severe depression, but one should attempt to cut the cost as low as possible. As a rule, even when there is some noticeable alteration of memory after a course of fits, it will gradually clear up during the succeeding few weeks.

A vexatious complication of convulsive therapy is translation of the depression into mania or hypomania. This is most frequently seen in the manic-depressive syndrome, and is a rare complication of treatment in involutional depression. When it occurs no harm is done, but the social aspects of treatment are altered, and admission to a mental hospital may have to be arranged. Fortunately by using tranquillisers or lithium we can usually damp down quite quickly the swing over into the opposite phase. In schizophrenics convulsive therapy may precipitate a schizophrenic excitement; this most readily occurs in the active stage, but will generally be avoided if sufficient doses of the tranquillising drugs are being given at the same time. The reverse of this is sometimes seen—an increase of the degree of depression after the first one or two fits. Such a thing would have to be greatly feared if it were more common, as there then might arise for the first time a risk of suicide; but in our experience it is a most unusual event. There is a small risk of developing epilepsy after treatment, but probably only in the predisposed and the cerebral dysrhythmic. There is as yet no evidence that the incidence is greater than it would be in a control group.

Other metabolic deficiencies may be revealed by the stress to which the patient is subjected by a course of ECT. Vitamin deficiencies, especially of the B group, may appear and need appropriate treatment. A woman, who had had a thyroidectomy some years before, and later developed a depression, was precipitated by ECT into an acute myxoedematous state with confusion, which responded to thyroid. Those who use this treatment must constantly keep their medical wits about them.

Alarm expressed in America that the combination of ECT with such drugs as chlorpromazine was dangerous has found no echo in Great Britain. In fact, it forms the basis of our present treatment of acute schizophrenia, in which each treatment without the other is relatively ineffective. Dangers are only likely to arise if patients are allowed to stand up or wander about after ECT, when under the influence of heavy doses of chlorpromazine. If they are kept lying down till fully recovered there are no such dangers; but if this is not possible, then no large dose of a phenothiazine should be given for three to four hours before the ECT.

Time to Begin and the Length of Treatment

Much of this ground has already been covered earlier in this chapter, and we may now summarise. Manic-depressive and involutional depressions should not be handled in their early stages in entirely the same way. In the old days, before the introduction of the antidepressant drugs, it was generally wise to put off giving ECT to the cyclothymic, at least for a time, since early in the endogenous swing it was often not very effective. This is still a consideration to be borne in mind; but as the combination of ECT with antidepressants is very effective, in a proportion of patients even in the first month of their illness, the motive for postponement of ECT is much less than it used to be. Accordingly, the patient will first be put on antidepressant medication; ECT will be tried with it if the indications are adequate; and after stopping the ECT, the antidepressant will have to be continued for some weeks or months to prevent relapse. If relapse occurs while the patient is on a full dose of antidepressants, more ECT should be tried.

Some (rare) cyclothymic patients suffer at times from a depression which does not respond to ECT, or to ECT combined with antidepressants, until the time of expected spontaneous remission is also approaching. Patients should accordingly be warned that if an earlier course of ECT has failed, they may still respond later on in the attack.

Although we must emphasise the need for caution with convulsion therapy in the depressions of earlier life, not a few will be met with where it is justifiable to start treatment fairly early, especially if drugs have failed to help, even when there is no sign that the patient is going down hill. These are the depressions which bear a symptomatic resemblance to the involutional depressions—an insidious course, an obsessional non-cyclothymic personality, typical sleep changes and diurnal rhythm, and a clinical picture in which retardation is well marked. These often react so well and so infrequently relapse when recovery has been attained that early treatment is very well worth while.

In the involutional depressions the earlier treatment is begun, as a rule, the better. This is especially the case if the antidepressant drugs have not helped enough to get the patient back to work. When he first comes for diagnosis he may have been ill for months, struggling in vain against his mounting difficulties. These patients, by reason of their rigid and obsessional personalities, usually do not give in at all until they are far gone in the illness. Further waiting for spontaneous remission is needlessly painful, and is contra-indicated by the probable deterioration of the physical condition. Chances of rapid improvement are much better when the patient's physique is still fairly well preserved than when he has become thin and feeble. Social aspects of illness can never be forgotten in psychiatry, and such considerations as the available amount of sick leave, the imminence of compulsory pensioning, or dismissal on medical grounds, the capital available, have all to be taken into account.

The good clinician will avoid set courses of treatment, which all patients are forced to undergo regardless of their individual peculiarities; he will rather govern his treatment by his increasing knowledge of how the patient reacts. The aim will be to give as few and infrequent fits as are sufficient to produce a progressive change for the better. One patient will report that for three days after a treatment he feels much better, but then it all comes back; and in such a case treatments twice weekly may well be required to get maximum benefit. Other patients will react more slowly and will report that for a day or so after the treatment they feel muddled and unable to concentrate, that they then begin to feel better, and a week later find themselves still improving. With such patients a much slower tempo will very likely prove best. The cautious physician will refrain from giving further fits while improvement continues, and will wait for the first sign of relapse before quickly countering it with another convulsion. This policy will prove itself again and again, and will provide some striking cures with very few administrations. As many as three fits a week need scarcely ever be given, except perhaps in the first week of treatment in a particularly severe case to get remission quickly under way, and generally no more than 12 fits in all; often less than half that number will be sufficient. The older the patient, and the severer the fit, the fewer should be given and the more infrequently. As has been emphasised, signs of any gross or continuing memory disturbance or confusion should lead to an intermission for a time, and reconsideration of the question whether the patient is really a suitable subject for this treatment.

Fewer mistakes would be made, and better results would be obtained, if psychiatrists did not apply the methods of treatment suitable to one class of depressive patient to all types. Severe, prolonged and recurrent endogenous depressions and manic-depressive syndromes may need longer and more intensive courses of ECT than others, and are often not so upset by them. But most true involutional depressions, and the reactive depressions which respond to ECT, are almost certainly different aetiologically and need different handling. In them, treatments should be more widely spaced and, of course, as few as possible. Patients of the former type often need several treatments before becoming aware of any benefit, whereas the suitable reactive depressive will feel a little better after the first fit.

We have also been finding recently (see Chapter III) that certain apparently depressive, anxiety, obsessional and even schizophrenic illnesses respond to long courses of ECT when given together with modified narcosis and anti-depressant drugs. These had not done well with shorter courses of previous ECT. Up to three months of combined sleep and ECT treatment may be needed to bring some of these patients into remission. This finding is still being investigated. A reasonably adjusted previous personality seems essential to success and these patients may well turn out to be mainly masked depressive illnesses of long duration.

Out-Patient Treatment

It is often better to treat a patient with electrical shock in an out-patient clinic than to admit him to hospital to receive the same treatment there. One of the main reasons for this lies in a conspicuous fault of modern hospital practice. It is sometimes the practice in mental hospitals to give patients courses of six or even a dozen fits, regardless of rate of improvement, or even before any attempt is made to find out whether improvement is occurring at all. There are a number of reasons for this. The first is that it is much easier to give a set course than to adjust the number of treatments exactly to the patient's requirements. The second depends on a misconception of the nature of the treatment. Convulsive treatment is thought of in the same way as the penicillin treatment of general paralysis, as a treatment of a disease, when in fact it is the treatment of a symptom and loses its justification when that symptom is no longer shown. The result is that in some hospitals many more fits are often given to the patient than is needed to set him securely on the road to recovery.

The same temptations and the same risks are not attached to treatment in the out-patient clinic. The observation between treatments is more informative than in hospital; for minor signs of improvement or worsening are noticed at once by the relatives instead of passing unnoticed against the general background of mental illness in a hospital ward. The patient is in the environment that is usual to him, and it is much easier to say whether he is now well enough to carry on without additional fits. In hospital it is usual to give two treatments a week; in many out-patient clinics the frequency of treatment may be once weekly. The lower frequency of treatment is much less likely to cause impairment of memory, even when the same total number of fits is given; and there is ample time between one treatment and the next to assess improvement. As a rule, it is found that some slight indication of improvement is shown after the first fit, even if it is only during the first 24 hours after the fit and itself does not last more than a few hours. After succeeding treatments the improvement persists for an even longer time, and a total of three or four fits may be all that is needed to produce recovery. Certainly it is a general experience that a smaller total of fits proves sufficient in out-patient than in-patient practice.

The advent of the antidepressant drugs has made wider spacing of fits, and reduction in their total, both more desirable and more possible. Out-patient practice should rely on the combination, and on continuation of drug therapy after ECT has been stopped.

Out-patient treatment has many other advantages. The most important is the avoidance of all the social repercussions of admission to hospital, and the stigma that is still felt to attach to it. It will also be found that a large new group of patients can be treated in this way. These are the milder depressions, in which neither the patient himself nor his relatives think he is ill enough to go to hospital. Where out-patient facilities are not available these patients struggle on, partially or wholly incapacitated, for many months before recovery, or before the need for hospital is admitted, and even then may evade the issue by suicide. Some of these cases are clinically very puzzling, and it is not easy to differentiate them from the anxiety neuroses and neurasthenic states occurring on a basis of psychopathy. Where one is in doubt, one or two electrical fits plus antidepressants may be used diagnostically. If there is a depressive element there will be some measure of response, even if it is only partial and of no more than a few hours' duration. On the other hand, the patient with an anxiety state will usually report that he has felt rather worse after the fit. However, diagnostic ECT is much less necessary nowadays, since the atypical case, especially in a person of good previous personality, will often respond to one or other of the antidepressant drugs.

Of course, there are limits to out-patient treatment which do not hold with in-patients. Nevertheless, we have been struck by the severely agitated patients who could be treated successfully, and who with the unremitting care and devotion of their relatives got through the worst stages of their illness at home. Furthermore, the risk of suicide with out-patient treatment is much less than might be thought. No doubt case selection has helped; but it seems likely that the feeling that the patient has of receiving active treatment controls suicidal inclinations, even before the treatment has had time to produce marked benefit.

In many mental hospitals a considerable proportion of the beds in admission villas is occupied by depressive patients who could have been treated as well or better at out-patient clinics. We believe that as more and more centres take up the provision of out-patient ECT an essential service will be added to the country's facilities for early treatment, especially in those areas where admission to the local psychiatric hospital is the only alternative.

Technique of Fits

There is no need for elaborate preparation of a patient for electrical convulsion. Especially because of the general use of muscle-relaxant drugs, vomiting must be avoided at all costs. No food should be taken for at least four hours before treatment. Atropine should also be given; and it has been shown at St. Thomas's that it is best given intravenously at the same time as the Pentothal and Scoline. The patient should remain in his ordinary clothes, but they should be loosened around the waist, jacket and vest should be removed, and the shirt opened at the neck. In women tight girdles should be removed. Before entering the treatment room the patient must empty his bladder and remove his false teeth.

If premedication is necessary because of the patient's apprehensiveness, Sodium Amytal, Seconal or other quickly acting barbiturate may be given by mouth an hour or more before the treatment is to be given. A few patients intensely dislike the short period of confusion after the fit before they come fully round. This can be avoided if necessary by giving more intravenous barbiturate, intramuscular phenobarbitone or intramuscular chlorpromazine after the fit is over. The patient then has a long relaxed sleep and wakes clear and refreshed. In hospital ECT may be given at bed-time; after the fit an intramuscular sedative secures sleep which is prolonged through the night.

The time has now passed when treatment should ever be given 'in the raw', without Pentothal and a muscle relaxant, unless for some very special reason. However, if it has to be done, the following routine should be observed. The treatment is given on a hard but padded couch; an ordinary clinical examination couch is quite suitable. The patient lies on his back on the couch with a pad beneath the dorsal vertebrae and a small pillow for the head. The aim is to provide support for the dorsal column and head, and a considerable but not excessive degree of hyperextension of the back.

The control of the patient's movements during the fit is very necessary if fractures are to be avoided without the routine use of muscle relaxants. There are two practical ways of securing mechanical control: either the patient is held down by a trained staff of nurses, or he is covered by a special canvas restraining sheet which they then hold down. This restraining sheet was developed by Sargant from the original use by Batt (1943) of a strait-jacket. The arms are crossed over the chest, and just before the fit is given the sheet is put over the body and held. While it allows a certain amount of limited movement to occur, it is sufficient to prevent the wilder and more dangerous bodily movements.

If nurses are used to restrain the patient instead of the sheet, they must be trained to play their correct part. One holds the feet in close adduction. One applies her weight to the pelvis, pressing it firmly to the couch. Two more stand on each side of the shoulders, and with their weight transmitted through their forearms keep the shoulders down on the couch. The patient's arms are kept close to the side of the body and crossed across the chest, being maintained in that position by the two nurses at the shoulders. A fifth nurse will control the head and jaw movements.

While the patient is being placed in position or the sheet put on, the nurse who stands at the head will be cleaning the forehead. The temples are left moist, though not wet, with saline, but the middle of the forehead should be dry. The electrodes, enclosed in lint pads soaked in 30 per cent saline, are then placed in position by the doctor. Electrode jelly may be substituted for saline if desired. There should be two inches between the electrodes in front. The nurse who cleans the head then inserts the gag into the mouth and asks the patient to bite on it, making sure for a second time that false teeth have been removed. The nurse at the head holds the mouth gag in place and the patient's chin firmly up on the gag, so that the jaw cannot open too far in the initial stage of the fit and risk a dislocation. The doctor glances round to see that all are in position, gives a word of warning, and then presses over the switch.

We have found any small portable machine which permits variation either of the length of time during which the current passes, or of its voltage, to be as efficient as any of the more complicated machines now on the market. There is no evidence that variation of the current used is of any therapeutic value, provided it is enough to fire off a fit. With an efficient machine, well cleaned head and good electrical contact, 90 volts with a duration of 0·35 of a second may be given as a start. If the duration is shorter, a higher initial voltage will probably be required.

An insufficient voltage will only produce a sub-shock, i.e. momentary loss of consciousness, but no convulsion. Several of these given at one session will sometimes produce cardiac irregularities and the patient may appear to stop breathing and collapse. Breathing may be re-established by pressure to the thorax, and the patient will generally rally in a minute. Nevertheless, too many of these sub-shocks at once are to be avoided. Patients may be more confused after several sub-shocks than after a major fit. If only sub-shocks are achieved, the patient may also wake up much more depressed. In an apparently resistant patient, a fit can generally be produced by giving two or three applications of current immediately following one another, rather than waiting some minutes between each application. Without increasing voltage or time, the repeated application brings about a fit.

All the time the fit is going on the movements are controlled. The most important part of this control is taking the strain of the initial jerk on the back and preventing flexion of it. When the fit dies down the restraining sheet is taken off so as not to restrict breathing. If breathing does not rapidly recommence after the fit a few rhythmic compressions of the chest will cause it to begin. For all patients as a routine, but especially for elderly patients and those liable to marked cyanosis after the fit, a face-mask with pressure-bag, delivering oxygen, is a useful adjunct. It is applied as soon as the fit stops, and the patient is given a few breaths to restore full oxygenation as soon as possible.

After the patient has taken several deep breaths he can be put on the trolley and got back to bed. A soft canvas stretcher may be better than a trolley. This is placed on the treatment couch before the patient lies on it, and the patient can then be lifted straight up and carried back to the ward. If struggling starts, the patient's movements are to some extent restrained by the sides of the stretcher and the nurses carrying it on either side. One wishes, however, to avoid excitement just at this stage, and it is often best to get the restless phase over in a room off the treatment room before returning the patient to the ward. In some cases the doctor should try to observe the patient during the post-convulsive phase, as his behaviour at that time is often very illuminating and may clear up a doubtful diagnosis. The true depressive generally remains quiet and pleasant as he comes round. The unsuspected schizophrenic may exhibit suspicious and aggressive behaviour and typical mannerisms. The hysterical and aggressive psychopath may show floridly hysterical and aggressive behaviour. All these manifestations diminish as full consciousness returns. Generally after an hour or two the patient is able to get up and, if he is being treated as an out-patient, to go home. But there may be some memory loss, and it is desirable that he should be kept under some supervision (by the relatives if he is an out-patient) for the rest of the day. Not infrequently there is a good deal of headache, and he will be well advised, if an out-patient, to go to bed when he gets home. The next day, however, he should be able to take up his usual activities, and may be able to go to work if that is his wont, especially if it is of a routine nature. Work should not be continued, however, if more than one fit a week is given.

UNILATERAL ECT

For some time we have experimented at St. Thomas's, as have many other clinics, with unilateral ECT. The electrodes are both placed on the head on the nondominant side. The lower is applied slightly above a line between the lateral angle of the orbit and the external auditory meatus; the upper electrode is placed 7·5 cm higher.

Undoubtedly there is less memory upset after unilateral ECT; unfortunately it is not so effective. More treatments are generally needed; and some patients have only finally recovered when full ECT was resorted to. Unilateral ECT should be thought of when retention of memory is very important. But a patient's recovery should not be jeopardised by sticking to it too rigidly, when it just isn't working, or when too many treatments are having to be given.

CARDIAZOL

Cardiazol has been found by some workers to be more effective than electrical convulsion in severely agitated depressions, some depersonalisation states, stuporous states with refusal of food, acute hallucinatory episodes and persistent paranoid states. It must be remembered that electrical fits and metrazol fits are produced by different mechanisms, since epanutin controls the former but not the latter, while tridione has the opposite action. Polonio and others with long experience of insulin therapy believe that combined insulin and metrazol are often more effective than combined insulin and ECT. A 10 per cent buffered solution is used, and injected intravenously as rapidly as possible. The initial dose is 5–7 ml; if within a minute no convulsion has occurred, a second injection increased by 1–2 ml is immediately made. If this also fails, the third injection, again increased by 1 ml, is given; but on one occasion no more than three such attempts should be made. Great fear may be experienced by the patients between the moment of the injection and the beginning of the fit, especially so if in fact no fit occurs. For this reason, if cardiazol is to be used, it should be given in insulin sopor or light coma, which abolishes memory of the episode. Hyoscine, barbiturates and nitrous oxide anaesthesia are other ways of reducing the unpleasantness of the procedure. The convulsion is usually more violent than with ECT, the risks of fracture are if anything greater, and the same precautions must be stringently observed. Out-patient cardiazol can be given under Pentothal and Scoline, but the dose of cardiazol needed to produce a fit is often then in the region of 12–14 ml.

MUSCLE RELAXANTS

Ever since the introduction of convulsant therapy, the possibility of fractures and dislocations, especially of the long bones or spinal vertebrae, plagued the therapist. If proper methods of restraint are used, fractures of the long bones are very rare and dislocations are most uncommon. Crush fractures of the spine are more difficult to avoid in muscular people, but fortunately the disability involved is temporary and usually of much less consequence than the condition for which treatment is being given. Even under these circumstances, however, up till the time of introduction of the muscle relaxants, there were patients clinically suitable for treatment, which could not be used because of possible complications; old people, sufferers from diseases of bones or joints, those with old fractures or spinal deformities, etc.

Curare was the first relaxant to be employed, and later synthetic preparations with a curare-like action. Then a number of them, such as d-tubocurarine chloride and Flaxedil, had a vogue. We have, however, now reached a position in which very short-acting muscle relaxants are almost ideal for use with ECT; muscular paralysis can be made almost complete and yet of little longer than five minutes' duration. It is important that those who use these drugs should first be instructed in the method of dealing with a patient whose respiratory muscles are paralysed, possibly for a long period. The techniques of resuscitation and aeration of the lungs with a pressure-bag are not difficult to learn. Whenever a trained anaesthetist is available, his services should be utilised.

TECHNIQUE. Succinylcholine ('Scoline') is such a reliable short-acting relaxant. If the patient is to be given this drug it is most important that no food is taken for at least four hours beforehand; for if vomiting occurs, the paralysis of the throat muscles will permit inhalation of the vomitus. If the patient is to have treatment at 10 a.m. no more than a cup of tea is allowed at 6 a.m., and *enquiry must always be made about the food taken, before the injection is given*. Atropine 1 mg is also injected subcutaneously 30 minutes before treatment, or given intravenously at the same time as the pentothal and scoline. The patient is laid on the couch in the normal way for ECT, but with the back pillow removed, and the usual precautions about such things as false teeth are taken. He must be comfortable and under no muscular strain which, when he becomes paralysed, would have to be taken by the ligaments. Scoline administration must always be preceded by unconsciousness produced by Pentothal, as the feeling of progressive paralysis which would otherwise be felt is terrifying.

The Scoline should not be mixed with the Pentothal, but both drugs should be injected through the same needle, one after the other, changing syringes in the process. Pentothal 0·2 grams, dissolved in 4 ml of water, is usually enough, but 0·25 grams in 5 ml should be given to a strong muscular subject. The injection should take 20 to 25 seconds. The syringe is then changed, and 30 mg of Scoline is injected immediately through the same needle; 40 mg or more will be used on subsequent occasions if the fit was not sufficiently modified on the first occasion. If very complete paralysis is required for a special reason, e.g. in the subject of severe rheumatoid arthritis, 50 mg will generally be necessary. Oxygenation of the unconscious patient is then started, and several breaths of oxygen are given by means of a tightly fitting anaesthetic mask and pressure-bag. After that the patient should have a satisfactory red colour, and muscle twitchings will be seen from the effects of the Scoline, which should have passed off thirty seconds after the time of its injection. When they have stopped, and the patient is a good red colour from oxygenation, the fit may be given. This will be about 60 seconds after the Scoline injection, but not more than three minutes after it, because the effect of the relaxant will then be beginning to wear off.

If the muscular relaxation is profound, it may be difficult to know whether a fit is taking place or not. Normally, however, the toes may be seen to be twitching slightly, and there may be slight movement of the facial muscles and blepharospasm. Adderley and Hamilton (1953) have described a technique of compressing the arteries of an arm with a tourniquet or sphygmomanometer cuff just before the Scoline is given, to isolate the limb, releasing the compression before the fit, which will then be shown by this limb when not by the rest of the body. However, the patient should not be so deep as to need such a manoeuvre.

After the fit, diaphragmatic movements are the first to reappear as the effects of Scoline wear off, and after them come intercostal movements. Further oxygenation may be necessary. The tongue should be kept forward by holding the jaw forward, the pressure-bag should be used, and some prefer to insert a Water's airway before the fit is given.

Using these doses, prolonged apnoea should be a rare occurrence; but Scoline sensitivity has been reported, and the doctor must be prepared to continue oxygenation of the paralysed patient for up to half an hour, if need be. There is no antidote to Scoline, which has some of the properties of acetylcholine, its effects being aggravated by prostigmine. Generally, however, the effects will be passing off in five minutes, and when breathing is re-established, the patient may be moved to his bed, or off the couch to rest in a cubicle. This has proved quite safe in an out-patient clinic.

The routine use of muscle relaxants and Pentothal now enables patients of over 80 to be treated safely; and it has greatly diminished the contra-indications to treatment on grounds of physical weaknesses of various kinds. It has also taken much of the unpleasantness out of the treatment, both for the patient and the spectator. Either an anaesthetist must be available, or the psychiatrist must have had special training in resuscitation techniques. With that proviso, one can say the method is a major advance, and should now be generally employed everywhere.

Adjuvant Therapy

In true involutional depressions, the patient often makes a full recovery after ECT and that is that. In most cases for which it is used, however, recovery is not so dramatic and the end of convulsive therapy does not mean the end of treatment. The patient may have to be persuaded he is fit for work again; he may need symptomatic treatment for insomnia, and perhaps some occupational therapy or some measure of family readjustment. Psychotherapy has unfortunately proved very disappointing as a prophylactic against later recurrences of depression in the periodic endogenous case, and so for that matter has ECT. But this is where modern psychotropic drugs come to our aid. Most depressives will need to continue with antidepressant drugs to diminish the chances of relapse; and schizophrenics will need maintenance on tranquillising drugs. If restoration of physique is needed, the schizophrenic may even be given modified insulin treatment on an out-patient basis, if facilities are available.

The need for after-treatment of a depressive illness in the form of an occasional 'maintenance' fit is not all that rare, even with the antidepressant drugs playing the major part in stabilising recovery. In the treatment of schizophrenia by the combination of ECT and tranquillisers, it sometimes happens that the patient after the course of treatment lapses into a depressed state, without recurrence of schizophrenic thought disorder. In such an event the tranquillising drugs may be interrupted; and return to normal may be brought about by giving antidepressants and a few maintenance ECTs.

Many patients are admitted to hospital presenting mixed syndromes in which depression, retardation and anxiety are all present. In such cases modified insulin and sedation may be most valuable additions, and can be given at the same time as ECT. During the course of a continuous narcosis ECT may be given, and the MAOI drugs—but generally not the tricyclic antidepressants which may cause severe constipation. Insulin may also be useful after ECT, if the patient has lost much weight.

Once improvement begins to show itself it should be reinforced by demonstrating its extent to the patient. Things that he could not do when the illness was at its worst he may now be able to tackle and he should then be encouraged to do so. A considerable step is taken when the patient realises his improvement for himself. Of course, discouragement has to be avoided, and he should not even try in the early stages of recovery to do anything that is likely to be difficult for him—a failure will reinforce his ideas of insufficiency and guilt. If he is in hospital he should be permitted to go home for a week-end as early as is safe, once substantial improvement has been shown. As the illness clears up the delusions or ideas of guilt lose their basis and become for the first time susceptible to argument and reason; then is the time to use such minor psychotherapeutic measures in clearing them out of the way. The patient will almost certainly have a number of problems of when and how to take up an active life and guard against a recurrence of symptoms and will need the physician's guidance in settling them. He has to be supported in any way of which he feels the need until full recovery is finally stabilised.

CHAPTER THREE

Modified Narcosis and Combined Treatment with ECT and Antidepressants

The treatment of mental upset by procuring sleep for long periods is probably the oldest method of treatment known to psychiatry. Alcohol has been the drug most freely used socially for this purpose; but in the nineteenth century cures of states of mania and melancholia were noticed with massive doses of opium and later with inhalation of ether and chloroform. Early in the twentieth century bromides and later chloral, long known as sedatives, came to be used for this purpose. With the advent of the barbiturates the possibilities of continuous sleep treatment came to be more thoroughly explored. The chief credit for the development of the technique goes to Kläsi (1922). During the succeeding thirty years, declining interest has been re-awakened every now and again by the publication of favourable reports from individual workers. However in the early 50s the technique suddenly became much safer and easier with the introduction of chlorpromazine; and since then its field of usefulness has been greatly enlarged.

Modified narcosis, given together with ECT and anti-depressants, has shown itself to be a valuable new form of treatment. Its use arose following the chance observation by Birley in 1964, in the course of a research follow-up, that St. Thomas's patients suffering from 'tension states', who had been treated by leucotomy, often developed clear-cut attacks of depression at varying times after the operation. It occurred to us that such chronically tense patients might really be suffering from undiagnosed depressive illnesses; so it was made a rule at St. Thomas's that, before leucotomy could be advised in such cases, the patients should first be treated with courses of ECT and anti-depressants of adequate length. Many patients, supposedly suffering from chronic anxiety states, improved on this regime; but others became more tense and distressed, and so were put on narcosis to enable further ECT to be given. With narcosis added to the regime more patients responded, and responded more favourably. Sargant, Walter and Wright in 1966 reported the results of such treatment of 55 patients presenting with 'chronic tension states'. Of those who had been treated with anti-depressants and ECT (but *not* narcosis) *less than half* subsequently required a leucotomy, though most of them had been referred for its consideration. The patients in the second group, where modified narcosis was given additionally, did even better: *less than 10 per cent* of them now needed leucotomy. One could hardly doubt that the addition of narcosis was in part responsible for the markedly superior recovery rate in the second group.

We have now examined the results in over 400 patients, all treated with one or more courses of modified narcosis combined with ECT and anti-depressants between 1962 and 1968, in the Department of Psychological Medicine at St. Thomas's Hospital or at Belmont Hospital. Ages ranged from 16 to 73 years, and the mean duration of symptoms was no less than 7·2 years. Most of these patients during their long illnesses had received many other types of treatment; almost half of them had been referred to St. Thomas's by other consultant psychiatrists for a second opinion, and in the majority of cases this was for consideration for a modified leucotomy. It has also been possible to compare the results of combined treatment of a smaller group of patients with the results in a control group followed up for five to eight years (Walter, Mitchell-Heggs and Sargant, 1972).

We have found that modified narcosis combined with ECT and anti-depressant drugs can bring about rapid symptomatic relief in many severely depressed, anxious and suicidal patients resistant to other methods. Many patients, unable to tolerate a long course of ECT, can do so when anxiety is relieved by narcosis. The best results are obtained in agitated depression and non-agitated depression; but, surprisingly, many patients with (so called) chronic tension and with anxiety states can also be helped. Even more unexpectedly, worthwhile improvements have also been obtained in obsessional neurosis, in schizophrenia and in schizo-affective disorders. The duration of the illnesses, which may have been one of many years, is not so important for the prospects of a remission as the evidence from the history on whether or not the patient has been able to cope with the environment adequately before the breakdown. What is also so valuable is that they generally have no memory about the actual length of the treatment or the number of ECT used after the treatment is finished.

Depression

There are many patients who, though primarily depressed, do not complain of depression but rather an anguish and an inner feeling of severe tension, and describe this as the main symptom. To give these patients ECT has often proved difficult in the past. After three or four treatments, they may ask for ECT to be discontinued because of an increasing dread of further treatment. Combining sleep with ECT avoids this, and with it the results have been very rewarding particularly in agitated depressions; and one can expect 75 per cent of the patients to be either symptom-free or much improved following combined treatment, even if they have been ill for many years, provided the previous personality had been adequate to cope with life's ordinary stresses. As a rule these patients should be maintained on combined anti-depressants (see Chapter I) for at least six months after stopping the narcosis. In the first two to three weeks, if symptoms begin to recur, the addition of a few more ECT is usually all that is required to prevent relapse. Some patients may later on require a second course of combined treatment before stabilising, and this is definitely called for if the first course of treatment produced a worthwhile improvement followed by later relapse.

Patients with non-agitated depression usually need rather shorter courses of combined therapy than those with agitated depression; the immediate results are just as good. When patients with such long-standing syndromes of either kind are treated by this method and followed up some years later, about half of them will be found to be either symptom-free or much improved.

The length of the course of combined treatment needed may be from one to two, and exceptionally three months. The treatment is only stopped when the patient in his waking state reports the lifting of the previous persistent tension and depression. For some resistant patients who may have been ill for years, up to 20 to 30 ECT during the treatment may be finally needed. Many failures of the past seem to have been due to breaking off the ECT too soon. One should base one's decision to continue with ECT or to stop it, in obsessional and schizophrenic patients as well as in depressed ones, on what one learns on questioning the patient in the waking state.

Obsessional Neurosis

Unexpectedly rewarding results of treatment have also been obtained with patients suffering from incapacitating rituals and ruminations, even though they may have been present for many years. Many leucotomies have been avoided. However modified narcosis and ECT may have to be continued for up to three months, assessing the patient's progress periodically during treatment, since the length of the narcosis will depend on the response. These patients may become disorientated and markedly amnesic, especially if the course is pro-longed; but confusion towards the end of the course is often the sign of good prognosis. The patients who respond best are those under 45 years of age who show a lot of anxiety about their rituals. The overall improvement rate is less satisfactory than in depressive ill-nesses. But one may hope that 40 per cent of those patients will be symptom-free or much improved immediately after treatment, and improvement is often maintained, if the personality before the onset of the illness was satisfactory. If relapse does occur, this may be when memory fully returns; but some relapsed patients can be further helped by a subsequent course of treatment.

Anxiety states and hysterias

Patients presenting with chronic anxiety of many years' duration do well initially with combined treatment; and one can expect nearly 60 per cent to be symptom-free or much improved at the end of a full course. But the long term results are much less satisfactory. These patients can be distinguished from those with agitated depression. They are usually anxiety-prone personalities, who have had attacks of acute panic in their twenties or thirties, attacks which recurred with increasing frequency until in the end there was a state of more or less perpetual agitation, and the patient was seldom if ever able to relax. With these patients the response to MAOIs such as phenelzine is also less satisfactory than with ordinary phobic anxiety states. After an initial favourable response relapses are not uncommon, and a limited leucotomy may finally have to be considered.

Patients with phobic anxiety present with circumscribed fears (e.g. of crowds, lifts, public transport, shops, restaurants or enclosed places); but they do not have the high levels of 'free floating' anxiety which distinguish the chronic anxiety states. Many of these patients respond to MAOIs and intravenous Valium injections. (See Chapter I.) Those who do not, under modified narcosis may take a course of ECT that would otherwise be refused; and the total treatment regime usually lessens the phobias for a time. Unfortunately the follow-up results are often disappointing. Much additional treatment is gener-ally necessary, and limited leucotomy may in the end be the answer.

In some cases of 'hysteria', where the previous personality has been good, a long illness has finally resolved under combined treatment.

But we can be sure that these patients were really suffering from depressive states in which hysterical symptoms eventually surfaced from the stress of the long illness. One such patient recovered after being kept for five months on modified sleep and ECT, mostly given once a week, after seven years of continuous illness. When she had a mild relapse a year or so later, it started as a clear-cut depressive illness and she was quickly better again with further treatment.

Schizo-affective Disorders and Schizophrenia

Those patients in this group who make no adequate response when treated with phenothiazines alone, or combined with ECT, should be tried on a full course of modified narcosis combined with ECT and anti-depressants; a third of them or more may become symptom-free or much improved. Here, as in other diagnostic groups, the illness may have lasted for years without prejudice to the prognosis if there was a good previous personality, and the affective state has not become markedly discrepant. One can speculate that the effect of combined treatment may be similar to that of insulin coma, but it is unlikely that just the same mechanisms are involved. In the patients we are thinking of, the illnesses have been of longer duration than those that used to respond to insulin coma alone; and some few patients have been found to respond to insulin coma or sopor following the failure of combined narcosis therapy, and these latter patients have generally had more recent onsets. The use of intramuscular fluphenazine enanthate (Moditen) or decanoate (Modicate) afterwards may help to prevent relapses.

Intractable pain, primary unreality and personality disorders

Patients in all these diagnostic categories have been given combined treatment, but the results have not in general been very rewarding. However, one or two patients with intractable pain, not responding to leucotomy, have been helped after years and years of misery, and leucotomy has been avoided in other cases of intractable pain. One is tempted to think that a depressive state has been the underlying cause of the pain, even though it did not respond even to leucotomy.

TECHNIQUE OF TREATMENT

This is much simpler than the old deep narcosis regime. It can be carried out in a general ward with the patients screened, or in a special small narcosis ward leading out of a general ward. All the three wards being used (by WS) at Belmont Hospital manage to care for three to six sleep cases at a time. The aim should be to achieve prolonged periods of light sleep, between 16 and 20 hours a day, from which the patient can be easily roused for meals, physiotherapy and nursing care. Drugs are given six-hourly and the patient must have **three full meals and two litres of fluid** during each 24 hour period. Careful records must be kept of the level of consciousness, blood pressure, temperature, pulse rate and respiration; fluid intake and urinary output and bowel function are also noted. A good standard of nursing is therefore essential. At regular intervals the patient is woken for a meal, at a time when the effects of the last dose of drugs is wearing off. Most patients are light enough to feed themselves; some may be encouraged to get up and have meals at a table. **Further drugs should not be given unless adequate food and fluid have been taken.** The patient should also be encouraged to walk to the lavatory, as this ensures some essential exercise. After the meal he is brought back to bed and the next dose of drugs is administered.

The major danger of treatment is from paralytic ileus. In view of this, regular aperients are used and the patient's **abdominal girth is measured daily**. Enemas are given immediately if there is any suspicion of failing bowel activity; routine daily enemas or enemas every other day may be the best solution. The patient should pass urine during every waking period.

ECT is given twice a week. Occasionally, however, three ECT a week may be given to speed up improvement, or in some resistant obsessional patients to produce therapeutic confusion.

Drugs used

Medication is given six-hourly at 7 a.m., 1 p.m., 7 p.m. and 1 a.m. The precise dose is left to the judgment of the senior nurse, who must be an experienced and responsible person. Chlorpromazine, 100 to 400 mg six-hourly, is the chief drug used. Doses at the lower end of the range are given if the patient is sleeping well, or is very drowsy at meal times, higher doses if the patient is agitated or not sleeping. The level of blood pressure is the other factor determining the dosage, and it may have to be taken before the drugs are given, both with the patient supine and erect.

Anti-parkinsonian medication is given as a routine, e.g. orphenadrine 50 to 100 mg six-hourly. A small dose of a short-acting hypnotic can be added to the chlorpromazine; but the choice is not easy. When the treatment was first introduced we used barbiturates, most commonly amylobarbitone sodium 100 to 400 mg six-hourly. Although anxiety was greatly reduced, this drug also led to confusion and a feeling of intense apprehension in the withdrawal period, and occasionally to withdrawal fits, and we now rarely use it in narcosis. Elixir of chloral hydrate, 5 to 20 ml six-hourly, has also been tried; but in many patients it was found to cause irritation of the mouth, and also indigestion. Welldorm (dichloralphenazone), 650 to 1950 mg six-hourly, has been used, but its effects are potentiated by chlorpromazine and hypotension may be increased. Nevertheless, it does produce a smooth narcosis, and much less tension in the withdrawal stage. The dose often has to be increased in the third week. Mandrax (methaqualone 250 mg with diphenhydramine 25 mg), one to three tablets six-hourly, has been the hypnotic most frequently used recently. It can produce some confusion, especially in patients over 40, but there are fewer withdrawal effects.

Very disturbed patients have required up to 600 mg chlorpromazine in an individual dose, or another drug such as haloperidol or promethazine, in addition, to the adjunct hypnotic; the dose of the latter must always be kept as low as possible.

Anti-depressants

For quite a long time both tricyclic anti-depressants and MAOI were given together during modified narcosis combined with ECT; but, as a result of the infrequent occurrence of paralytic ileus during treatment, this is no longer done as routine; generally MAOI is given as the only anti-depressant during narcosis. Paralytic ileus has been described elsewhere as a rare complication of treatment with amitriptyline alone. However, as soon as the narcosis is completed, the tricyclic is added to the MAOI again. MAOI drugs most commonly used are phenelzine 45 mg daily, or tranylcypromine 30 mg daily. If, for special reasons, a tricyclic is going to be used in conjunction with the MAOI during the narcosis, the MAOI is given during the day in three divided doses, while the tricyclic anti-depressant, either amitriptyline or trimipramine 100 to 150 mg is given in a single dose at night. To avoid bowel complications in cases where combined anti-depressants are being given, enemata should be given daily.

Additional treatments

Vitamin supplements are given to prevent the development of angular stomatitis, which is commonly seen during narcosis. On the days when ECT is to be given, the drugs are withheld until after the ECT. Occasionally modified insulin therapy can usefully be added to the regime. Prophylactic physiotherapy is valuable to reduce the risk of chest infections.

Withdrawal of drugs

At the end of the course of treatment, drugs are gradually withdrawn over a period of four to seven days. The hypnotic is withdrawn first. If barbiturates have been used, this reduction must be carried out very slowly, and phenobarbitone 30 mg daily should be given to reduce the likelihood of withdrawal fits. We have seen much less withdrawal tension when Mandrax has been used. The dose of chlorpromazine is then slowly reduced. ECT may continue to be given during the withdrawal phase. Following the completion of treatment, the patient is as a rule maintained on combined antidepressants with the minimum of sedatives.

Side effects

Hypotension may require a reduction in the medication, and occasionally also raising the foot of the bed. Drug rashes may be due to chlorpromazine, barbiturates or Mandrax, and may call for the withdrawal of the drug and the use of an antihistamine. Urinary retention is generally overcome by reducing the anti-depressants.

Obstinate constipation, impacted faeces **high up,** and paralytic ileus have all occurred. The tricyclic anti-depressants have been held chiefly responsible for this effect; but it can occur without them. The abdomen becomes distended; bowel sounds may be reduced or absent; and if the patient vomits, the danger of inhalation of vomitus is considerable. Even if there have been bowel motions, at the first sign of abdominal distention **all drugs and oral feeding should be stopped immediately**. The stomach contents may be emptied, if necessary, through a Ryle's tube. In severe cases an intravenous infusion of isotonic saline or 4 per cent dextrose with N/5 saline is set up, and maintained until the distention has subsided completely and normal bowel sounds have returned. Attempts have to be made to dislodge faeces which may have become impacted high up while the rectum itself is empty.

A few patients in our series developed lower limb deep vein thrombosis; this is largely prevented by ensuring that the patients walk to the lavatory at least four times a day.

Diarrhoea is a not uncommon occurrence, and can be treated with a bland diet or mist. kaolin (without morphine). Chest infections may require antibiotics and a lightening of the narcosis; but regular physiotherapy should help to prevent this.

Actually we have experienced only four deaths during 679 courses of treatment lasting up to three months, and in one case five months. The deaths were all due to bowel complications. There have been no suicides. There has been one further death from bowel complications since stopping the use of tricyclics in narcosis; so constant vigilance about the bowels still seems necessary.

Other uses of narcosis

Apart from the combined treatment described at length above, narcosis, using predominantly chlorpromazine, is very useful in controlling acute psychotic illness in patients admitted to unlocked open units. All sorts of treatment can be given while the patient is kept sleeping, including a variety of drugs and ECT, while the acute illness is brought under control. One can give, for instance, antischizophrenic drugs and many other things the patient may need for recovery.

Some patients with anxiety and depression have been helped by a long course of sleep, alone and without ECT; but it is difficult to pick these patients with assurance. We have occasionally seen sleep and anti-depressant drugs successfully used when full combined treatment had failed.

Finally, the circumstances of the life to which the patient is returning will have to be reviewed in every case, and the point examined whether they both require and are susceptible to some modification. What are the patient's normal powers of resistance? Were they reduced at the time of the onset of the illness by any physical process? What were the predisposing and the precipitating factors, and were they exceptional or inherent in the patient's constitution or way of life? No psychiatric treatment can be considered satisfactory unless it is designed for more than the immediate emergency, and is at every point adapted to the most thorough-going diagnostic and prognostic consideration.

In the combined treatment, the hypnotic drug and the ECT together generally induce considerable memory loss for the period under narcosis. As a rule the patient does not know how long he has been asleep, or what treatment, even including ECT, he has been given. Under sleep, in the acute or in the chronic patient, one can now give many kinds of physical treatment, necessary but often not easily tolerated. We may be seeing here a new exciting beginning in psychiatry, and the possibility of a treatment era such as followed the introduction of anaesthesia in surgery. Our aim, surely, must be to get the suffering patient well again, if possible with little after-memory of what may have been a long and otherwise distressful illness and treatment.

Full statistical data and clinical details of the treatment of over 400 patients by modified narcosis, ECT and anti-depressant drugs is being published in the *British Journal of Psychiatry* this year (Walter *et al.*, 1972a, 1972b).

CHAPTER FOUR

Prefrontal Leucotomy

In medieval Rome, Robert Burton relates, they had already observed that insanity might recover after a sword-wound to the head in which the brain-pan was broken; and they tried, with occasional success, to cure it by boring the skull to let out the fuliginous humours. Authority, however, went against them; Alexander Messaria, a Professor in Padua, held that the humour was too stiff and too thick to be so eva-porated, and the method fell into desuetude. So it has often been since, when humanity has blandly refused to permit a beautiful theory to be killed by an uncomfortable fact. It is now many years since observant brain surgeons recognised that operations which interfered with the anterior part of the frontal lobes had remarkably little ad-verse effect. Yet it was still believed that this part of the brain, being the most recently developed, must be the organ of the highest intel-lectual and spiritual activities of man, and, when not actually diseased, should be sacrosanct against deliberate damage.

Our knowledge of the function of the frontal lobes, though still scanty, has now reached a rather more advanced stage; and we can say with some preciseness what are the mental attributes which are likely to be affected by the operation of prefrontal leucotomy, and which will most probably escape. Intelligence, as measured by intel-ligence tests, generally shows no diminution whatever. With the older types of operation, now obsolete, the more subtle powers of the intellect, such as its intuitive and imaginative qualities, were some-times thought to be affected. It was difficult to be sure, since little call on these qualities would ordinarily be made in the routine life of day to day. Nowadays the dangers are fewer. In well-chosen material and with suitable operations, troublesome sequelae will be shown by only a small minority of patients, and those ones in whom the cut has been too extensive or has gone too posteriorly. In general, the better pre-served the personality, and the more reluctant the doctor is to use the treatment on that account, the better the end result will be.

Over 50 years ago Burkhardt (1890) attempted brain surgery in the region of the parietal lobe in one patient with mental symptoms, and in a second attempted section of the fibres between the central area and the frontal lobe. His efforts were not well received, and current objections on philosophical grounds resulted in the work being abandoned. Later, when Freeman and Watts in the U.S.A. attempted to develop Moniz's original work, they met with similar difficulties. It was the publication of further work in Britain which helped to convince a growing circle of Americans of the possibilities of this approach to the treatment of mental disorder; and since then progress has been consistent.

Moniz (1936) began his work on the hypothesis that in mental disorders certain synaptic paths were controlling the abnormal behaviour patterns, and he hoped to interrupt these pathways. His first method was to introduce alcohol into the subcortical white matter in the anterior part of the frontal lobes. Later a steel leucotome was used, and cores of white matter were separated but not removed. The technique of the operation has since been developed in various directions.

In their original work Freeman and Watts felt that, if the operation was to be successful, some temporary confusion had to be produced. As a result a 'standard' operation, with rather too posterior a cut, was performed which, though relieving symptoms, too often led to unnecessarily severe personality changes. The ill effect was enhanced by the fact that at first it was the usual practice to select only the most chronic and deteriorated patients, and the personality damage done by the operation was added to that caused by prolonged mental illness, usually schizophrenic. Opinion has since changed and is still changing.

In careful experiments on animals Fulton (1952) has shown that significant emotional changes can be produced with little adverse alteration in other aspects of behaviour (e.g. in tests of discrimination), provided the inferior medial quadrant of the frontal lobe is alone interfered with. Other workers in America, France and England have brought evidence from human subjects that open or closed operations in this area can cause a reduction of emotional tension without serious side-effects. It is possible that some patients may need to be emotionally blunted to some extent to tolerate his abnormal drives and ideas without an excessive reaction in behaviour, especially as even a full leucotomy may leave his delusions and hallucinations unaffected. However, even in such a case one will probably do better to carry out a modified operation, and stabilise and maintain the improvement by tranquillising drugs. In patients in whom the operation is done before the personality has suffered severely, a reduction of tension alone may suffice for recovery, the abnormal ideas tending to die out for lack of emotional reinforcement. Modified operations should therefore always be tried in the first place. In the case of failure a second operation can always be undertaken, perhaps by a different approach.

Many different approaches are still being tried. Freeman and Watts (1942) originally advocated a closed operation from the side. Poppen (1948) and others have done equally extensive operations by opening the skull from above, and sucking out tissue from the frontal lobe. However, better results were achieved, even in schizophrenics, when damage was limited to the upper and lower medial quadrants (Greenblatt and Solomon, 1953). Scoville (Scoville *et al.*, 1951) undercut the cortex of the frontal lobes, and reported that intellectual impairment and undesired changes were least when the grey matter of the orbital aspect of the frontal lobes was undercut; however, the change produced may be insufficient in some schizophrenics.

A recent development of orbital undercutting has been bifrontal stereotactic tractotomy, produced by placing radioactive yttrium seeds in the substantia innominata reported by Knight in 1965. The consequence is a flat lesion, 2 cm long, 1 cm wide and 0·5 cm deep, below the head of the candate nucleus, which interrupts the ascending thalamo-frontal radiation.

The Limbic System and Leucotomy

In 1937 James Papez wrote a classical paper in which he postulated that the anatomical basis of emotion involved the hypothalamus, anterior thalamic nuclei, gyrus cinguli, hippocampus and their interconnections. In monkeys it was found that electrical stimulation of anterior cingulate area 24 led to pupillary, respiratory and cardiovascular responses; and lesions in this region produced tamer, less fearful and less aggressive animals. Fulton, in 1947, at a meeting in Glasgow of the Society of British Neurological Surgeons, suggested that 'were it feasible, cingulectomy in man would seem an appropriate place for limited leucotomy.' Sir Hugh Cairns then began the operation of anterior cingulectomy and it was later found by Lewin (1961) that patients with obsessional neurosis were significantly improved. 'Cingulectomy may interrupt a reverberating circuit formed by hippocampus, fornix, mammillary bodies, anterior nucleus of thalamus and cingulate gyrus, and it is interesting that it is the obsessional disorder which seems to respond best of all to this particular operation.' Le Beau in 1954 also obtained good results with anterior cingulectomy, and Foltz later (1968) stereotactically ablated the cingulum fasciculus, and found this beneficial in patients with depression and anxiety. Stereotactically placed lesions in the lower rostral portion of area 24 gave beneficial results in intractable psychoneurosis and affective psychosis with negligible surgical risk according to Hunter Brown and Lighthill (1968), while lesions in the anterior cingulum above the roof of the lateral ventricle resulted in improvement in patients suffering from anxiety, depression and obsessional neurosis according to Ballantine *et al.* (1967).

Livingstone (1969) in a recent review of the physiology of the limbic system states: 'It has been clinically established that a variety of anatomical lesions of the frontal lobes can produce beneficial change in the affect and behaviour of patients suffering from severe psychiatric and psychoneurotic disorders. It has been further demonstrated clinically that the areas most effective in producing such change are discrete regions of the medial and orbital frontal cortex, and demonstrated experimentally that stimulation of these "effective" frontal areas produced autonomic responses which presumably reached outflow pathways to the hypothalamus and brain-stem through intermediate limbic circuits. On the basis of this evidence it could be postulated that the key to understanding the effects of frontal lobotomy lay in the elucidation of fronto-limbic relationships—the mechanism by which frontal lesions may alter limbic system function.' He suggested that the effect of leucotomy was to a large extent attributable to 'the disconnection of relatively discrete functional areas of the orbital and frontal cortex from intermediate limbic circuits leading to autonomic outflow pathways through the hypothalamus and brain stem'. 'By 1953 the technical feasibility of restricting the lobotomy lesion to the autonomic effector areas of the frontal lobe had also been established.' (Livingstone, 1969.)

STEREOTACTIC LIMBIC LEUCOTOMY

The risk of adverse personality change has been the major problem with open or blind modifications of standard leucotomy, and misplaced cuts may lead to failure of the operation. Stereotactic techniques have largely overcome this problem, and if small lesions are made, the risk of hæmorrhage, epilepsy or adverse personality change are reduced to a minimum, and unnecessary destruction of white matter is avoided. A better understanding of the limbic system and new surgical techniques now enable operations to be designed for individual patients. Mr Alan Richardson at Atkinson Morley's Hospital (St. George's Hospital) uses a cryogenic probe which can produce small permanent lesions up to 1 cm in diameter, by freezing white matter to −70°C. Multiple lesions are made by a stereotactic method in different areas of the limbic system depending on the patient's psychopathology. In anxiety and depressive states bilateral lower medial quadrant lesions are made at points 1 cm in front of and 1 cm above the base of the anterior clinoid process, 6 mm and 12 mm from the mid-line (Figs. 1 and 2).

This site overlaps part of the target area of bifrontal tractotomy. 'The postero-medial angle of the plane to be implanted lies 0·5 cm in front of the plane of the tuberculum sellae, 1 cm above the orbital roof and 1 cm from the midline.' (Knight, 1965.) The lower medial quadrant target area corresponds to the medial and deepest part of the division of white fibres produced by a rostral (McKissock, 1951), or Harvey Jackson (1954) leucotomy. With the older operations there were considerable variations in the operation site in the anterior-posterior plane. Lesions in anterior cingulate area 24, have also been found to be beneficial in anxiety state and depression. In obsessional neurosis four lesions are made on each side in the anterior cingulum above the roof of the lateral ventricles. A perpendicular line is drawn upwards from the base of the anterior clinoid process, and a pair of lesions placed on it 5 mm above the roof of the lateral ventricle, and a variable distance from the mid-line, depending on ventricular size and shape, and another pair of lesions made 1 cm posterior to these points—sites 1 and 2 (Figs. 1 and 2). Patients with anxiety and obsessional symptoms have lesions made in the lower medial quadrants and in the cingulum bundle (sites 1 and 2).

The patients are admitted to the psychiatric ward for full clinical, psychological and physiological assessment since some of these measurements may predict a good clinical result (Kelly et al., 1972). If leucotomy is advised, the patient is seen at a joint interview between psychiatrist and neurosurgeon and the target sites chosen for the individual patient. At the time of operation a lumbar air encephalo-gram is performed to outline the lateral ventricles, as the cingulate lesions are related to this landmark, and to determine the mid-line of the ventricular system. Continuous physiological recordings of heart rate, forearm blood flow, respiration and skin resistance are made during the operation, and stimulation performed in the target zone before lesions are made. The predicted target site may be changed

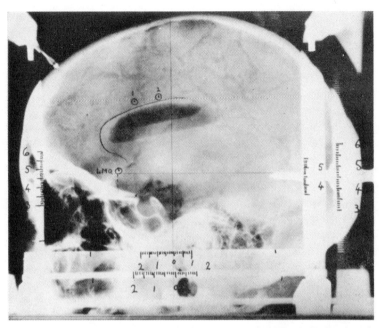

Figure 1. Stereotactic Limbic Leucotomy. Lateral x-ray of the skull showing air in the lateral ventricles (dark shadow), and the stereotactic frame in place. The corpus callosum is outlined and lesion sites 1 and 2 in the anterior cingulate gyrus marked. The pituitary fossa can be seen with a cross at the base of the anterior clinoid process. The lower medial quadrant site is 1 cm in front and 1 cm above this mark (LMQ).

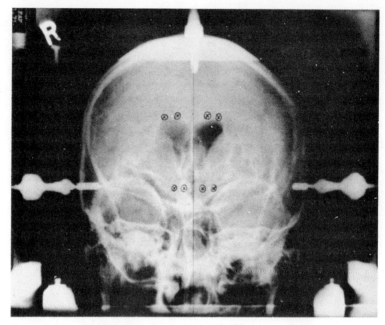

Figure 2. Stereotactic Limbic Leucotomy. AP view of the skull with air in the lateral ventricles (dark shadow). The cingulate lesions are above the roof of the lateral ventricles, while the lower set of crosses mark the sites of lower medial quadrant lesions in the frontal lobes.

if it is not an 'active area' physiologically, thus individual variations in anatomy can be taken into account.

Post-operative Care

After operation, routine recording of vital signs and assessment of the level of consciousness, orientation and neurological state are performed every half hour for the first 12 hours; and these observations are repeated at progressively increasing intervals until the standard four-hourly level is reached. The patient may complain of headache and nausea for some time, as most patients do after lumbar air encephalography, and an intravenous infusion is continued for 24 hours, and food and fluids by mouth restricted. Routine antibiotics are given post-operatively for five days, codeine phosphate is given for headache, and prochlorperazine may be necessary if nausea is severe. Patients usually notice no change in their mental state immediately after operation, but over the course of days or weeks improvement becomes apparent; maximum benefit may not occur until months after operation. In the immediate post-operative period appreciation of the passage of time may be altered, and disorientation can occur. Urinary incontinence is occasionally seen for a few days but always clears. Perseverative behaviour may be observed transiently. Anticonvulsants are given prophylactically for six months. The patients generally get up after two to three days and return to the psychiatric ward between the third and fifth postoperative day. A post-operative rehabilitation programme usually begins 10 days after operation. If the patient was agoraphobic, a series of graded excursions are instituted, with the patient going progressively greater distances from hospital, at first accompanied by a nurse and later alone. Bus and train journeys may be planned in the same way. If obsessional symptoms were the reason for operation, close supervision by the nursing staff is employed to remodel previous ritualistic behaviour. Rehabilitation usually takes at least six weeks, and the patients are then reassessed clinically, physiologically and psychologically.

The object of surgery is to remove or modify severely incapacitating symptoms when all other methods had failed; and limbic leucotomy often enables further treatment to be much more successful. Our experience has mainly been with the older type of lower medial quadrant operations which have given very satisfactory results, assessed over many years. With any operation, and especially with limbic leucotomy, selection is of paramount importance.

The Selection of Patients and Results

It is not easy to discuss the results obtained by other authors, because of their great differences one from another in method and outlook; different diagnostic criteria are applied, different operations are
carried out, and standards of recovery are differently assessed.
Furthermore, clinical expectations after operation have been greatly
improved by the recently introduced stereotactic techniques. However the symptoms and the disabilities which one hoped to influence
for the better with old-style operations are still the ones most
accessible to the modern precision approaches. The clinical experience of earlier years is, in fact, still relevant. An exhaustive knowledge
of the literature is not needed for purely practical purposes. The
selection of the most promising patients for surgery offers no overwhelming difficulty, if certain principles are kept in mind.

DEPRESSIVE STATES

Many of our long-standing depressive patients are now being
treated in neurosis centres and in the psychiatric wards of general
hospitals, and there is a much greater unwillingness to accept
chronicity for any patient. The introduction of the antidepressant
drugs has altered the indications for modified leucotomy. The
patients who do not respond to ECT alone, who made up a considerable part of the candidates for leucotomy in the old days, may now
do much better when ECT is combined with an antidepressant, or
both with modified narcosis. Moreover, these drugs used as maintenance treatment often prevent the relapses after ECT which, in
earlier days, were one of the other main indications for operation.
Lithium carbonate, also, may prevent or modify relapses in some
patients. Frommer (personal communication), examining the case
records of patients admitted under the care of one of us at Belmont
Hospital for consideration of leucotomy in the years 1959–61, found
that in 41 out of 85 patients it had been possible to avoid leucotomy,
mostly by the further use of ECT with antidepressants, but sometimes by the proper use of antidepressants without ECT. Most of
these patients had been sent in by other psychiatrists who felt that
everything had been tried apart from operation. Of 73 such patients
suffering from chronic tension states, Sargant, Walter and Wright
(1966) found that 67 per cent improved markedly with further treatment of the underlying depression. Of the 37 patients treated with

ECT and antidepressants alone 15 still needed leucotomy in the end;
but only three of the 36 patients who were given modified narcosis in
addition. The uses of combined therapy are discussed in Chapter
III.

Depressive illnesses are of a different nature from schizophrenic
illnesses, and there is no evidence that, however long they last, they
necessarily have a destructive effect on the personality. Total recovery
with no obvious impairment may occur spontaneously after years of
illness. Furthermore, the personality is usually of a more dynamic
kind than in the schizophrenic, and in very many cases the quality of
the previous personality is the critical issue on which the success of
leucotomy depends. It is in the long-standing depression that leucotomy may achieve its most spectacular results.

Depressive illnesses are of many kinds, and with some leucotomy
is much more apposite than with others. The involutional depressive,
whose illness occurs on the basis of a rigid and constitutionally
obsessional personality, rarely fails to recover with convulsion
therapy and the antidepressant drugs, especially if retardation is an
obvious symptom. In these patients leucotomy should not be performed until these have failed. But there is another group of depressive illnesses which tend to occur about the same time in life, not in
the obsessional but in the chronically anxious person, in men often
of social and extroverted type. In their illnesses also symptoms of
anxiety and tension, both in the psychological and the somatic fields,
are prominent. These patients often respond badly to ECT, unless it is
combined with narcosis, because, when the depression is relieved, its
place is taken by an enhanced state of tension or even agitation. These
patients usually do well with one of the monoamine exidase inhibitor
group of antidepressant drugs, combined with Librium or small doses
of a tranquilliser, even after ECT has failed to help. However, if
neither ECT nor the antidepressant drugs succeed, nor both combined with narcosis, a modified leucotomy should eventually be considered, as its prospects of bringing about recovery at negligible cost
to the personality are excellent. Tension symptoms that may still
remain will now be found to respond to therapy with antidepressants
and tranquillisers; and they provide an effective treatment of any
recurrence after the leucotomy.

Another type of depressive illness that may be helped by leucotomy
is the reactive depression in which environmental factors of an irre-
mediable kind are involved. A depressed woman, for instance, may
owe her illness to a psychopathic husband who cannot change and

will not accept treatment. Separation might be the answer, but is ruled out by other ties such as children, by the patient's financial or emotional dependence, or by her religious views. Patients of this type are often helped by antidepressant drugs. But in the occasional case where they do not work, we have seen patients enabled by a leucotomy to return to the difficult environment and cope with it in a way which had hitherto been impossible.

Other reactive depressions are caused by physical illness. Thus some patients with Parkinson's disease become depressed and obsessed with their disability, and ECT only increases their tension. A group of patients by which we have been particularly impressed is that of the sufferers from tinnitus, however caused. Most patients with this trouble are able to accept it philosophically, but there are some who find the noises in the head intolerable. They too, like some of the cases of Parkinsonism, derive the greatest benefit from a modified leucotomy. Individual patients with other physical maladies, who develop severe and chronic psychological reactions to their troubles, may be very favourable subjects for modified leucotomies when everything else has failed. But again the various tranquillisers and antidepressant drugs, are making these an increasingly infrequent group (Sargant, 1951b).

In addition to the particular types of late depressive illness already mentioned, there are numbers of involutional and other long-standing depressions which will have to be considered at times. These are the patients who as a result of therapeutic inertia have been left too long, or who have failed to react to convulsive therapy and the drugs, or have reacted more than once in an initially satisfactory way but who have subsequently relapsed. Perhaps, after each fit, the patient is better for a few days, but then slips back into gloomy repetitive thoughts. With the evanescent lift of mood there is no alteration in the ideas, which starting in the early and acute stage of the depression have now become deeply ingrained and are accepted as part of everyday experience. With the persistence of the illness the prognosis has become progressively gloomy. Though the depression persists, it is not as deep as the ideas the mind dwells on would warrant. The suffering of these patients is extreme and prolonged; and for the onlooker the picture is made painful by the indications of continuing good preservation of the personality and of an elan and responsiveness if the patient's preoccupation with his miseries can for a moment be diverted. These patients provide both a sufficient justification and a sufficient hope for surgical interference, and the results of this treatment show a high percentage of recoveries.

Nevertheless there are reasons for caution. In a follow-up of patients treated at St. Thomas's Hospital, Birley (1964) found several of our patients who were having recurrent attacks of depression after the operation; they also quickly responded to ECT and drug treatment. Reviewing their past histories, it was found that they had had courses of ECT which might have been inadequate. Since then our patients with severe symptoms of tension and depression have been given longer courses of ECT and drugs combined with modified narcosis before being submitted to operation (Chapter III). Some made unexpected recoveries with continuation of ECT after the twelfth treatment, and operation has been avoided, despite a duration of illness as long as seven years (Sargant *et al.*, 1966). Considering whether to continue ECT in such patients beyond the normal length of course, one should take account of the memory. If disturbance of memory is slight in relation to the number of treatments, one may give more; if it is not to be regarded as slight, then continuation of ECT may not be advisable, unless therapeutic confusion is desired.

The indications for operation in the recurrent endogenous depressions and manic-depressive psychoses have to be differently assessed. Even at the symptomatic level there are noteworthy contrasts. The depressions we have so far discussed as particularly suitable for leucotomy, show prominently the signs of anxiety, agitation and obsessional rumination but an absence of severe retardation. As a rule they can be distracted from their miseries for a short time if sufficient effort is made. Psychological precipitation and reactive elements may also have played a part.

In recurrent endogenous depressions and manic-depressive psychoses a different pattern may prevail. Retardation and the depressed mood may persist unchanged in any environment, only to lift unpredictably for no apparent reason. Depression may swing over abruptly into elation without any change in the environment and circumstances. In these patients the body build is more often pyknic, instead of, as in the others, asthenic or an asthenic-athletic mixture. The results to be expected from leucotomy are also different. In clear-cut manic-depressives, who have had swings of mood of both kinds, a less numerous group than those subject only to recurrent depressions, leucotomy may lead to the replacement of depressive attacks by attacks of hypomania, though illnesses of both the manic and depressive type are often shorter and milder than before operation. These hypomanic attacks, however, respond well to the tranquillisers, lithium or haloperidol. The operation may be worth while if attacks of either elation or depression are severe and frequent, as sometimes the swings of mood will cease completely and quite frequently they will lessen in frequency and severity. Moreover, after operation it is usually much easier to get good control of mood swings by drug therapy than it was before.

One should also distinguish among recurrent depressives between those who do and those who do not expect, in the intervals between their attacks, ever to be ill again. Those who have had hypomanic interludes frequently dismiss the possibility of a return of depression. Others in their more normal periods show much anxiety and apprehension about the return of illness, so much so that individual attacks may be facilitated under the influence of environmental stress or bodily illness. A modified leucotomy may then be a useful safeguard against recurrence, although antidepressants, lithium or tranquilliser drugs will sometimes prove very effective, the patient himself increasing doses as soon as he feels a return of symptoms. Some patients who suffer from periodic endogenous depressions do not seem to be ætiologically related to the manic-depressives, but to be rather nearer to the schizophrenias. They may show schizophreniform symptoms in their attacks, or have a depresive mood without the usual daily variations from morning to evening in depth, may sleep more deeply than normal, or show elements of confusion or unreality. Even then, recovery from each attack may be complete. One of our patients, who was subject to three weeks of agitated depression and three weeks or more of relative normality coloured by apprehensiveness, and who had had a succession of such cycles for fifteen years, had only very modified mood swings for several years after a modified leucotomy and was helped further by the antidepressant drugs and tranquillisers.

A trap of which one should be wary is offered by the recurrent depressive whose moods are of some months duration, who has been treated by ECT at the beginning of an attack with no success. Not infrequently these patients are then referred for an opinion on leucotomy, when all that is required is to wait a little longer and try ECT again. For this reason very careful enquiry should be made to elicit the history of previous attacks, which may have been so mild that they have not been mentioned, and to discover their average duration and variability in length. These are patients who are also now recovering much earlier when the antidepressant drugs are given with the ECT and kept on afterwards for some months to prevent relapse.

Bearing all these considerations in mind, the result of surgery in carefully chosen cases of depressive illness can be most rewarding. High percentages of recovery and improvement have been recorded by many workers. Stengel (1950) reported on 16 recurrent depressives that leucotomy provided a full remission in 13, mitigation in 2 and no change in the last; and that among 24 patients who had had both manic and depressive phases, full remission was obtained in 18. The patients with predominantly depressive tendencies did better than those whose attacks were mainly manic, of whom only 5 out of 10 remitted. Stevenson and McCausland (1953) have also reported that 18 out of 22 patients with recurrent manic-depressive illnesses were enabled to leave hospital though the follow-up was insufficient to say much about the tendency to relapse. In the Ministry of Health Survey (Tooth and Newton, 1961) the depressives also did spectacularly well.

In our view, when the patient has been liable to attacks both of excitement and depression, and is of a pyknic build, and shows the other classical features of a manic-depressive, operation should not be considered except in extreme circumstances. These arise when, despite the use of ECT and drugs, the patient is ill for longer periods than he is well, or when permanent hospital life has become inevitable. Then there is little to lose and much to gain. In well preserved depressives, modified procedures confined to the medial inferior quadrants should always be chosen. A second operation is always possible, but too extensive an initial operation cannot later be remedied.

When modified operations are used, it is very largely the previous personality which determines the quality of the result. With the older more extensive operations one had to avoid operating on patients with any obvious hysterical admixture in their depressions; however, very good results can be obtained with the modified operation in such cases. It is not the extent to which hysterical symptoms are shown in the presenting picture which matters, but the personality underneath. If this has been of a generally satisfactory type, with perhaps some obsessional tendencies tending to prolong the symptoms of illness, then the hysterical symptomatology can be seen for what it is—a reaction to long illness and incapacity. There are many patients like this in neurosis centres and in the psychiatric wards of general hospitals. They present a most difficult treatment problem, and leucotomy should be considered if combined narcosis, drugs and ECT have also failed (Chapter III).

Site of Operation and Results

In depression very good results have been achieved with lower medial quadrant leucotomy and bi-frontal tractotomy. The surgical method of approach is different in the two operations but the target sites overlap one another. In a recent paper by Kelly, Walter, Mitchell-Heggs and Sargant (1972) it was found that of 26 patients with either non-agitated or agitated depression, 23 (88 per cent) were improved six weeks after lower medial quadrant leucotomies. All but one of the patients who were followed up and re-assessed 18 months after the operation had maintained their initial improvement. In the most recent report of the effects of bi-frontal stereotactic tractotomy on 210 patients followed-up by Ström-Olsen and Carlisle, (1971), the best results were obtained in depressions, both recurrent and other forms with 56 per cent of patients recovered and much improved, the latter category including patients for whom no treatment was required but slight residual symptoms were present.

At Atkinson Morley's Hospital limbic leucotomies are being performed on depressed patients and multiple lesions placed stereotactically in the lower medial quadrants of the frontal lobe and anterior cingulate gyrus with good results (Figs. 1 and 2, p. 102). Much smaller lesions are needed than with the older type of operations because of increased accuracy of placement, and the risks of operation and adverse personality change are considerably reduced, if a stereotactic technique is employed.

ANXIETY STATES

Needless to say, all other methods which hold out hope of relief should have been tried first, and the patients who are to be selected should either be incapacitated or have been made permanently miserable by their condition. Psychopathic traits, such as those of aggressiveness, explosiveness in the absence of stress, lack of emotional control, or at the other extreme, emotional flattening, should be regarded as contra-indications. With these provisos, better and more certain results may be obtained in the chronic anxiety states than in obsessionals. The modern operation leaves the personality intact, the personality itself is of a more flexible and adaptable kind, and the symptoms are of the kind for which leucotomy is particularly suited. Middle-aged patients are better subjects than younger ones, because of their more matured personalities, and still older patients may do better still. We have seen excellent results between the ages of

60 and 75. One anxious and depressed patient, operated on in 1943 at the age of 68, was still hale and hearty at 87 and in full possession of his faculties. He had had no further attack of anxiety and depression despite severe environmental stress. In patients of older age groups the operation seems to have a rejuvenating effect, so that they remain young for their years with their less harassed appearances and lives.

Patients in whom anxiety is the central feature of their illness often describe intense feelings of apprehension or dread, but are unable to say what it is that frightens them. Their symptoms often began many years previously with an acute attack of panic, which was so severe that they feared they would lose control, pass out or even die. Panic attacks are usually associated with autonomic concomitants of fear such as tachycardia, palpitations, tremor, sweating, shortness of breath, a dry mouth, pallor, a sinking feeling in the stomach and weakness of the legs. The attacks may gradually become more and more frequent until the patient avoids circumstances which he thinks may precipitate an attack. Common situations are—enclosed spaces, crowds, shops, cinemas, theatres, restaurants, buses and trains, lifts and the hairdresser's. The patient may become agoraphobic and be nervous of leaving the house, or may be afraid of being left alone. A chronic anxiety state may be diagnosed when the patient is in a constant state of apprehension and is seldom able to relax. Other patients with circumscribed phobias may be able to relax normally at times, but become acutely fearful in specific situations. They may be afraid of animals, birds or insects, or be fearful of blushing or vomiting in public, or be afraid of flying, or of thunder, heights, water, etc.

One of the most constant clinical findings after leucotomy has been a reduction of anxiety and tension. It is known that electrical stimulation of certain parts of the limbic system, such as the hypothalamus and amygdala may produce intense anxiety in patients, while the defence reaction is produced in animals. This is in preparation for either 'fight' or 'flight', and blood is redistributed from the viscera and skin to important structures such as skeletal muscle, the myocardium and brain. Stimulation of the hypothalamus, amygdala and a band of interconnecting fibres, as well as the central grey matter and tegmentum in the mid-brain, produce muscle vasodilatation which is an essential part of the defence reaction.

It has also been found by Kelly and Walter (1966 and 1968) that in the resting state anxious patients show evidence of defence reaction arousal and have a high heart rate, and forearm (muscle) blood flow (Kelly, 1966; Kelly and Walter, 1968). Livingstone (1969) has recently visualised 'a great fronto-limbic—hypothalamic/mid-brain behavioral axis'. He goes on to say 'It is not unreasonable to postulate further that a functional hierarchy exists within these limbic circuits, exerting differential modulating effects on the hypothalamic and mid-brain outflow that finds expression in behaviour.'

Leucotomy undoubtedly reduces anxiety and in a recent series of 78 consecutive patients examined before and again six weeks after operation, there was a significant reduction in the Taylor Scale of Manifest Anxiety, and anxiety self-ratings, while the forearm blood flow and heart rate under resting and stressful conditions also decreased to a highly significant extent. It has also been found that the patients who did best clinically, had a larger change in these measurements than the group who did less well, and forearm blood flow was the best physiological predictor of a good clinical result (Kelly, Walter and Sargant 1966; Kelly, Walter, Mitchell-Heggs and Sargant, 1972).

In this series, of the patients suffering from chronic and phobic anxiety who had lower medial quadrant leucotomies of the Harvey Jackson or rostral type, 83 per cent were improved six weeks after operation, but by 18 months this figure had fallen to 61 per cent.

Anxiety may be reduced by lesions in a variety of limbic circuits and the lower medial quadrants and anterior cingulate gyrus are favourable sites, while stereotactic tractotomy resulted in 41 per cent of anxiety states recovered or improved at follow-up according to Ström-Olsen and Carlisle (1971). At Atkinson Morley's Hospital limbic leucotomies are performed and lesions placed stereotactically in the lower medial quadrants and anterior cingulate gyrus, resulting in a gradual reduction of anxiety. Physiological recordings are made during the operation and the target area stimulated to find a physiologically active area, before the lesion is made. Rehabilitation is particularly important with these patients, and a special programme is designed for each individual so that they are gradually exposed to situations which formerly engendered considerable anxiety; in this way once the high level of 'free floating' anxiety has been reduced by the operation, deconditioning can proceed over the course of weeks or months.

OBSESSIONAL NEUROSIS

The enthusiasm which was aroused by the results of leucotomy in obsessional neuroses, when this method of treatment was first tried,

has somewhat diminished. It is now clear that some types of obsessional neurotic maintain many of their symptoms even after operation.
Nevertheless, all observers are agreed that in properly chosen cases the
results can be excellent, and are sometimes brilliant. In our experience the best results have been obtained when the operation was performed with some reluctance, e.g. on the man of sterling worth whose
severe neurosis should have responded to psychotherapy in theory,
but in fact did not. The least satisfactory results, not unexpectedly,
have been seen in those patients where the justification of the operation was regarded as most ample, because of the chronicity of the
complaint, the severe degree of mental disability, and the lack of any
other possible method of handling the case. No two obsessional
patients are exactly alike, and excellent or unsatisfying results will
depend on the degree of care with which the patient's personality and
symptoms are analysed.

In a recent study by Kelly, Walter, Mitchell-Heggs and Sargant,
(1972) about 50 per cent of patients with obsessional neurosis were
found to be improved six weeks after lower medial quadrant operations. This was a less satisfactory result than had been obtained in
patients with anxiety and depression. There was a tendency, however,
for further gradual improvement during the next 18 months, and very
similar improvement rates have been found at follow-up after stereotactic tractotomy. Considerable interest has been shown in the cingulate gyrus by Cairns, Lewin, Le Beau, Hunter Brown, Ballantine and
others who have operated in this area for obsessional neurosis. At
Atkinson Morley's Hospital (St. George's) a limbic leucotomy is performed by Mr Richardson stereotactically in the anterior cingulate
gyrus above the roof of the lateral ventricles, (Figs. 1 and 2), with
good results in patients suffering from rituals and ruminations. If
anxiety is a prominent component of the patients' psychopathology,
which is usually the case, lower medial quadrant lesions are made in
addition. Rehabilitation after operation again plays an important
part in the total treatment programme and usually lasts for six weeks.
The compulsion to perform rituals repeatedly is considerably
diminished after the operation, and the secondary anxiety which arises
if rituals are resisted is also reduced. Against this background of
improvement, gradual exposure to washing or cleaning situations no
longer produces the emotional tension that it did before, and retrain-
ing can proceed smoothly. The patient then goes home for weekends,
and is exposed to the familiar environment in which obsessions are
invariably more severe than in hospital. After two or three weekends

at home, with encouragement from the nursing staff to resist her rituals in the interval, and an active occupational therapy programme, the patient is usually able to leave hospital and resume normal activities.

One of the character traits to which attention should be paid is the energy of the personality. Leucotomy, even in a modified form, is likely to affect this to some degree initially; and if the patient is naturally of an anergic type, after operation he may not have the drive to get out of his old habits. A second quality of importance is rigidity. If the whole of the patient's life is governed by obsessional routines, which are not so much symptoms as ways of fixing and standardising the environment with which he has to deal, long ingrained habits for avoiding the causes of anxiety and tension, then the operation must be planned to cope with this situation. With modern stereotactic techniques cingulate lesions will be called for, but not necessarily any increase in size of lesion; and good results can be hoped for even when the rituals are severe and incapacitatary. But with older types of operation, a fuller cut may be necessary. The effects of a fuller cut are sometimes to produce an undesirable change of personality, which may spoil the benefits of symptomatic relief, as when the previously scrupulous man becomes inconsiderate and demanding. The outlook is much better when, in addition to obsessional traits there are others indicating some responsiveness to the environment, tendencies to reactive anxiety, suggestibility, even hysterical traits. With these patients, in pre-stereotactic days, a modified cut was generally all that was needed. However stereotactic operations are certain to replace even modified prefrontal or rostal leucotomies for these patients.

The course and duration of the illness should also be taken into account. One reason for this is to avoid the unnecessary operation. Some obsessional neuroses run a phasic recurrent course, and if this past history is found a spontaneous remission may be hoped for. The combination of an antidepressant with Librium or with small doses of the tranquillisers is particularly effective in these phasic obsessionals, especially where depression is marked, and obsessional ruminations rather than rituals predominate. We have also known obsessionals, whose symptoms began at a fairly definite time of onset, to recover after five years or more of illness. At the other extreme is the patient whose first obsessional symptoms were shown early in childhood, and who has become increasingly bound down by them ever since. We have found that patients whose symptoms began in the twenties or thirties, having had previously well adjusted personalities, do much better than those whose tendencies were manifested in the first or second decades. In the former a relatively normal personality did mature and stabilise to some extent, and they have a base line of a more normal kind to which they may hope to return. Some of our most impressive results have been obtained in patients between the ages of fifty and seventy. In them the fully stabilised personality is relatively little affected by the operation, although obsessive thoughts and the distress caused by symptoms are much mitigated (Sargant and Slater, 1950). However, many of these patients are depressives whose obsessions will get better when the depressive aspect of the illness is adequately treated (see Chapter III).

The young patient offers another risk. In him the obsessional pattern may be a sign of defence mechanisms of the personality against the disrupting effects of a psychosis. We have seen young obsessionals, after a leucotomy, pass into an obvious schizophrenia. Study of their case records has shown that schizophrenia has been suspected before the operation, though that diagnosis might have been rejected; or, in one or two cases, the patient had actually concealed the existence of pathognomonic schizophrenic symptoms. One should, therefore, be more cautious with the young patient, and make careful examinations for any signs of schizophrenia, for instance, under the influence of an intravenous injection of methedrine. Paranoid tendencies, particularly, demand caution, as even when they are not associated with a schizophrenia, they may emerge into greater prominence after operation. Fortunately now, such drugs as chlorpromazine can generally control the schizophrenic symptoms emerging after operation, making this a lesser risk than it used to be.

This has brought us to the indications and contra-indications provided by the symptoms themselves. Obsessional ruminative tendencies, phobias, and co-called sensory symptoms, all tend to be favourably affected by operation, whereas the so-called motor symptoms, obsessional rituals and the like, are not so easily overthrown. Neurotic epigastric and somatic discomfort is generally abolished, and gains of weight may be marked. Intractable symptoms of depersonalisation, as Shorvon (1947a) has shown, either in an obsessional setting or without it, have also responded to this treatment when everything else has failed. Freeman has had the same experience. One of our patients is now free of these symptoms, after 15 years without relief. Either the feeling of unreality itself disappears, or the patient ceases to be so distressingly preoccupied with it. But this is not always so.

There are certain symptoms which tend to contra-indicate operation. One of these is any abnormality of sexual behaviour, although
obsessional fears of a sexual nature are not a contra-indication. Any
social disinhibition after operation may bring people with sexually
abnormal tendencies into conflict with society, and ruin them. This
applies to the fetishisms not infrequently shown by obsessionals, and
we have generally avoided the operation in their cases. Undoubtedly
there are some patients in whom the sexually deviant behaviour is or
has become obsessive, and they might be helped. The difficulty is to
pick them out from the others. In some young patients with homosexual traits, we have seen what was well controlled before operation
emerge into overt manifestation after it. If so, stilbœstrol and Librium
may be needed. Of all such symptoms, those denoting constitutional
aggressiveness are of the worst omen. Markedly aggressive personalities should never be operated on, and the only tragedy we have seen
resulted from ignoring this prohibition. Although in the neurotic
patient aggressive tendencies, previously well controlled, may be
released by the operation, catatonic patients liable to impulsive
aggressive outbursts usually lose these tendencies and become quite
meek and sedate. The apparent contradiction is understandable when
one remembers that the operation predominantly affects states of
tension. If the aggressiveness is the direct consequence of tension
arising endogenously or from morbid thoughts, leucotomy will probably diminish it; if it is a primary characteristic of the personality, it
will not.

In monosymptomatic ruminative tension states, which do so
brilliantly with a modified operation, even that may now be avoided
by the use of modified narcosis combined with antidepressants and
ECT (see Chapter III).

Long follow-up has shown that modified leucotomies reduce the
ability of the individual to build up new and self-perpetuating patterns
of abnormal thinking and behaviour, and similarly that long-standing
abnormalities may gradually disperse. These are grounds for expect-
ing that long follow-up results will be every bit as good with the
much more precise stereostatic operations of today.

SCHIZOPHRENIA

In recent years there has been a marked diminution in the numbers
of patients treated by leucotomy, both in England and America, and
the reduction of numbers has been greatest with the chronic schizo-

phrenics. In England this has been largely on pragmatic grounds. The advent of the tranquillising drugs such as chlorpromazine has meant that many fewer schizophrenics have become chronic. The enormous backlog of chronic patients suitable for operative treatment has largely been worked through. And there has been a growing revulsion against the old standard operation in hospitals where, for lack of facilities, a switch to the new modified surgical techniques was not always possible. In America, much more than in Britain, ideological issues have been involved. The domination of therapy by ideas derived from psychoanalysis has been a force constantly tending in the opposite direction, so that in recent years leucotomy has been used less and less, even though there is nothing else done for the patient in its place.

The point has now been reached where the swing towards conservatism has gone too far. The tranquillising drugs have not enabled many chronic patients to be brought out from the back wards of mental hospitals; too often they have succeeded only in muffling the cries for help coming from those wards, where the patients may now accept their chronic state more placidly. If, as Pippard has suggested (1962), half the mental hospitals, even in England, are now doing no leucotomies, we can have no doubt that hundreds of patients are being cheated of the excellent chances of great improvement which can be provided by the combination of a modified operation with after-treatment with tranquillisers. In America the numbers must be legion. In Scotland, always more conservative than England in psychiatric therapy, there are probably also some hundreds of patients who could be satisfactorily treated.

It must be admitted that, of all groups of patients submitted to leucotomy, schizophrenics provide the slenderest chance of a completely first-class result, such as one hopes, for instance, with a depressive illness. Yet even with old-style operations worth-while improvements were obtained with a good proportion even of the most hopeless cases. Mayer-Gross and his colleagues (Gillies *et al.*, 1952) got about a quarter of their patients of this degree of severity back to work and to an almost normal social life; and Solomon and co-workers at the Boston Psychopathic Hospital (Greenblatt and Solomon, 1950) succeeded similarly with about one patient in five. Similar trends were seen in the large-scale studies, including the Ministry of Health report on over 10,000 patients leucotomised in England and Wales between 1942 and 1954. In this survey (Tooth and Newton, 1961) over 30 per cent of all schizophrenics operated on were able to leave their hospitals.

A striking controlled study was reported by Friedman and others (Friedman *et al.*, 1951). They contrasted the fates of two groups of patients, mostly schizophrenics, who had been chosen as suitable for leucotomy, permission for operation being refused in the case of 100 and given for the remaining 254. The two groups were well matched, more than half the patients in each group having been ill for 5 to 12 years; refusal of permission for operation in most instances could only have been on ethical grounds. After two years only 2 per cent of the control group had been released from hospital, compared with 37 per cent of the operated group; and only 3 per cent of the control patients experienced any significant improvement during the two-year period, in contrast with 58 per cent of the operated patients.

The critics of leucotomy, while perhaps accepting these figures, are likely to point to the success in getting the long-stay patient back to his home which has been achieved by such methods as active training and re-socialising therapies in the chronic wards, recreating contacts with relatives and countering social isolation. The present authors have also been greatly impressed by this work; but it is essentially the same kind of therapy as is given in the after-treatment of the leuco- tomised patient, and is accordingly very familiar to them. Such treat- ment is often quite useless when given before operation, but begins to work wonders when the rigid morbid patterns of behaviour have been broken down by leucotomy. We cannot but think that the opponents of leucotomy would change their attitude if they could see the results of modern modified operations, with which a clinically observable post-operative defect of personality is nearly always avoided al- together. They would then find that operation played its part in just those processes of rehabilitation in which they are specially interested. But the clinical results of operation depend not only on the vital after- treatment, but also to a great extent on skill in selection and on the proper design of the operation.

The main effect of leucotomy in the schizophrenic patient is a reduction of tension. Delusions may die out for lack of emotional reinforcement, or, if maintained, are held with lesser force and con- cern. Hallucinations very often persist, but worry the patient less. The patient becomes more extraverted, as his own feelings are less in the centre of the picture for him and he is more responsive to the external world. The continued refusal of food is rare after leucotomy as, like other abnormal attitudes, it cannot be so persistently maintained.

On the other hand purely negative symptoms, those of defect and loss, are little affected by the operation. Some clinicians will not accept a diagnosis of schizophrenia unless emotional disintegration has become complete; in these patients, in whom ideas which should cause intense anxiety no longer do so, only poor results will be achieved.

The time factor is also extremely important, and those patients do best who have not had to wait for years before someone had the courage to advise operation. Of course it is unwise to step in prematurely, but clinical experience suggests that no hard and fast rules should be made. If one abandons, as one should, all other forms of operation on the frontal lobes in favour of an approach which concentrates on the thalamo-frontal radiation in the medial inferior quadrant, then operation becomes legitimate at an earlier date than with the old standard operation. However, some schizophrenic illnesses run a cyclic course, the patient recovering after each attack. In such a case leucotomy is to be considered only as a prophylactic against a later attack, and tranquillisers and lithium may be better for that purpose. Other periodic schizophrenics deteriorate a little more after each attack, and in them the prophylactic operation, before deterioration has gone too far, may arise as a serious possibility.

Some of the most remarkable symptomatic improvements of old days were obtained in the overactive catatonic patients. These were among the most distressing sights that the hospital had to offer, as for years on end they would remain destructive, restless and impossible to communicate with. Many of these patients are now greatly benefited by the tranquillisers. If by drugs alone the improvement obtained is insufficient, then a modified operation should be tried, with a return to tranquillisers during after-care.

All observers are agreed that the chronic hebephrenic, in whom there is poverty of affect in greatest degree, seldom benefits from the operation and is generally not suited to it. Chronic hallucinations usually remain unchanged, except that the patient is less worried by them; but here again the tranquillisers may be found more effective after operation than before.

Other types of schizophrenia provide much better results. Catatonic patients often do well, especially those who have periods of normality between their attacks of stupor or excitement, and who show some preservation of the basic personality. In paranoid schizophrenia the results are more favourable still and may be spectacular, especially in paraphrenia and 'paranoia', where the personality is maintained almost intact, despite delusional systematisation. Disabling hypochondriacal organ-sensations and the tendency to project them in paranoid delusions are especially amenable to relief. It is important to operate before delusional ideas become too fixed. Later on, one will still hope that the delusions will die out in time by lack of emotional reinforcement, but if firmly fixed they will certainly persist for a long time and prejudice discharge from hospital.

Although their illnesses are so susceptible to control by the tranquillisers, it is the paranoid and paraphrenic patients who so frequently make difficulties about taking them. After a modified leucotomy, this attitude is often completely altered; and now maintenance on tranquillisers may be all that is needed to keep that patient well indefinitely.

In most types of schizophrenia older patients do better after operation than younger ones. This is particularly the case if the illness has affected a matured and well integrated personality. Our follow-ups suggest that the premorbid personality is of the very greatest importance, and is very often decisive. One needs to know to what old patterns of behaviour the patient is likely to return, when more recent ones have been shed. Previously one had to be very cautious about operating on young patients with a marked obsessional component to the schizophrenic illness, in case with a reduction of obsessional symptoms the schizophrenic ones came more to the fore. The use of post-operative and maintenance chlorpromazine, or similar drugs, makes this now a less real risk. Hoch (Hoch et al., 1955) has reported excellent results, with a modified leucotomy, in what he terms pseudo-neurotic forms of schizophrenia. These patients are dominated by diffuse anxiety, and show phobias, obsessions and numbers of neurotic symptoms of a bizarre type, combined with a tendency to withdraw from reality. It is important, however, that they should have remained basically well preserved and without emotional flattening.

It is unfortunate that the tranquillising drugs such as chlorpromazine are so ineffective in dealing with obsessional symptoms. And one of the main indications now for a modified leucotomy in schizophrenia is when delusions or other abnormal thoughts or behaviour are being maintained by a marked obsessional element in the total picture. When this element has been modified by leucotomy, the tranquillisers can be expected to deal with the remaining symptomatology much more effectively.

The number of schizophrenic patients who need leucotomy has been greatly reduced from what it once was. The use of combined therapy, i.e. narcosis, ECT and drugs, obviates the need for operation in some cases. Even if the illness has gone on for as long as five years a remission by this means may be obtained in a patient of originally adequate personality. Moreover, some of the 'chronic schizophrenics' one is asked to see, show themselves as suffering from an atypical depression, in which the appearance of schizophrenic deterioration has been produced by prolonged use of tranquillising drugs.

Nevertheless those who have claimed that the tranquillisers have abolished the need for leucotomy in schizophrenia, can only be thinking of the permanently hospitalised patient. Some schizophrenic patients reject drugs, unless forcibly given, and on leaving hospital refuse to continue with them and relapse. Polonio has pointed out that one of the great uses of leucotomy in such patients is the change in attitude towards co-operativeness which it brings. After operation these paranoid patients are much more amenable to taking maintenance drug therapy, and are much more willing to continue under follow-up care, so that for the first time they can be kept under control outside hospital. Those who at this date are content to leave permanently 'tranquillised' in the back wards of their hospitals, patients who are capable of recovery with a modified leucotomy, should remember the principle that we should always treat our patients as we would wish to be treated ourselves, if we were so placed.

PSYCHOSOMATIC STATES AND HYSTERIA

Hysterical patients have to be chosen with some care; it is useless or worse to operate on the bland and contented hysteric who develops symptoms in the absence of any stress. If, however, hysterical symptoms are clearly being produced only in situations of stress, and pass off of their own when tension is relieved, then there may be a good case for operation. This will especially be the case in patients whose personality was good and contained obsessive traits before the start of the attacks of recurrent hysterical illness. We have had some excellent results quite unexpectedly in such patients. We have seen both hysterical attitudes to the environment, and episodes of hysterical dissociation brought on by emotional tension, lessened or abolished after operation.

The opportunity to work with conditions of these kinds comes to the psychiatrist who is closely connected with general medicine. But the observations we have already been able to make have important implications, and seem to suggest that some fundamental concepts of the current psychoanalytic view-point may have to be revised (Sargant, 1951).

The sufferers from asthma, skin diseases, hypertension, rheumatism, and other conditions which are now often called psychosomatic, are very numerous; but most of them do not get obsessed by their symptoms, or mentally incapacitated to a much greater degree than their physical state would account for. In some of them, however, psychiatric aspects are important, especially in patients of a somewhat obsessional disposition, and the question of leucotomy may arise. Skin conditions provide excellent examples of the part played by tension and an obsessional temperament in maintaining a compulsive scratching, so that the lesions originated by allergy may be maintained when the allergic cause has, perhaps, ceased to operate. Improvement has been obtained by modified leucotomy in long-standing cases of eczema and asthma. After the operation it may be that the attacks recur; but they are then shorter, are not maintained by emotional tension, and they may show a tendency to die out when deprived of emotional reinforcement. Good results have also been obtained in severe chronic effort syndrome. After the operation the patient still has for a time his usual attacks of palpitation, but he loses the fear of death associated with them. Later on the attacks themselves diminish, and he ceases to link attacks with new conditioned stimuli. Patients with chronic rheumatism, obsessed by their discomforts and disabilities and by a dread of total incapacity, may still suffer from the purely physical symptoms after the operation, but become able to return to work as all the psychiatric aspects fade away. Fortunately, the need for operative treatment in such intractable psychosomatic disorders can be avoided or greatly reduced in incidence by drug treatment. The monoamine oxidase inhibitors, combined with such drugs as Librium or small doses of the tranquillisers, and the increased use of cortisone, have proved effective controls.

Reports from various workers have shown that anorexia nervosa, may be aided by leucotomy. One of our patients regained normal periods after an illness of 20 years, characterised by amenorrhoea, persistent worry, obstinate constipation and refusal of food. Another patient had used enemas for the same length of time, and there had been no normal bowel action. It needed six months after a modified leucotomy for the bowels to regain their normal activity. Yet another patient, suffering from some degree of organic disability, had come to believe that he was to all intents blind, though he could see much better than he thought he could. Three months after a modified leucotomy he found it impossible to retain this fixed hysterical attitude, and reported that he was able to see much better again. All previous attempts to convince him of his powers had failed for a long time.

In the earliest stages of such conditions, sensible handling by the physician is sufficient to prevent the association between physical symptoms and the patient's fears of what they may imply. Later on, but still early in what may prove to be the total duration, psychotherapy and drugs may be capable of breaking up the conditioned neurosis. But gradually, it seems, the neurotic dysfunction may become incorporated into the nervous organisation of the individual, not to be unseated by anything less than a structural change.

ORGANIC ILLNESS

The principles which apply to the purely psychiatric uses of leucotomy may also guide us in its application to organic states where psychological precipitation does not enter. Pain cannot be diminished by leucotomy, but the patient's preoccupation with it, his apprehension and his distress may be. Intractable pain from carcinoma may be found more tolerable, and the use of morphia and other pain-killers can sometimes be abandoned, often diminished. In this case the life of the patient is not likely to be greatly extended, so that it is of no great consequence if there is a tendency for the ameliorating effects of leucotomy to wear off after a while. This is not the case where leucotomy has been advised for the pain of tic douloureux or post-herpetic neuralgia. In some of our patients suffering from these conditions there has only been rather temporary relief; but though the patient, if asked, will say that his pain is as bad as ever, he may still live a more normal life, complain less and look less pinched and harassed. But again, antidepressant drugs like Nardil have been found to give almost complete relief to some of these sufferers from facial pain (Webb and Lascelles, 1962).

We have already mentioned the favourable effects we have observed in cases of tinnitus made miserable by the noises in the head; in some of them the tinnitus has itself diminished, even to the point when it is heard only on waking in the morning and lying down at night. This is unusual, and the ordinary effect is to ameliorate only the mental distress. Worthwhile relief has also been observed by us in cases of torsion dystonia due to disease of the basal ganglia. In some of these patients the attacks of muscular spasm are not only painful but intensely distressing; in two such patients, though there was little change in the pattern of motor behaviour, there was a complete temperamental reversal from tense depression to cheerfulness and placidity. In lesser forms of these diseases, for instance in a case first showing as a torticollis but exhibiting later small abnormal movements of face, arms and hands, the movements themselves were greatly lessened for several years, so that a man who had been unable to walk down the street because with his head twisted he could not see where he was going, was enabled to take up whole-time work again.

Hypertension and arterial disease provide cases where leucotomy may be of great aid. A patient with angina was enabled by leucotomy to enjoy the last few months of his life, before it was cut short by the fatal attack he had rightly anticipated and dreaded through years of worry and addiction to opiates. Another patient in our care, of intensely worrying disposition, and with marked hypertension, had been given a fatal prognosis by one neuropsychiatrist of distinction, and by others regarded as a purely social problem. Certainly she over-reacted to a husband's brusqueness, a daughter's marriage, and other everyday events to a degree which endangered her bodily health. Every attempt at psychotherapy and at social readjustment, almost invariably successful for a few months, broke down in due course. After leucotomy she had three years of happiness and content, before she had a stroke at a Masonic banquet. Freeman (Freeman and Watts, 1950), however, considers that the risk of a vascular accident is also reduced by leucotomy. Certainly the symptoms complained of by the hypertensive diminish, and though the blood-pressure may not remain permanently at a lower level after operation, the progressive increase to death may be slowed down.

Undesirable Sequelæ and Complications

Before the operation is performed, the most careful enquiry must be made into the neurotic or psychopathic tendencies whose appearance might be facilitated by the frontal damage. The family history and the past history of the patient must be gone into with this in mind. The elderly patient, who already shows some slight signs of mental impairment, can be expected more than the ordinary patient to show some changes in this field. The man with homosexual tendencies, held under control by associated feelings of guilt and anxiety, may be freed of these safeguards without losing his innate homosexual tendencies. Pre-existing traits of aggressiveness, ruthlessness and egoism may be enhanced by the operation. It is probable that nearly every individual after operation is happier than before, but this may sometimes be bought at too great a cost, not only to himself but to society. If the claims of society and those of the individual seem likely to conflict, then those of society should not be forgotten. But one need not unduly fear the development of antisocial trends where there has been no evidence of them in the previous personality; and this practically never happens with modified operations in which there are no complications such as a misplaced cut or hæmorrhage.

Apart from the release of neurotic and psychopathic traits, with the older types of operation one may have to enter on the debit side a certain degree of deterioration. How much there is of this will depend on the extent of damage to the brain. Unless the operation has been too extensive, or there has been some hæmorrhage into the brain, intelligence is not significantly altered, and alteration in the personality is very unlikely to take a serious form. Earlier fears that all the highest qualities of the mind must suffer have not been borne out; and even the impression that post-operative irritability and inadequacy of control must be counted on has proved too gloomy a view. Post-operative irritability occurs, but it is usually of temporary duration, except in ill-chosen cases where the personality showed these tendencies previously. With stereotactic leucotomy all these risks are reduced.

After fuller operations the patient may, of course, become demanding in his desires and imperative in their expression. There is a tendency to increased extroversion, which has as its reverse side a lessened capacity for sympathy to others. The patient worries less about the future, and lives much more for the present. He thinks less himself, becomes more orthodox and matter-of-fact in his view-point. He may become free and easy in his manner, lacking in self-criticism, but willing enough to give opinions on his environment, sometimes so tactlessly as to give offence. Furthermore, there may be damage to the personality where its good qualities have to a considerable extent been dependent on an obsessional drive and persistence. These fuller operations are now very rarely necessary.

Much has been made of the possibility of changes in the religious and ethical aspects of the personality, which were pointed out by Golla as occurring after full cuts. These changes have not been found when neurotic patients were subjected to limited undercutting rather than to a full operation. We have not seen such losses of ethical principle except in the cases of too extensive operations or wrongly selected patients (Shorvon and Sargant, 1947). What we have observed is that religious beliefs tend to become more concrete; one of our patients, for instance, left his Methodist chapel for a fuller emotional life by becoming an ardent Salvation Army worker. Ethical loss need not be expected in good personalities subjected to a modified operation, nor loss of religious feeling, unless religion has been solely an attempted escape from neurosis and not the manifestation of a fundamental need of the personality. Freeman has pointed out that in the professions, where fine qualities of personal appreciation of the feelings of others are so necessary, more caution in recommending operation should be exercised than when the patient comes from the world of business and commerce. A little ruthlessness can be an asset in business, when it is a liability in a profession. We have not found that our leucotomised patients have become unsympathetic, but rather that they confine their sympathies to practical modes of expression, refusing to be troubled over-much if there is nothing to be done. Marked emotional blunting after a modified leucotomy is seldom seen except in schizophrenic patients, and then is most probably a sequela of the illness itself which has been allowed to progress too far.

The actual dangers of the operation need not be unduly stressed. In skilled hands the mortality should not exceed 1 per cent, and is less with modified procedures and with better preserved patients. In the survey by Ziegler (1943) of 582 patients, mostly schizophrenic, treated in the U.S.A., there were only 11 deaths from the operation, while 235 patients were got back to work. Maclay (1953) notes only 180 deaths reported to the British Board of Control in over eight thousand operations done by a variety of experienced and less experienced surgeons on all types of mental hospital patients. Of these 56 were attributed to cerebral hæmorrhage and 20 to respiratory complications. Surgeons with special experience get much better results than the general average. Harvey Jackson, for instance, has had one death only in a large number of modified operations done since 1948. With sterotactic operations all risks, including mortality, are very much less than with older operations; adverse personality change after operation is rare.

A later complication, seen rarely now, is the appearance of epileptic fits. Although experience of the subsequent histories of these patients is that fits, when they appear, are usually only temporary, disappearing as reparative changes proceed in the brain. Residual fits can nearly always be fully controlled by suitable medication; and where epilepsy was present before operation the tendency to fits does not seem to be increased. When a modified operation has reduced tension, they may even be diminished. With stereotactic operations, brain damage is almost entirely restricted to that planned and produced at the site of the lesion, i.e. a very much smaller volume than that involved in more haphazard old techniques. The risk of epilepsy is accordingly greatly reduced.

The Board of Control Report (1947) shows that older patients have done rather better than younger ones, and that half of those after the age of 65 remitted. Leucotomy, which has been found of value in old and agitated patients, is now rarely needed; tranquillising drugs such as chlorpromazine can usually be depended on to control senile agitation without depressing mental life.

The great benefits which can be obtained from a rational approach to leucotomy, especially in the prevention of chronicity, are made evident by the Ministry of Health enquiry (Tooth and Newton, 1961). The figures show that 46 per cent of over 10,000 patients were enabled to leave mental hospitals in England and Wales, although a high proportion had been ill for six years or more and many of these patients were among the most difficult ones in the hospital. To be sure, efforts short of surgery, but involving very heavy burdens on doctors, nurses, occupational therapists and others, are being made to get the long-stay patient out of hospital and back to the care of his family; and considerable success has been attained. Such efforts would not be possible at all without the aid of drugs, and even so are often very temporary; if the patients go out of hospital, a high proportion soon return. The part that might be played by judicious psycho-surgery in these rehabilitation schemes has been unduly neglected. Of one thing we can be sure: the combination of a leucotomy effect with a drug effect goes farther than the sum of what each can do separately. The current neglect of these potentialities of treatment can only be put down to the widespread feeling that leucotomy is an assault on the personality. Those who are familiar with the effects of the modern modified operation carried out by highly skilled hands, know that this idea is out of place. The damage done, even to a mature and differentiated personality, as a rule is so slight as to be beyond detection by clinical methods; the relief of symptoms can be of the order that makes a sane man of a lunatic.

After-Treatment

After the operation the patient is, as a rule, in a more suggestible, malleable frame of mind and in a more favourable condition for rehabilitation. Psychotherapy, which had not helped previously, may now be effective. Some patients, particularly those who have not been socially incapacitated so long, are able to make their own readjustments; but others need its help. Psychotherapy after operation may have to be conducted in a different way. Previous conditioned reactions may have been abolished, so destroying the basis for analytic attempts to build new patterns by mobilisation of older ones, and to provide the patient with insight into the present by understanding the past. But with his progressive freedom from old habits of reaction to stress, the patient may more easily be trained into new ones. We have seen an intelligent male nurse help to disperse the residual delusions of a leucotomised schizophrenic, when intensive psychoanalysis had totally failed beforehand. After leucotomy, psychotherapy must be fully realistic and based on the present and the future rather than the past. The antagonism of schools of psychotherapy to leucotomy, as well as to other physical methods of treatment, is especially to be regretted when we are faced with the problem of rehabilitation, as the two approaches could so easily be mutually complementary.

If the patient has been ill for a long time before the operation, he will have made many adjustments and concessions to his fears; although the emotional tension that was the dynamic force is no longer felt, the old patterns may persist. The hand-washing obsessional, for instance, may continue as of old habit to wash his hands abnormally often, but no longer becomes anxious if accident prevents his doing so. He may have to be trained into new ways, and forced to discover for himself how much he can now do that would have been impossible before. He must not be allowed to go back into the old rut. In psycho-somatic conditions it may be months or years before deeply ingrained patterns of behaviour finally disperse from lack of emotional rein-forcement. The willingness of relatives to take patients home to build them up anew is often the critical factor in success in long-standing cases. Early discharge from the mental hospital is usually desirable, though one should feel one's way with schizophrenics. After dis-charge continued advice and supervision are necessary, and the environment will often have to be a protected one at first.

Leucotomy only deals with symptoms of a certain order; and in many patients, even after operation, there will be others which will need further treatment along different lines. If in a schizoid personality paranoid symptoms are untouched, or even brought out into the open, then ECT and the phenothiazines may be called for. Persisting depression in the involutional depressive can now be expected to respond to antidepressants. Residual anxieties in the patient with a chronic tension state will now be alleviated by much smaller doses of drugs, or by a change in social circumstances which would previously have been ineffective.

After operation and successful rehabilitation there is still a possibility of relapse, greatest in the recurrent affective psychoses but a tangible risk in all cases. Fortunately, suitable drug therapies are capable of preventing most of them. As a general rule, for instance, schizophrenics after a modified leucotomy should remain on a stabiliser such as chlorpromazine for long periods.

In some cases of relapse, as also in some of the obvious failures of leucotomy, the operation may have failed to find the most important fibres. Post-mortem examination has shown on occasion that the brain-needle or leucotome has not gone where it was meant to go, or has severed fibres only along a narrow tract. With the older types of operation, the risk of missing the right tracts becomes greater as the extent of operation is more and more restricted. This is one most important disadvantage of the old-style modified leucotomy. Even when some degree of organic personality change can be seen, the persistence of tension, or its return after an interim, may show that the critical part of the thalamo-frontal radiation has been missed or only partly damaged, so it may have to come to a second leucotomy. The enormous advance which has been made with the far greater precision of stereotactic surgery is made painfully evident.

It is sometimes difficult to judge the eventual success of the operation by the results seen in the first three months. Some of the patients do well from the beginning and never look back. Others begin as apparently complete successes, but later develop some undesirable symptoms. And yet others only begin to improve some months after operation and continue to do so steadily during the ensuing years.

For too long leucotomy has been considered a last desperate recourse, the failure of which means the end of all hope. Neither the one view nor the other is justified. The consideration of a leucotomy, especially a stereotactic leucotomy, should not be delayed until the patient's state is desperate. Even if, exceptionally, direct benefit does not result, symptoms are made more labile and become more readily influenced by other lines of treatment. Even small improvements are important, and can make a critical difference to the patient's happiness, or his working capacity, or his adjustment. There are three rules to be borne in mind in connection with leucotomy: first, try other treatments first; secondly, fully exploit any improvement, even if it is a small one; thirdly, remember that after a leucotomy the patient's constitution has been changed. One is, so to speak, back to square one, with avenues, previously closed, opening again on all sides.

CHAPTER FIVE

Modified Insulin Therapy

As a result of his experiences in the American Civil War, Weir Mitchell developed a method of treatment for neuroses which achieved a spectacular success. He stressed the importance of removing the neurotic immediately from the causes of his breakdown, and during the period of enforced rest of devoting attention to the complete restoration of normal physique. 'If I succeed in first altering the moral atmosphere which has been to the patient like the very breathing of evil, and if I can add largely to the weight and fill the vessels with red blood, I am usually sure of giving relief to a host of aches and pains and varied disabilities. If I fail it is because I fail in these very points or else because I have overlooked or under-valued some serious organic tissue change.' It was not every neurotic that he chose for treatment by this method. He describes the suitable patient in the following quotation: 'A woman most often between twenty and thirty years of age undergoes a season of trial or encounters some prolonged strain. She may have undertaken the hard task of nursing a relative and have gone through the severe duty with the addition of emotional excitement, swayed by hopes and fears, and forgetful of self and what everybody needs in the way of air and food and change when attempting this most trying task. . . . No matter how it comes about, whether from illness, anxiety, or prolonged physical effort, this woman grows pale and thin, eats little, and if she does eat does not profit by it. Everything wearies her—to sew, to write, to read, to walk—and by and by the sofa is her only comfort. Every effort is paid for dearly and she describes herself as aching and sore, as sleeping ill and awakening unfreshed and as needing constant stimulus and endless tonics. Then comes the mischievous tale of bromides, opium, chloral and brandy. . . . If such a person is by nature emotional, she is sure to become more so, for even the firmest woman loses self-control under incessant feebleness. Nor is this less true of men, and I have many times seen soldiers who have ridden boldly with Sheridan or fought gallantly with Grant, under the influence of painful nerve wounds, as irritable and hysterically emotional as the veriest girl.' He goes on to point out that this type of patient may end by exhibiting the grossest forms of hysteria despite an originally sound and conscientious personality (Weir Mitchell, 1885).

Weir Mitchell secluded his patients and gradually increased their diet to a point seldom reached nowadays. Over two quarts of milk were, if possible, given daily, and in addition three full meals with extras such as meat juices, soup and fruit juices in between. To make this possible he prescribed very heavy massage lasting at least an hour a day, supplementing this sometimes with electric stimulation of the muscles. This promoted sweating, increased appetite, and probably also increased the metabolism of ingested food. Otherwise it is doubtful whether such quantities could have been absorbed. Prodigious gains of weight occurred—up to 36 lb. in one underweight girl—and in successful cases the patient's whole metabolism was changed. He describes the return of colour to the cheeks, an improvement of the complexion and texture of the skin, an increased physical energy, and with these a lessening of the neurotic symptoms that till then had persisted despite many and highly suggestive forms of therapy. During the régime he tried to deal with psychological problems and to adjust the patient's life so that emotional upsets should not start anew the old vicious circle of anxiety and physical deterioration.

The Weir Mitchell method suffered eclipse and was gradually forgotten. No one remembered that he picked his cases, and the treatment was applied to all and sundry, whether of good or poor previous personality. Attention was switched from the restoration of normal physique to rest, isolation, massage, and diet as treatments in themselves. Greater interest was developed in the psychopathology of the neuroses. The results of Weir Mitchell, who as T. A. Ross says 'cured them by the hundred', were attributed to suggestion and to his forceful personality, and its effects on patients and followers. Ross (1937) remarked that while he believed in the treatment he used it with success over a period of five years; but when relapses occurred he began to doubt its efficacy, and it then seemed to lose its beneficial effects on his patients. But Weir Mitchell's results cannot be attributed entirely to suggestion. That there was something more in his method than that is shown both by his case reports and the long period of success it enjoyed. He had grasped the fundamental fact, subsequently forgotten in the energetic development of the psychological approach, that the mental and somatic aspects of an illness can never be entirely disentangled and that physical factors may be the critical ones in preventing recovery from psychological symptoms.

The last war provided confirmation of Weir Mitchell's views. The sporadic case of breakdown under physical exhaustion of peace time appeared under the stresses of war with epidemic frequency. It was rare to find soldiers or civilians of good and stable personality, who had fallen ill with symptoms of anxiety, hysteria and depression, without having lost a considerable amount of weight before the final collapse. Even many of those of neurotic disposition had fought against their symptoms until worry and strain had reduced them well below their physical par. On the other hand, in the chronically hysterical or anxious person in whom the neurosis is a lifelong habit rather than an acute illness, such losses of weight are much less common; the individual retires from the conflict before any real stress has been met.

It is easy both for the physician and the psychotherapist to miss alterations in physique. Changes in weight, even though striking in degree, often escaped observation during the war; and their significance as the starting point of a neurotic illness was missed. In peace-time practice they are still more likely to be ignored. Yet they are easy to detect, and are one of the more obvious signs of metabolic changes which in many forms may alter the predisposition of the individual to mental illness, or his susceptibility to emotional changes. Pavlov (1941) found that some dogs were only susceptible to conflict situations after such a change of predisposition; it might be caused by debilitation, by fevers or intestinal upset, or be induced by castration. It is not without significance that physical debilitation has been a method used throughout history to initiate changes in outlook. Some devils are only to be cast out by prayer and fasting; and in the reports of religious conversion, the time when revelation occurred, and the mind was opened to new ideas, was when the individual was in a lowered physical state (Shorvon and Sargant, 1947).

One must not think, however, that a large drop in weight inevitably produces a neurotic reaction. Even in the neurotic patient of good previous personality one can often find the indications of some degree of constitutional instability in a family history of neurosis or psychopathy or an account of neurotic traits in childhood. In the potentially unstable individual neurotic symptoms lie just below the surface. They may be brought out by such varied causes as head injury, loss of sleep, influenza, or the gradual physical debilitation described by Weir Mitchell. In contrast to them we meet the unusually stable person who can undergo great loss of weight and pass through stress, anxiety and exhaustion unshaken. They are endowed by their heredity with nervous mechanism of finer calibre, and are not thrown out of adjustment by metabolic changes or the transient autonomic disturbances of emotional upset. It is wise to assume that most persons have an optimal physical and metabolic level in which they show their most steady response to environmental stresses. Where this point lies is not so easy to ascertain, since most people, especially the middle-aged, carry excess weight; but it probably lies near their weight at the peak of physical fitness enjoyed by young men and women in their early twenties. Where this optimum weight has been departed from by a large margin, an attempt should be made towards its restoration. The over-weight individual is most usually a problem for his general physician; and the depressive and anxiety reactions are more likely to lead to loss of weight, and to bring the patient to the psychiatrist.

In earlier years, perhaps too much importance was laid on the restoration of weight in patients suffering from neuroses, and modified insulin therapy was the development of an effort to restore normality. Nowadays, when the main line of attack is likely to be made with chlorpromazine and the antidepressants, under-weight patients usually regain weight easily, and many become too fat. The role of modified insulin therapy has, accordingly, largely been taken over by standard drug therapy. However, there are always the cases in which quick recovery of weight is important. A modified insulin course can be given combined with antidepressants and chlorpromazine, or ECT, or following or before narcosis. In our psychiatric wards there are generally one or two patients being helped in this way, but nothing like the numbers we used to have.

The Selection of Patients for Treatment

Independently of Weir Mitchell, whose results were examined in detail later, it was found that the patients who responded best to a modified form of insulin therapy developed by Sargant and Craske (1941) in treating cases of war neurosis, were those that he has also picked for his treatment. They were men and women of fairly good personality, even though some signs of constitutional instability might be present, who had been through a prolonged period of stress and put up a good fight against it before breaking down into a state in which anxiety, hysteria and depression of a reactive type were the most prominent symptoms. The stress might have been along physical or emotional lines, and was not infrequently of a nature that might have been quickly dealt with by judicious psychotherapy and sedation, before physical deterioration had arisen to deepen and complicate the picture. In normal health these patients were of a calibre to deal with these stresses; but once some one to three stones in weight had been lost, abnormal patterns of response were released in circumstances which would previously have left them unmoved. They commonly retained insight—even to some extent into their hysterical symptoms—sought advice and were anxious to get well.

The fluidity of the affective response may suggest the desirability of psychotherapy; but though some improvement may be gained by this means, it is unusual to get recovery until normal physique is also restored. Such patients were common in war-time, after severe fighting or prolonged overwork or even worry alone. Thus by the end of the last war Kelly and Thompson (1947) were able to report a series of 15,000 such cases, satisfactorily treated by insulin, in the U.S. army in Europe alone. In peace time, though less common, these patients are familiar to the general practitioner; and his recommendation of a long holiday may permit the condition to right itself of its own accord. Removed from stress, the tendency is in any case towards spontaneous recovery, but if stress continues even in a mild form this may be very delayed. The advantage of the treatment is that it accelerates these processes of normal recovery, aids psychotherapy, and prevents further aggravation of the existing condition.

Prolongation of symptoms is in any case to be guarded against in the anxiety hysteric, owing to the likely development of conditioning effects and the possibility of hysterical motivations making their effect more and more noticeable. **As a matter of interest, it is patients of this kind, people of good personality with recent anxiety, hysterical and fatigue reactions, who have been found to respond to the monoamine-oxidase inhibitor group of antidepressant drugs.** Treatment by these drugs may well avoid the necessity for modified insulin therapy in some cases, or be combined with it in others.

The chronic neurotic, if he has lost no weight, is quite unsuitable for this method of treatment; its use in such persons will only bring it into disrepute. It is not suitable as an initial measure for the patient suffering from a hyperacute anxiety state, who is best first treated by a period of continuous sleep, or by its modern equivalent—large doses of tranquillisers combined with smaller amounts of sedative and with modified insulin therapy. When the worst of the agitation has been subdued, modified insulin treatment may be a most useful measure of physical rehabilitation. Gross hysterical conversion symptoms, fugues, amnesias, paralyses, etc., should be dealt with and got out of the way before treatment is started or while it is proceeding; the role of the insulin treatment will be to put an obstacle in the path of their recurrence. Some patients need abreaction before the insulin becomes effective. The potential hysteric is much more likely to manifest such symptoms when in a reduced physical state, and physical rehabilitation will increase his powers of resistance and diminish the likelihood of further dissociation.

Patients suffering from a severe degree of depression with agitation, or retardation, especially those in middle or later life, do not react well to the treatment. These are the endogenous depressives, and their response is quite different from that of the reactively depressed. The difference can be used diagnostically; and the failure of a depressed patient to improve with insulin combined with an antidepressant drug of the monoamine oxidase inhibitor group may mark him as a patient who will do well with ECT. In general, the depressives who are benefited by insulin have an opposite sleep rhythm and diurnal mood variation to those of the patients who are helped by ECT. Retardation is less prominent; instead of waking in the early hours of the morning, they have difficulty in getting to sleep, and they feel worse in the evening than they do in the morning. It is this group who are helped, not only by modified insulin, but also by the monoamine oxidase inhibitors. One may see elements of endogenous and of reactive depression combined in a single case, and then the patient will improve more quickly with a combination of insulin and ECT than with ECT alone. In depressions where retardation and anxiety symptoms are combined, once convulsive treatment is started gain in weight with insulin therapy may be rapid. But depressives of the type that is responsive to ECT may gain little weight under insulin treatment alone until ECT is used. With any depressive, if there has been considerable loss of weight, as is often the case, it is well to build up the normal physique again before discharge from hospital, even if the affective state seems to have returned to normal. In general, however, the endogenous depressive does not need more in the way of specially directed physical treatment than the antidepressant drugs with or without ECT.

Depersonalisation, whether accompanied by obsessional, depressive or anxiety symptoms, is little helped by modified insulin, despite any gain in weight which may occur. In fact, unreality symptoms are often temporarily made worse by insulin treatment.

The reaction of patients of obsessional constitution to insulin treatment is a matter of importance. Obsessional neurotics who have lost weight, and patients suffering from anxiety states with obsessional features, are frequently given this treatment. The results are, however, far from satisfactory. Tension is often relieved during the hypoglycæmic state, but returns later in full force. The contrast with patients suffering from anxiety states on a hysterical basis is very marked. There is much evidence to suggest that obsessional personalities feel tension less when in a physically run down state, and may even debilitate themselves to obtain some symptomatic relief. If their bodily vigour is built up with a course of modified insulin treatment, their tension and other symptoms become more acute.

Since modified insulin treatment was introduced, it has been widely used in the treatment of anorexia nervosa. Patients suffering from this illness often present a superficially hysterical or even psychotic impression when in a debilitated state; but as they regain weight under treatment, the underlying obsessional component of the personality sometimes comes more clearly to the fore. As their bodily condition improves, their resistance to treatment may mount. Now it should be used mainly as an adjuvant to large doses of chlorpromazine.

The contribution of obsessional factors to the causation of anorexia nervosa may account for the success of modified leucotomy operations, when they have been tried with chronic and intractable patients (Sargant, 1951b). However, the illness is no longer so intractable as it was; and operative treatment is rarely needed, if the method devised by Sargant (Dally et al., 1958) is applied. The technique, as described by Dally and Sargant (1960), is fully dealt with in Chapter VII. It involves combining modified insulin treatment with very large doses of chlorpromazine, from 300 to 800 mg daily, under which most patients with anorexia nervosa gain weight very rapidly.

Other states of mixed organic and psychogenic nature do well with the treatment. Interestingly enough it has been found to have surprisingly beneficial effects on certain patients with post-concussional states, though there has been no marked loss of weight, and no great gain in weight occurs with the treatment. This may perhaps be connected with the autonomic disturbances which are found in these patients, which may be influenced in some way by the treatment. The drawn face becomes more relaxed, the colour improves, and there is a lessening of tension, irritability, and lethargy. In other post-concussional syndromes with an accompanying loss of weight an improvement after insulin treatment is more easily explained. The initial head injury has started a vicious circle. The patient has tried to return to work before he was fit; the somatic responsiveness to anxiety-producing situations, such as are normally met with, has remained heightened; conditioned phobias are added to the original disabilities; lethargy, headache and loss of appetite and weight contribute to a progressive mental and physical deterioration. In such a man the treatment may leave the post-concussional headaches untouched, but put him in better trim to tolerate them and other symptoms of like origin. Insulin treatment has also been found very useful in patients with hysterical vomiting, nervous dyspepsia, nervous colitis, and even gastric ulcer when a restricted diet or vomiting have produced physical deterioration. In some cases the artificial appetite created by hypoglycæmia overcomes the repugnance to food, and success may be attained when other treatments have failed. The method should also be useful after a physical illness when convalescence is hanging fire, and in the nervous disabilities that follow illnesses like pneumonia and typhoid. Experience has shown that it is perfectly easy to manage in a general hospital ward.

Kersley and his co-workers (1951) have reported the beneficial effects of insulin treatment in rheumatoid arthritis. Here again anxiety and loss of weight may gravely aggravate the disability directly caused by the illness; and the vicious circle of psychological and somatic changes mutually aggravating each other may be effectively interrupted by an insulin course. Patients with asthma may also obtain considerable relief from this treatment. The hypoglycæmia sometimes temporarily benefits the asthmatic symptoms; and restoration of physique tends to lessen the autonomic irritability which is conducive to the attacks.

In previous editions of this book we have taken the view that modified insulin therapy had only a limited part to play in the treatment of schizophrenia, and that it should rarely or never be used instead of full comas. But the position seems to have been altered radically by the advent of the new tranquillising drugs. While the combination of these drugs with ECT provides the brunt of the attack on the illness, modified insulin therapy in addition plays a most valuable role. Its primary purpose is to restore lost weight, to get the patient's weight above normal, and to fortify the bodily constitution against relapse. In addition it will be found that some patients benefit when the modified insulin therapy is taken to the depth of a few light sopors. Restoration of normal weight is a main aim of the treatment and should be achieved before treatment stops. Sometimes, of course, chlorpromazine and ECT alone attain this end.

Another form of modified insulin treatment, not that described in the section below, is required in other cases where a full exploitation of the sedative effect of insulin is desired. This method may also be used when the sedative effect of insulin is to be used for abreactive purposes. Insulin in sub-coma doses has a powerful effect on anxiety and tension and is often a better sedative than the barbiturates, even for excited psychotic patients. Fifty units of insulin or more can be given two or sometimes three times a day, not necessarily with the production of sopor. Sakel also used insulin with great success in the withdrawal treatment of drug addictions. And in delirium tremens, two or three sopors a day, immediately interrupted by glucose, have brought about a return to clarity in as little as 48 hours. A combination of modified insulin and light narcosis is also of value in the acute anxiety states, particularly where the dangers of intoxication with barbiturates are to be feared, as in the severely excited patient whose state is insufficiently controlled even by large doses of drugs. Special precautions have to be taken against the occurrence of hypoglycæmic coma. An experienced nurse can, however, readily distinguish this from the sleep produced by drugs. The comatose patient generally sweats freely and cannot be roused. But the danger should be avoided by ample glucose and regular feeding during the twenty-four hours. Nowadays smaller doses of insulin can be given, if they are combined with large doses of tranquillising drugs such as chlorpromazine. These drugs are a valuable aid in damping down the withdrawal symptoms which arise in the treatment of alcohol, barbiturate and even morphia addiction.

Technique

The treatment can be given to 20 patients in a ward with the minimum of extra staff. When the staff have been trained the doctor need not be present, though he should be at hand in case of emergency. At 7 or 7.30 a.m. the patient, who has fasted from 8 p.m. the previous night, is given the insulin; 20 units are injected intramuscularly as a starting dose, and this is increased by 10 units daily until a dose of 100 units is reached, provided that the patient is still able to eat the food given to him at the end of three hours. The room can be kept in semi-darkness and the patient at complete rest. In these doses insulin has a sedative effect; sweating may be profuse, and the autonomic changes are obvious. If at any time the patient shows signs of slipping into a state when he could no longer take food, he is immediately sat up and given a glucose drink or sugared tea. The staff can be trained to recognise and anticipate this point, so that actual coma is never reached, and one of them should be constantly observing the behaviour of the patients during treatment. The glucose will bring the patient sufficiently round for him to be able to eat. Only rarely will an intravenous interruption be necessary. For if an emergency should arise, both coma and sopor can be quickly terminated by 1 mg glucagon given intramuscularly. Within 10 to 15 minutes the patient will become sufficiently responsive to take glucose by mouth, which should then be given without delay. In an emergency the doctor can be called, but there is no need for flurry as it will be some time before the patient will be in any danger from the induced hypoglycæmia. In the meantime the nurse can, if necessary, pass a stomach tube and give sugar solution. If on one day the treatment has had to be interrupted early by sugared tea, the dose of insulin should be reduced next day by 10 units. The aim is to stabilise the dose at one just short of producing sopor or early coma, though 100 units should not generally be exceeded. In many patients 50 units are sufficient to produce autonomic changes and satisfactory increases of weight, and some patients like the smaller doses better. Three hours after the injection the patient is roused and given a full breakfast with sugared tea, and when it is desirable to put on as much weight as possible in the shortest time, potatoes mashed and flavoured as a supplement. A vitamin B preparation such as Bemax may also be given. After the meal the patient may get up, make his bed, and help in the ward cleaning. He is given a full lunch at 1.30 and a good tea and supper; he is encouraged to eat as much food during the day as his increased appetite will allow him. After-shocks in the afternoon are very rare, but it is well to keep the patients under supervision though actively employed. On Saturday, to allow the patient to go out, the dose is reduced to 20 units, and no treatment is given on Sunday. Strenuous exercise in the afternoons is encouraged.

We have found at St. Thomas's that modified insulin can also be given on an out-patient basis. The patient attends fasting; the insulin treatment and a meal after it are given; and the patient is sent home accompanied by a relative. Sugar is always available for the patient to take with him, and to take at home if needed, with the same protective régime as is used by the diabetic, who is taking insulin and is liable to a hypoglycæmic episode later in the day.

The treatment is continued until normal weight has been regained, until further improvement seems unlikely and other measures are indicated, or until, after an initial large rise, the weight seems to be stabilised although the normal level seems not yet to have been regained. No attempt should be made to force the weight above the normal level when in good health; any excess gained in this way is rapidly lost when the treatment stops. Even part of the weight gained below the normal level may be lost, unless psychotherapy and environmental readjustments have dealt with outstanding difficulties. If insulin is being specifically used to combat anxiety, or to antagonise the excitatory effects of ECT, it will of course be continued as long as is necessary for these purposes.

A rare complication reported by Kersley and others (1951), and also seen by the authors, is the occurrence of one or two attacks of spontaneous hypoglycæmia some days after the course of treatment is finished. It is, perhaps, more likely to happen in those who have had more than one course of treatment. Patients leaving hospital very soon after treatment should be warned of the possibility, and they can be recommended to take, as a prophylactic, a high protein diet and an extra meal at bed-time for three weeks after the end of treatment. The hypoglycæmic attack itself should, of course, be dealt with as soon as it is recognised, or even suspected, by taking sugar.

In the predisposed patient fits may occasionally complicate the hypoglycæmic stage in treatment. No harm will be done if the patient is prevented from biting his tongue and other usual means of first aid are employed; but the fits should be prevented by giving phenobarbitone 60–120 mg daily, or Epanutin.

Suggestion plays a considerable part in the treatment, especially in the early stages when the patient is in a suitable frame of mind. Other patients in the ward who are doing well help to instil confidence. The staff should be enthusiastic. The very fact that a definite treatment is being given is not without psychological effect. No advantage is gained in suggesting to such patients that their condition is a purely psychological one. The dual mechanism should be explained to them, and the plan of treatment and what is expected of it carefully outlined by the doctor. The psychogenic aspects of the illness should, of course, not be forgotten. It is the physician's duty to analyse the precipitation of the illness to see how far similar future causes of breakdown can be eliminated and how to prepare the patient to meet them. The active co-operation of the patient will be demanded. Not infrequently, however, with the neurotic as with the schizophrenic and the depressive, it will be found that the immediate apparent precipitating cause fades into insignificance as improvement occurs, and that what the patient took to be the reason for his breakdown was merely a premonitory sign of its imminence.

Results

The results attained by treatment will vary from individual to individual. Often a stone or more is gained in a few weeks, and up to seven pounds in the first week is not an unusual finding where the right patient has been chosen. The rapid gain in weight in a patient suffering from anxiety and hysterical symptoms or from a reactive depression contrasts strongly with the slower gain in the endogenous depressive, who as a rule does not do well with this treatment alone. The weight chart may supply the evidence for a revision of the diagnosis. This gain in weight is usually accompanied by a considerable access in feeling of physical well-being, which can be used to support other measures directed more specifically towards the removal of neurotic symptoms.

Poor results will be obtained if the wrong patients are chosen, such as endogenous depressives, or obsessionals, or those who have never suffered any physical deterioration. Results will be improved, if the treatment is combined with other methods specially selected for the individual case, such as, on occasion, ECT, and the antidepressant drugs, etc.

Gain in weight and psychological improvement do not always go hand in hand. Neurotics of poor personality may make big and even dramatic gains in weight without much change in their mental state and their attitude; whereas relatively moderate increases may be all that is required in other patients, especially when not much weight has been lost originally. The quality of the remission has to be measured against the quality of the pre-existing personality and the environmental stresses which have been and will have to be met. However, it must be remembered that the makeup of the personality has not been in any way changed by the treatment, and even symptoms of illness, such as conditioned phobias, are usually unaltered, although the somatic manifestations of anxiety are for the time being considerably lessened. The treatment provides no guarantee against the liability to relapse, and the effort to guard against this will have to be directed along other lines.

As has been mentioned, **the antidepressant drugs,** whether used alone or in combination, often cause a craving for food, especially carbohydrates. Drug therapy, therefore, **may replace modified insulin therapy**, or modified insulin and drug combinations, **in anxious and depressed patients**.

CHAPTER SIX

The Use of Drugs in Psychotherapy

It is a commonplace that under the influence of alcohol a man reveals tendencies that remain hidden in everyday life and may become suggestible, obstinate, euphoric or boastful. Tongues are loosened by drink; critical judgment is suspended and secret aspirations, damaging confessions and dramatic falsifications of previous events come pouring out. Primitive religions have made use of such mechanisms, with an added therapeutic effect. The emotional release that occurs under alcohol or other drugs may be followed by a decrease in tension and the relief of feelings of depression. The naïve savage feels he has been through an experience of religious significance, that he is spiritually renewed and that his troubles have dropped from his mind. Sailors, after long voyages, feel the need of a prolonged alcoholic spree to relieve the accumulated emotional tension. Psychiatry in its turn has discovered the value of these methods both for treatment and for exploration; and what have sometimes been called 'narcoanalysis' (Horsley, 1943) and 'narcosynthesis' (Grinker and Spiegel, 1945) resemble on the one hand the catharsis of religious intoxication, on the other hand the method employed from time immemorial by the colonel in the mess to discover the qualities of the newest subaltern.

Instead of giving alcohol by mouth, when the effects take some time to appear, and are unreliable and difficult to control, we can employ a whole range of agents more certain in their action and more varied in their effects. These include intravenous barbiturates or methedrine, and inhalants such as ether, nitrous oxide and high percentages of carbon dioxide in oxygen (Meduna, 1950). Powerful hallucinogenic drugs such as lysergic acid diethylamide (LSD 25) have also been used. Most of these drugs have some of their effects in common. Both in the normal, the neurotic and the psychotic, the tendency is to abolish inhibitions and allow underlying thought processes and preoccupations to appear. In addition, any associated anxiety may be abolished or reduced, or in some instances greatly heightened. The great value of the intravenous barbiturate for diagnostic purposes in the psychotic is sometimes not sufficiently realised. Under the influence of a suitable dose, the retarded depressive may become free, able to talk and even cheerful. Delusions or ideas of suicide, which may have been deliberately concealed or merely un-expressed as a result of the inhibition, may freely appear; and the doctor may be put in a position to see how much of the illness is due to the momentarily abolished disturbances of mood, how much to some specific environmental situation, how much to more fundament-ally determined delusional beliefs. The procedure may also be a useful indication of the amount of benefit to be expected from convulsion therapy, as the latter brings about over a longer period of time what the barbiturate can do only for a space of minutes. In a case of simple stupor the method may provide diagnostic indications which are invaluable. The catatonic schizophrenic is freed from his inhibitions as efficiently as the retarded depressive, and may then for the first time reveal the true nature of his illness, by his description of halluci-nations, delusions and thought disorder hitherto unsuspected.

An excitant, such as intravenous methedrine, may also release schizophrenic symptoms, which then appear in clear consciousness and in a tense rather than a relaxed state. Symptoms of an unsuspected schizophrenic state may also appear under the administration of ether or CO_2.

In neurotic states chemical aids can be used for both diagnostic and therapeutic purposes. The anxious neurotic has less difficulty in dis-cussing his fears in a semi-drunken state produced by a barbiturate, when he is protected against the most disagreeable manifestations of anxiety, than in a state of completely clear consciousness. Even ordi-nary reserve tends to melt under the influence of the drug, and the shy individual, preoccupied with ideas and experiences he feels ashamed to mention, no longer finds difficulty in discussing the subject which is on his mind or which the doctor wishes to explore. Hours of investigation and questioning may be saved in this way. In some re-spects the method resembles that of free association, as practised by analysts, in that both depend on procuring mental and physical relaxation. But in the drugged state the time available is strictly limited, and has to be employed by the purposive drive of the doctor. It is now, in fact, being used increasingly to shorten the laborious process of a full-scale analysis, by helping to overcome resistances in a shorter time.

In the acute neuroses of war, the use of intravenous barbiturates proved of great value in dealing with functional amnesic states of all kinds and with conversion symptoms of abrupt and recent onset. Beneficial abreaction of emotionally laden incidents is facilitated.

Their use in acute battle casualties was reported after Dunkirk by Sargant and Slater (1940) and became widely used as a front-line technique. Such conditions are less frequent in peace, when most neuroses are the developments of months or years, but they do occur. Abrupt onset of conversion symptoms then usually has to be dealt with by a general physician called, for instance, in a hurry to see a hysterical girl on her bridal night, to a pit explosion or to a traffic accident. In usual psychiatric practice with neurotic patients the method has a more restricted application, but is still useful in selected patients.

Its chief use is undoubtedly in dealing with hysterical conversion symptoms; and it obviates alike the delays and difficulties of hypnosis, for which in any case only a minority of psychiatrists are temperamentally adapted, and the need for the mobilisation of medieval engines of torture, such as the faradic battery and the electric wire brush. The mode of action of the barbiturates is far from clear, but it probably not only has a directly sedative chemical effect on the cells of the brain but also an effect on the vasomotor system. After the precipitating event, a car crash perhaps (during the last war it was usually after a bomb explosion), the individual blanches, starts to sweat or tremble, and shows either quickening or slowing of the pulse. At the same time the amnesia appears, or the functional loss of use of a limb. 'Paralysed with fright' is a far from inaccurate description; and the escape mechanisms, presupposed by theory, frequently cannot be demonstrated at that time. Many soldiers whom we have observed, and who have gone through this experience, have been thrown on their own resources, and have struggled to regain the use of their limbs or memory. The motivated manipulation of the symptom is a mechanism which usually appears some time later; and often enough the patient has made a recovery on his own initiative in a few hours, relapsing later perhaps when circumstances favoured it. If, as sometimes happens, the patient can be caught in the preliminary stage, soon after the first abrupt appearance of the symptom, the intravenous injection of the barbiturate may bring about, even as the drug is injected, the changes that might have occurred spontaneously hours or days later. The drawn face of the patient relaxes, colour returns, and memory or full use of the limbs also returns without any suggestion having been made to that effect. In cases that have lasted longer, and the behaviour pattern has become more fixed, forceful suggestion may be required as well as the relaxing effect of the drug; or it may prove better to proceed at once to abreaction of the traumatic incident. Such events are, of course, not at all common in peace-time. Crisis psychiatry, so important during the last war, is less needed, but still sometimes needed; and in that field abreaction is most valuable.

Although the hysteric also becomes more open to suggestion and reassurance under intravenous amytal, no true hypnotic state is produced. Post-hypnotic suggestion is not possible with amytal narcosis in normal subjects, and postures are not maintained as in hysterical trance states. But in both states there is reduction of the critical sense, an enhancement of rapport, and often a pouring out of both truth and fantasy equally. Aggressive feelings, which would terrify the individual in his normal state, can be expressed without excessive anxiety, and the emotional experiences of the past can be lived anew.

Intravenous methedrine has a different effect. It is a rapid one, so that the patient may be taken unawares; tension is heightened and the flow of talk greatly increased, while consciousness remains clear. If good rapport is first obtained, the patient may bring out problems which have been repressed for years, and methedrine may bring success in this way even when the relaxing effect of barbiturates has failed. Inhibited persons of obsessional disposition often respond very well. The increased possibilities of contact should be made use of from the beginning, and the first two or three interviews are often the vital ones. The effect of the drug is prolonged, and sometimes the patients can hardly be prevented from talking to all and sundry for some hours after the injection.

Other drugs, nitrous oxide, ether and carbon dioxide can also be used. Nitrous oxide causes a rapid and short anæsthesia, on emerging from which abreaction in a fairly clear state of consciousness can be produced. Ether is useful in cases where some degree of excitation is desired to aid in abreaction, or where one wishes to bring aggressive feelings to the fore. The rapid dissociation caused by carbon dioxide is useful when a quick attack on a hysterical symptom is needed; and it is often a successful aid in bringing out, early in a course of treatments, problems whose very existence may not have been suspected. The psychological effects of all these drugs have much in common, and there are patients for whom each is more suitable than the others; the skill of the therapist in using them is the critical factor.

Technique with Barbiturates

In the acute hysteric the treatment should be begun as soon as possible after the appearance of the symptom; the probabilities of success diminish with time, and the method is much less successful with long-standing cases. The treatment should be regarded as a method of first-aid, to abolish a hysterical symptom before the nervous system is habituated to it and before its possible advantages have become apparent to the patient. Every attempt should be made to get rid of the hysterical symptom at the first interview, and powerful suggestion, in the form of explanation of the purpose of the procedure, may be necessary as the patient lies on the couch and his arm is prepared for the injection. The drug used may be Sodium Amytal, or Pentothal Sodium; choice will depend on the predilections of the clinician, but as each drug has slightly different properties, it is best to get used to one. If Sodium Amytal is used, 500 mg are dissolved in 5 ml or 10 ml distilled water. The injection is made slowly, 100 mg a minute or even less being given. Conversation is continued throughout, not least in order to know the exact stage in anæsthesia reached. What is desired is a state of complete relaxation and euphoria, without slurring of speech or mental confusion. The dose required will differ from patient to patient, and in the same patient at different times. If he is very anxious, more will be needed than if he is calm and placid. As emotion is aroused during the conversation, more of the drug may be needed from time to time to damp down the anxiety and consequent resistance to further disclosures. The full effect of each ml as injected may not be apparent till a minute or two after it is given, so that it is easy to overshoot the desirable endpoint.

It is as well to warn the patient, as the injection is being made, that he will feel a little dizzy in the head. The first outward sign that the drug is starting to take effect is a heavy sigh and a change to a steadier and deeper respiration from the small and shallow breaths usual to the hysteric. Facial expression becomes more relaxed, placid and friendly, and mobility returns; tears may even well into the eyes. At this stage questioning may be allowed to become more direct. The doctor should gain complete control of the proceedings and quietly dominate the patient. If an amnesia is to be recalled, the patient should be questioned about his memories around that time and be brought gradually nearer the episode. All the time the idea is being conveyed to him that he can think more clearly and his memory is returning. He may now be asked whether he has any suspicions of what happened, whether any vague and fragmentary incidents come to his mind. Sometimes, especially where the illness is of very recent onset, none of this may be necessary, and memory will come back of its own accord in the early stages of the injection. Once isolated incidents have been recalled they can be used as bases for the exploration of other gaps. Sometimes the blockage occurs after a large part has been regained, and this usually means that a critical traumatic incident has been reached. If so, then the patient will display great emotion, and may need deepening of the anæsthesia and pressure from the doctor before memory returns with a dramatic emotional abreaction. When the story is complete, it should be run over again and again until it can all be talked about, even if the conversation is almost sinister in its drunken recital of harrowing experiences shorn of their appropriate affect. It is unlikely that the patient will reveal vital secrets, even under amytal, unless he is prepared to do so. It is hopeless, for instance, to expect a confession from the malingerer, who usually under this treatment only becomes abusive and truculent. A friendly emotional *rapport* should be retained throughout, and 'beating up' the patient will defeat its own ends.

If there is much repressed material, two or three sessions may be necessary to obtain the whole story; and it is important that the whole story should be obtained. Even if a large part of the forgotten memories has been recovered, and the patient does not get well, a gap in the story indicates that treatment has been incomplete. We have seen a number of patients who had been treated in this way with partial success by an earlier therapist, but who remained subject to persistent symptoms until renewed exploration brought out the last of the repressed material. Manipulation of the amount of drug used at each interview may be difficult, because the amount of drug needed to bring out an experience associated with intense anxiety will lead to drunkenness and confusion when the affective outburst has blown over and the patient is relaxed again. When that happens, the interview should be ended and a smaller amount of drug given the next time. Sometimes the treatment, which has begun with an Amytal narcosis, can be continued in subsequent interviews with ordinary hypnosis and suggestion.

The hysterical instability under biochemical stresses may be exploited in another way, by causing the patient to hyperventilate, which in itself induces a state of suggestibility; overbreathing may also be used to supplement the effects of the barbiturate. Other drugs may also be employed. During a barbiturate interview, if things are hanging fire, Methedrine may be injected intravenously. This will increase the flow of talk and the degree of tension which is engendered as emotionally laden topics are discussed. The combination can be very effective in skilled hands. In the same way, ether inhalation can be given during the barbiturate interview; depending on the patient and on the way he is handled, there may be either an increased degree of excitement or more confusion.

When memory has been restored it should be kept on the surface. The patient should not be allowed simply to go off to sleep. It is wise to let him return to the ward (he will still be able to walk though drunkenly) and sit by his bed; and an hour later he may be seen again and the conversation renewed. Memories will then be retained into a state of clear consciousness and so fixed. If the patient is allowed to go to sleep at the end of the interview, he may very well forget the whole episode and all will have to be gone through again. Similarly, if the method has been used to break down reserve in simple therapeutic exploration, the patient who is once aware that he has effectively broken the ice is not likely to experience the same difficulties again. Often the doctor will be told fantastic stories under the drug, straight from the world of nightmare. The falsity of these will be apparent on the surface. But it may also be that he will be told quite plausible and circumstantial stories which are no less the product of dream fabrication. Truth and fantasy will have to be sifted when the patient is in a state of clear consciousness, events seen in reasonable perspective and, shorn of exaggerated affect, integrated with the rest of the patient's experiences. A cautious and sceptical attitude on the part of the doctor will save him from swallowing all of his patient's hocum, hunting Snarks, and exploring mare's nests.

For hysterical conversion symptoms the same procedure is adopted, attention then being concentrated on the loss of function of limb or voice. Hysterical tremors may also subside; indeed if they are not controlled under intravenous Amytal the outlook for their rapid subsidence is not good. Even if they disappear under Amytal to return later, the prognosis for fairly rapid relief is better. It is best, when the doctor is trying to restore the use of an arm or leg, to start by helping and suggesting movements of unaffected limbs as the drug takes effect. Thereafter attention may be gradually directed to the affected limb. It is first passively moved by the doctor, and then the patient's more active co-operation is invited. Sometimes considerable resistance is shown to acknowledging the regained function. When this occurs, it is as well to take the patient back into the ward while still in his euphoric state and make him exercise the limb in front of other patients, and movements are continued as he gradually emerges from the drugged state into full consciousness. Once the patient finds himself committed, relapse is less likely to occur, unless further stress or a return of insecurity occurs. If treatment has been unsuccessful during the interview, it is wise to give the patient enough drug at the end to put him to sleep, so that the interview may be forgotten or blurred when he awakes. The doctor will then have to decide whether to repeat the attempt later or use another method.

Excitatory Abreaction

A fundamentally different management of the abreactive technique has led to interesting and valuable results. This consists in adding to and stimulating the patient's excitement, rather than damping it down, when it will often reach a climactic phase and pass into a state of temporary general inhibition. Relief from tension and hysterical symptoms, when it occurs after this, is often very dramatic (Shorvon and Sargant, 1947).

An excitatory abreaction can be obtained under hypnosis, and it may occur during the course of an analysis as traumatic events are uncovered. Where circumstances are favourable, it may be deliberately induced with the aid of barbiturates, ether, nitrous oxide, Methedrine or CO_2. We found during World War II that excitatory abreaction not infrequently occurred in recent battle casualties with little help on the part of the therapist. It then usually happened soon after the injection of the drug, while the circumstances of the breakdown were being recounted.

The great benefit that is often felt by the patient after a fortuitous abreaction like this has usually been interpreted by Freudians among others, as due to the release of emotion tied down to the traumatic incident itself and subsequently repressed. But we have made observations which suggest that physiological mechanisms may also play a large part (Shorvon and Sargant, 1947; Sargant, 1957b). The abreaction need not always be around a real experience; a fantasy may be exploited just as well. In order to bring about the right degree of excitement, the patient may be put back into a past which has been modified by the therapist's invention. In his drunken state the patient accepts a false version of the facts as if it had been the truth, experiences the appropriate emotional response, and the abreaction is attained. More important than the nature of the real life experience, or even than the emotional response it occasioned at the time, is the nature and the degree of the patient's emotional excitation during the course of the therapeutic interview. It seems to be important that emotions of anger, as well as those of anxiety, should be brought to life. Abreactions which end in weeping are not so successful.

The patients who have benefited from this treatment have been of a rather limited type. They are mostly men of previously stable personality who have been subject to persistent anxiety, and to depressive and hysterical symptoms, after one or a series of traumatic incidents. Emotional lability, a general sense of fatigue, listlessness or lack of initiative, persistent rumination on the past, nightmares, conversion symptoms, headaches and outbursts of irritability are often seen. With these men a recital of the traumatic events while anxiety is dulled by barbiturates may bring no relief, even if the recall of an amnesic period is attained. But the state of violent emotional excitement, which is more easily induced under a drug like ether, is more effective; and if the previous personality has been fairly stable it may be hoped that the return to normality will be a permanent one. Success can sometimes be attained even after two or more years of illness.

The technique of the treatment is aimed at producing an artificial excitement of mounting degree. Ether is probably the best drug for the purpose. It is poured on a mask and held, initially, slightly away from the patient's face. He is encouraged to start talking about past experiences which, from his history, may be expected to arouse powerful emotions, particularly those of anger and fear. As he becomes absorbed in his story the mask is brought nearer to his face. When he becomes slightly intoxicated and starts to abreact, the excitement is deliberately stimulated by the therapist until the man may be shouting and struggling. In this stage nurses will very likely be needed to hold him down, and the physical restraint adds to his excitement. This rises in a rapid crescendo to a climax when it passes abruptly into a state of collapse: the man suddenly goes limp and lies quietly for a minute or two, during which he is unresponsive. With many patients this final state of collapse is needed for success in treatment, and abreactions which do not go so far are ineffective. When the patient comes round his manner is composed and rational, and there is no sign of persisting excitement or intoxication. If the treatment has been successful he will then say that he feels as if a burden had been lifted from his mind.

Observations of a very similar kind were made by Pavlov on dogs (Frolov, 1938; Pavlov, 1941). He found that they showed a similar disruption of recently formed conditioned behaviour patterns when they were excited emotionally to the point of temporary cortical inhibition. Those animals who showed signs of a constitutional instability were only made more unstable by such an experience; but in others of more stable constitution, who were subjected to the experiment, the abolition of recent conditioned patterns of behaviour permitted the return of pre-existing habits and the easier formation of new ones.

So it is with the human being. The patient who has undergone an excitatory abreaction has no doubt that something vital has happened to him. The terms in which he describes his previous and his present state bear often a striking resemblance to the miraculous conversions of the revivalist meeting. After the emotional storm, not only is the slate wiped clean, as it were, but the patient is left in a more impressionable state than before. The situation is familiar also to the analyst, who can expect a heightening of the transference when repressed emotions have been abreacted. The enhanced suggestibility of the patient after abreaction can be used by the therapist for the implantation of new ideas, for processes of reconditioning, the nature of which will be decided by his social, psychoanalytic or religious predilections. The extent, however, to which these new behaviour patterns will be retained will depend on the constitutional stability of the patient and on the after-treatment (Sargant, 1957b).

This method of treatment is rather more limited in its application than the other techniques discussed. The chronically anxious and the severe constitutional hysteric are not helped; indeed it may only increase their instability. Obsessional symptoms are rarely abolished, unless they are recent and occur in a setting of hysteria or reactive depression. Obsessional neuroses and obsessive tension states can, in fact, be made much worse by excitatory abreaction with ether, and therapists should be very cautious about using this method in all but hysterically predisposed persons. Endogenously depressed patients do not respond well, and usually cannot be made to abreact. The more widespread and deeper inhibition seen in them needs a more powerful excitant, such as electrical convulsion (Sargant, 1957b). Depersonalisation, however, may respond better to abreaction than to convulsion therapy if hysterical features are also present in the personality. For it is above all the hysterical patient, or fairly stable personality, who has broken down under severe stress, who does well with these methods. It is because abreactive techniques have been, time and again, extended beyond their main field of application—the traumatic hysterical syndrome as formulated by Janet and later by Breuer and Freud, that they have so repeatedly fallen out of favour, only to be rediscovered when wars and disasters furnished a fresh crop of the most suitable kinds of patients.

Abreactive therapy is not often needed in peace-time practice. In recent years we have found that patients, of the kind we used to abreact, have done very well by other means, used with the aim of putting traumatic material under the surface rather than bringing it out. When we are well, we mostly repress our fears, which are eventually forgotten, and do not normally need to ventilate them. As a general approach to this group of patients, we have found the MAOI and tricyclic antidepressants more valuable than abreactive therapies.

Technique with Intravenous Methedrine

We have described the use of drugs to abolish recently implanted conversion symptoms, and to disrupt hysterical behaviour patterns by excitation. Drugs may also be used as aids in one or other of the established psychotherapeutic procedures, in which a series of problems in the past and present life of the patient is quietly worked over. For this purpose, intravenous Methedrine is probably now to be regarded as the drug of choice, though other adjuvants may be used with it, or separately, to produce particular effects. Claims have been made that Methedrine injections *per se* provide a useful treatment for neuroses. These claims have not been validated, and the best that can be said that Methedrine used in the way described below is a good abreactive agent.

Methedrine, which is a derivative of amphetamine, was originally used to raise the blood-pressure during spinal anæsthesia. Later it was reported by Simon and Taube (1946) to have interesting effects when used intravenously as a substitute for the barbiturates in psychological exploration. Since 1947, when it was first used in this country at Belmont (Sargant, 1948), much work has been done there and at St. Thomas's Hospital to define its usefulness in relation to the other abreactive procedures, especially by Shorvon (1953).

The dangers of using ether abreaction or the inhalation of carbon dioxide in obsessionally anxious patients have already been stressed in this chapter. All too often there is a great increase in tension which may aggravate the symptoms instead of relieving them. The same risk does not apply to intravenous Methedrine. The obsessional patient does not have the same fear of losing consciousness; and under the influence of the drug obsessive ideas may lose some of their hold, inhibition is reduced, and the patient frequently finds it much easier to discuss his personal difficulties. However, obsessional rumination may sometimes be increased; and if paranoid features are brought into the open or unsuspected schizophrenic symptoms come to light, one should stop the treatment immediately. In the first or second interview there may be an outpouring of conflicts and problems, not previously discussed, which it might take months to arrive at by the ordinary psychotherapeutic discussion. The factors which come to light are usually not buried very deep, and Methedrine is less successful than, say, ether, in bringing out deeply repressed material.

The use of Methedrine has been restricted under the Drug Acts, since it has proved to have strongly addictive properties. At one time, in some clinics, patients who had gone through a 'course' of Methedrine-assisted abreactive therapy, continued to attend and reattend with urgent demands for another session. Some patients, in fact, once they had been introduced to it, continued to come mainly for the 'kicks', but were exceedingly difficult to wean. Methedrine is very useful on occasion, given only in one or two sessions for exploration, abreaction and suggestion. But a strong warning must be given not to continue it too often.

This method can also be employed with hysterical patients, especially those with some obsessional features, who have been found only to become more anxious with the more violent abreactive techniques; and it is also valuable in monosymptomatic obsessional phobic states and obsessional personalities with mild depersonalisation symptoms. Certain skin conditions, in which there is much repressed tension, can be helped, as also other psychosomatic disorders where unreleased aggression or anxiety seem to be contributing to their aggravation or perpetuation (Shorvon *et al.*, 1950).

The therapist must be prepared to give the patient a full hour or more of his time. The initial dose of the drug, given into the vein, should be 10 to 20 mg, but has to be adjusted to circumstances. In some hysterical patients any large dose will cause an almost intolerable tension, and may bring about a flare-up in the symptoms which will be difficult to control for some hours afterwards. On the other hand, it must be remembered that the first one or two treatments will probably be the critical ones, and that an initial dose which is also an effective one is much to be desired. If too small a dose is given at the first interview, and the initial barrier is not then broken through, the hope of doing so on a second occasion is the less. In some cases doses of 40 mg or more may be needed, or the combination of Methedrine with another drug such as ether; but large doses, and the combination of drugs, should be attempted only after trial, and by those experienced in such methods. Where Methedrine is found to produce too much tension, this may be combated by heavy sedation afterwards. Methedrine may also be combined with amytal or with pentothal.

The effect of Methedrine lasts some hours, and after he has finished with the therapist the patient may sometimes go on talking about his most private problems with anyone who is there to listen to him. Special precautions to prevent him causing himself embarrassment in this way, may, therefore, be needed. The effect of the drug will not, as a rule, have entirely worn off by bed-time, and a strong sedative should be prescribed to be taken then to avoid a disturbed or sleepless night. If a short-acting barbiturate is given, it must be remembered that there is a synergic action, so that when the sedative is taken there may be a further release of repressed emotions. The actual sedative used will therefore have to be adjusted to the individual patient. At St. Thomas's Hospital facilities are now provided by which the patient rests in his own cubicle or a special waiting room for as long as is required after treatment before returning home.

It is most important not to give intravenous Methedrine to any patient who is taking a monoamine oxidase inhibitor, or who has been on such a drug during the preceding two to three weeks. The combination of these two drugs is dangerous and may cause a hypertensive encephalopathy, from which fatal results have occurred.

Carbon Dioxide Inhalation Therapy

This treatment, the inhalation of 30 per cent CO_2 and 70 per cent O_2 was introduced by Meduna (1950); and as he was responsible for the earlier introduction of convulsive therapy, it is hardly surprising that it aroused immediate and wide-spread interest. Claims that the method is of value in the treatment of neurotic patients of many kinds, are, we think, uncritical and over-enthusiastic. Apart from the discovery that obsessional patients are often made worse by the treatment, little effort has been made to sift out those neurotic states or symptoms which respond to such treatment and those which do not. Psychiatry cannot make any steady progress unless the fields of application of new methods are mapped, so that they can either fit into the gaps left between the fields of application of existing methods, or shown to be valid replacements.

In recent years we have only used CO_2 therapy occasionally, as an abreactive agent or to break up a hysterical conversion state. Essentially it provides the means of an excitatory abreaction, and is useful in those patients for whom this type of abreaction is helpful; and in some of these patients it offers advantages over other drugs.

Among the best patients for CO_2 treatment are the traumatic hysterical states in which hysterical dissociation is prominent. Repeated abreaction with Pentothal or ether can be exhausting to patient and to therapist alike. The inhalation of CO_2 in such patients often produces a speedy dissociation with little effort, and a vivid re-living of the traumatic episode. In subsequent treatments this can be repeated again and again until the emotions connected with the incident are discharged or dispersed. One of the advantages of the method is that for a part of the time the patient is likely to be quite out of contact with the therapist, so that events may then come to the surface which have been unsuspected by either. Or phantasies may be spontaneously abreacted which have been as much the cause of the breakdown as any real happenings. Dream-like experiences are frequent, but are usually only recalled with difficulty when the treatment is over.

Recently implanted hysterical symptoms, such as stammer, hiccough, aphonia or paralysis may be relieved dramatically by one or more treatments. Such symptoms, however, may recur later. CO_2 also proved useful in long-standing anxiety-hysterias dating from the last war. Incidents not brought out by Pentothal abreaction have emerged under CO_2. In some patients it is not possible to abolish the traumatic neurosis, but CO_2 may still be useful, as a weekly or fortnightly maintenance treatment, in allowing a periodic discharge of tension sufficient to safeguard a reasonable level of work and family life.

Another use of CO_2 is, during an ether or Methedrine abreaction, to bring the patient rapidly up to the climactic phase. With these other methods of abreaction the patient may become very excited, but fail to reach the climax; a switch to CO_2 inhalation may then bring this about. When this has happened, he should not be further stimulated, nor the inhalation be continued, since the strain may be too severe. Combined methods such as this should only be used when experience has been gained into the limits and the dangers of each of the techniques which it is proposed to combine.

Many patients are unsuitable for CO_2 treatment. Obsessional conditions are often made much worse by the treatment, and anxiety states with obsessional features may also be aggravated. Hysterical patients with obsessional features also quickly learn to fear the treatment, and they may wake up at night in a state of panic, re-living the experience of the treatment given during the day.

In treatments that were given to some hundreds of patients at St.

Thomas's and Belmont Hospitals, the method proved very safe. The amount of oxygen in the mixture ensures that the patient remains a good colour, even if 50 or more breaths are taken; and any blueness calls for an immediate stop. Pure oxygen should be available, but will have to be used only rarely. Caution must be exercised in those over 45 years of age; but the only patient who suffered from a severe collapse in our experience was one who had been given a combination of CO_2 with intravenous Pentothal and a prolonged treatment.

The mixture of 30 per cent CO_2 with 70 per cent O_2 is delivered from a special cylinder into a tight-fitting face-mask with re-breathing bag and an expiratory valve to prevent a rise of pressure. The patient should not have had food for three hours before treatment. Before the treatment the bladder is emptied, dentures are removed, and the collar is loosened. The treatment is given with the patient lying on a couch. He is warned that as he breathes and begins to go unconscious he will feel short of breath. Fear of going unconscious and the unpleasant sensation of shortness of breath may be combated by an induction with nitrous oxide, with the switch to CO_2 when consciousness becomes clouded. Ether may also be used for induction, but only just enough should be given to cause mild euphoria and intoxication and not unconsciousness. In patients who get very anxious neither of these stratagems may be enough, the patient waking later under the CO_2 after only a few breaths. If much anxiety is felt, the method will have to be abandoned.

Some workers have given a set course, with two or three treatments weekly. Abreaction is not specifically encouraged, but is allowed to occur. Meduna believed that up to 100 treatments might be needed in some patients, though if there is no improvement after 20 treatments, one should reconsider the use of the method. We have also tried this technique, slowly increasing the number of breaths taken at each treatment where necessary; but we find that, in regard to the patients one can expect to help, the field of application is no larger. If one merely wishes to abreact a known incident, one may either talk to the patient about it as he is going under so as to start an immediate abreaction, or one may do the same when he is coming round after unconsciousness. Some of the most impressive results obtained with CO_2 have been achieved when quite unexpected material was forced to the surface by the combination of deep unconsciousness, which may be produced by CO_2 and, its strong excitatory effects. But this should rarely be attempted in obsessionally anxious patients.

Carbon dioxide may also be used in such a way that only a few breaths are taken, consciousness only slightly clouded, and tension heightened, before the mask is removed and the patient's fears and problems are discussed. But other methods already described, nitrous oxide, Pentothal, Amytal, ether and Methedrine, are just as useful for the purpose. In clinics where all such methods are available. CO_2 will be used relatively rarely, because of its tendency to cause anxiety and its lack of advantage over other methods, except for a limited group of patients where it can be of great value.

The Use of Hallucinogenic Drugs

Until recently increasing use as an aid to psychotherapy was being made of drugs which cause severe states of confusion, disordered consciousness and hallucinatory experiences, such as LSD 25, mescalin and some mushroom derivatives. Foolish claims of the value of this technique have been made: and equally foolish interpretations are often offered of the material which emerges from the patient's chemically disordered brain. Some therapists claim that they elicit the contents of the patient's subconscious or unconscious mind and repressed memories which can then be used for interpretative therapy. But experience shows that what often comes out is often determined by the interests and beliefs of the therapist himself; if he believes in birth trauma and the re-living of birth experiences, then delusional memories of such events may become gratifyingly available. Both strict adherents of Freud and those who depart in some respect from his tenets find the material that fortifies their faith. The patient's personal interests also influence the chaotic fantasies produced by these drugs. Thus men with religious convictions have had experiences in which they believed they saw and spoke with God; the anthropologist has relived aeons of time, and mimicked the behaviour of the primitive reptile he felt he had become; and those who have been through an analysis have produced fresh material of a fruitfully psychoanalytic type.

A very sceptical attitude must accordingly be taken if any deductions are to be drawn from the psychotic experiences of such a drugged state. The main value of these drugs is not for that purpose. But intense states of belief may be created in some of those who go through the hallucinated confused state, which is afterwards felt to have been of tremendous emotional significance. Such states of belief can, of course, be used therapeutically, for instance to compel faith in psychoanalytic doctrine, or to bring the patient to accept the insights which his therapist has evolved. Even articles of faith which are patently false or imposed from without will be taken as the patient's own.

All abreactive techniques make use of the force of suggestion, the methods which use drugs perhaps even more than the others. Both false memories and true can be equally effectively used in this way. The production of a state in which confusion is complicated by massive hallucination does not mean a departure from this primary principle, and the essentials of treatment with hallucinogenic drugs do not differ markedly from those of other drug abreactions. The same sort of patients can be helped, and the same sort of results will be obtained. Patients with anxiety hysteria are the ones most likely to be helped. Obsessional patients are helped only rarely, and are often made worse as they may become disturbingly obsessed with some of the bizarre material that emerges in the drugged state. Depressive patients are left with their depression untouched; and schizophrenics not only derive no benefit but are nearly always made worse by the addition of artificial psychotic symptoms to their spontaneously occurring ones. Persons of schizoid disposition should not be put in danger by the administration of a hallucinogen.

Lysergic acid may bring into the open schizophrenic symptoms which have been lying unsuspected beneath the surface, it may release manic tendencies, or cause aggressive uninhibited behaviour in predisposed individuals. It is, in fact, very easy to make mistakes in selection and to be surprised by an undesirable reaction. All cases should be carefully selected with these risks in mind, and the treatment has to be given under medical supervision, preferably as inpatient therapy. In England official sanctions now restrict the use of lysergic acid to a few selected persons who are given special leave to use it, mainly for research. Elsewhere there are no regulations, and in many countries there is nothing to stop its abuse or to protect patients against its dangers. If, for good reason, the drug is to be used, the technique is as follows:

On the first day at 9 a.m. 25 micrograms are given orally in 5 ml of water, after which the patient lies quietly on his bed, with the nurse or doctor at hand. On subsequent days the dose is increased by 50 micrograms a day until reactions occur, which is usually between 75 and 150 micrograms. It is important to make sure that no phenothiazine drugs are given in the preceding 24 hours, as they will antagonise the effects of lysergic acid.

Effects begin to be felt within 30 to 60 minutes, and reach a peak after three to four hours. The first changes are autonomic; dizziness, palpitations, nausea, headache, dryness of mouth, and often a peculiar numbness around the mouth. Changes in perception follow, and there may be heightened awareness of certain colours and even synæsthetic reactions. Distortion of body image, disturbance of time sense and drowsiness are common, although consciousness is never really impaired. The mood may vary from fatuous euphoria to deep but transitory depression. There may be silence, the patient apparently engrossed in a world of fantasy, or bursts of laughter, or signs of panic or anger. Forgotten childhood memories may be recalled with great vividness, and past experiences, traumatic or otherwise, may be re-lived and emotionally abreacted. These abreactions can be heightened or prolonged by appropriate intervention on the part of the doctor. Effects begin to fade after about 6 hours, but they may still be present 24 hours later. At any time it is desired to stop them, chlorpromazine can be given either orally (100 mg) or intramuscularly (25–50 mg).

Good results are sometimes obtained without the production of significant material or emotional upheaval having been in any way apparent. In other cases, particularly when there are strong hysterical traits in the personality, it seems that the emotional re-living of past events, actual or fantasied, is essential for a good result. It is sometimes possible to increase the likelihood of this happening, by inducing a state of apprehension and excitability immediately before treatment. Intravenous Methedrine (15–30 mg) given at bedtime for two or three nights is often very effective in this way.

The day after treatment should be used to discuss his experiences with the patient in the light of his history, interpreting and explaining any difficulties he may raise. Usually he is still in a state of heightened suggestibility, and is able to talk freely and without inhibition. Suggestions can now be offered and will be accepted, which would have been rejected out of hand before treatment. It is sometimes desirable to have the conversations and the abreactions which occurred under LSD recorded on tape, and play them back next day or later in order to reinforce therapeutic suggestions.

If necessary, treatment with the same dose of LSD can be repeated three or four days later, if there are still doubts in the patient's mind which need to be settled. We have never seen very much gained by continuing beyond six such treatments.

In recent years, mainly as a result of the abuse of the drug by highly unstable people taking it for 'kicks', there has been increasing worry about the risk of late or immediate psychoses in the drug-takers. LSD is by far the most toxic of the commonly used hallucinogens; and these dangers are not to be pooh-poohed. LSD must be used, if at all, with the greatest care and the maximum of supervision, at the time of administration and for some weeks after. Its therapeutic value is very small; it is contra-indicated in the psychoses, and in the neuroses is quite unsuitable for those who are obsessively unsuggestible.

The most valuable application of the hallucinogens is likely to be in the conduct of an experiment, to be made under guidance, by a normal individual who seeks a new valuation of his life by the aid of an artificial mystical experience. The new view-point taken up after the experience may well be one which is suggested by the therapist. It is because such experiences can be used to this end that hashish and mescaline have been the servants of a variety of religions all over the world.

Differential and Combined Usages

These several uses of drugs in psychotherapy may at times be applied at different stages in the treatment of the same patient. Traumatic incidents may, for instance, be revealed during an exploratory session with barbiturates or Methedrine, which will then need excitatory abreaction with ether or CO_2 to abolish the associated hysterical symptoms; a final covering of the ground under the original drugs may then permit the doctor to be sure that residual sources of tension have been adequately dealt with. Different patients will derive benefit more from one treatment than the other, according to their constitution, the nature and the duration of the symptoms. Very recent anxiety hysterical syndromes may be easily reversed with Amytal or CO_2, whereas ether or Methedrine may be needed in the more long-standing case. A lot will also depend on the handling and the skill of the therapist with any particular drug. Sometimes the best results will be obtained by using an exploratory or abreactive method during a course of light narcosis. The effects of suggestion or the implantation of 'insight' are often more easily obtained with one of the hallucinogenic drugs. It may also be easier when the patient is in a low state physically, debilitated by illness or emotional exhaustion. In the treatment of alcoholism, for instance, the idea that it is absolutely necessary to be teetotal is much more easily fixed in the patient's mind during the state of revulsion and weakness induced by the aversion treatment when injections of emetine and apomorphine are used. Indeed, cases have been reported in which patients have recovered repressed memories after a convulsion treatment, when these other methods had failed. Non-convulsive electrical stimulation of the brain under intravenous pentothal is another technique which has been used in the neuroses. Abreaction often occurs; but again we have seen valuable results only in that limited group of patients in whose cases abreaction is likely to have a curative effect.

Psychotherapy with and without Drugs

In this chapter we have described the ways in which drugs may be used to aid psychotherapy. The therapeutic effects of the drugs is only one part of the picture; and often the main part they are called on to play is to induce in the patient a state of mind in which he is particularly open to a psychotherapeutic procedure, whether of suggestion or exploration or abreaction. What then matters is the psychological impact made by the therapist on the patient while this susceptible state of mind lasts. It is becoming increasingly obvious that psychoanalysis itself scores its greatest successes in just the limited groups of patients who are also those most readily helped by psychotherapy with the aid of drugs. The same qualitative changes can be observed with the one as with the other method—increase of transference, abreaction, the breaking up of old patterns of thought and the implantation of new ones, even an increase in 'insight'. To be sure, the degree of 'insight' registered will depend on the theoretical opinions of the therapist, and the extent to which he is convinced that the patient has adopted his own view of the case.

Drug-aided psychotherapy is not successful with the graver states, schizophrenia and endogenous depression, nor even with the severer anxiety states and obsessional neuroses, for which more specific methods are required. But it is becoming ever clearer that psychoanalysis also fails with these conditions. It is normal people, or those who are only mildly ill, who are the most suggestible, and the most accessible to psychoanalysis; partly for that reason, the best conversions to whole-hearted belief in psychoanalytic doctrine have often been in the young doctors who subject themselves to a training analysis. The more ill the patient is mentally, whether psychotically or neurotically, the less suggestible he is, and the less easily to be helped by these methods. The lesson which we think is to be learned is that physical aids are a legitimate recourse in psychotherapy and should not be neglected on merely doctrinaire grounds. It is only the prevalence of authoritarianism in psychiatry which prevents the closer integration of all methods which have a common field of application and a common aim.

CHAPTER SEVEN

Diet, Vitamins and Endocrine Therapy

by JOHN POLLITT

Over a century ago doctors working in mental hospitals realised the need to provide psychotic patients with an adequate diet; and ever since there has been a succession of schools of medicine, as well as of nature therapy, which have sought to make use of dietary modifications in psychological medicine. No substantial advances were made, however, until we began to understand the primitive defence mechanisms of man and the role of nutrition in homoeostasis and central regulation. Probably the commonest of all psychological disturbances is the premenstrual syndrome. The attention this has aroused, and the research in this area which has borne fruit in the wide use of oral contraceptives, have brought scientific methods to bear in a field previously governed by enthusiasms, prejudices and unsupported hypotheses. What now follows will be based on the growing systematisation of our knowledge, but will be limited to the discussion of practical approaches which have been well tried and found helpful.

General Dietary Considerations

Subtle variations of a physiological kind probably determine differences between individuals, and between states of mind in the same individual at different times, yet nutrition is often viewed only in relation to absence, deficiency or slimming regimes. Cultural differences show extremes even in the presence of plenty, and there is much variation in the timing and consumption of meals between countries and continents. Although people will often repeatedly miss meals when slimming or when actively engaged, failure to eat is one of the reasonable grounds for compulsory detention of a patient. Dietary deficiency may turn an active man into a sluggard, neurasthenic or hypochondriac. Idiosyncrasies of diet such as life-long avoidance of fats or protein may have a biological protective function. In the healthy, if a meal is delayed, gradually increasing irritability and fatigue may be noticed. Minor changes in blood sugar may produce loss of morale, irritability, alterations in judgement and perspective and accident proneness. A good square meal is often the best tranquilliser.

Psychological stress, tolerated for a time by the man of balanced personality, produces eventually some degree of physical deterioration and reduction of powers of resistance. As every experienced soldier knows, persistent severe dietary deprivation weakens morale, determination, the power to strive and the sense of judgement. Nutritional deprivation has been used for positive aims. Fasting and deliberately induced debilitation have been employed in many cultures to change the psychological state, to lay the basis for religious experience, or to open the mind to new ideas and insights. Depending on the personality structure a stage is reached when even the previously robust individual is particularly vulnerable.

In clinical work pathological reactions following weight loss commonly take the form of depression. This tendency appears whether the patient's previous weight can be viewed in general medical terms as excessive or not, and regardless of the means by which weight is lost. Careful inquiry into the histories of many young people with atypical depression reveals loss of weight through slimming, physical illness, surgical operations and periods of overwork or neglect of nutrition, before the onset. In earlier ages, starvation with consequent emaciation and secondary infection in mentally ill patients perpetuated their mental reactions and prevented them from benefiting from such medical and nursing care that could be given.

The underweight patient, whether under treatment or not, recovers more slowly than one who regains his normal weight. For example, despite the use of electroplexy, the patient who remains in a poor physical condition often fails to gain more than transient benefit. In endogenous depression and schizophrenia where much weight may be lost during the illness, the prognosis often depends upon whether weight is regained during treatment. A depressed patient may fail to respond to all therapeutic measures with the exception of leucotomy, if a severe state of physical debilitation has prevailed during their use. So it is very important to build up the patient's weight as an essential part of the treatment of under-weight patients with psychiatric illness.

In the choice of a correct diet it is a question of quality and balance rather than quantity alone. There are idiosyncrasies of which we know very little, and individuals vary in their requirements of particular foods. Some patients seem to be at their best with relatively large amounts of protein, others with a greater preponderance of fat or carbohydrate. As Gjessing (1938) has shown, some schizophrenics do not metabolise the average amount of protein assimilated by the normal person. On an ordinary diet they are subject to periodic phases of retention of nitrogen which are concurrent with their attacks of excitement or stupor.

In mental disorders, both mild and severe, there is usually an alteration of appetite. As with normal people, the sight of attractively and unattractively prepared food will have a very different effect. In psychiatric hospitals, where anorexia is commoner than elsewhere, and the diet is provided by mass-production methods, it is extremely important to maintain a strict supervision of the feeding arrangements and to see that the food served is as dainty and appetising as possible. Weekly weight charts should be kept. The weight to be aimed at is the one the patient showed when in his time of health and happiness, and is not to be determined by general averages. Where the patient's weight is low or falling the amount of food taken should be recorded daily and accurately. For reliable control of difficult patients a standardised diet is desirable. When one has to try to get the patient to take more food than he feels inclined for, one must look out for evasion by subterfuge. When the usual routine fails, the patient may have to be kept in bed to improve supervision and reduce requirements. Wherever possible, one should investigate and treat the cause of the anorexia; observation may show that alterations in the metabolism of the ingested food have to be studied.

To help patients to gain weight, much can be done in a few weeks, even in an out-patient clinic. In depressive illnesses, including atypical forms with secondary neurotic symptoms, tricyclic antidepressants, usually given in the evening, will often promote appetite for carbohydrate and gain of weight. The combined use of antidepressants is often more effective, but particular care must be taken to warn patients against incompatible foods and alcohol. If much weight has been lost, the addition of small doses of phenothiazine derivatives to tricyclic antidepressants, and the use of anabolic steroids, either by mouth or intramuscular route for a period of three weeks will often start recovery of weight. The sublingual administration of stanolone 25 mg t.d.s. for this period is often most effective in less severe cases. This hormone should not, however, be given for more than three weeks or during pregnancy. Where much weight has to be gained, it is necessary for the patient to rest during the day and to take a dietary complement largely in the form of protein. This should be given in as great amounts as the patient can tolerate just before going to bed, so that appetite and normal food intake during the day are not interfered with.

If the patient's circumstances are such that rest and taking proper meals in the day cannot be achieved at home, one can consider modified insulin treatment in out-patients or a day hospital setting. The patient attends as early as possible in the morning having taken no food since the previous evening, and lies in bed throughout the treatment. Insulin is given shortly after arrival, the initial dose being 5 units; the amount of insulin is increased slowly over the next 10 days. The patient attends for five days a week, if possible. A large carbohydrate meal is given as soon as he shows early signs of hypoglycaemia, such as sweating, or after one hour if no signs have appeared. The patient then rests for the remainder of the morning, taking lunch at the hospital. One must explain the treatment fully to the patient, and warn him to take oral glucose should symptoms of hypoglycaemia appear later in the day. In milder cases one can get the patient to put on weight even by giving him large meals regularly at the hospital without prior medication.

Tube feeding is now rarely necessary, even for severely ill and debilitated patients in hospital; it should be resorted to only when all other methods have failed. It tends to impair rapport between patient and physician, and to upset others in the ward. As large amounts are frequently regurgitated, and then cannot be measured, there is no accuracy of dietary control. In the majority of severe endogenous depressive states and schizophrenic stupors, energetic treatment of the psychosis avoids the need for tube feeding. However, if other methods have failed or are not available, this technique may be life saving.

In psychosis, if tube feeding is necessary, it is better to do it when the patient is unconscious, provided that particular care is taken. For example, it is easier to feed the patient immediately after ECT, than to struggle to administer a feed and delay ECT for some hours because the stomach is not empty. Tube feeding can be done with the minimum of discomfort to the patient, if nasal tubes are used of 12 to 14 bore rubber, which are reasonably stiff and not yet soft with repeated boiling. The patient's head is bent forward, the jaw held up to avoid the point of the tube entering the mouth or larynx, and the tube should be well oiled before insertion. Once in position a little fluid should be aspirated and its reaction tested with litmus, to make sure the tube has reached the stomach. Any necessary sedatives, aperients and other medicines as well as the food are then given. Tube feeding should be carried out twice daily. The standard feed is composed of: 30 oz. (850 ml) milk, 2 eggs, 2 oz. (60 g) sugar, $\frac{1}{2}$ oz. (15 g) Horlicks, and 1 teaspoonful Marmite in alternate feeds. The juice of one orange should also be prepared and given separately.

Tube feeding is always regrettable, and efforts should be made to deal with refusal to eat by other means, so as to avoid it altogether where possible or to reduce the time for which it is necessary. This is best done by energetic treatment of the psychotic state. In psychoses, as in most psychiatric disorders, anorexia is central rather than peripheral in origin, and centrally acting treatments are both reliable and essential to maintain nutrition and restore physical well being. The endogenous depressive will often begin to put on weight following a single ECT, although taking the diet that proved insufficient before. Similarly electroplexy will often interrupt a catatonic state and restore normal feeding; and it is rare for a schizophrenic to fail to eat and maintain weight once insulin therapy has begun. The modified form of insulin therapy has the widest application today, and if given with relatively large doses of the phenothiazine drugs this combination produces dramatic weight gains. The technique is described fully in the treatment of anorexia nervosa. More recently the introduction of thymoleptic drugs, such as imipramine and the monoamine oxidase inhibitors has provided a solution to many types of depressive illnesses. The action of these drugs in stimulating appetite and weight gain commonly avoids the need for ancillary methods, particularly in the less severe cases. The patient suffering from a severe and acute anxiety state will often take large quantities of food under a continuous narcosis when neither modified insulin nor a psychotherapeutic approach have had any effect. Finally, it is rare for the leucotomised patient to persist in refusing food after the operation; and in the chronic hospitalised patient, or the patient who seems determined to starve herself to death, leucotomy may sometimes be considered.

Anorexia Nervosa

The most marked examples of debilitation in psychiatric disorder are seen in patients suffering from anorexia nervosa—an illness which highlights the importance of personality in determining the type of mental breakdown accompanying weight loss. In this illness, practically confined to young females, once a stone or two (5 to 15 Kg) have been lost, the combination of obsessive and hysterical personality traits appears to compel the patient to avoid consuming sufficient food to maintain a healthy body weight. Her constant activity despite debilitation exaggerates her unfilled anabolic needs. The illness is characterised by low blood pressure, blue and cold extremities, complete amenorrhoea, obstinate constipation, low metabolic rate, dry and papery skin and a growth of new downy hair on the back and extensor surfaces of the limbs. These and many other facets of the illness have been studied by Dally (1969) in relation to prognosis.

These patients, unlike most hysterical personalities but like obsessionals, tolerate their symptoms well. They are frequently brought for advice by anxious relatives rather than making a spontaneous bid for help themselves. The dominant symptom is an aversion for food in general, often with a special loathing for fats, accompanied by a fear of eating and of becoming obese. Although these patients seem unable to accept the fact that they are harming themselves by failing to eat, they cannot be regarded as deluded; indeed the absence of delusions of guilt, of suffering from gastro-intestinal disease, of being poisoned or other bizarre preoccupations, helps to distinguish anorexia nervosa from the secondary anorexias. The differentiation of Simmond's disease or pituitary cachexia is equally important. In Simmond's disease, no weight is gained despite a normal intake of food and there is an atrophic appearance of the breasts and external genitalia indicating the endocrinological aetiology of the illness. Two physiological tests first used in combination by Fraser and Smith (1941), help to exclude Simmond's disease where clinical doubt exists. In anorexia nervosa the urinary ketosteroids often reach low values, but never reach the extremes seen in pituitary cachexia where they are indeed generally absent. The insulin resistance test also shows significant differences in that patients with anorexia nervosa show normal curves in contrast to the extreme sensitivity of those with pituitary deficiency. Dietary preparation is usually necessary in anorexia nervosa prior to this test.

Although the onset of anorexia nervosa is commonly determined by psychological factors, the disease takes on an autonomous characteristic which is largely unresponsive to a purely psychological approach. It is for this reason that restoration of body weight by physical methods is the first essential in treatment.

Fortunately the days when milk mixtures and stomach tubes were commonly necessary have passed and these methods have been replaced by a technique developed at St. Thomas' by Dally and Sargant using phenothiazine drugs, modified insulin therapy and a normal or high calorie diet (Dally et al., 1958; Dally and Sargant, 1960). In this change, the phenothiazines, particularly chlorpromazine, have contributed most. Before that, even with modified insulin therapy, psychiatrists were often unable to do more for these patients than could be done in a well-nursed ward of a general hospital. Successful treatment depends in the last resort on the efforts of the nursing staff. Patients will adopt every subterfuge to avoid consuming or retaining food. Their persistence in deceit when in hospital—one aspect of their obsessive character—is in striking contrast with their usual reliability and conscientiousness before the illness. Unless they are carefully watched, they will hide food in lockers, vomit out of the window, into bed-pans or hot-water bottles, or simply soak their bed sheets with the milk mixture before helpfully changing these sheets in the usual routine. Their persistence and over-activity will outwit and wear down an uninformed or ununited nursing staff long before an ounce of weight has been gained. It is for this reason that treatment, to be effective, must be given in hospital.

Instruction to the nursing staff must be thorough and encompass all facets of the feeding required and the patients' behaviour patterns. The aim of treatment and its importance in maintaining life should be explained to every nurse likely to come into contact with each patient. The difference between a firm 'caring' approach and bullying is hard to define, but will be appreciated best by example: an anorexic patient who would vomit copiously after each meal was made to take another meal immediately. This was done on successive occasions. She did not vomit the last of these meals, and her vomiting did not recur later in treatment. After this she regained her normal weight rapidly.

The regime is started by putting the patient on absolute bed rest. The patient's resistance to this instruction should be countered immediately by giving an outline of the whole treatment. This means a frank explanation of facts, such as the greater and more rapid weight increase noticed with complete rest, the need to avoid deceptions of any kind, which will only prolong treatment and hospitalisation, and which can best be prevented by complete rest. The need for drugs, which will also be resisted, may be explained as necessary not only to reduce the activity which promotes weight loss, but also to make the programme more acceptable to one who is unaccustomed to resting. Once the patient is on bed rest, chlorpromazine is given in increasing daily doses. The individual variation in sensitivity to chlorpromazine makes it difficult to indicate dose levels, but 300 to 800 mg daily in divided doses are usually sufficient to enable the patient to gain weight on the modified insulin therapy, 20 to 100 units each morning, which is given concurrently.

The modified form of insulin therapy most useful for the treatment of anorexia nervosa consists in preparing the patient beforehand by giving no food after the evening meal. At 7 a.m. next day 5 units of soluble insulin are given intramuscularly, continuous observation being maintained by the nursing staff thereafter. The patient's pulse rate is taken at 10 minute intervals and a watch is kept for hypoglycaemic symptoms and signs. When sweating begins, a large carbohydrate meal is given and its ingestion supervised throughout. Care should be taken to give food before the patient shows slurring of speech or other signs of interference with volition, lest hypoglycaemic coma supervenes. The treatment is given five days a week, and the dose of insulin is raised slowly until the period between the injection and the onset of hypoglycaemia is 30 to 45 minutes. It is rarely necessary to exceed 60 to 80 units. If signs do not develop within one hour of injection, a large meal should be given. Patients should not leave the ward unaccompanied on a treatment day; and they should be warned about symptoms likely to develop if a delayed hypoglycaemic reaction occurs, so that a nurse can be informed immediately. Some patients are extremely sensitive to insulin; and if this is suspected, an insulin sensitivity test should be carried out before commencing treatment.

The chlorpromazine is increased until the patient's resistance lessens markedly. Strict supervision of the ingestion of tablets is, however, still necessary, as patients may conceal them under dentures or delay swallowing them so that they may later dispose of them down the sink. Alternatively chlorpromazine can be given as an elixir and drunk in front of the nurse. In all cases in which chlorpromazine is used, orphenadrine 50 to 150 mg daily, or benzhexol 6 to 10 mg in divided doses, should be given to prevent the distressing symptom of akathisia. In very severe cases the amount of food given should be increased slowly during the first few days to avoid acute gastric dilatation.

The aim of treatment is to enable the patient to reach a body weight near to her highest level ever reached. If this is below the average figure for age and height, the latter should be used as a guide, although not a binding one. It is falsely economical to aim too low and the target should be set at the maximum expectation. To know as soon as possible what is happening to the weight, the patient is weighed daily. Weight is recorded on a chart showing by three horizontal lines the admission weight, the average weight before the illness, and the highest weight reached at any time. The latter, if not the high mark of an earlier pathological obesity, is usually the goal to be reached before discharge from hospital. Once the average weight has been reached the patient is allowed up for increasing periods each day, provided that she does not then start to lose weight. If she does, activity is again curtailed and further bed rest may be required. The dose of chlorpromazine may be reduced gradually as she becomes more ambulant, so that a suitable maintenance dose of 150 to 200 mg daily is reached by the time she leaves hospital.

The increase in weight during this treatment is commonly in the region of 2·5 kg a week. The dramatic expressiveness of these weight charts are most helpful, not only to the patient who can see clearly the rapid progress towards the weight goal, but also to her relatives and to the nursing staff. They can all quickly see the rewarding improvement in physical state, long before the difficulties in management are lessened. Explaining of ideal results of this kind, and showing her the successes made by other patients in a short time, will greatly encourage a newly admitted patient and help her to cooperate.

As weight is gained, the previous personality gradually emerges again, and the patient finds it easier to eat what is required. The initial battle at every meal becomes less as she responds; but vigilance should not be relaxed lest she should take advantage of the increased opportunities to deceive, and then inevitably slip back. Such a failure destroys morale in both patient and staff, and the hard work has to be started again.

Occasionally symptoms of endogenous or physiological depression appear during treatment, such as depressed mood, feelings of hopelessness and even suicidal ideas. Physical treatment is likely to be needed for the depression if there is insomnia, a marked diurnal variation in mood, demeanour or behaviour, and a 'plateau' or reduced incline on the weight chart. In contrast to the initial restless rebellion, a state of apathy gradually supervenes. The reaction may be due to the worsening of an underlying depression, not recognised earlier because of the patient's denials, but a main cause of the anorexic syndrome. It may also be a depressant effect of the large doses of phenothiazines and insulin therapy given over several weeks.

In mild cases this depression can be cleared up by antidepressants. Both tricyclic drugs and monoamine oxidase inhibitors are often helpful. Although particular care must be taken with MAOI drugs to avoid incompatible foods, a satisfactory diet for weight gain can be maintained without difficulty, since a high calorie diet need not contain foodstuff likely to cause hypertensive reactions. If progress is slow, ECT should be given, for this treatment usually corrects the depressive reaction rapidly and avoids prolonging the patient's hospital stay.

Although in principle the patient is induced to eat against her will, her resentment will be less if she is given support and psychotherapy concurrently. The physician's firm approach and adherence to the course of treatment provides a helpful basis for the development of a therapeutic relationship. If psychotherapy is not undertaken, the patient may eat to please while under supervision in hospital, and then often start to starve again after discharge. The underlying psychosomatic factors should be investigated in hospital. Delayed psychosexual development is common; one should go into this carefully, as well as the past and current attitudes of parents. In some cases one may have to treat the parents or the family as a group, to make sure that their contribution in restricting and belittling attitudes is gently dispelled. If one goes into her case along psychological lines, the patient will be much more willing to keep in contact as an out-patient afterwards.

This follow-up is in many ways the most important part of management as patients will find ways of avoiding further medical supervision, and may not only relapse into debilitation, but alternatively may commence to over-eat with as much compulsion as they previously deprived themselves. Regular out-patient supervision is necessary for at least two years, even if the earlier stages are uneventful. There should be appointments at weekly or monthly intervals until one is certain that after a longer gap between visits there will not be a considerable weight loss, which will be irretrievable under out-patient care. Contact should be continued until one is reasonably sure the patient can get on independently. It is unwise to discharge patients before menstruation returns, for relapse is liable to occur. If regular periods have started, the risk of relapse is much smaller and any subsequent recrudescence is usually milder.

Amenorrhœa frequently requires no treatment in those who have responded well. Menstruation will generally return within a year after full weight has been regained, but in a few patients many years elapse before menstruation starts.

The Overweight Patient

In twentieth-century culture the ideal woman is of a slim and willowy body-build. Improved standards of living and better understanding of the principles of a healthy diet, disseminated through television programmes, magazines, newspaper columns and advertising addressed to women, have all tended in this direction.

Although most of the patients who come to the psychiatrist are under- rather than over-weight, not infrequently he has to face the problem of investigating the psychological factors contributing to obesity. If the patient is only moderately overweight, it is his perhaps excessive concern that will have to be dealt with; one of the standard diets will be all that is needed physically, and that can be supervised by his general practitioner. Sometimes, however, patients become grossly overweight, and the failure of ordinary methods of weight reduction leads to psychiatric referral. The compulsive overeating of patients recovered from anorexia nervosa has already been mentioned. Rarely, episodes of overeating and starving are seen in alternation in such individuals, who find a balanced state impossible to maintain. In some tense and obsessive subjects and in anxiety states, increased food intake appears to allay tension or anxiety symptoms, whereas in others fear and anxiety make eating impossible. In otherwise good personalities, this large fluctuation in food intake is transient and related only to periods of particular stress, weight returning to an average level subsequently. In markedly obsessive subjects, and occasionally in inadequate and psychopathic individuals, the compulsive overeating becomes practically an addiction. The patient is unable to follow advice which restricts his intake and adopts subterfuge of a childish kind and apparently without internal moral censure to obtain food when under observation. Probably the commonest underlying reaction to be found in cases of chronic weight increase in previously healthy subjects is an atypical depressive state in which the basic changes of the functional shift are in part in a positive direction. The mood is one of tension, irritability or anxiety and the prominent features are those of a neurosis; the basic regulation of sleep, appetite, weight and libido are altered in a direction opposite to that seen in classical cases of depression. These patients are mostly female and relatively young; and their concern about loss of figure and attractiveness may be rationalised as the sole complaint. Occasionally the same reaction occurs in women taking oral contraceptives.

Although many of these patients respond to antidepressants or

ECT, in extreme cases the former may increase weight further, and both treatments may produce only temporary benefit while the weight remains high. In such instances, drugs of the amphetamine group have often been tried, but tried in vain. They carry the risk that addiction for food may be transferred to the euphoriant drug.

If the patient is physically fit, a reducing regime, otherwise similar to that used for anorexic patients may be started under strict supervision. The principles of hospitalisation, setting a goal, daily weighing, observation of food intake and initial bed rest are the same as for anorexia nervosa. Indeed chlorpromazine is used in the same way, but instead of insulin therapy, a low calorie diet. Carefully administered, this method produces dramatic weight falls far beyond the expected initial fluid loss. The patient's craving for food is lessened once the chlorpromazine dose is sufficiently large, and the low calorie diet is tolerated with equanimity. In obesity complicated by cardiac failure the method should not be used, and chlorpromazine is contraindicated.

Vitamins

As a deficiency disease group, the neuroses and psychoses arising from vitamin lack are the most readily reversible. They provide some of the most gratifying responses to purely physical treatments. In fact, empirical treatment for clinical psychiatric deficiency states has become so effective that interest and research have not kept pace. In vitamin deficiency psychological symptoms often precede obvious physical signs because the cerebral neurones, being dependent upon vitamins constituting their complex metabolic enzyme systems, are probably the most sensitive indicators. Although gross evidence of vitamin deficiency can be readily recognised and treated, an appreciation of the principles involved in the physiology of brain function enables the physician not only to detect incipient and minor examples, but to prevent the development of deficiency states and iatrogenic syndromes during physical treatment for psychiatric disorder and indeed in general medicine.

Although the influence on cerebral functions of all the known vitamins is not yet clear, lack of the members of the vitamin B complex is known to produce the majority of the most severe deficiency states seen in practice. It is for this reason that aneurine and nicotinamide have been termed the 'psychiatric vitamins'. In the following section the effects of each of the known vitamins will be considered in turn.

Lack of vitamin A and D may cause night terrors in children. Lack of vitamin A is related to night blindness. The desirable dose of vitamin A is 5000 international units a day, and this amount should not as a rule be exceeded. Little or nothing is known of the psychological effects of vitamin C deficiency. Persons of stable constitution can develop scurvy unaccompanied by psychological symptoms. The neurotically predisposed, on the other hand, may show lassitude, loss of appetite and fatigue, though it may be that these symptoms are dependent on sub-clinical deficiencies of other vitamins. If vitamin C deficiency is suspected, saturation of the body can usually be attained by giving 500 mg of ascorbic acid daily for two or three days followed by a maintenance dose of 100 mg daily.

From the point of view of the severity of the mental symptoms that may be caused by their deficiency, the vitamins of the B group are by far the most important. This group provides enzymes essential for normal cerebral neurone function, being associated with the metabolism of carbohydrate. Deficiency leads to neurotic and psychotic changes. It is a matter of supply and demand, the supply being dependent on intake, absorption and storage, and the demand depending on body weight, the amount of carbohydrate in the diet, the activity of the individual and the metabolic rate. The normal intake and absorption, sufficient for ordinary needs, may be inadequate when the metabolic rate is raised in hyperpyrexia or thyrotoxicosis. The reduced intake of the alcoholic may be adequate whilst sufficient alcohol is taken to lower the metabolic rate of the cerebral neurones *pari passu*, but once alcohol is withdrawn, psychological symptoms determined by vitamin deficiency may quickly appear. Vitamin deficiency therefore should be suspected as the basis for any mental reactions occurring in the setting of an increase in cerebral metabolic rate, and reduced absorption or storage of vitamins. Usually the deficiency is not pure, but involves several members of the B complex. A population exposed to the same dietary lack shows a spectrum of clinical pictures rather than a single pathological syndrome. Only a third of cases of fully developed pellagra show evidence of severe mental disturbance. The chronic manifestations depend on the spectrum of deficiency of members of the B complex, the parts of the nervous system affected dominantly, and on the patient's constitution and previous personality.

Apart from the more common examples of pellagra and beri-beri in impoverished populations, both in peace and in war, vitamin deficiency from dietary causes may occur in elderly patients living alone who do not provide themselves with adequate meals. This is more likely to occur if they get depressed or begin to dement. Under these circumstances a pyrexia with consequent increase in metabolism and vitamin need will bring on suddenly the symptom of vitamin lack. In alcoholics, reduced intake and storage may lead to chronic deficiency which may become acute when the individual stops eating but continues to take large quantities of alcohol, whose high calorie content requires large amounts of vitamin B. Withdrawal of alcohol may also precipitate acute deficiency symptoms. Even in healthy individuals, endogenous depression may lead to chronic deficiency because of refusal of food, poor intake or poor absorption. Unsupervised self-imposed diets, and fads may produce a similar state.

In the general medical wards particular care is required to avoid vitamin deficiency when feeding the unconscious patient, in all parenteral feeding and when any diet is imposed. Cases of hyperpyrexia, thyrotoxicosis, recovering myxœdema and all postoperative subjects are potentially vitamin B deficient. A certain but unknown quantity of vitamin B is synthesised in the gut by bacteria; but administration of antibiotics may destroy these and precipitate acute deficiency in those patients whose minimal supplies enabled them to function adequately before. In psychiatric treatment, attention to vitamin intake is essential during and after the induction of continuous narcosis, in the treatment of anorexia nervosa and during the treatment of alcoholism by aversion therapy. Occasionally, additional vitamins are required when using certain antidepressant drugs. It must be stressed that the named vitamin B deficiency diseases are extremes of the range of lack of thiamine (B_1) and nicotinic acid (Niacin) respectively. Many of the symptoms attributed to these illnesses overlap, and it is safer, from the therapeutic point of view, to regard any vitamin B deficiency as involving both, and commonly riboflavin as well.

CHRONIC DEFICIENCY

This is dependent on reduced intake of vitamin B over a long period, and it is seen in geographical areas in which specific food shortages are likely. In more fortunate societies, where a balanced diet is generally within reach, chronic shortage is likely to be associated with special factors, such as alcoholism, fever, senility and psychosis.

The clinical state depends on the degree of deficiency and the length of time it prevails. The early symptoms resemble the neurasthenic picture which is to be distinguished from atypical depression (pp. 42 to 44); and later, as the illness develops, multiple symptoms mimic other psychiatric syndromes. In predominant thiamine (aneurine, B_1) deficiency, anorexia, insomnia, headache, depression, suicidal ideas, irritability, sighing, nausea, constipation and abdominal discomfort may be seen. Efficiency at work falls; there is some loss of memory for recent events and unreality feelings may exist throughout. Numbness of the hands and feet and dysmenorrhœa may occur. If cardiac incompetence and/or peripheral neuritis (polyneuritis) accompany these symptoms of cerebral beriberi, the diagnosis is clear; but in doubtful cases a therapeutic trial with vitamins should be undertaken. Thiamine is a co-enzyme involved in the breakdown of pyruvic acid. In deficiency states, the serum pyruvate level is raised and estimation of this in chronic conditions will confirm the diagnosis.

Nicotinic acid is co-enzyme 1 concerned in the breakdown of lactic acid to aceto-acetic acid. In chronic nicotinic acid deficiency a similar and overlapping constellation of symptoms is seen. Feelings of fatigue, depression, difficulty in concentration, restlessness, forgetfulness, anorexia, apprehension, vertigo, paræsthesiæ and palpitations may occur in the pre-pellagrous stage, remitting and recurring over long periods. In most long-standing conditions other features of pellagra will be evident, glossitis being well developed and accompanied by cheilosis. The characteristic skin eruption is initially erythematous and affects parts of the body exposed to sunlight. Lesions of the spinal cord similar to those of subacute combined degeneration may develop.

Acute vitamin B deficiency states may occur when marginal deficiency has existed for some time, but it may also be precipitated in previously healthy subjects when demands are greatly increased. Sydenstricker and Cleckley (1941) have reported confusion and lethargy or excitement from this cause after such varied conditions as hemiplegia, peptic ulcer, prostatectomy, fractured femur and pneumonia. All their patients did well with nicotinic acid therapy. The onset of mental disorder may be abrupt, or preceded by a mild neurasthenic picture. The physical signs of pellagra are nearly always absent, but there may be a characteristic glossitis. Delirium, hallucinations, confused behaviour, often with partial insight, are seen. In other patients a condition resembling uraemia may occur, and there may be clouding of consciousness, increasing drowsiness and coma without any rise in the blood urea. The acute clinical picture is delirium tremens with clouding of consciousness, hallucinations, illusions, confusion, disorientation, tremor and mood changes. The affective response and behaviour will depend on the patient's previous personality; whereas many are fearful, even terrified by their psychotic experiences, others may be amused by them and view them objectively although without insight. Despite the alarming nature of the symptoms, this state is reversible if there has been no chronic deficiency and if treatment is begun early.

Vitamin deficiency may be a factor in a confusional state primarily determined by other causes. Thus it may arise during a course of continuous narcosis, if insufficient attention has been paid to vitamin intake, when other foods have been forced on the patient; or if large quantities of glucose saline infusions have been given without adequate vitamin B cover. It may be a part factor in confusional states with a toxic cause, including delirium tremens. Agitated, exhausted and under-nourished patients, who start to eat ravenously after ECT or leucotomy, may temporarily need additional vitamin cover for their increased carbohydrate intake. In older people suffering from bromide or barbitone intoxication or senile confusional states with dehydration, the intravenous administration of large amounts of fluids and salines may be life-saving; but in every case they should be accompanied by adequate amounts of vitamin B, to prevent a depletion of reserves below the danger point.

Wernicke's syndrome, an encephalitis, is the result of capillary lesions in the grey matter of the brain stem and structures bordering the third and fourth ventricles. It is associated with dominant thiamine (B_1) deficiency in alcoholism, hyperemesis gravidarum, pernicious anæmia and gastric carcinoma. The condition shows itself in clouding of consciousness, confabulation and even coma; the cause is at once recognised from the co-existing ophthalmoplegia. Korsakoff's psychosis, the result of irreparable damage to the cerebrum, is associated with hæmorrhages in the mammillary bodies. It may appear insidiously or during the subsidence of delirium tremens and is commoner in mid-life and in females. It is characterised by amnesia, disorientation for time and place, confabulation; and is associated with peripheral neuropathy, cog-wheel rigidity and grasping and sucking reflexes. The structural and permanent changes in the nervous system in both Wernicke's encephalopathy and Korsakoff's psychosis indicate the need for immediate treatment with vitamins to prevent further damage and to allow such recovery of cerebral tissue as is still possible. The differential diagnosis may be difficult, especially in the disturbed mental states of elderly people; and similarities may be presented to frontal lobe tumours, G.P.I., vascular brain disease, brain abscess and bromide intoxication. The last condition is, of course, easily excluded by an estimation of the blood bromides. Where there is any doubt in the physician's mind, energetic treatment must be begun without delay. Vitamin therapy can do no harm, even though it may prove to have been unnecessary. Death may occur in a high proportion of patients showing these acute symptoms, unless nicotinic acid is given immediately; and if the treatment is not adequate and the state is allowed to continue too long, there is the risk of permanent mental impairment.

Although psychological symptoms of vitamin B_{12} deficiency usually occur in the presence of readily detectable macrocytic anæmia, they may occur before the anæmia is recognisable (Smith, 1960). In these cases the only positive finding, apart from mental changes, may be abnormalities in the EEG. Neurasthenic symptoms, headache and malaise may appear at this stage, and call for early investigation and treatment. Vitamin B_{12} in large doses parenterally is also the treatment for depression accompanying macrocytic anæmia or subacute combined degeneration. This vitamin has also been found helpful in restoring appetite in patients when no vitamin B_{12} deficiency has been found.

Early treatment is essential in any vitamin-deficient state. Some delay is inevitable in chronic cases; but since functional changes in the form of psychological reactions precede organic damage full recovery is possible, if only treatment is early and energetic. Vitamin B deficiency should always be regarded as multiple, and it is wise to treat all syndromes by giving a combination of all members of the vitamin B group, thiamine (B_1) and nicotinic acid (Niacin) being of prime importance.

If possible the vitamins should be given parenterally. Not only is the oral route technically difficult in the comatose, restless or psychotic patient, but the poor absorption from the gut in many cases in which vitamin deficiency is likely to occur, leads to unjustifiable delay. The intravenous route is best, although the intramuscular may be substituted. 2 to 6 mg (500–1500 I.U.) of thiamine and 400 to 600 mg of nicotinic acid should be given daily in divided doses, the latter in the form of the amide to avoid distress and hypotension from vasodilation. This dose should continue for 72 hours unless improvement has already been satisfactory, after which the dose should be halved and continued until the condition has remitted or reached a stationary level. Preparations made up in small volume are available, one or two injections daily being sufficient to supply all the important vitamins proportionately.

If no parenteral preparation is available, 10 to 50 mg of thiamine and up to 1000 mg of nicotinamide may be given by mouth during 24 hours; these doses can be lowered after three days and halved for maintenance purposes later.

Whether parenteral or oral route is used, it is necessary to add dextrose and the patient's diet should be enriched as soon as practicable, to supplement supplies.

Neurological complications are uncommon effects of the anti-depressant drugs, but flaccidity, paræsthesiæ, twitching, neuralgia and even convulsions have been reported. A much more common side effect is œdema of the ankles, and this and the above neurological changes have been ascribed to vitamin B deficit. In animal studies much more marked toxic effects have been found when monoamine oxidase inhibitors have been given with a pyriodoxine deficient diet. In practice it is wise to give pyridoxine hydrochloride (vitamin B6) in doses up to 50 mg daily if neurological side-effects develop.

Endocrines

In recent years the role of the endocrine system in the organisation of both bodily and psychological defence has been clarified. We no longer believe that the disturbance of one or other endocrine gland could be a primary cause of a functional neurosis or psychosis. But we recognise the role of the endocrines in maintaining health, for their wide use in the treatment of endocrine disorders, in gynaecology, obstetrics, in general medicine and for contraception has produced new problems in the psychiatric field.

The psychological effects of endocrine disturbance in adults are characterised by wide variation in kind and degree. While many are unaffected, the mental disturbances that may follow myxœdema or pituitary disease, the depressive manifestations that accompany the menopause, the mental lassitude of the sufferer from Addison's disease, the euphoria or the psychotic reactions sometimes precipitated by ovariectomy, or the therapeutic use of corticosteroids, show broad patterns. The reaction in such patients is determined not only by their vulnerability to the stressful effect of endocrine change, but as in functional psychiatric disorders, it is coloured by the constitution and personality. A general tendency in myxoedematous states to the development of confusional symptoms goes with neurasthenic pictures and states of depression and anxiety, with or without a paranoid aspect. The specific cause produces in the psychological field only non-specific changes, and diagnosis has to be based on the physical findings.

In more subtle form, a similar variety of change is shown in the reactions of women at times of marked endocrine activity. Many patterns are seen premenstrually, postpartum and at the menopause. So it is that depressive reactions are much commoner in women; that the time of greatest disparity in incidence between the sexes is during the child-bearing period of life; and that the puerperium and the menopausal years are associated with a relatively raised incidence.

Recent investigations have led to contrasting results in the functional psychoses. Whereas evidence for endocrine changes in schizophrenia has so far been sought in vain, in depression there are raised plasma cortisol levels (Gibbons and McHugh, 1962), and the residual sodium is usually raised (Coppen and Shaw, 1963; Coppen, 1965).

Perhaps the most useful way to bring together our knowledge of endocrine changes and psychological effects is to think in terms of central regulation by homeostatic mechanisms. It seems that mood and outlook, and endocrine activity, are both monitored and regulated by the hypothalamus; and that this collection of nuclei is responsible for both physiological defence and the level of psychological adjustment. It seems likely that changes in one group of nuclei affect others, and that peripheral endocrine disturbance monitored by the hypothalamus causes changes in the homeostatic levels maintained for its other functions. The subsequent efferent effects of, say, alteration in mood or sleep pattern would then be coloured by the individual's constitution, and depend on the nature of the pathway, clinical effects on thought, feeling and behaviour, being a synthesis determined by the personality.

Although no less important, the psychological manifestations of endocrine disorder are secondary; for the full investigation and treatment of the primary organic illness collaboration with an endocrinologist is essential. Nevertheless, treatment of severe psychological disorder should not be delayed until endocrine treatment has been completed. Once normal endocrine function has been restored, existing stress will have less effect; but as with psychological precipitation, an illness which began during the endocrine disturbance may become autonomous. It must be remembered also that with the appearance of symptoms the process of conditioning begins, and if physical readjustment takes too long, they may become fixed, and persist when the endocrine balance has been restored.

The most urgent application of hormones in psychological disorder is required in cretinism. The gross retardation consequent on failure to promote metabolism prevents the normal development of brain function and maturation to such a degree that any delay in administering thyroid lowers the maximum intellectual and emotional potential even if the deficiency is made good later. The condition is usually present at birth and the importance of early recognition is obvious. Once recognised, the condition cannot be treated too soon.

The parents of a cretin should know that continuous dosage throughout life is essential and that it may be necessary to increase a dose, that has long kept a child or adult stable, in the event of pyrexia or pregnancy. Immense care is necessary if such individuals are away from home or move to come under the care of medical men unfamiliar with the full history of their condition. Occasionally the essential prescription is withheld by an incredulous doctor faced with an individual healthy in every respect, but the sad effect of such a mistake cannot be made good.

Myxœdema may present with symptoms of lethargy, excessive fatigue, mental retardation, depression and paranoid attitudes or delusions. The use of thyroxine is required and, as in cretinism, it is better controlled by regular independent examinations by a general physician. Restoration of the normal metabolic rate does not always abolish the psychological symptoms, and persisting depressive or hypochondriacal symptoms must then be treated by other measures such as ECT. Thyroid deficiency may be aggravated by ECT. We have seen this occur in one patient who had previously had a subtotal thyroidectomy; ECT given for a depressive state, upset the precarious balance and caused confusional symptoms and the appearance of a frank myxoedema, subsequently corrected by giving thyroxine.

There are many other conditions met with in ordinary psychiatric practice where collaboration with an endocrinologist can be of great help. Functional hypoglycaemias are characterised by psychiatric as well as physical symptoms. They are often missed in the standard glucose tolerance test unless the test is continued for four hours instead of the usual two. The physiological anomaly and the symptoms which result from it can be corrected by more frequent meals, or by a high fat and protein diet. In the less severe cases of spontaneous hypoglycaemic attacks from pancreatic insulinomata, psychological symptoms are usually the prominent feature (Todd *et al.*, 1962).

At the present time corticosteroids have no primary place in the treatment of functional neuroses or psychoses. Severe depressions, confusional states and schizophrenic symptoms are occasionally observed when these hormones are given for general medical conditions. Such complications call for immediate psychiatric treatment. Whereas a symptomatic psychosis or depression so caused may respond dramatically to ECT, and paranoid symptoms to ECT and phenothiazines, the question of withdrawal of corticosteroids must always be considered. This is a complex matter, for in certain cases withdrawal carries a high risk of recrudescence of life-threatening physical disease; in others reduction can be implemented only gradually and not without hazard. The total picture must always be carefully weighed in consultation with the general physician treating the patient. In this context the *post hoc ergo propter hoc* fallacy must be borne in mind. Depression and schizophrenia occur often enough in patients not receiving corticosteroids, and symptomatic psychoses are not uncommon in patients with severe organic disease. It is well not to assume that corticosteroids are responsible for psychological changes until other common causes such as vitamin B complex deficiency, virus infections and organic brain disorder have been excluded.

SEX HORMONES

Among the hormones most used in the past in the attempt to alleviate every type of mental disturbance are those associated with sexual function; and there is one large group of patients who greatly benefit from such endocrinological treatment. For women who show psychological changes during the last week or 10 days of the menstrual cycle, progesterone and its derivatives are of particular value. The commonest reaction is simple premenstrual tension, and both the phenomena and treatment have been carefully investigated by Katharina Dalton (1959, 1960, 1961, 1964). The patient complains chiefly of tension, feelings of wanting to scream, irritability, headache and increased sensitivity to noise for 2 to 10 days prior to the onset of menstruation. Usually the intensity of these symptoms increases as the onset of menstruation approaches, but subsides once the flow starts. The severity of mental disturbance is not necessarily related to manifestations of a bodily kind such as oedema of the legs, swelling of the neck, breasts or abdomen, but the neurotic symptoms may vary markedly over a short time in the same individual. Such premenstrual changes may appear for the first time several months before the onset of a clinical episode of depression; and the severity of any mental disturbance which develops independently, e.g. schizophrenia, may be greatly modified during the premenstrual phase. In otherwise healthy subjects the premenstrual psychological symptoms may take the form of depression rather than tension, and rarely this may appear as a classical depressive syndrome. An increase in irresponsible behaviour consequent upon increased tension, impaired judgement and impulsive acts may be seen at this time.

Acute schizophrenic episodes in women appear to be more common in the premenstrual phase than at other times in the menstrual cycle. Flare-up of a pre-existing depression, schizo-affective disorder, or schizophrenic illness in women without obvious cause, such as cessation of phenothiazine drugs, is often found during the week before menstruation. The exacerbation of hysterical illnesses, obsessional neuroses, chronic anxiety, unreality or tension states is well known.

It seems likely also that in a number of cases of recurrent depression the onset of individual depressive episodes occurs during the premenstrual phase. In such instances there is usually a history of premenstrual depression even during long free intervals. An unusual manifestation of this periodic disturbance is seen in a few women after hysterectomy, when detection depends on careful observation of the timing of the psychological disturbance. It also occurs rarely after the menopause.

In all these circumstances, recognition of the periodic nature of the symptoms or their exacerbation may enable the physician to reduce their effect by anticipatory administration of drugs. Such an association may be reported only by observant and intelligent patients after a period of supervision; more commonly, the patient (or relative) has already noticed the relationship but needs to be asked about it to produce what has been regarded by them as coincidental or too far-fetched to be medically acceptable. If any doubt exists the patient (or relative) should be given a menstrual chart on which to record accurately each day of the menstrual cycle, the menstrual period and the manifestations of changed psychological state or behaviour causing concern. A number of patients recognise the important relationship only after this has been done. If depression and premenstrual tension co-exist, the depression should be treated first, and if necessary the premenstrual symptoms treated subsequently.

The treatment of premenstrual symptoms may be approached in a number of ways. The most satisfactory method is to give progesterone by intramuscular injection for 10 days preceeding menstruation. When marked evidence of water retention accompanies premenstrual symptoms, it may be preferable to use a diuretic for 10 days before each period. These substances have the advantage that they rarely affect the menstrual rhythm.

Monoamine oxidase inhibitors such as phenelzine or isocarboxacid combined with Librium also are effective in treating premenstrual tension and depression. Phenelzine 15 mg with 5 to 10 mg of chlordiazepoxide may be given throughout the cycle, the dose of the former being raised to 30 to 45 mg and of the latter to 20 to 30 mg for 10 to 14 days premenstrually. There is no need to stop these drugs before menstruation commences.

Progesterone is often effective in mild early puerperal depressions. Such depressions while largely subclinical may take on a chronic course and become associated with premenstrual tension for the first time. In such chronic mild depressions the chief complaints are exhaustion and fatigue, lessened affection for the children, irritability, tension and disinterestedness, lack of libido dating from the confinement, and a vague feeling of frustration commonly rationalised as due to the strain of their children's behaviour.

Since oral contraceptives have been widely adopted, the psychological effects of regular periodic use of combinations of female hormones have been much studied. The benefits women have received from these methods of contraception are undoubtedly great, and do not need to be stressed. Only the pathological psychological effects are considered here. Lewis and Hoghughi (1969) and Herzberg and colleagues (1970) have shown that between 5 and 10 per cent of women may develop depressive reactions apparently due to the taking of oral contraceptives. These depressions are often of the atypical variety and symptoms include sleep disturbance, irritability, tiredness, tension, appetite and weight changes, and even loss of libido. The reaction often develops insidiously, so that the association with the oral contraceptive is unrecognised and the woman does not appreciate the change in personality until it is marked and threatens to disrupt her life. Loss of libido may be so complete that sexual advances are totally refused; yet the patient resists withdrawal of the 'pill', which has now lost its purpose. In general, in any case in which adverse personality changes, physiological disturbances or pathological psychological changes are linked in time with the use of an oral contraceptive, it is wise to withdraw the latter as a therapeutic trial.

It must be remembered that withdrawal of the hormones once a true depressive illness has developed will not by itself necessarily cause the illness to resolve. If it does not, the depression must then be treated. Likewise, if a patient who is taking an oral contraceptive has a depressive illness or anxiety state and does not respond to appropriate treatment, or relapses as soon as treatment is discontinued, it is best to withdraw the 'pill' until the illness has resolved.

Careful consideration should be given before resuming an oral contraceptive after recovery. Women who have suffered from a depressive illness are more likely than averagely to develop a depressive reaction while taking an oral contraceptive; and if a satisfactory alternative can be found, the risks are far less. If she already has the family she wants, and the risks of further pregnancy are great, the operation of sterilization is justified. Much has been written about the relative psychological effects of oral contraceptives containing more or less oestrogen or progesterone. The broader biological effects should be borne in mind, for the central disturbance associated with psychological changes may be a result of regular rhythmic alteration of endocrine levels, rather than to the actual levels of either progesterone or oestrogen.

Indications for the empirical use of hormones in the treatment of psychiatric disorders are few. Many involutional depressions are not related to menstrual abnormality; they either precede the menopause by some years, or come after it, there is no evidence that oestrogen is effective, or that with it the recovery rate is better than the spontaneous remission rate. Certainly ECT and antidepressant drugs have been very much more effective.

However, there are situations in which such treatment has not yet been superceded. Gjessing's syndrome, consisting of recurrent episodes of catatonic excitement or stupor with an associated disturbance of nitrogen metabolism, has been successfully treated by giving large doses of thyroid during the attack. Continuous administration of the hormone may also prevent or minimise future attacks. If the onset of attacks can be predicted, a small maintenance dose of thyroid can be used during the interval of freedom, this dose being increased greatly at least three weeks before the earliest expected onset of the next illness. Alternatively, rapidly acting tri-iodothyronine or l-thyroxine-sodium may be given just before or even during a catatonic episode. Attacks can often be further minimised by adding a tricyclic antidepressant or by giving phenothiazine derivatives, such as chlorpromazine.

In the past androgens were often used in the treatment of impotence in the absence of testicular deficiency. There is, however, no evidence that male sex hormone is efficacious in functional impotence or in restoring loss of sexual drive. Androgens sometimes improve the physical state with increase in weight and accompanying feeling of well-being, but they may inhibit the activity of the anterior lobe of the pituitary, and spermatogenesis can be reduced temporarily when they are given. In almost all cases of functional impotence, treatment of an associated functional neurosis or depression or investigation of the underlying psychological problems is much more likely to be helpful than the use of hormones.

One physical treatment for impotence is occasionally useful. Various forms of penile splints are available, and these are of particular value when impotence is partial (Loewenstein, 1947). The splint by supporting the penis and to some extent restricting the venous flow, enables the patient to complete the sexual act when partial erection and difficulty in insertion would otherwise lead to failure. While their use is limited, they provide help in circumstances for which psychotherapy and drugs are of no direct practical value; and in many instances the patient is able to continue normally without the apparatus once confidence is restored and 'impotence anxiety' allayed.

We know that some homosexuality is constitutional in origin, and that many male homosexuals are feminine in manner and build; but few can yet be treated by systems of endocrine replacement. The best that can be done is to examine physically for signs of endocrine disorder, carry out hormone assays, and correct deficiencies where possible. For the rest, treatment must proceed along psychological and environmental lines. Much homosexual activity is facultative in nature, even where the environment includes adequate numbers and varieties of persons of both sexes, and the relative importance of constitutional and psychological causative factors has to be investigated. Homosexual activity may appear for the first time in conditions of mental anxiety, fatigue and exhaustion, and recede again on remedy of the causes. Reinforcing the powers of the individual to suppress and repress undesirable instinctual impulses may be as effective and far quicker than psychological exploration and explanation.

Stilboestrol is useful in reducing libido in the treatment of sexual abnormalities of the male. Given in sufficient doses, it markedly diminishes the libido, whether it is normal, inverse or perverse. Up to 15 mg a day may have to be given to some patients before the libido is temporarily abolished, while in others much smaller doses are enough. When the drug is discontinued, libido usually returns quite rapidly; but if it is continued for long the theoretical risk of causing infertility must be borne in mind. However, it is unlikely that stilboestrol will be indicated unless equally great issues are at stake. Lowered fertility is perhaps a small price to pay to avoid anti-social behaviour and prison sentences, or complete sexual incapacity, or final break-up of an otherwise happy marriage.

Aggressive psychopaths and sexual psychopaths of other kinds often suffer under the inordinateness of their sexual appetites. The continual state of tension in which they live, the need to seek the sexual object again immediately when the urge has just been satisfied, the guilt associated with temporary satisfaction or the vain attempts to keep sexual needs under control, may all be diminished or abolished if the libido itself is brought down to a low level.

It is best to start with small doses of 2 to 5 mg daily and increase this fairly rapidly until it proves sufficient. Swelling and induration of the nipples may occur, but usually disappear again when the dose is lowered. If there is nausea, other oestrogens may be substituted for stilboestrol. After two months, one should consider lowering the dose or interrupting therapy; but longer courses can be given provided that the implications and the risks are fully appreciated by the patient and the doctor.

There are occasions when hormones should not be used in the mentally ill. Attempts to induce ovulation and menstruation in patients with depressive illnesses are unlikely to initiate a regular menstrual cycle, while the illness continues. After treatment for the depression menstruation often begins spontaneously, provided the patient is not under weight. One should not use stilboestrol even to restart menstruation after recovery, as this often brings the depression back again. Stilboestrol given during a puerperal depression occasionally evokes a change from the mild affective symptoms to those of severe classical depressive states. Stilboestrol is also generally contra-indicated when insulin is given, as sensitivity to insulin appears to be unpredictably increased in some subjects, and collapse is more common. Only with the greatest caution should one ever use androgens to increase libido in elderly people, particularly women. Occasionally a surge of libido is followed by continued insatiably heightened sexual feeling, leading to intractable pruritus and perhaps delusions of influence and guilt.

Although dietary, vitamin and endocrine considerations often arise in isolation, an exceptional illustration of the influence of all three in one unfortunate patient may help to show the rewarding results which can be reached if the possibility of these disorders are borne in mind.

A woman in her mid-thirties had been in large psychiatric hospitals periodically for psychotic episodes, in which she would impulsively thrust her arm through a window, or exhibit sudden physical violence suggestive of hallucinatory experience. Before the illness began she had been a well adjusted mildly extroverted person, happily married and engaged in normal social life. When she finally came to be investigated, she was 19 kg below her previous heaviest weight. She was given combined antidepressant drugs and ECT in narcosis, but during this treatment, despite normal oral intake of vitamins, she developed a raw beef tongue and was found to be vitamin B deficient.

Further investigation showed that the absorption for vitamin B in the gut was impaired and this was attributed to earlier tropical illness. The vitamin deficiency was controlled to begin with by intravenous vitamin injections, and later by the regular use of oral vitamins.

Attempts were then made to increase her weight by giving chlorpromazine and insulin; but although she made good progress for three weeks, psychotic behaviour developed suddenly. This outburst occurred 25 days after the previous violent episode; and careful study of the time relationship showed that similar exacerbations had been at intervals of about one month. As hysterectomy had been performed, a menstrual chart could not be drawn, but on the assumption that this was a premenstrual syndrome equivalent, progesterone was given regularly in the 'ghost' premenstrual phase. After regaining two stones in weight she continued to do well and, although it has been necessary to give progesterone, vitamin B complex and small doses of antidepressants regularly, the patient has been virtually symptom-free for six years.

CHAPTER EIGHT

Drug Treatment in Childhood and Early Adolescence

by EVA FROMMER

The first systematic descriptions of psychiatric illnesses in childhood by clinicians in the last century linked them with conditions that were also known to occur in psychiatrically ill adults. (Maudsley, 1863; Emminghaus, 1887). At that time, no effective physical treatments were available; and as paediatrics developed as a separate speciality, few clinicians continued to take a separate interest in the psychiatric disorders of childhood. However, Homberger (1926) published a detailed and highly sophisticated account of child psychiatric disorders and the clinical tradition has been developing increasingly in Europe since his time. A different impulse came into child psychiatry from the United States following the First World War with the start of the Child Guidance movement. This was based on the ideals of preventive and educational social work, and the psychiatrist took part in this as a team member, not necessarily as a clinician. But he was the person responsible for establishing the diagnosis in a disturbed child and his family, and he then either undertook psychotherapy or supervised this for the patient. He was also responsible for various administrative decisions about the child, e.g. with regard to school placement.

Psychoanalytic theories became more intimately incorporated in this approach to the management of psychiatrically ill children during and after the Second World War; and interest in treatment centred for a while almost exclusively on the problems of relationships between mothers and children. Recently, this situation has altered and new developments are taking place in child psychiatry (Korenyi and Whittier, 1967). Since the advent of the modern psychotropic drugs, simple and effective treatments have been placed in the clinician's hands. It has become vital to recognise the children whose illness might benefit from them; and it has again become important to be able to recognise the common patterns of mental illness in children and to realise their similarities to adult affective and schizoaffective disorders (Frommer, 1968).

This chapter deals with the drugs which can be used with children; and it is written on the basis of experience of those psychiatric illnesses of childhood that have responded satisfactorily to medical treatment.

It is essential to remember two aspects of clinical diagnosis which are peculiar to child psychiatry. The first concerns the child who is brought for treatment. It is very important that thorough physical investigations are carried out in any children who develop psychological symptoms which cannot readily be explained as reactions to identifiable emotional traumata. It is common for physical illnesses in childhood to be accompanied by symptoms of depression or emotional disturbance. Variations in the level of attention or even consciousness also occur. For instance, a child of 7, who was small for her age, was referred to a psychiatrist because the doctor thought that her moodiness, fluctuating attention and listlessness were due to depression. However, it soon became clear that antidepressant treatment was having no effect. Meanwhile, concurrent investigations into her general health brought to light a large primary pulmonary TB focus. Another child, a boy, developed troublesome behaviour while under observation as an in-patient, which was clearly out of character. He was found to have an intracranial tumour.

Many children, who in fact are suffering from a psychiatric illness, complain in the first place of a physical pain. Most often this is abdominal; sometimes it is a headache, or some other physical symptom. This can lead to lengthy negative physical investigation for an answer which persistently eludes one, with increasing anxiety and distress to the child and his parents. Operative procedures may even be undertaken without relief of the physical symptoms, if these are not recognised as part of an emotional illness.

The second aspect concerns the families of children who are psychiatrically ill. There may be important reasons within the family setting which determine why a particular disturbed child is brought for help to a psychiatrist. Several studies have shown (Gath, 1968; Ryle et al., 1965; Shepherd et al., 1966) that there are many psychiatrically ill children in the population, yet only some are brought to a doctor for help. The determining factor in many cases seems to be less the child's need for skilled help or its availability, than the parents' decision that action should be taken. This decision is often made by parents who are themselves anxious and feel unable to cope. It has certainly been our experience that a high proportion of the parents, notably of the mothers, are themselves psychiatrically ill at the time that the child is brought for help. Most suffer from depressive illnesses. Many of the children's depressions seem to respond to drugs of the same group that helps their parents (Pare *et al*, 1962). Psychiatric illness may also be found in one or more siblings. For these reasons, as well as the further management of the case, a full history of the whole family is desirable in addition to details of the medical history and symptoms of the child himself.

Sedatives

The Phenothiazine Derivatives*

CHLORPROMAZINE (Largactil). This drug is particularly useful in the treatment of children who are troubled by hallucinations. These may occur in quite young psychotic children, who show by their behaviour that they are being distracted and disturbed in their activities by auditory or visual experiences. They may hold their ears intermittently, or cower in a corner, shouting to something invisible to others to go away. For young children from age 4, the syrup has been used, starting with 5 mg and increasing the dose until the symptoms were controlled without inducing undue drowsiness. Sometimes, it is possible to distribute the drug so that the bulk is given at bedtime with only one or two small maintenance doses during the day. Sometimes the doses must be evenly spread out to maintain control.

Children from age 10 to 11 may develop a schizophrenic illness as they enter puberty. This can take the form of a sudden explosive breakdown, with hallucinations affecting any of the senses but commonly vision and hearing. There is accompanying thought disorder, incongruity of affect and paranoid ideas. Sometimes the onset may be slow and insidious. The illness may follow an earlier phobic or depressive episode or a juvenile obsessional illness. Occasionally, it follows an earlier state of neurotic withdrawal or of severe anxiety. The symptoms of illness may appear more fleetingly in children than in adults, and a very careful account must be elicited from them and their parents. The child may have an accompanying suicidal depression and should, where possible, be treated as an in-patient. Unfortunately, this is often not feasible. If the family can be adequately supported, it may be possible to succeed with outpatient treatment.

---

* The doses in the following section represent those commonly used in this clinic. Other doses may be calculated with the aid of a paediatric prescriber (Catzel, 1966).

The treatment of this illness in an adolescent is similar to adults. However, it must be remembered that there is a very wide variation in tolerance of the psychotropic drugs in adolescents so that one may be equally surprised by the small amounts of drugs required to control the illness in some and the relatively very large doses that are needed and tolerated by others.

Chlorpromazine up to adult doses may be needed. If there is accompanying depression, one of the tricyclic antidepressants should be added. If the patient becomes too drowsy on the amount of chlorpromazine needed to control his illness, the maximum tolerated dose can be given at night and a less sedating phenothiazine, e.g. trifluoperazine added as a supplement by day. If high doses are being used, an anti-Parkinsonian drug should be added to control side effects.

If depression is severe, ECT may be needed. Its use must be determined by the depth of illness and failure to respond to other treatment. Maintenance ECTs may continue to be needed for some time. One patient aged 14 needed more than 25 treatments in all before recovery became established.

Chlorpromazine also helps patients with anorexia nervosa as described in another section of this book.

Some overactive children (Weiss *et al.*, 1968) improve when they are treated with chlorpromazine, though it may not help those with associated brain-damage. If the child improves, the dose is determined by the clinical response, but the drug should not be pushed to toxic levels in the hope that a response might occur.

Care is needed when giving phenothiazines to brain-damaged children. Occasionally very severe Parkinsonian effects appear following a very small dose.

Chlorpromazine also helps some neurotic children who are distracted from their school work and their play by severe chronic anxieties. They often have sleep problems but are not depressed. These are rare cases. They may soil or wet themselves; in a group of children, they are likely to stand out because of their lack of involvement or persistent demands for attention from any adults near by. A small dose given at night, say 10 mg to a 6 year old, up to 25–50 mg to a 12 year old, may well prove sufficient for the anxiety to subside. The child then becomes more confident and noticeably more able to cope with the demands of everyday life. Eventually, the drug can be discontinued.

Chlorpromazine should not be given to depressed children even if they appear to be severely anxious. It is a depressant drug and will inevitably make such a child worse.

TRIFLUOPERAZINE (Stelazine). This is particularly helpful if children have feelings of persecution or frankly delusional ideas, e.g. that their food may poison them or that they are dying. Persecutory feelings are often found in children with a chronic depression who have a hostile antisocial attitude. The commonest complaint about such children is that they are aggressive, hard or impossible to please and spoil every family treat. They are at loggerheads with others in the family, most usually their mother. If a small dose of Stelazine, 1 to 2 mg daily, is added to the antidepressants in such cases, there is usually rapid improvement; and provided that other members of the family are prevented from perpetuating sour relationships by constantly reminding and provoking the patient, harmony can eventually be restored. It has not been given to children under 8 years old.

Some children hallucinate particularly at night. They may be anxious, as previously described, or they may be suffering from a depressive or an obsessional illness. The common factor is the deep and chronic state of anxiety. This does not show itself in them in agitated behaviour, but by a general tendency to under-function for their ability with poor concentration and learning and a lack of self-confidence. Difficulties in getting to sleep or disturbed sleep are the other usual problems in these cases. They do not usually mention their hallucinatory experiences unless they are asked about them directly. Common presenting symptoms are obsessions and compulsions, depression, developmental disorders (soiling or wetting) and learning problems. The condition seems to occur most often between the ages 6 and 12, and is not accompanied by any other frankly psychotic symptoms. It responds very satisfactorily to Stelazine, 1 to 4 mg daily being enough to control things in most cases. Anti-depressants may also be needed if the depressive component is severe. So far, it is not clear how long treatment must continue in these children. Where the hallucinations are part of a depressive illness, they disappear once that has resolved. The prognosis for the others is at present still very uncertain.

The schizo-affective and schizophrenic illnesses of adolescence may respond better to Stelazine than Largactil in some cases, particularly if there is a strong depressive component and little agitation. Doses then may have to be calibrated as in adults, but it should be remembered that some adolescents still metabolise the psychotropic drugs like children and may need much smaller doses at first. As they grow up, their drug requirements may then alter drastically to adult amounts. Duration of treatment is determined as in adults. Some patients will probably need to continue on a phenothiazine for the rest of their life.

Some psychotic adolescents benefit from being given combined Largactil and Stelazine.

Side-effects can become troublesome in children on relatively small doses of phenothiazines, and it is wiser always to prescribe an anti-Parkinsonian drug such as Disipal if big doses of Largactil or Stelazine are given.

LITHIUM CARBONATE. This has been found useful for the treatment of some children who have chronically excited behaviour and sleep disturbances (Gattozzi, 1970). These children are young, between 4 and 8, and the parents complain that they are never still, may have to be barricaded into the house, are liable to accidents, sleep badly, and that they are an uncontainable unteachable nuisance at school. These children have to be differentiated from over-active or epileptic brain-damaged children, from children who have a temporary anxiety state, and from neglected or rejected children who get into scrapes. There is often a family history of affective disorders and even at 8 or 9 the child may show the characteristic pyknic configuration of a manic-depressive. Lithium carbonate can be given to young children from the age of 4, 50 mg once or twice daily being a convenient starting dose. For older children, 125 mg once or twice daily can be given and the dose built up to a clinically effective amount. In young children, small doses are usually sufficient to control the mood and bring about greater stability. However, depression may suddenly occur, when an antidepressant must also be given. Amitriptyline given at night may help to improve sleep as well as control the depression. Sometimes Largactil may be needed in combination with lithium carbonate. So far in this group, it has not been necessary to monitor every case with blood-level estimations. However, these have been done when bigger doses were given. Some excitable young children have only required treatment for a few weeks before settling down. Some, however, have had to continue with treatment for years in the same way as would an adult patient with a manic-depressive illness.

Lithium carbonate also helps some older children who go through episodes of uncontrollable aggression during a depressive illness. These children may become seriously destructive during such an episode, smashing furniture and tearing curtains. The parents are usually terrorized by the child's eruptive tendency. The child is frightened and upset about these rages, particularly because he has no means of controlling them and he may actually fear that he is going mad. Lithium carbonate, 125 mg to 250 mg once or twice daily added to the antidepressants may have a dramatic effect in preventing such outbursts and relieving the tension from which they seem to spring. It may only be needed for a few weeks and warning should be given to reduce or omit it if it seems to be aggravating the depressed mood. On the whole, children have proved to be remarkably reliable about using this drug in this condition. They usually know when they need it and will insist on having it, but leave it as soon as their need for it has gone. Nevertheless, medical supervision must continue as long as a child remains on any psychotropic drugs.

Other Sedatives

PHENERGAN is a useful sedative to help infants and young children over a period of acute anxiety. The barbiturates have not been used for this purpose in this clinic.

CHLORDIAZEPOXIDE (Librium) can be given in combination with antidepressants to children who are very anxious as well as depressed. It may make them very drowsy and occasionally there are complaints that it has precipitated weepiness and an unpleasantly depressed mood. For this reason, it has been used cautiously. Children from the age of 6 may be given 5 mg once or twice daily, from 10 more may be needed. It has usually been combined with a MAOI, particularly in the treatment of phobic states in children and adolescents (see later).

DIAZEPAM (Valium) is a minor tranquillizer like Librium, and has the advantage that it does not cause drowsiness in small doses, nor usually the depressive mood swings that may occur in children who are given Librium. Valium has been used in small doses, 2 mg once to three times daily, with MAOIs for children with an anxious depression.

Valium also helps some children with an anxiety state. These are children who are restless, attention-seeking, demanding of time and materials, and difficult or impossible to teach at school. They characteristically sleep very badly and may constantly seek someone in the family to share their bed at night. In some cases, Valium 1 to 2 mg up to three times daily may help the child to settle down over the course

of a few months, provided that the family are stable and other up-
heavals do not precipitate a fresh anxiety attack.

Intravenously, Valium helps to control fits in children with status
epilepticus and this is an important use of this drug in paediatric
emergency practice. Recently it has been used intravenously for a few
acutely anxious phobic adolescents as for adults (see p. 33).

The Barbiturates

Apart from the control of epilepsy, this group of drugs has very
little place in child psychiatry at present. In children, as in adults,
medical treatment of psychiatric disorders must be directed to dealing
with the cause of disordered behaviour where possible, or at least at
those biochemical processes that might be connected with it. Barbiturates produce a global effect on the nervous system. One can certainly drug a child into more or less insensibility and so eliminate some
inconvenient behaviour, but the medical grounds for such treatment
must be at least questionable.

Stimulation

Monoamine Oxidase Inhibitors (MAOI)

This group of drugs is particularly useful in the treatment of
children with anxious depressions and with phobic depressions.
Despite dietary restrictions, children take them regularly once they
feel that they are being helped by these medicines. They are often more
careful about these restrictions than are adults. So far, no other
antidepressant has proved to be as effective for these clinical groups
as the MAOIs.

PHENELZINE (Nardil) has been given to children from the age of
8 years. A usual starting dose is 15 mg once or twice daily. For adolescents, 15 mg three times daily may be needed. If there is a great deal
of anxiety Librium or Valium may be given with the antidepressant.

Children with anxious depressions may be weepy and clinging or
immobile and quiet. They commonly complain of persistent abdominal pain and may also have headaches. It is unusual for the pain to
waken them at night. Weepiness, irritability and lack of a sense of
humour are all characteristic, but usually only mentioned if the
doctor specially asks about them. The presenting feature is nearly
always the pain and this may have led to endless negative physical
investigations from IVPs to a laparotomy. The illness has often

followed some physical or psychological shock or a series of various shocks. The child is usually conscientious and normally extremely reliable. The breakdown into depressions is often hard for such a child to bear. During the illness, he may become extremely clinging, even insisting on sharing the parents' bed. Once the illness has re-solved, this behaviour subsides and the child returns to his previous conscientious reliable behaviour. Although the child may appear to be hysterical while ill, this must not lead to his being mistaken for a hysteric. Treatment must continue until he feels well and no longer wants the medicines.

ISOCARBOXAZID (Marplan) is less powerfully antidepressant and stimulant than Nardil and has some calming qualities which make it particularly useful for treating phobic children over the age of 6 years. It can be used in small doses as the tablets are scored and easily halved. A usual starting dose would be 5 mg once or twice daily and this may need to be increased for older children to 10 mg twice daily for an 8 year old and 10 mg three times daily for adolescents.

Phobic illnesses in children commonly begin during a change in their life-routine, most commonly after moving from primary to secondary school, sometimes on first entering school at 5 years old. Some phobic illnesses are precipitated by physical or psychological shocks in sensitive children, e.g. a burglary or road accident. How-ever, in children who break down into a phobic illness simply on changing schools, the symptoms may be the outward sign of severe personality problems which make the ultimate outlook gloomy. Many of these children do not manage to complete a normal school career and while some may mature out of their fear of life, many others continue to lead a restricted existence. A working life is more easily adapted to the restrictions imposed by a phobic personality disorder, than are normal school requirements. For this reason, some anxieties and problems of phobic children seem to disappear once they leave school. Others mature out of their difficulties. However, some continue to be ill and a few break down into a psychotic dis-order.

The use of MAOIs in the treatment of this condition is similar in children and adults. Once the panic attacks and the physical symp-toms are under control, in about 10 days from the start of treatment, the child should extend his activities and get back to school as soon as possible. A change of school may be necessary. However, changing schools by itself will not solve the problem of the school-phobic child and usually serves only to procrastinate treatment and education. In some cases, home tuition may be the only possibility of getting education restarted.

Other MAOIs

Where Nardil helps to some extent and depression persists, *iproniazid* (Marsilid) may be more effective. This has been given to severely depressed children and adolescents from the age of 12 upwards. There is great flexibility in dosage because of the scored tablets.

TRANYLCYPROMINE (Parnate). This drug has not been used for children. It is extremely powerful. When it has been given to young adolescents, side effects of headaches and dizziness have been troublesome. It can be very helpful for older adolescents from the age of 16 years. As the tablets are coated, it is very difficult to modify dosage.

General Comments

These drugs have been avoided in asthmatic children and where there was a history of infective hepatitis. Apart from postural giddiness in a few cases, there have been few problems with side-effects.

Tricyclic Antidepressants

AMITRIPTYLINE (Tryptizol). This is the most useful member of this group in child psychiatry. It helps children with chronic depressions and younger children with anxious depressions.

Depressive illness in infants and toddlers causes persistent grizzling, weepiness, insomnia and sometimes failure to thrive. From the age of 18 months, such infants have been treated with syrup amitriptyline, the beginning dose being $2\frac{1}{2}$ mg given at night. This can be cautiously increased if necessary in these very young children, to 5 mg. From 3 to 5 years, a bigger dose can be given, 5 to 10 mg per 24 hours and progressively larger amounts for older children. Usually the effective dose is less than would be calculated by Catzel's chart (1966) up to age 12 years.

A depressed young child will not continue to improve if the mother is suffering from a concurrent untreated depressive illness or if the family life is otherwise disorganised.

In older children, chronic depression may be accompanied by developmental disorders, wetting, soiling, learning problems, underfunctioning at school, and sometimes antisocial behaviour. Aggression and destructive outbursts may occur as previously described. There may be weepiness, but there is always irritability and the child is intolerant of teasing and never really enjoys anything. Abdominal pain or headache may occur but are not usually a main feature as with children with anxious depressions.

Sleep may be deep in children with chronic depressions, but more usually there is difficulty in getting off, or waking in the middle of the night, perhaps screaming from a nightmare.

Some children suffer from endogenous depressive illnesses like those seen in adults, with typical variation of mood from gloom or irritability in the morning to normal or even cheerful behaviour in the afternoon. It sometimes helps in the diagnosis to see such a child in a morning and in an afternoon clinic. These children may complain of feeling depressed. They often have severe abdominal pain, characteristic sleep disturbances with early morning waking and psychomotor retardation. They look pale and ill. Suicidal ideas and feelings may occur in any childhood depression, notably after age twelve, but can be particularly severe in this group.

These children are all helped by amitriptyline. However, this may make the endogenous depressive too drowsy and then an alternative should be sought.

IMIPRAMINE (Tofranil). Imipramine has rarely been used in this clinic. It helps children with a clear-cut endogenous depression as described above. It does not have a sedative side-effect, but acts as a stimulant and is therefore particularly helpful for these retarded miserable children. From the age of 8, the dose has been 10 mg two or three times daily, increasing for older children and adolescents up to 25 mg three times daily.

TRIMIPRAMINE (Surmontil). This is a milder antidepressant than either of the previously mentioned drugs and has a less potent sedative side-effect than amitriptyline. It can be a great help for a chronically depressed child who is made too drowsy or nauseated by amitriptyline. Dosage for a 4 to 5 year old begins with 5 to 10 mg daily. As with amitriptyline, the main dose can be given at night.

NORTRIPTYLINE (Allegron). This drug is very useful for depressed children who sleep well and feel bad during the day. It does not usually have a sedative side-effect in children. It can also be used to supplement treatment with amitriptyline at night if the full antidepressant dose of the latter that is needed to control the illness makes the child too drowsy. Dosage is as for amitriptyline. It has not been given to children younger than 6 in this clinic.

OPIPRAMOL (Insidon). Opipramol has a strong tranquillising side-effect and helps some children who have an anxious depression of recent onset. It is well worth a trial before using MAOIs for such children. Dose from 6 years old, 10 mg two or three times daily to 10 years old, 25 mg three times daily.

Side effects

Apart from nausea and constipation, there have not been problems with side-effects of tricyclic antidepressants in children in this clinic.

CHILDREN WHO BECOME WORSE ON ANTIDEPRESSANTS

A few children react with hysterical outbursts when antidepressant treatment begins to be effective. In these few cases, the depression is probably a defence against some continuing anxiety and once this is broken, the anxiety bursts through. These children usually need intensive psychotherapy to deal with their illness and drastic modification of their environment may also be required.

Switching and Combined Antidepressant Treatment

Some children improve only to some extent on drugs from either group of antidepressants. Anxious depressives characteristically may improve for six weeks on tricyclic drugs and then stick. A change has to be made to a MAOI if there is to be further improvement. Usually such a change from tricyclic to MAOI is simply done but if the switch is from imipramine it may be better to allow a few days to elapse without treatment before commencing MAOI. It is generally recommended that there should be 10 days' interval when changing from MAOI to a tricyclic antidepressant.

Some children, like some adults, are not adequately helped by drugs from either group alone. Depression persists, or the insomnia, or the pain. It has been found safe to combine Marplan or Nardil with Tryptizol or Surmontil in children from the age of 8, and in some cases this has been essential for their recovery. In rare cases where even a combination of Nardil and Surmontil has only partially relieved a depression, Marsilid has been substituted for the Nardil.

Duration of Treatment

In children with depression, it is usually safe to let the child himself determine when he no longer needs antidepressants. This does not always hold good for paranoid depressed children who may stop treatment in a fit of antisocial spite and it would be a dangerous policy with schizoaffective and schizophrenic disorders.

Relapses may occur. In depressives these are easily treated. However, if a phobic child relapses, particularly if the relapse occurs in adolescence, the outlook is probably gloomy for the outcome of the phobia.

Other Stimulant Drugs

Amphetamines have been used for the treatment of various child psychiatric disorders. They have proved useful in the management of some hyperkinetic children (XII). They may also be found useful for some brain-damaged children who are torpid and inaccessible but not depressed.

Amphetamines have been used to lighten the sleep of persistently enuretic children, so making them more aware when their bladder is full and about to empty spontaneously. They have only a very limited use for such cases, however, *e.g.* for a set well-organised re-training programme. One may otherwise find children tolerating large doses without visible benefits.

Depressed children and adolescents in whom the diagnosis has been missed, may experience a temporary lightening of mood following amphetamine but with a severe depressive after-effect. They may therefore rapidly become addicted to amphetamine compounds.

Other Treatments

ECT may be needed by a severely depressed child or adolescent and for some with schizophrenic disorders. The youth of the patient is then no guide to the amount of treatment that may be required to get him better. One 12 year old depressed girl with an illness of more than five years' duration who had failed to respond to combined anti-depressants, finally came out of her illness after more than 20 ECT. It has not been given to children under 12 in this clinic, and only rarely, but it is the severity of illness and not the youth of the patient that should decide the use of this treatment.

Modified sleep treatment as described elsewhere in this book, may greatly help a panic-stricken younger child who is hallucinated, or a suicidal phobic adolescent. It has only been used for short periods in children, a combination of Largactil, Stelazine and Tryptizol being most useful.

Abreactions are only rarely needed by children. However, occasionally a child with conversion hysteria may require abreactive treatment as in adult cases. Excitatory abreactions with, e.g. Ritalin, will be found most useful but great care must be taken that the child has adequate support from the nursing staff between treatments, as otherwise fear may attach to the treatments which will counteract any benefits.

CHAPTER NINE

Treatment of Epilepsy

by ERIC WEST

This chapter will deal mainly with the type of treatment required by the patient with epilepsy treated by psychiatrists dealing with adult mental illness. Child psychiatrists will see children with epilepsy who also show behaviour disorders; forensic psychiatrists will see some epileptics who are delinquent. The paediatrician will see quite a number of children with minor epilepsy of the petit mal type. The neurologist will tend to see epileptics who attend as out-patients, and who are reasonably well motivated to take their anticonvulsants, and whose behaviour will not, on the whole, be disturbed. The psychiatrist tends to see patients whose epilepsy affects their personality directly and indirectly. He also has to handle the epileptic who takes an overdose and reaches the psychiatrist by referral from the physician after resuscitation. Most area mental hospitals have a small population of epileptics as chronic inmates. In these patients, problems of institutionalisation are added to those of controlling the epilepsy. About a quarter of the patients in hospitals for the mentally subnormal have epileptic fits either continually or at some time. Sometimes psychiatric patients with a non-epileptic diagnosis have an occasional major epileptic fit which requires investigation. The antidepressant drugs and the phenothiazine tranquillisers can evoke epilepsy occasionally in patients with a low convulsive threshold (Betts *et al.*, 1968; Dallos and Heathfield, 1969; Houghton, 1971) plus, perhaps, a pharmacogenetic factor leading to a different metabolic handling of the drugs.

Patients who have been given the diagnosis of schizophrenia may be found collapsed. These episodes may be due to hypotensive reactions to phenothiazine drugs; they may be due to the effects of alcoholic or barbiturate addiction, but the possibility of an epileptic fit from the effects of phenothiazine drugs must be remembered. Also, any schizophrenic who has a fit must be considered for diagnostic reformation. Sometimes temporal lobe epilepsy can mimic schizophrenia. Patients with temporal lobe epilepsy may have few or no motor fits, the attacks consisting of disturbances of sensation, perception, mood or behaviour. There may be a chronic or intermittent psychosis (Slater *et al.*, 1963).

Alcoholics suffer from convulsive seizures (Walsh, 1962; Lees, 1967) and the problem is to decide whether the fit is a direct effect of the alcohol, or whether the alcohol has activated fits from another brain lesion. Barbiturates commonly produce convulsions in barbiturate-dependent patients, and again the problem is to decide whether there is another lesion which the barbiturates have brought to light.

Classification of the Epilepsies

Epilepsy can be classified as symptomatic or non-symptomatic ('idiopathic'), as major or minor according to the type of attack; or we can use information from electroencephalographic (EEG) studies to typify the site of origin of the epileptic discharge as follows:

1. FOCAL CORTICAL EPILEPSY. The seizure starts in a localised part of the cerebral cortex, and the EEG correspondingly shows a local abnormality, usually a spike or a sharp wave discharge. Clinically, there may be an aura. The seizure can be marked by the briefest interruption of consciousness or result in a disorder of sensation, and extend to major motor convulsions if the discharge from the focus spreads to involve both cerebral hemispheres. Temporal lobe epilepsy is a common form of focal cortical epilepsy, and is the type most likely to be met by the psychiatrist.

2. PRIMARY CENTRENCEPHALIC OR SUBCORTICAL EPILEPSY. This could be called idiopathic epilepsy. There is a genetic element, not strong, but greater than in other forms of epilepsy. It is typified by the petit mal attacks of childhood, not beginning at birth, but often starting around the age of 5 years. Clinically, there are brief interruptions of attention and consciousness. There is no aura. There are no clinical or psychometric signs of coarse brain damage. The personality is usually not grossly disturbed at the outset, but as major fits often start later in the illness, all the usual difficulties the epileptic patient has over employment, marriage, holding a driving licence, etc., may lead to secondary personality upsets. The EEG in centrencephalic epilepsy usually shows bilaterally synchronous 3 Hz (Hertz, i.e. c/sec) spike and wave, often more prolonged on hyperventilation.

3. MIXED OR INDEFINITE TYPES OF EEG FINDINGS OCCUR. In secondary subcortical epilepsy there may be generalised bursts of irregular spike

and wave superficially resembling the paroxysms of petit mal, but the discharges are secondary to a primary focal cortical focus, perhaps in the medial parts of the temporal lobe. In some patients' EEGs there may be multiple spike discharges from scattered bilateral cortical foci. The EEG may show excess slow wave activity in some patients with epilepsy without constancy of localisation on repeated records.

4. THERE ARE VARIOUS TYPES OF REFLEX EPILEPSY. The one most often seen is photosensitive epilepsy. The patient may have had a seizure whilst watching a badly adjusted television screen. These seizures nearly always end in unconsciousness. The EEG may be abnormal in the routine record, but is usually more definitely abnormal when the patient is exposed to a flickering light from a stroboscope lamp, spike and wave paroxysms being evoked at a critical flicker rate.

Appraisal and Investigation of the Epileptic Patient

The following points should be borne in mind when a patient with epilepsy has been referred to a psychiatrist:

1. First of all, exclude the possibility of an intracranial lesion, particularly in patients whose epilepsy starts after the age of 25, even though most of these late starting epilepsies will not be found to have a gross expanding lesion. Always consider the possibility of a meningioma, because it is treatable by surgery. Few will be found in a whole clinical lifetime, but the search should always be on as some are missed (Elbanhowy et al., 1963). Petit mal with 3 Hz generalised spike and wave in the EEG should be identified at the outset because the drug treatment is different from other types of epilepsy. Few will actually come to the psychiatrist, but some will. Occasionally, very prolonged petit mal seizures seem to trigger off major seizures, and the control of the petit mal element helps to control the grand mal indirectly.

2. Establish whether there is an aura or not. Leading questions may have to be asked to confirm some of the psychic phenomena of temporal lobe attacks. A woman with a visual hallucinatory experience in temporal lobe epilepsy told a marriage guidance counsellor about the experience but not her doctor. Patients, and even their families, may suppress information about epileptic attacks. One patient's girl friend was the only reliable witness of a major fit in an epileptic who developed a paranoid psychosis. The mere fact that a patient can recall some kind of brief but unfamiliar episode but finds it very hard to describe is suggestive in itself of cortical epilepsy.

3. Find out if there are any precipitating causes such as light-sensitivity, menstruation or emotion. Disturbed emotional experiences and fear may be part of a temporal lobe attack, but emotion seems to fire off epilepsy in some people. Increased epileptic attacks have been reported in children in the Ulster rioting of 1970 and 1971. One woman's first temporal lobe attacks began with brief repetitive feelings of unreality which she found nearly impossible to describe, and which first began when her husband started openly flirting with another woman at a picnic party. The attacks started again when her husband left her. She had had mastoid sepsis from a middle ear infection as a child, and the EEG showed a spike focus on the same side as the middle ear disease.

4. It is assumed that a full psychiatric history and physical and neurological examination will be made as a routine with corroboration from relatives and friends (with the patient's agreement). It is well worth obtaining hospital records at an early stage if the patient has been investigated and treated elsewhere. Also find out, if possible, what the response has been to anticonvulsants and at what dose level. This is particularly necessary where an epileptic is brought before the courts or is in borstal or prison, and where information about the early medical history is hard to obtain. Enquiry should be made about status epilepticus and how it was treated. Febrile convulsions in infancy may cause anoxic damage to the hippocampus and medial temporal lobe.

5. Be aware that temporal lobe epilepsy particularly may be first diagnosed as some other condition—as an anxiety state, hysteria, mania, depression, schizophrenia, aggressive psychopathy. A lot depends on the words first used to describe the attacks; 'panics' may be the word used to describe the sensations of fear; the dissociation in a minor epileptic attack may lead to the assumption that the patient has hysteria.

6. This chapter deals mainly with treatment, and standard neurological text books should be consulted for advice on the investigation of a person with epilepsy, but it can be said that clinical information will often give as precise information as to localisation (a sensory attack always in one limb, or dysphasia always being present in an attack) as will later investigations.

7. The Advisory Committee on the Health and Welfare of Handicapped Persons in its 1969 report *People with Epilepsy* recommends the multidisciplinary approach to epilepsy and the setting up of Epilepsy Clinics in District General Hospitals. Psychometric testing

is part of the assessment. Initial testing can provide a baseline against which later change can be judged. If possible, besides cognitive testing, tests for attention span and psychomotor speed should be done.

8. The concept of low convulsive threshold is a useful one. Anyone can have an epileptic fit. A fit occurring after an alcoholic bout in someone fatigued with travel may have less significance than one occurring in more usual circumstances. A patient may have a fit on a tricyclic antidepressant drug and not otherwise. The epilepsy may have been provoked because there is a lesion, but the attack may have occurred because of a low convulsive threshold. Conversely, tricyclic antidepressants need not necessarily make established epilepsy worse.

9. A person with epilepsy may have some other psychiatric condition. There may be doubt at times whether the mood change is directly due to epilepsy or to the effect of anticonvulsants or, perhaps, to low serum folate levels. Where mood changes are noticeable over short periods it is sometimes possible, by getting the patient and an observer to complete a daily mood rating scale, to relate swings to changes in the EEG. One patient always rated herself depressed when the EEG showed generalised slow waves. This kind of evaluation depends, of course, on the easy availability of an EEG department.

General Management of the Person with Epilepsy

The initial assessment scheme will have shown whether the epileptic patient has enough warning of an attack to get out of danger, admittedly an unusual situation, or whether the attacks occur only in sleep, or just before menstruation. Usually, the beneficial effects of anticonvulsants are exerted over a long period, and although dosage may be increased in the evening or before a menstrual period, the beneficial effects from doing this are not always striking.

Many epileptics have no warning of their major attacks, and some have fallen on to fires and burnt themselves. Although death by suffocation in attacks occurring in bed is rare, a few cases have been reported where the patient has been found dead with the face buried in a soft pillow. Worster-Drought (1970) reports three such deaths, all males, and also two female deaths by drowning in the bath. He reports a further male death of an epileptic who had apparently drowned by falling, during an attack, into a shallow river whilst fishing. Some patients have attacks in the street and so get taken to

hospital on numerous occasions. The British Epilepsy Association*
issues a card that can be carried by epileptics liable to have attacks in
the street. Advice is given on the card for first aid treatment, and the
doctor or hospital treating the patient are named on the card.

Little need be done at the height of an attack except to clear a
space around the patient and to see that the airway is unobstructed.
It is difficult to remove dentures during muscle contractions. Dentures
can be removed as soon as relaxation sets in. If recovery is long-
delayed, the decision must be made to give the patient's next dose of
anticonvulsant intramuscularly or intravenously.

Epileptic children may find it difficult to continue in a normal
school, although every attempt should be made for normal school
placement. The report *People with Epilepsy* already referred to
(Advisory Committee on Health and Welfare, 1969) suggests that a
multidisciplinary team be based at the hospital on which the divi-
sional educational authorities should be represented.

About 40 per cent of epileptics have difficulty with employment.
The Ministry of Labour (now Ministry of Employment and Produc-
tivity) issued a pamphlet in 1967 entitled *Employing Someone with
Epilepsy*. Leaflets on employment and other problems can be obtained
from the British Epilepsy Association. General practitioners and
doctors advising in industry can help by defining the type of job which
it is safe for an epileptic to do. Clearly, they must be kept away from
power-driven machinery, and not climb ladders or work at heights or
near pits containing water or industrial cleaning solvents, but they
may work in stores and in warehouses away from moving vehicles.

The Disablement Rehabilitation Officer should also be a member
of the multidisciplinary team at the hospital. Registration as a disabled person does not guarantee employment to an epileptic, the
terms for job security being the same as for other workers. Epileptics
do not seem to be more often absent from work as a group than non-
epileptics, and may, indeed, strive to stay at work whenever possible
for fear of dismissal.

Epileptics are covered for industrial injury in the same way as any
other worker under the 1946 National Insurance Act.

Possibilities for emigration are restricted for epileptics, or for a
family wishing to emigrate to, say, Australia if they have an epileptic
member.

Epileptics have difficult problems with getting employment with
organisations such as banks with rigid superannuation schemes.

* 3–6 Alfred Place, London, W.C.1.

They are barred from the services and the police. They have difficulty in getting on to a permanent superannuation basis in local government.*

Although epileptics have problems in obtaining life insurance, the life expectation of idiopathic or non-symptomatic epilepsy is not very different from the non-epileptic population. Epilepsy is, of course, often merely a symptom—where there is brain injury or associated mental defect, the primary illness may be the determining factor for morbidity and life expectancy. Status epilepticus is the main threat to life in epileptics, but only some, usually with a lesion in certain areas of the brain, are liable to status.

Pregnancy has a variable effect on seizures. They may increase in frequency or stay the same. Anticonvulsants do not appear to affect the foetus, although the subject is one that is being currently investigated. Although it has been reported that phenytoin (Epanutin) is possibly teratogenic in producing oral clefts in offspring, some of the parents were obviously taking the phenytoin for epilepsy, possibly symptomatic, and might be carrying genes for multiple defects; the defects in the children, therefore, need not have been due to the phenytoin. Nevertheless, the simplest combination of anticonvulsants should be used in pregnancy, and the lowest dosage compatible with control of the seizures. Breast feeding is probably unwise where there are seizures still occurring, mainly because of possible injury to the child if the mother is breast-feeding the child whilst alone and has an attack without warning. Anticonvulsants are excreted in the milk, but this is a lesser reason for advice against breast feeding. Patients should, nevertheless, be assessed individually. A woman who has only had a few attacks in her sleep might be given different advice from that given to one with a regular weekly fit pattern of major convulsive type. The same would be said for a woman who had only had brief minor psychic temporal lobe attacks.

Advice on marriage is difficult to give. The question of the inheritance of epilepsy cannot be answered without defining the type of epilepsy and the circumstances. Epilepsy in the family must also be defined. There is a difference between a grandparent's epilepsy following cerebral arteriosclerosis and, say, two cases of classical centrence-

* Information about the above and related matters in this country can be obtained from the British Epilepsy Association, the address of which has already been given, and information abroad from the International Bureau for Epilepsy, also at 3–6 Alfred Place, London, W.C.1. (Telephone: 01–580–2704/5) There is a Scottish Epilepsy Association, 24 St. Vincent Place, Glasgow, and an Irish Epilepsy Association, 30 Leeson Park, Dublin.

phalic petit mal in the same family. The same reservation would apply to epilepsy beginning after a head injury. It is necessary to find out, then, how 'spontaneous' the epilepsy was. Petit mal with 3 Hz spike and wave in the EEG, and 'low convulsive threshold' leading to febrile convulsions in infancy with possible anoxic causation of later mesial temporal sclerosis, are two distinct situations, but in both there is some evidence for inheritance above the normal expectation for epilepsy. If one of a procreating couple has one of these two conditions, there is a 1 per cent to 1·5 per cent chance of a child having epilepsy of a similar kind, as contrasted with an 0·5 per cent expectation in the population. These figures are very approximate because the exact distribution of the different types of epilepsy is not accurately known. If both parents have a spontaneous (non-symptomatic) type of epilepsy this will further increase the chances of a child being affected.

An even more difficult situation arises where a couple seek advice before marriage. One is a known epileptic. If this patient has either petit mal or had febrile convulsions of childhood which have led to manifest clinical temporal lobe epilepsy due to presumptive mesial temporal sclerosis, then there is the slightly increased risk already referred to. If the partner without clinical epilepsy is aged about 25 and unlikely to develop idiopathic epilepsy in the future, what advice does one give if the partner's EEG is, nevertheless, paroxysmal? I have met this problem on two occasions. It was as if there was some kind of prospective assortative mating. One would have to make more careful enquiries in this case to see if there was any metabolic disorder, earlier brain injury or infection to account for the paroxysmal EEG in the partner on an environmental basis. Finding an environmental cause would make the situation genetically neutral. If there proved to be a case of petit mal or febrile convulsions in the partner's first degree relatives, this would add a very slight increase to the genetic risk.

Advice is sometimes asked by epileptics and their families about the general management of their lives. Advice given is not always advice taken. A young lady with an abnormal EEG who has only had fits after drinking alcohol at parties may decide to go on drinking alcohol and risk further fits, and even disbelieve the explanation. Nevertheless, alcohol should not be taken by epileptics on any occasion as it is liable to increase fit frequency. Alcohol may cause fits directly, by causing drowsiness, or by over-hydration. Some perceptive epileptics—sometimes businessmen subject to what at one time were called expense account lunches—know this only too well. In general, drowsiness and inactivity lead to fits. One adolescent epileptic noticed that he had more fits in summer when he played cricket than in winter when he played rugger. It is not clear whether tobacco smoking has any effect on the frequency of fits.

Driving and Epilepsy

The doctor may be asked to advise about driving in epilepsy. Some epileptics conceal their epilepsy and go on driving. This is known to clinicians, and has also been documented by Murray Falconer and David Taylor (1967).

In this country, new regulations came into force on June 1st, 1970 allowing an epileptic to drive if

(1) he has been free of epileptic attacks when awake for at least three years prior to the date the licence is to take effect;

(2) an applicant who has had such attacks whilst asleep in the previous three years must also have had them before the period of three years;

(3) the driving of a vehicle by him is not likely to be a danger to the public.

The County Medical Officer of Health is to advise the Licensing Authority on information provided by the general practitioner.

The decision is not always easy. One may suspect that an epileptic who is strongly motivated to have a driving licence, say, one working in a garage, would be tempted to say nothing about a very occasional epileptic attack. His family might not wish to be drawn in as informants either. The epilepsy may be controlled, but only by rather high doses of anticonvulsants—although, providing these are not leading to psychomotor retardation, the high dosage itself may be no bar to driving. Attempts to get independent information from the EEG are not always decisive. Whereas in general a very abnormal EEG in a known epileptic usually corresponds to a likelihood of frequent attacks, in a borderline situation there may be no clinical attacks and in the EEG a moderate amount of rather non-specific paroxysmal activity. In the end, the judgment must be clinical, after taking reasonable care to get as much information as possible without destroying the doctor-patient relationship by infringing confidences. In the future, a better method might be for the epileptic patient to appear before an independent medical board which would advise the Medical Officer of Health.

Before this change in the Act in 1970, the patient was deemed to be suffering from epilepsy if he needed drugs for its suppression. The new regulation is more liberal, but must be judged on experience of accident proneness in epileptics whilst driving.

Prevention of Epilepsy

Wars produce a crop of epilepsy, from penetrating injuries of the brain as well as from closed head injuries. Apart from prevention of head injury, controlling febrile convulsions and preventing anoxic brain damage from them, and controlling brain-damaging infections such as meningitis and encephalitis, or at least trying to mitigate their effects, there is little to be done in epilepsy prevention. We cannot prevent because we do not know the causes of non-symptomatic epilepsy.

Road accidents and industrial head injuries add to the quota of post-traumatic epilepsy. The wearing of protective helmets on industrial and building sites, and the wearing of seat-belts in cars would make some reduction in head trauma. Boxing is one way of producing repetitive minor head traumata, leading occasionally to cerebral damage but rarely to epilepsy.

Use of Anticonvulsant Drugs

Sodium bromide succeeded the folk remedies for epilepsy, but caused mental dulling and rashes. Phenobarbitone displaced bromides as an effective treatment for grand mal about 1912, having a marked anticonvulsant effect without causing unacceptable sedation. The next effective anticonvulsant was discovered in 1937 by the effect on electroshock threshold in a laboratory animal by placing an electrode inside a cat's mouth and another on the top of its head, and measuring the minimal stimulus required to produce an electroshock-induced convulsion before and after the administration of the substance. This substance was 5,5-diphenylhydantoin (phenytoin, 'Epanutin', 'Dilantin') discovered by Merritt and Putnam.

The first effective drug against petit mal was found in 1944 among the 2,4-oxazolidinediones using the anticonvulsant effect against animal convulsions provoked by pentylenetetrazol ('leptazol', 'Cardiazole', 'Metrazol'). The first drug in this series to be clinically effective against petit mal, although not against grand mal, was 3,5,5-trimethyl-2,4-oxazolidinedione (troxidone, 'Tridione'). Recently, the succinimides have been found to have an action against petit mal.

Primidone ('Mysoline') is an effective drug against grand mal, and was developed chemically by replacing the urea carbonyl group of phenobarbitone by a methylene group.

Drugs effective against major seizures often contain the acylamide grouping:

$$C_6H_5.\underset{\underset{R_1}{|}}{\overset{|}{C}} - CO - \underset{\underset{R_5}{|}}{N}.CO -$$

R_1 is ethyl in phenobarbitone, primidone and methoin (i.e., an alkyl grouping), and in phenytoin R_1 is phenyl.

Other substances have been found to have anticonvulsant action, e.g., chlormethiazole ethandisulphonate ('Heminevrin') with a thiazole (sulphur-containing) 5-membered ring structure.

After identification of possible anticonvulsant activity from chemical structure, laboratory testing now includes measurement of the effect of the drug against convulsions produced by minimal and maximal electroshock, by leptazol, Megimide, strychnine, insulin and other agents. Simulated irritative focal lesions can be produced in certain areas of the brain by aluminium oxide crystals or alumina cream, and the effect of a new drug on the EEG abnormalities from such a focal lesion can be assessed.

ONE OR TWO FITS. Should anticonvulsants be started if there has been only one fit? The answer, as always, depends on what sort of fit and at what age. There is the single fit in a baby with a rising high temperature at the start of an infectious illness. There is the fit in a baby who is found to have a chronic cerebral condition with associated mental subnormality. Treatment may be postponed in the first situation, but will probably be needed in the second.

A child of 5 to 10 years of age suffering the first major fit may be found to have the EEG of petit mal; careful retrospective enquiry may then reveal minor attacks, supposed inattention at school, and poorer school performance than the intelligence level would predict. There is more of a case for starting treatment in this situation, because the minor attacks should be reduced, and the succinamide drugs used for control of minor seizures may not prevent major attacks.

The holidaymaker abroad who has a fit after unaccustomed wine drinking may give a clear account of post-ictal headache and stiff muscles to suggest the genuineness of the attack as a convulsive major seizure. In a case like this a wait-and-see policy is best, though perhaps an EEG should be done to see if there is a localised abnormality suggesting an early lesion.

Some situations are complex. The sufferer from migraine may have had the usual pattern of attack for years, perhaps with a complex aura distinguished from an epileptic aura by the slowness of its course and the sequel of hemicrania and nausea; but one day, this migraine subject has what appears to be an epileptic attack soon after the onset of a migraine episode. One can speculate that occasionally in migraine the vasoconstrictive phase may produce enough local brain anoxia to fire off an epileptic attack. In such a case one would look for a focus in the EEG, and only start anticonvulsants if epileptic attacks continued. The other possibilities are that both the migraine and the epilepsy are caused by the same lesion; or that the migraine is what it always was, but there is a new lesion beginning elsewhere in the brain which has fired off the epilepsy by inducing slight temporary anoxia.

Mention has already been made of the psychiatric patient receiving amitriptyline or chlorpromazine who has an epileptic fit. These drugs are epileptogenic in a few people and not others, presumably depending on pharmacogenetic individuality. Again, an EEG may help to exclude a lesion which has been up to now latent. In some cases it is possible to do an EEG before and after a dose of the suspected epileptogenic drug and see the appearance of paroxysmal abnormality follow its administration. One woman had 'hysterical' turns and blackouts on chlorpromazine. These ceased when she was taken off the drug. One EEG was normal, another distinctly paroxysmal. If the patient needs the offending drug for the psychiatric state, and if there has been only one seizure, it may be justifiable to continue treatment providing the patient will not be driving a car or be hazarded in any other way. Change can be made to another similar drug which may prove to be slightly less epileptogenic in a particular patient, or an anticonvulsant drug can be given as well, but it should be remembered that the metabolic breakdown by the liver microsomes of one drug may induce the more rapid breakdown of another drug.

ANTICONVULSANTS IN ESTABLISHED EPILEPSY. Two situations arise for the psychiatrist. He may become involved in the treatment of an epileptic patient who is already having anticonvulsants, where some other situation has arisen—a behavioural disturbance, or depression leading to overdose, or some other psychiatric problem. Some patients have their favourite drugs and resist changes in them, even if these drugs are not those that would be particularly recommended by the interim clinician. A patient may, for example, be quite adamant that only methyl phenobarbitone works in his case and not phenobarbitone, or that he finds acetazolamine a very effective drug. It has been shown (Gibberd *et al.*, 1970) that epileptic out-patients prescribed phenytoin had a lower serum phenytoin concentration than in-patients. The groups were comparable for dosage, age and sex distribution. The serum phenytoin levels of the out-patients rose to very near the in-patient level when they were more closely supervised. If epileptic patients are unreliable in taking their anticonvulsants in the doses prescribed, they will probably be more unreliable if changes are made in their medication without explanation and close supervision. If the epilepsy is not grossly out of control, and there are medical notes elsewhere documenting previous drug regimes, it is best to obtain the previous notes and see which drugs have been most successful. Situations do change. As has been mentioned, one drug may affect the action of another given with it; phenobarbitone may, by induction of enzymes on the liver, have the effect of causing another drug to be broken down more rapidly, although on the whole, anticonvulsants are compatible with one another. Also, an adverse reaction to a drug such as primidone may have been because the starting dose was too high and caused unpleasant, unwanted effects that could have been avoided by a cautious start with low dosage. Mention will be made later of the effect of folic acid which may reduce serum phenytoin levels in some patients. A drug which has caused a serious toxic reaction, such as a blood dyscrasia or exfoliative dermatitis, should not, of course, be tried again.

ANTICONVULSANTS IN THE NEWLY DIAGNOSED PATIENT WITH EPILEPSY. If, after investigation and consultation with a neurologist, anticonvulsants are to be given for the first time, the following drugs are in use:

1. For the suppression of petit mal seizures (with 3 Hz bilaterally synchronous spike and wave in the EEG)—ethosuximide.

2. For the control of all other types of seizure, including motor, sensory and psychic attacks, both minor and major:

> phenobarbitone
> phenytoin
> primidone
> pheneturide
> sulthiame.

3. Alternative drugs for the suppression of petit mal:
   troxidone
   paramethadione
   mepacrine
   diazepam (for petit mal status)
   chlordiazepoxide.

4. Alternative drugs for the control of other types of seizures:
   ethotoin
   methoin
   carbamazepine
   beclamide
   acetazolamide
   bromides.

5. Where there is a myoclonic element:
   diazepam
   nitrazepam.

6. For status epilepticus:
   diazepam
   some of the above in category 2 given
        intramuscularly or intravenously
   paraldehyde
   sodium amylobarbitone
   chloral hydrate (in children)
   trichloryl (in children)
   chlormethiazole
   lignocaine
   general anaesthetics in conjunction
        with muscle relaxants.

It is better to get to know the actions and limits of dosage of a few drugs than continually to change, and one should try not to use more than two or three drugs in combination. Table I gives a list of anti-convulsant drugs under their brand names.

For petit mal, ethosuximide ('Zarontin', 'Emeside') should be tried first. Available in 250 mg capsules or as a syrup of 250 mg per 5 ml. For children, the recommended daily dose is 15 to 50 mg per kilogram (kg) of body weight, so for a child of 5 years weighing 19 kg the daily starting dose would be one 250 mg capsule a day, or 5 ml of the suspension, going up to three or four capsules a day according to response; for a child of 10 weighing 31 kg the daily dose could start at two 250 mg capsules a day. For children from 12 to 14

TABLE I

Name and Manufacturer	Approved Name	Oral Dosage		Indication and Comments	Unwanted Effects
		1-10 years	Over 10 years		
GARDENAL, May and Baker (also GARDENAL SODIUM)	Phenobarbitone tabs. 15, 30, 60, 100 mg; Sodium Phenobarbitone tabs. 30, 60 mg	15-60 mg b.d.	30-120 mg b.d. or t.d.s.	All seizure patterns apart from petit mal. Synergistic with phenytoin. Do not use alone in psycho-motor epilepsy	Somnolence. Rashes. Slow excretion if taken in overdose. Some children and adults made depressed and irritable. Rarely megaloblastic anaemia. Contra-indicated in porphyria
PROMINAL, Winthrop	Methylphenobarbitone tabs. 30, 60, 200 mg	30-60 mg b.d.	60-180 mg b.d. or t.d.s.	As for phenobarbitone but preferred by some patients. May be less prone to aggravate behaviour disorders	Less hypnotic than phenobarbitone, but the advantage may not be great in the end as more methylphenobarbitone may have to be prescribed for equivalent anti-convulsant effect
RUTONAL, May and Baker	Phenylmethylbarbituric acid tabs. 200 mg	30-60 mg b.d. or t.d.s.	60-300 mg b.d. or t.d.s.	As for methylphenobarbitone but individual preferences may determine choice	As for methylphenobarbitone. Occasional rashes
METHARBITAL (GEMONIL), Abbott	Diethylmethylbarbituric acid tabs. 100 mg	50-100 mg b.d.	50-300 mg b.d. or t.d.s.	As for methylphenobarbitone	Less hypnotic than phenobarbitone
EPANUTIN, Parke-Davis	Phenytoin sodium capsules 50, 100 mg	50-250 mg daily N.B. Suspension can be used for children 30 mg per 5 ml. In status epilepticus the parenteral form (vials of 250 mg) can be given i.v. at 4 mg per kg body weight.	150-450 mg daily	All seizure patterns apart from petit mal. Therapeutic dose near toxic dose, but toxic effects usually reversible. Pharmacogenetic variation in response	Pruritus, morbilliform or haemorrhagic skin eruptions, nystagmus, ataxia, diplopia, tremor, vertigo, nausea, hypertrophic gingivitis, hirsutism in girls, folic acid deficiency
MESONTOIN, Abbott	Methoin tabs. 100 mg	100-400 mg daily	200-600 mg daily	As for phenytoin but action stronger. Use with caution. Watch for sore throat, haemorrhages petechie. Should not be combined with troxidone	Drowsiness, allergic rashes, agranulocytic anaemia. Pigmentation. No hirsutism or hypertrophic gingivitis
PEGANONE, Abbott	Ethotoin tabs. 500 mg	0·5-2 g daily	1-3 g daily	For all seizure patterns apart from petit mal	Similar to phenytoin
GAROIN, May and Baker	0·1 g phenytoin sodium 0·05 g phenobarbitone sodium tablets	Tabs. ½ to 1 b.d.	Tabs. 1 to 2 b.d. or t.d.s.	For all seizure patterns apart from petit mal. Can be used when mixed therapy established	As for phenytoin and phenobarbitone

Drug	Preparation	Dose	Dose	Use	Side effects
HYDANTAL Sandoz	0·1 g methoin 0·02 g phenobarbitone	Tabs, ½ to 2 daily	Tabs. 2 to 4 daily	For all seizure patterns apart from petit mal. Can be used when mixed therapy established	Same as with methoin and phenobarbitone
MYSOLINE I.C.I.	Primidone tabs. 250 mg also suspension 250 mg per 5 ml	125 mg b.d. Begin with small doses and increase cautiously	0·75–1·5 g daily	For all seizure patterns apart from petit mal. Can be used with phenytoin. Avoid use with phenobarbitone. Sometimes effective when phenobarbitone is not	Nausea, ataxia, drowsiness, rashes; rarely megaloblastic anæmia and lowered serum folate. With long continued use as with some other anticonvulsants, raised serum alkaline phosphatase levels and disturbance of calcium metabolism, reversed by calciferol
MYSOLINE with PHENYTOIN I.C.I.	Primidone 250 mg Phenytoin sodium 100 mg tablets	½ tab. once daily late evening cautiously increasing by ½ daily to 1–2 daily	½ tab. once daily late evening cautiously increasing until control obtained. Maximum 6 daily	For all seizure patterns apart from petit mal. Can be used when mixed therapy established	As for primidone and phenytoin
PHENURONE	Phenylacetylurea tabs. 500 mg	0·5–1·5 g daily	2–3 g daily	Can be tried for psychomotor seizures which have not been controlled by other anticonvulsants. Too toxic for general use	Personality changes, liver damage, skin rashes leading to exfoliative dermatitis, blood dyscrasias
BENURIDE Bengue	Pheneturide quartered tabs. 200 mg	6/12 to 1 yr. 50 mg daily. 1–5 yrs 100 to 200 mg daily. 5–12 yrs 200 to 600 mg daily	600 mg to 1·0 g daily	All seizure patterns apart from petit mal, but try in cases of temporal lobe epilepsy. Relatively free of side effects in brain-damaged children with epilepsy	Ataxia and anoxia. Drowsiness not usually marked. Occasionally leucopænia. Rare possibility of aplastic anæmia. Raised serum alkaline phosphatase levels after prolonged use as with some other anticonvulsants, reversed with calciferol (Richens and Rowe, 1970). Discontinue in first trimester of pregnancy
TRINURIDE Bengue	Pheneturide 200 mg Phenytoin 40 mg Phenobarbitone 15 mg tabs		1–5 tabs. daily. Increase cautiously	All seizure patterns apart from petit mal. Try in cases of temporal lobe epilepsy	As for pheneturide, phenytoin and phenobarbitone
OSPOLOT F.B.A.	Sulthiame tabs. 50, 200 mg also suspension 50 mg per 5 ml	Start with ½ tab. daily or use the suspension 10–15 mg per kg of body weight daily in divided doses	200–600 mg daily	All seizure patterns apart from petit mal, but particularly in temporal lobe epilepsy. Some use is being made of this drug in behaviour disorders in children	Paræsthesiæ hyperventilation, anorexia, loss of weight, psychic changes. Side effects are usually not serious, and are not always related linearly to dosage, but may prevent the use of drug in individual patients

Name and Manufacturer	Approved Name	Oral Dosage 1–10 years	Oral Dosage Over 10 years	Indication and Comments	Unwanted Effects
TEGRETOL Geigy	Carbamazepine tabs. 200 mg	Begin with 100 mg (½ tab.) daily, increase cautiously to 200 mg daily younger children and 600 mg daily in child of 10	Begin with 100 mg (½ tab.) daily, increase gradually to 800 mg daily. Exceptionally to 1·2 g or 1·6 g daily	In seizures other than petit mal. Try particularly in psycho-motor epilepsy	Rashes and ataxia. Contra-indicated with or 2 weeks after the prescription of monoamine oxidase inhibitor drugs. Withold in first trimester of pregnancy
NYDRANE Rona	Beclamide tabs. 500 mg	0·5 g b.d. or t.d.s.	0·5 g to 1·0 g t.d.s.	In grand mal and psycho-motor epilepsy or epilepsy associated with behaviour disorders. Used in combination with phenobarbitone	Relatively non-toxic. Transient renal changes reported
ZARONTIN Parke-Davis	Ethosuximide caps. 250 mg or syrup 250 mg per 5 ml	250 mg. Increase if necessary	500 mg b.d. Increase if necessary	Petit mal, the drug of first choice	Nausea, indigestion, drowsiness, dizziness, headache
EMESIDE Labs. for Applied Biology	Ethosuximide caps. 250 mg also syrup	250 mg Increase if necessary	500 mg b.d. Increase if necessary	Petit mal, the drug of first choice	Nausea, indigestion, drowsiness, dizziness, headache
CAPITUS Berk	Ethosuximide caps. 250 mg	250 mg Increase if necessary	500 mg b.d. Increase if necessary	Petit mal, the drug of first choice	Nausea, indigestion, drowsiness, dizziness, headache
CELONTIN Parke-Davis	Methsuximide caps. 300 mg	4–15 mg per kg of body weight	300 mg per day first week increasing if necessary by weekly intervals to a daily dose of 1·2 g	For petit mal. Less effective than ethosuximide	Minor side effects similar to ethosuximide. Rarely, renal or hepatic toxicity
MILONTIN Parke-Davis	Phensuximide caps. 250, 500 mg	500 mg to 2 g daily	Up to 3 g daily	For petit mal. Less effective than ethosuximide	Skin rashes, drowsiness, nausea, hæmaturia, blood dyscrasias
PARADIONE Abbott	Paramethadione tabs. 300 mg	300 mg to 1·2 g daily	Up to 2·1 g daily	For petit mal, myoclonic jerks, akinetic attacks in children. Use if suxinamides or troxidone ineffective	Toxic effects similar to troxidone

TRIDIONE Abbott	Troxidone caps. 300 mg	300 mg to 1·2 g daily	Up to 2·1 g daily	For petit mal, myoclonic jerks, akinetic, seizures. Use only if suxinamides ineffective for petit mal, and if nitrazepam ineffective for myoclonus	Morbilliform rashes, blood dyscrasias, nausea, vomiting, vertigo 'glare'
DIAMOX Lederle	Acetazolamide tabs. 250 mg		250–500 mg daily for up to 5 days at a time	Occasionally useful for petit mal and other forms of epilepsy, e.g., pre-menstrual. A carbonic anhydrase inhibitor and diuretic, it may have a direct cerebral effect	Drowsiness, thirst, polydipsia. Contra-indicated where diuretics would exacerbate renal hyperchloretic acidosis or known depletion of sodium and potassium
HEMINEVRIN Astra	Chlormethiazole edisylate tabs. caps. 500 mg also i.v. infusion Chlormethiazole edisylate 8 mg Glucose 40 mg	i.v. infusion has been tried in status epilepticus as 1·5% solution of chlormethiazole 60–80 drops per minute to control convulsions until 1·2 to 1·6 g chlormethiazole administered	Status epilepticus. Limited evaluation so far	Tingling sensation in nose and sneezing. Rapid infusion will produce apnoea and may produce fall in blood pressure. Superficial phlebitis at site of injection
XYLOCAINE Astra	Liquocaine hydrochloride for injection	i.v. infusion in saline at rate of 100 mg per minute (1 ml of a 1% solution contains 10 mg). A maximum of 5 mg per kg body weight as a slow single intravenous injection	Status epilepticus. Limited evaluation. Will sometimes stop seizures	Overdose may evoke more seizures

This table is based on that compiled for the previous edition by Professor A. H. Crisp.

years of age the lowest range of the adult dose would be given, one to two capsules of 250 mg. The dose can be increased at the rate of 250 mg weekly or fortnightly until the optimum effect is obtained. Although the upper limit is sometimes eight capsules in an adult (2·0 g) the more usual dose is three to five capsules (0·75 to 1·25 g). About 70 per cent of petit mal patients can expect to have their minor attacks improved or controlled. Unwanted effects of the drug at high dosage, such as abdominal pain, hiccup, nausea, drowsiness and ataxia, may occur in about a third of patients, but in practice, etho-suximide is sometimes combined with another anticonvulsant— phenobarbitone, primidone or phenytoin—because ethosuximide, whilst it may not provoke grand mal, does not have a marked effect in controlling major fits. Unwanted effects may, therefore, be the result of a combination of drugs. Rashes, drowsiness and photo-phobia due to ethosuximide may recede if the dose is reduced.

A child with classical petit mal, where the distinction has been clearly made from minor temporal lobe epilepsy, may be treated at the start with ethosuximide alone. Drugs effective against grand mal can be added later if major attacks begin. Although it is sometimes said that anti-petit-mal drugs may increase grand mal, I have seen un-doubted cases where better control of prolonged petit mal attacks with ethosuximide has reduced major motor attacks in a patient with-out increase of other anticonvulsants. The drug may be continued in pregnancy, but at the lowest dosage possible. The incidence of foetal abnormalities in children of epileptic mothers taking anticonvulsants is currently being investigated, and at the moment it is not possible to say whether the suximide group are implicated or not. At present, the dangers of stopping the anticonvulsants in pregnancy seem greater than continuing them.

If ethosuximide does not give good control of petit mal, first make sure of the diagnosis. If alternative anti-petit mal drugs are to be given there are two other suximide drugs available, methsuximide and phensuximide. Methsuximide ('Celontin') in 300 mg capsules can be begun at 300 mg a day for an adult in the first week, increasing by 300 mg weekly to a daily dose of 1·2 g. For a child, the dose would be roughly 4 to 15 mg per kg of body weight. Phensuximide ('Milontin') is in 250 mg capsules given in a dose of 250 mg daily for an adult, with weekly increases up to a limit of 2 to 3 g daily. For a child the dose is 40 to 50 mg per kg daily.

Troxidone ('Tridione'), in 150 mg tablets and 300 mg capsules, is more toxic than the suximides. Unwanted effects can be nausea, vomiting, vertigo, 'glare', rashes and mood changes, but more serious are blood dyscrasias, exfoliative dermatitis and nephrosis. The drug is useful to have in reserve for patients who do not respond to suximides. For a child, a rough guide to dosage is 30 mg per kg. For an adult, start at 300 mg and increase weekly to 900 mg daily and estimate the effect of this dose for a time, although the drug can be given up to a limit of 2·1 g daily in divided doses.

In myoclonic epilepsy, diazepam ('Valium') has been found useful in children at a dosage of 0·5 to 4·4 mg per kg as a rough guide. For a child of 9 months weighing 9 kg the trial dose would probably be in multiples of 2 mg tablets up to 6 mg, judging by the effect. Unwanted effects are weakness and somnolence. If these prove minimal, higher doses may be used. The related benzodiazephine drug nitrazepam ('Mogadon') is probably more effective, although in small children more likely to produce drowsiness and weakness. Nitrazepam should be given in a dose of 0·5 to 1 mg per kg.

For all other types of seizures the most commonly used drugs are phenobarbitone, primidone and phenytoin.

Treatment remains very much a matter of adjusting doses and drugs for optimum control. Tolerance is an individual matter. There has been increasing recognition of pharmacogenetic individuality. Some patients may lack the optimum level of enzymes to metabolise certain anticonvulsants. Nearly all the anticonvulsants effective against major convulsions can be combined.

Phenobarbitone, the oldest established anticonvulsant in common use, is often the drug of first choice to try for the control of seizures of all types, apart from petit mal. Phenobarbitone may make children irritable and exacerbate behaviour disorders; some adults may become depressed on it, but these are minor drawbacks to what is a cheap and effective anticonvulsant.

Phenobarbitone is available in 15, 30, 60 and 100 mg tablets, and as an elixir with 15 mg in 5 ml. For children, a guide to dosage is 5 to 10 mg per kg of body weight. For adults, 30 mg is given night and morning, increasing to 120 mg daily is necessary for optimum effect. If control is not achieved at this dose, the choice is between going up to 180 mg daily, which can be done if the unwanted effects are minimal, or, alternatively, keeping the dose of phenobarbitone at around 120 mg and adding another drug such as phenytoin. Phenobarbitone is a dangerous drug when taken in overdose because of its slow excretion. This point must be taken into account when prescribing for epileptic patients of unstable personality where there is a likelihood of deliberate overdose.

Phenytoin ('Epanutin') is the most commonly used drug of the hydantoin group. It can be used alone or in combination. Phenytoin is available in 50 and 100 mg capsules. For children, a rough guide to dosage is at the rate of 5 to 7 mg per kg. In adults, the effective dose is near the toxic level, the effective dose range being between 200 and 400 mg daily with a usual level of 300 mg daily. Wide variations in serum phenytoin have been found in patients taking approximately the same dose. Differences in absorption and metabolism may be responsible. The substance used in the capsules has been found to influence absorption. The concomitant use of other drugs, for example, chlorpromazine or anticoagulants, may cause the level of phenytoin to rise. Precise serum levels at which unwanted effects occur have been described, e.g., nystagmus at 20 μg/ml and ataxia at 30 μg/ml (Behrman, 1969). Suggestions have been made that epileptic patients on phenytoin should have their dose level controlled by serum estimations, but this is not practical in most centres at present. Providing it is recognised that individual variation occurs and intolerance may develop, many difficulties can be avoided. In addition to nystagmus and atazia, other unwanted effects are hypertrophy of the gums in young people; allergic reactions with rashes, joint pains and lymphadenopathy; in continued dosage hirsutes may develop in women, and is a well known finding in women in epileptic colonies.

Too much should not be made of the unwanted effects. In many patients phenytoin is well tolerated for many years.

Phenytoin is often given with phenobarbitone. The usual recommendation is to give the two drugs in separate preparations, although combinations are on the market. These combined drugs made up in one tablet may occasionally be of the convenient dosage for effective control of seizures, and may serve a purpose when it is desirable to cut down the number of tablets a patient has to remember to take. One preparation ('Garoin') contains 100 mg phenytoin sodium and 50 mg sodium phenobarbitone in one tablet.

Primidone ('Mysoline'), similar in structure to phenobarbitone, is sometimes effective when the barbiturate is not. It is very important to introduce primidone slowly, since some patients show diplopia, vertigo, dysarthria and ataxia on quite small initial doses, and may be put off what is an effective drug. It is commonly recommended not to give primidone and phenobarbitone together, and this is a good principle. Many established cases will be found to be controlled by phenobarbitone, primidone and phenytoin in combination, and if this is working well there is no point in removing one of the drugs. For the new patient, however, it is best to avoid primidone and phenobarbitone together if control is possible by other combinations of drugs.

Primidone is available in 250 mg tablets. As a guide in deciding children's dosage, 20 to 30 mg per kg is suggested. For adults, start with half a tablet at night, i.e., 125 mg, and increase by half a tablet a day, or every three days if there is marked intolerance. Ultimately, the drug may be well tolerated, dose levels of 750 mg to 1·0 g being quite common. It is possible to increase primidone up to 2·0 g daily.

Apart from the side effects mentioned, there may be rarely a megaloblastic anaemia.

Some more recently introduced anticonvulsants are now available. They are quite frequently used in combination with established anticonvulsants. Clinical trials of new anticonvulsants present methodological problems of how to decide what is a worthwhile reduction of fit frequency, and whether we should calculate an absolute reduction of the number of fits or a proportionate decrease, for example, by using a logarithmic transform of the number of fits plus one (to deal with the problem of what to do about zero fits in a trial). One method is to add two new anticonvulsants to existing medication in two separate groups of patients, and make comparisons between the decrease in fits due to the two new drugs.

Pheneturide ('Benuride'), structurally similar to phenacemide ('Phenurone') but less toxic, is available in 200 mg tablets. Pheneturide is recommeneded for temporal lobe epilepsy. Like all other anticonvulsants, pheneturide is successful in some patients, either alone in gradually increasing doses from 200 mg daily up to 1000 mg daily, or when added in small doses to existing medication, but whilst some patients tolerate it well, others do not get on with it. Pheneturide combines well with phenytoin in some patients. For children, the recommended dose is 15 mg per kg.

Side effects are ataxia and drowsiness, but serious side effects are seldom seen. Pheneturide like other anticonvulsants has recently been implicated in disturbances of calcium metabolism.

Pheneturide is available in a compound tablet containing 200 mg pheneturide, phenytoin 40 mg and phenobarbitone 15 mg, and can be given in doses of one to five daily.

Sulthiame ('Ospolot') is mainly advocated for use in temporal lobe epilepsy, and is usually added in small doses to other anticonvulsants. It is claimed that sulthiame combines better with phenytoin than with primidone. Chemically, it is a sulphonamide derivative. Sulthiame is available in 50 and 200 mg tablets. Ospolot is claimed to be effective in psychomotor attacks in children, for whom a dose range of 10 to 15 mg per kg is recommended. In practice, one 50 mg tablet can be given to babies, 75 mg ($1\frac{1}{2}$ tablets) to small children, and to school children 50 to 150 mg daily.

Sulthiame is apt to evoke unwanted effects different from most other anticonvulsants. Dyspnœa, drowsiness, paræsthesiæ, headache, nausea, anorexia, photophobia and unsteadiness have been complained of. Psychic changes are reported—confusion (or of lesser degree, inability to think clearly) and excitement.

Carbamazepine ('Tegretol') in 200 mg tablets is occasionally effective, either alone or in combination with other drugs, in temporal lobe epilepsy and major motor seizures. Carbamazepine is sometimes useful in children since it does not affect behaviour as phenobarbitone sometimes does. The drug should be introduced cautiously to avoid drowsiness and gastrointestinal upsets. For children, 20 mg per kg of body weight is a rough guide. For adults, half a tablet may be started, i.e., 100 mg once daily for a few days, increased to 200 mg daily, with a usual dose of 800 mg daily, and occasionally 1·2 g daily. Some patients may show a sensitivity reaction to carbamazepine; jaundice, rashes and blood dyscrasias have occurred. Carbamazepine should not be used with monoamine oxidase inhibitors.

Sometimes a patient with temporal lobe epilepsy associated with aggressive behaviour will show a response to carbamazepine with concomitant improvement in the EEG.

Beclamide ('Nydrane') differs chemically from other anticonvulsants. It is a benzylamide and the molecule contains chlorine. Beclamide has a weak anticonvulsant action. It is available in tablets of 500 mg. Beclamide is expensive, and should be used for patients who have not responded to other drugs or have troublesome unwanted effects on other drugs. Beclamide can be added to phenobarbitone when phenobarbitone alone or in combination with other drugs has produced side effects. In some patients phenobarbitone can be gradually reduced as beclamide is added, at first 500 to 1000 mg three or four times daily. Children aged 5 to 12 should receive half the adult dose; children below 5 should receive a quarter of the adult dose. Beclamide is relatively non-toxic.

If a number of changes of anticonvulsants and the addition of the newer compounds does not reduce the frequency of seizures, go on trying, but remember that the lack of control may be because the patient has an expanding brain lesion. Remember also that reduction of more potent anticonvulsants and the introduction of weaker agents may provoke status epilepticus.

There are a number of drugs which a few patients may benefit from. Acetazolamide ('Diamox') may have an anticonvulsant effect by acting as a carbonic anhydrase inhibitor in the brain and not by its diuretic effect. The dose for an adult is one or two 250 mg tablets daily. Acetazolamide is sometimes useful because it lacks depressant side effects.

Amphetamine sulphate in 5 mg doses is occasionally useful to off-set the drowsiness of anticonvulsants if reducing them leads to more fits. The dangers of dependence must be remembered. It is possible that side effects of anticonvulsants are linear, e.g., drowsiness, but the anticonvulsant effect follows some other law, e.g., logarithmic. There comes a dose level when drowsiness rapidly increases but the anti-convulsant effect does not. Some forms of epilepsy are provoked by drowsiness. In these situations amphetamine may be helpful. Never-theless, it is best to avoid amphetamine if possible by adjusting com-binations of anticonvulsants.

Alternative forms of standard drugs are preferred by some patients and doctors. Alternatives to phenobarbitone are methylphenobarbi-tone ('Prominal') which has to be given in higher doses, 200 to 600 mg daily; 10 mg per kg for a child. Methylphenobarbitone is available in tablets of 30, 60 and 200 mg. Occasionally, epileptic patients take this and other barbiturates in higher doses than prescribed, having deve-loped dependence on the drug.

Phenylmethylbarbituric acid ('Rutonal') is another barbiturate marketed as an anticonvulsant, given in a dose of 200 mg b.d.

There are two additional hydantoins. One is ethotoin ('Peganone') 500 mg tablets with a daily adult dose range of 2 to 3 g. It is less effective than phenytoin, but in some patients less toxic. The dose range for children is 15 to 50 mg per kg.

Methoin ('Mesontoin') is the second hydantoin, but is sometimes more toxic than the other two. Methoin is presented in 100 mg tablets with a dose range from 50 mg (half a tablet) to 600 mg daily. For children, 2 to 10 mg per kg can be given.

Paramethadione ('Paradione') is an alternative dione to troxidone, although less effective than troxidone against petit mal. Parameth-adione tablets are 300 mg., and the dose is 900 mg to 2·1 g daily, with a child's dose range calculated from 15 to 25 mg per kg.

Discontinuance of Anticonvulsants

This may be considered if there have been no attacks for two or three years. After initial stabilisation on one or two drugs, the first thing is to try to get the dose adjusted so that it can be given twice a day, morning and evening. The drug taking is less likely to be forgotten by the patient if reduced to twice a day. If after this stabilisation period no seizures occur for three years, cautious reduction can be begun. Some clinicians use EEGs to help decide whether to reduce drugs or not. The EEG is not an exact guide to this. Further seizures can occur after the finding of a normal EEG. Attacks can remain quiescent clinically in spite of an abnormal EEG. Nevertheless, an EEG is of some help; a normal EEG on repeated occasions is a stronger indication for reduction of anticonvulsants than a very abnormal one, but the final decision must be based on clinical assessment.

Long-term Anticonvulsants, Folic Acid and Calcium Metabolism

Epileptic patients on phenytoin, primidone and phenobarbitone have been found to have low serum folate levels. It has been suggested that some epileptic patients who develop mental deterioration or a psychosis do so because of the low blood folate. Mental deterioration due to low folate is far from inevitable however (Grant and Stores, 1970), and the problem of individual variation arises. Furthermore, some epileptic patients who were given folic acid to combat a low serum folate had more fits; but, again, not all folic acid treated epileptics had more fits. These findings seem now to have been explained. Baylis, Crowley, Preece, Sylvester and Marks have shown (1971) that plasma phenytoin levels fall after 10 days of folic acid therapy, at times enough to impair control of the fits. The recommendation is made that folic acid replacement therapy should be monitored biochemically.

Long-term anticonvulsant therapy has recently been shown to be associated in some cases with low serum calcium levels but further work will show whether this is important or not.

Treatment of Status Epilepticus

The definition of what constitutes status epilepticus varies. One definition is that there is no recovery of consciousness between fits; in the USA the designation prolonged motor seizure activity is sometimes used, and status is assumed if there are three fits in half an hour, or a general or focal seizure lasting more than 10 minutes. Status epilepticus still has an appreciable mortality, and any increase of fits in a patient should be regarded as potential status and preventive measures should be taken.

It is said that in a number of epileptic colonies and hospitals the incidence of status has been reduced in recent years. Generally improved management and a wider range of anticonvulsants may be one factor, and also better control of intercurrent infections.

It is best to make arrangements in advance for the possible event of a patient going into status. Establish in the area you work in where the nearest intensive care unit is; get the views of the local neurologist; discuss the matter with the local anaesthetic division; then, when status occurs a plan is ready.

Occasionally a patient goes into status epilepticus when taken off anticonvulsants for an EEG test. Patients should not be taken off their drugs if the epilepsy has been difficult to control. If an established epileptic goes into status epilepticus it may have been a recurrent event, and the medical case notes may contain information on the treatment the patient has reponded to in the past. If a patient's first manifestation of epilepsy is to go into status, suspect a lesion of the frontal or fronto-temporal areas. Patients with epilepsy secondary to brain lesions are often more difficult to control than non-symptomatic cases.

If a patient with a known fit pattern starts to get prolonged motor seizures, say three in sequence, give the next dose of anticonvulsants as an intramuscular injection. If the patient is a child already on high doses of anticonvulsant, a different substance, e.g., chloral, trichloryl or paraldehyde may be given. In all situation of early status look in the ears and examine the patient for an intercurrent and possibly silent infection. Take the temperature at the outset.

If status becomes established, the most important thing is to stop the motor seizures and reverse anoxia. Notify the local intensive care unit that a case of status epilepticus has occurred. Make sure of the patient's airway, and arrange assisted ventilation if necessary, and deal with aspiration of mucus or vomitus.

Intravenous diazepam ('Valium') is the drug which should be tried as it is often effective in terminating seizures (Parsonage and Norris, 1967). The effectiveness of diazepam in status is one reason for avoiding its widespread use as an oral treatment of all kinds of epilepsy over a long period, although there may be good grounds for using oral diazepam in myoclonic epilepsy. Start with 10 mg diazepam intravenously in an adult. In children, give either 0·25 mg or 0·5 mg per kg of body weight, or 1 to 2 mg per year of life. If there is difficulty in finding a suitable vein in a baby give the drug intramuscularly. A scalp vein may have to be employed.

Once the initial dose of Valium has been given, arrangements can be made for transfer to a special intensive care unit, but a doctor should accompany the patient. If there is no intensive care unit, but a portable EEG is available, EEG monitoring can be started, but this is much less important than combating anoxia and stopping the seizures. If a single 10 mg intravenous dose is not effective, the best thing is to set up an intravenous infusion with 100 mg of diazepam in 500 ml of saline, adjusting the rate to control seizure activity. If the EEG is available, the disappearance of seizure waveforms can be used as a guide for rate of infusion. Up to 200 mg of diazepam can be given in an adult over 24 hours. The blood pressure may fall and respiratory depression may occur as a result of the diazepam, and the rate of administration of the drug must be controlled to avoid rapid fall of blood pressure or marked respiratory depression.

If the seizures persist in spite of the Valium, check once again for intercurrent infection, which may be cerebral, or for toxicity from previous anticonvulsants, such as the onset of jaundice or early liver failure; consider again the possibility that the epilepsy has been in fact due to an expanding brain lesion.

As time goes on, diazepam becomes less effective in controlling persisting seizures, and paraldehyde, phenytoin or phenobarbitone may be given intramuscularly or intravenously.

If there is persisting anoxia or obstruction to the airway, get in touch with an anaesthetist colleague and arrange for intubation. In very persistent seizures with deterioration in the general condition, a general anaesthetic may have to be given with neuromuscular paralysis from muscle relaxant drugs such as curare.

In children, the dose is calculated as given above, the initial rate of injection being 5 mg per minute for doses of 5 mg and above. If seizure activity is not stopped by the initial dose, 4 mg of diazepam can be given per hour in an infusion. In children, as in adults, supplementary treatment with phenobarbitone or paraldehyde will often be necessary.

Sodium phenobarbitone can be given in an intramuscular injection of 6 mg per kg of body weight. Paraldehyde can be given intramuscularly as 0·1 ml per kg of body weight. Paraldeyde solution should be checked for stability, and is more likely to be a stable solution if it has been stored under cool conditions in the dark; *it must be given in a glass syringe*, as it reacts with the plastic substances used in disposable syringes. Paraldehyde may have to be repeated after 10 to 20 minutes. If it is going to be effective, there should be some reduction of seizure activity in 10 minutes. The repeat dose should be injected in a different site.

Treatment of Post-epileptic Automatism and Prolonged Psychomotor Automatism

In the relatively brief automatism following a fit the patient may need to be gently restrained and, if possible, manoeuvred into lying down. Forceful methods may evoke anger, resistance and violence. If the recovery is delayed, intravenous diazepam or intravenous sodium amylobarbitone 300 to 400 mg may have to be given to control the patient.

A more prolonged automatism may ocur which, in a hitherto undiagnosed epileptic, may be mistaken for a psychosis. If the condition is suspected, try if possible to get an EEG done immediately. The EEG will show generalised slow activity at about 4 to 6 Hz., and will at once distinguish the case from a non-organic psychosis such as schizophrenia. The patient in prolonged automatism may show motor over-activity such as chewing movements, or experience sensory over-stimulation with complaints of buzzing or banging sounds or flashes of light.

Even though clouding of consciousness exists, its detection may be difficult, and the patient may be clinically diagnosed as a schizophrenic. This is likely in the few cases who experience hallucinations and paranoid ideas. Some patients show variable psychomotor retardation and excitement, and some patients show posturing with hands outstretched, usually with upward gaze and chewing movements going on at the same time. The patient may be regarded as a case of the now rare acute catatonia.

Sometimes the automatism suddenly stops, with the emergence of an affectively warm person, different from the schizophrenic's more withdrawn personality. Recovery, also, is usually much more complete than in schizophrenia.

Where there is aggression or prolongation of the attack, intravenous diazepam or sodium amylobarbitone may be tried. One or two electroconvulsive (ECT) treatments may terminate the attack.

After recovery from the acute episode, one of the newer drugs, phenturide, sulthiame or carbamazepene can be added to standard anticonvulsants. Although the final value of these drugs is difficult to assess, they are claimed to be of help where psychomotor attacks occur.

Use of ECT in Epilepsy

Apart from the use of one or two ECT to terminate a prolonged psychomotor attack, the question sometimes arises whether to use ECT in a more chronic epileptic psychosis or in a depressive bout in an epileptic patient.

If the psychosis is accompanied by generalised slow activity in the EEG, first consider adjustment of anticonvulsants, toxic side effects, or a hitherto undiagnosed metabolic or other disorder. Folate deficiency is probably not a frequent cause of severe psychosis, but estimation of serum or red blood cell folate should be done.

Sometimes, when in spite of adjustments to anticonvulsants increasing tension and irritability build up, and the EEG findings suggest that an epileptic attack is likely to occur in the near future, the attack can be aborted by giving one or two ECT with subsequent improvement in the mental state. When EEG monitoring is done immediately after the ECT, episodes of slow waves or spike and wave similar to the pre-ECT tracing begin to reappear after about 20 minutes, but do not become so persistent or generalised. These post-ECT waveforms are to be distinguished from abnormalities induced by the ECT itself.

This use of ECT to improve mood changes should not be used routinely merely to try to discharge fits before they occur. The treatment should only be used in selected cases where the mood changes have led to aggression or to severe depressive mood swings with suicidal attempts.

It is sometimes asked why it is that an epileptic who has, in a sense, a built-in convulsive therapy, should benefit on occasion from externally induced electrical convulsions. It is true that a fit or a series of fits occurring spontaneously do improve the mental state temporarily, but it is not true that epileptics do not suffer from depression. Their fits do not always occur at the right time to elevate the mood, or do not always relieve depression when they do occur.

Epileptic Personality and Persistent Epileptic Psychosis

It is still disputed whether there is an epilpetic personality or not

(Keating, 1961; Guevvant *et al.*, 1962). There are many different kinds of epilepsy, varying in impact from one fit in a lifetime to frequent psychic and major attacks in temporal lobe epilepsy, so that it is not surprising that it is difficult to identify a single type of epileptic personality. Epileptics living under the more traditional epileptic colony regimes can become institutionalised, as can any other patient. In some colonies which originally admitted the patients under the designation 'sane epileptics' the patients, on the whole, remain non-psychotic even after many years, but may show such institutionalised behaviour as having a favourite chair or favourite activity, and they may become quarrelsome if their territorial beat becomes invaded or their favourite activity threatened. Sometimes feuds develop. In larger colonies, this sort of behaviour can be ameliorated by moving patients around from time to time and by active occupation.

Whereas not all epileptics are religiose, there seems no doubt that some do become so, either due to the type or site of the lesion causing the epilepsy, or perhaps due to the area of the brain affected by the electrical discharges. I have seen a sanctimonious religiosity develop in a naval officer (not previously intensely religious) who suffered a penetrating brain injury during the D-day landings in 1944 with epilepsy supervening. Dewhurst and Beard describe sudden religious conversions in temporal lobe epilepsy (1970). In the present climate of religious disbelief these sudden religious conversions are striking, so much so that if any one in psychiatric care becomes religiose suspect schizophrenia or temporal lobe epilepsy and have an EEG investigation done.

The psychiatrist will be required to treat epileptics with general personality disorder, aggressive behaviour, depression, neurotic and paranoid reactions to social rejection and employment difficulties. The schizophreniform psychosis of epilepsy may provide a considerable treatment problem. Slater, Beard and Glithero (1963) present the arguments for considering the psychosis as an outcome of the epilepsy rather than as the chance occurrence of two separate diseases in the same patient. The onset of the psychosis was, on average, 14 years after the onset of the epilepsy; there was a tendency for the psychosis to begin when the fit frequency was falling. Although most cases of schizophreniform psychosis are associated with temporal lobe epilepsy, some centrencephalic epileptics show psychotic phases of hebephrenic type.

Although there is relative preservation of affect in the schizophreniform psychosis of epilepsy compared with schizophrenia, and some cases recover, the majority tend towards chronicity. Snaith, Mehta and Raby (1970) found low serum folate in half of their cases of schizophrenia-like psychosis of epilepsy, but this low serum folate was found in other states of mental illness in epilepsy, and also in some, though proportionately fewer, epileptics without mental illness. Although serum folate levels should be investigated in the schizophrenia-like psychosis, and any megaloblastic anaemia treated if it is also present, the effects of folic acid treatment are unlikely to be to reverse the psychosis.

Courses of ECT with phenothiazines or haloperidol can be given in an effort to control the psychotic illness, but are usually only helpful in the short term. Although phenothiazines are mildly epileptogenic, they provoke major attacks in only a few patients, and are worth trying to control florid delusions or episodes of aggressive behaviour. The anticonvulsants should be continued, but increasing the anticonvulsant does not usually improve the psychosis, although gradual adjustment of anticonvulsants with substitution of one of the newer drugs, sulthiame, pheneturide or carbamazepene, should be tried and may produce marginal benefit.

Surgical Treatment of Epilepsy

Apart from the removal of tumours, surgery is used to excise more indolent lesions of the temporal lobe, to excise the atrophic seizure-producing hemisphere in infantile hemiplegia, and to section the corpus callosum to prevent the spread of epileptic discharge from the focal origin in one hemisphere to involve the opposite hemisphere.

Surgery is only considered in temporal lobe epilepsy (excluding cases due to large or expanding tumours) if adequate anticonvulsant treatment has failed to control the fits, and if the patient's *habitual* seizure can be localised to one side of the brain. To do this, all the evidence has to be considered—clinical, EEG, radiological, psychometric. Sphenoidal electrode EEG recordings will often need to be done under thiopentone anaesthesia to see the spike or sharp wave discharges more easily. After some years, a mirror focus may develop on the opposite side making localisation more difficult.

The assessment of patients with temporal lobe epilepsy for surgery can only be done in specialist centres. The operation is done primarily to control fits, but coexisting psychosis or other mental illness is not necessarily a contra-indication to operation. Schizophreniform psychoses of an insidious kind with social withdrawal are, on the whole, less favourably influenced by operation than paranoid aggressive reactions with preservation of affect.

Over 100 cases of temporal lobectomy have been studied in detail by Murray A. Falconer and his colleagues in patients both with and without psychotic and other mental illness (James, 1960; Serafetinides and Falconer, 1962; Falconer and Taylor, 1968; Taylor and Falconer, 1968).

Blakemore, Ettlinger and Falconer report on the cognitive changes in relation to the frequency of seizures before operation and the type of lesion found at operation (1966), and the long-term effects of temporal lobectomy on certain cognitive functions have been studied by Blakemore and Falconer (1967).

Mesial temporal sclerosis was found in 47 of 100 consecutive cases treated by anterior temporal lobectomy (Falconer and Taylor, 1968), with hamartomas, small cryptic tumours, nonspecific gliosis, scars and infarcts making up the rest of the lesions. 50 per cent of the patients with mesial temporal sclerosis were completely fit-free after operation compared with 33 per cent of the remainder.

An auditory verbal learning deficit appears after removal of the dominant temporal lobe which may start to recover after three years (Blakemore and Falconer, 1967).

Hemispherectomy for infantile hemiplegia began to be done in the 1950s (Cairns and Davidson, 1951). Some patients with infantile hemiplegia have epiliptic fits whereas others do not, but usually those with fits show greater depression of intelligence than do those who are free of fits.

Improvement in behaviour and maintenance of, and even improvement on, intelligence scores have been reported in an average follow-up period of 10 years after hemispherectomy (Griffith and Davidson, 1966). *Surgical disconnection of the cerebral hemispheres* has been carried out for intractable epilepsy, the major interhemispheric commissures being divided. Luessenhop and his co-workers report improvement following this procedure (1970).

The Use of Electroencephalography

The EEG has been a disappointment to psychiatry. Too much was expected of it. The chief disadvantage of the EEG is its lack of specificity and its variability between different occasions. The usual routine scalp EEG causes no discomfort to the patient and can usually be completed in half an hour, but three minutes hyperventilation followed by photic stimulation are usually included as activation procedures. Hyperventilation, if vigorously carried out, washes carbon dioxide from the lungs, and with depleted CO_2 the cerebral vessels constrict, causing relative anoxia. Hyperventilation will sometimes provoke petit mal, and may accentuate or reveal for the first time the EEG changes of focal epilepsy.

Leptazol, bemegride, imipramine, chlorpromazine are potentially convulsant substances which have been used to activate foci in the EEG when given intravenously. Leptazol is the most reliable, but in practice is little used except in special units where the preliminary assessment for surgery is carried out. Sleep activation is more commonly used to reveal temporal lobe foci or sleep-sensitive epilepsy. The new drug chlorimipramine ('Anafranil') which is given intravenously for depression, is the kind of drug which warrants investigation as an EEG activator in epilepsy, but pharmacogenetic variability of response and problems of defining convulsive threshold will probably limit its usefulness in this field.

In spite of its limitations, the EEG is sometimes the only special test to reveal a neoplasm in late-onset epilepsy. The EEG should nowadays be combined with an ultrasound scan to determine the position of the brain mid-line structures. Ultrasound should be available in all EEG departments. A straight X-ray of the skull and lumbar puncture should be done next. If a pneumoencephalogram, arteriogram or radioisotope scan are contemplated, these can be arranged in consultation with a neurologist.

Some of the drugs used in psychiatric treatment suppress epileptic waveforms in the EEG. Particularly potent in this respect are diazepam, chlordiazepoxide and nitrazepam, even though they are not consistently potent anticonvulsants when given orally. All the standard anticonvulsant drugs suppress EEG activity, including the newer drugs carmamazepene, sulthiame and benuride. Barbiturates, the diazepenes, chloral and paraldehyde evoke low voltage fast activity in the EEG. It is best to stop all drugs three days before an EEG, but anticonvulsants should not be stopped if the epilepsy has been difficult to control as this may provoke status epilepticus. ECT evokes abnormal waveforms in the EEG for six weeks and longer. The fact that it has been given is often not stated on the EEG request form, and patients sometimes use the terms EEG and ECT interchangeably.

A series of EEGs should always be done before concluding that there is no support for epilepsy, particularly if the clinical evidence is strong.

Conditions Allied to Epilepsy

There is a group of disorders more often formulated under the heading of minimal brain damage or, in the USA, as minimal brain dysfunction (Stevens *et al.*, 1967). Children with the minimal brain damage syndrome (MBD) include those with over-active distractible behaviour, the hyperkinetic syndrome; children with right-left disorientation and specific learning disabilities; impulsive, emotional children with a short attention span who cannot delay gratification. It is difficult to know what should be included under MBD, and what they become as adults. The relationship with epilepsy is tenuous, but some have non-specific EEG abnormalities. Presumably some area of the brain has been damaged, interfering with control of volition, emotion and perception; but coarse neurological signs are absent. Amphetamine sulphate in 5 mg doses may help hyperkinetic children; phenobarbitone may make such children more irritable.

In adults there is the group who have minimal non-specific EEG abnormalities as seen in MBD. These are a mixed bunch. Some may show extreme behaviour deviation, such as arson, under circumstances of relatively minor resentment; others only step out of line after taking six to eight pints of beer. Some transvestites show these MBD type EEG changes, and it has been hypothesised, admittedly at a very speculative level, that they may have some body image ambiguity which causes them to dress as women, their male body image concept not being fixed.

Those patients who show extreme aggression, out of character, after alcohol should have EEG studies before and after taking the amount of alcohol which has caused them trouble. In the MBD cases, minor paroxysmal features in the EEG may be accentuated, but this is only meaningful if the patients do not become drowsy and remain with a normal alpha rhythm in the EEG. In those who become disturbed after alcohol but who lack abnormalities in the routine EEG, only the appearance of paroxysmal activity in the EEG should be regarded as possibly significant, as the background frequency may change from drowsiness or metabolic effects of large amounts of alcohol, and this cannot be regarded as abnormal.

There exists a group of people with behaviour disorders, including some aggressive psychopaths, who show slow wave abnormalities in the parieto-temporal areas of their EEGs but whose clinical picture does not add up to temporal lobe epilepsy. There is probably a mixed bag of pathology underlying these conditions, from 'cortical immaturity' to brain damage, possibly from viral infections. Cleobury, Skinner, Thouless and Wildy have found an association between herpes simplex virus (type 1) antibody and psychopathic disorder (1971). They have not yet shown that high antibody titres are associated with EEG abnormalities, and aggressive psychopaths from a prison population are, anyhow, likely to show high virus antibody titres as prison inmates are liable to cross infection.

There remains a group of psychiatric patients who show aggressive or quasi-automatic behaviour, who do not show the sharp wave or focal spike activity of temporal lobe epilepsy in their EEGs but, whose EEGs nevertheless show slow wave abnormalities in the temporal areas, and who remain difficult to diagnose. They do not readily fit into the psychopathic or organic group, and the clinical picture falls short of frank temporal lobe epilepsy.

Because of behaviour disorders with abnormal EEGs, some frankly paroxysmal, yet without clinical epileptic attacks, anticonvulsant drugs and also amphetamines have been tried. Recent controlled studies of giving phenytoin to delinquents have not supported the belief that phenytoin is effective in these situations (Connors et al., 1971). In one study (Lefkowitz, 1969) the 'Hawthorne effect' was found—both groups, control and drug-treated, improved due to the extra attention received from the research process.

CHAPTER TEN

The Treatment of Alcoholic and Other Addictions

ADDICTIONS OTHER THAN TO ALCOHOL

Although the number and varieties of these addictions have been increasing in recent years, with more and more young people endangered, neither singly nor lumped together do they create more than a small fraction of the social and medical problems caused by alcoholism. For that reason it seems best to deal with them in this chapter fairly shortly to begin with, before turning to the matters of graver importance.

During the past ten years there has been a steep rise in the numbers of drug addicts in the United Kingdom. The use of cannabis (marihuana, hemp, 'pot'), of the amphetamines, of lysergic acid diethylamide, of cocaine and heroin, have all increased. We may also reflect that the consumption of cigarettes has not diminished; dependence on tranquillisers is wide-spread, even if under satisfactory medical control; barbiturate dependence is as common a problem as ever it was. We shall only be able to discuss a part of these numerous problems, and that briefly, from the therapeutic point of view.

Addicted patients have to be handled with particular caution. If an unknown patient presents himself asking for a further supply of drugs, it is wise to check with the doctor who prescribed for him previously, or with the dispensing chemist, or with the Dangerous Drugs Branch of the Home Office (telephone 01-930 8100). If possible the patient should be referred to a special drug dependency clinic for treatment. The early signs of opiate withdrawal are anxiety, restlessness and a running nose, accompanied by a craving for drugs.

Treatment of the addict is difficult and usually proceeds in a number of stages; but the initial withdrawal of the drug should always be carried out in hospital. Thereafter the form of treatment to be given will depend on a number of considerations, and we shall not go into details here; excellent accounts are given in the Report of the Interdepartmental Committee on Drug Addiction (1961), and in a WHO Study Group report on the treatment and care of drug addicts (World Health Organisation, No. 131, 1957).

Bewley (1967, 1968) has given a good account of the treatment of opiate withdrawal. Heroin withdrawal symptoms are best treated with morphine or methadone (Physeptone), given in a linctus so that the patient does not know the amount given: I mg methadone is equivalent to heroin 1 mg, morphine 3 mg, pethidine 20 mg, codeine 30 mg, laudanum (1 per cent morphine) 0·3 ml. In a doubtful case 10 mg methadone can be given, and if there is no improvement in withdrawal symptoms within one hour 20 mg should be administered. This can be repeated after another two hours, but 50 mg should be sufficient to cover the next twelve hours.

LSD may produce psychotic states with hallucinations, acute anxiety or severe panic, depression, or toxic confusional states. These acute symptoms are best treated in a hospital ward with intramuscular chlorpromazine.

The extent of addiction and habituation to barbiturates is hard to assess, but the use of these drugs has increased in recent years. Most neurotic patients, who need barbiturate sedation for the combating of their symptoms, adjust themselves to reasonable levels of medication and remain so adjusted. But from time to time one sees patients who gradually increase their daily dosage, until it is all too apparent that habituation has gone on into addiction. If then states of mild confusion occur, further large doses may be ingested, sometimes with disastrous results. The treatment of an addiction of this kind is usually fairly easy, unless the patient has a very abnormal personality, or unless large amounts have been taken for too long. Withdrawal must always be gradual, otherwise there is a risk of increasing anxiety, of cardiovascular collapse, and sometimes of disorientation, followed later by epileptic fits and confusion. The tranquillising drugs such as chlorpromazine have proved very useful in damping down these withdrawal symptoms and combating insomnia. Some patients benefit from being maintained afterwards on small doses of a tranquilliser with an anti-depressant (of either or both groups). If one of the sedative tricyclics, such as amitriptyline (Tryptizol) or trimipramine (Surmontil), is given in a single dose at night, sleep is generally improved, without risk of addiction.

Dextroamphetamine (Dexedrine) is often taken by barbiturate and alcoholic addicts to wake themselves up, and there is little doubt that the combination of Dexedrine and Amytal is particularly liable to cause addiction. A practising doctor we treated took an average of 20 Drinamyl tablets a day, amounting to 100 mg of Dexedrine and 640 mg of amylobarbitone, as well as an additional 900 to 1200 mg of amylobarbitone daily. In the U.S.A. the problem of 'goof-balls', as this combination is called, has reached serious proportions, particularly in young people. Toxic psychoses, often resembling schizophrenia, may occur when more than 50 mg of amphetamine is habitually consumed during the day. A urine test is sometimes useful in confirming the diagnosis.

Stimulant drugs can be stopped immediately, since no withdrawal symptoms occur, although depression and irritability are often troublesome for some days and require sedation. Sometimes an antidepressant is also helpful, and it will prevent the craving from becoming overpowering in the months following withdrawal of the drug.

Marihuana smoking has become very much more common lately. Usually there is a period of stimulation followed by sedation; but there is wide individual variation in the response to the drug. Effects are unpredictable, and range from extreme elation to severe panic or depression. There is usually vasodilatation of the face capillaries, pupillary dilatation, and a rise in heart rate and blood pressure. Illusions and hallucinations may occur, and auditory perception and the experience of time may be altered. Severe adverse reactions may require treatment with chlorpromazine.

ALCOHOLIC ADDICTION

The evils of addiction to alcohol are of a higher order of magnitude to those caused by the drugs we have mentioned, both in their social extent and their threat to the mental and physical health of the individual. They are, in fact, only exceeded by the evils of cigarette smoking (which rarely presents as a problem to the psychiatrist). The fact that the only limitation on the consumption of alcohol is the depth of the consumer's pocket has meant that in all countries and at all times alcoholism has remained a major social and medical problem. It is out of the virtues of alcohol that its dangers arise. Taken in reasonable amounts and at suitable times, its effects are largely beneficial; its disinhibiting effects are valuable in social converse and in taking the edge off many of life's unavoidable tensions. The fact that though helpful to the many it may be disastrous to the few has often promoted the demand that its use should be prohibited or very strictly controlled. When this has been tried, however, the disadvantages have proved more far-reaching than the advantages.

As has just been said, it is only a minority of drinkers who are seriously endangered, and no discussion of treatment is worth while till this group is more clearly defined. Many people who are not abstainers go through life without ever running into excess; those who do can be classified into three groups which to a certain extent overlap. There is first the occasional and reasonable drinker who now and again oversteps the mark. As a general rule no harm is done, but sometimes it will happen that in a drunken state he offends against the law, perhaps with very serious personal consequences. For a long time in this country there were large numbers of men who got drunk regularly once a week, on the evening of pay-day. Today, perhaps, their place has been taken by the 'expense account' drinker. The problem here is mainly a social and legal one; medical complications are not common in this group.

Secondly, there is the heavy and steady drinker who may become dependent on the drug but does not lose his ability to keep its consumption under control. The addiction, in fact, is not compulsive. He is quite able to reduce the amount he takes if he is convinced that it is necessary, though he may be a little hard to persuade. The amount he takes may be a financial drain, and in course of time his physical and mental health may begin to suffer; but he does not appear on the scene drunk on important occasions, or pull down his life in ruins in the course of a few months. While the capacity for control is still present, and the addiction is reversible, treatment once begun in a co-operative spirit is fairly easy. The main danger arises from the fact that if consumption has been heavy over a long time, changes will have taken place in the nervous system and in the personality which may prove irreversible. A certain proportion of drinkers in this class graduate into the third group.

It is the third group which provides the main problem, for in their case treatment is urgently needed, is often exceptionally difficult, and may yet be outstandingly successful. The drinkers in this class are they who, once started, seem unable to stop drinking until drunkenness supervenes. The predisposition to this reaction may be acquired, for instance, after a head injury or even after damage of the constitution from a more normal type of over-indulgence in alcohol; but very often it seems to have a genetical basis. Positive family histories are often obtained if carefully enquired for. A son may be a teetotaller having seen his father develop the disease, but fails then to confide the true reason to his own children, who in turn fall prey to the condition. Social and environmental factors certainly also play a part; a society like ours which encourages drinking as an aid to social intercourse and relaxation will bring to light a high proportion of its constitutionally endangered members. In some animals under experimental conditions it has been found that increased voluntary intake of alcohol, amounting virtually to craving, may occur. This suggests that there are physical as well as psychological factors involved in alcoholism. It may well be, therefore, that the answer to this problem will eventually be found to lie in individual differences in nervous and metabolic organisation.

Compulsive drinking may start early or late in life. The man affected is often noted in his youth for a particularly hard head; he can out-drink his friends without showing undue effects—though even early on he may have shown the tendency, after a certain amount of alcohol has been taken, to continue drinking in an uncontrolled way when the normal drinker will stop. Later, and this may vary from a few months to several years, loss of control occurs, which is the hallmark of addiction. From now on the alcoholic travels steadily and inevitably down the road to disaster. Now the first drink taken sets up a pathological and irresistible craving for more which continues until supplies run out or the drinker becomes inebriated. With increasing age sensitivity develops and ever smaller quantities of alcohol cause intoxication. At first the loss of control only occurs after taking the first drink, and the alcoholic is still able to control to some extent whether or not he will drink at any one time; characteristically these patients will recall how they went 'on the water wagon' for long spells of time after a particularly heavy or prolonged drinking bout. But as time goes by these 'dry periods' cease. Hangover effects become increasingly severe and now call for a drink immediately on waking, so setting off the craving for more. Social and economic factors now intrude as the alcoholic tries to arrange his life around his drinking. He drinks secretly, drops his friends, quarrels with his family, perhaps loses his job. His libido diminishes and he begins to behave jealously towards his wife. 'Blackouts' and other forms of memory disturbance become prominent; even a few drinks so impair the ability of retention that next day he is unable to remember anything of the previous night. Capacity for recent recall, judgement and insight are affected even when sober and there may have occurred a marked change of personality. Insomnia, hallucinations and increasing waves of fear may herald the approach of delirium tremens and impending disaster. Finally a stage may be reached when the taking of quite small quantities of alcohol will lead to the abrogation of all judgment and control and a catastrophe is inevitable.

When a patient of this kind comes for treatment it must be made absolutely clear both to him and his relatives that there is no alternative to complete abstinence, however it is obtained. In the young psychopathic group this aim may be very difficult to achieve. Impulsiveness, neurotic traits leading to unhappiness, or the inability to stand stresses of any kind, are very likely to lead to relapse, or to the substitution of another drug for alcohol. Chances of success in treatment are much better in those patients who are normal when sober and only develop abnormalities after the first drinks. The outlook is also better with the patient who has recurrent bouts of depression, and only drinks compulsively during such phases. It is now sometimes possible with the antidepressant drugs to prevent or modify such attacks, and the alcoholism then ceases to be a major problem. But in selecting patients for treatment it is not only the nature of the drinking phases which have to be enquired into, but also the quality of the personality. If this is of a strong and driving kind, as is not infrequently the case, if there have been periods of abstinence with a normal adjustment, and especially if these periods have been secured by personal resolution, the prognosis is hopeful. If the personality is at all times abnormal or neurotic, there will only be hope of success if the abnormality is itself of a kind which can be treated after the patient has been induced to become teetotal. In any case the failure of treatment will be ensured if the doctor tries to put the compulsive drinker on a ration of alcohol. Such half measures must be tried only with the controlled but steady drinker who has been overdoing it, but with him are sometimes successful.

The compulsive drinker will always need some psychological preparation before beginning treatment. He must be convinced that total and permanent abstinence is his only hope for the future, and that a cure of his idiosyncrasy, permitting him to have an occasional drink, is impossible. It is justifiable therefore to appeal to his moral sense, his sense of responsibility towards his family, and to arouse fear by stressing the very real dangers of physical disease, dementia, social disaster and death, that may result from alcohol. Until he realises his plight and is prepared to co-operate fully in the treatment, it is generally useless to undertake it. It is better to tell the patient to go away and return when his inevitable downward progress has at last convinced him that nothing but treatment followed by total abstinence will save him from the gutter.

All physical and psychological treatments of compulsive alcoholism have this single aim, of bringing about a stable habit of abstinence. The selection of one method rather than another will depend accordingly on the special skills of the therapist, and on the personality, the circumstances and the particular needs of the patient.

We believe that the treatment of established alcohol addiction can only be given satisfactorily in hospital. Very few patients can be treated at home, and psychotherapy alone is generally ineffective while the patient is drinking. However, there are exceptions, and it is essential to be adaptable in one's approach and to assess each case individually.

When he is admitted to hospital, the patient has often had a last desperate drinking bout and arrives in a semi-intoxicated state. He is put to bed and no further drink is allowed. Withdrawal symptoms occur, and their nature and severity depend partly on the individual, partly on the recent alcoholic intake. Tremor, weakness, perspiration, nausea, anorexia, insomnia and irritability develop in the first 12 hours; hallucinations may appear within 24 hours, and convulsions after 24 to 48 hours. Delirium tremens comes on about the third or fourth day unless prevented. Drugs such as Librium 20 to 30 mg three times daily will control most of these symptoms; but if there are reasons to fear delirium tremens it is better to give large doses of chlorpromazine for the first five days after stopping alcohol intake.

Sleeplessness may be troublesome; but it is best to avoid barbiturates, except in an emergency, as the alcoholic is susceptible to addiction to these drugs. Heminevrin is a very useful drug when withdrawing alcohol, and controls the withdrawal symptoms (see p. 29).

Opportunity is taken during this withdrawal phase to assess the patient's physical and mental state, to give large doses of vitamins and a high protein diet (unless liver function is seriously impaired), and to prepare him psychologically for the treatment to follow.

An established method is to treat alcoholics by aversion techniques combined with psychotherapy, with a prolonged follow-up whenever possible. Patients are carefully selected. They are mostly over 40 and of good basic personality, with enough drive and ability to have made a satisfactory social adjustment before their lives began to be affected by drinking. Aversion therapy is not so successful in the younger psychopathic group, and these patients are probably better handled by group therapy, combined in some cases with Antabuse or Temposil.

The treatment serves a twofold purpose. It provides a method of deconditioning the patient, by associating the taking of alcohol with highly unpleasant consequences; and, perhaps more importantly, it produces a state of physical debility and heightened suggestibility, allowing old patterns of thought to be broken up and new ones sub-stituted. Even the most hard-headed, the most fixed in their beliefs and most unreceptive of arguments or appeals, can often be indoctrin-ated while in this state. This is shown by the success of suggestion in this technique after months or years of intensive psychoanalysis have failed. This and similar methods may eventually be found useful in some other neurotic states in which a fixed mental pattern, a phobia or delusion, has to be destroyed; some experimental work is already proceeding along this line. The old psychiatric and religious literature is full of reports of success from purges, starvation, and other debilita-ting procedures. In our own time we have witnessed the most remark-able conversions, achieved behind the Iron Curtain, by which, by extreme methods of debilitation and continuing suggestion, stable personalities, fanatical Bolsheviks and pillars of a Church, have been brought to confess their past crimes and adopt new faiths.

Technique. We have already emphasised the psychological build up which is such a necessary preliminary to the treatment, and which indeed has to continue throughout its course. If the patient is to be brought to a total and irreversible change in his way of life, every factor in his personality and his situation which can be brought to bear will have to be mobilised. While the treatment continues he will have to be isolated from all old associations, and visitors will be for-bidden; the necessity for this will have to be put to the relatives in a full and frank explanation. One particular doctor should conduct the treatment throughout. He will have to obtain a very full account of the patient's background and, for instance, find out the sort of situa-tions which are particularly difficult for him to face without the support of alcohol. Incidents in his past life, connected with his drink-ing, about which he feels particularly ashamed should be explored in detail, and gone over again and again to inspire and to heighten the sense of guilt. These incidents will be used again later during the actual aversion treatment.

Suggestibility can be heightened by keeping the room in semi-darkness and spotlighting bottles of alcohol placed at the foot of the bed. A pint of warm saline containing 120 mg of prepared ipecacuanha (B.P.) starts the treatment each morning, and is immediately followed by an intramuscular injection of 60 mg of emetine. The patient sits in bed with a blanket over his shoulders and a vomiting bowl near at hand. The pulse rate should then be recorded every three minutes, and the blood pressure at five minute intervals, until vomiting begins. Ten minutes after the injection the first drink is poured out with due formality and handed to the patient. This should be an ounce of neat whisky or gin, preferably the spirit to which the patient is accustomed. He is told to smell it and to remember the pleasures of the past, the pleasure of the first drink of the day, the relief of tension, the escape from the sense of responsibility; all the information the therapist has gained about the patient can now be used. After fifteen minutes, or sooner if the pulse rate starts to increase, the patient is told to drink, and further drinks are pressed on him.

Under this psychological pressure the patient may at first defend himself, even pugnaciously; but once vomiting starts what is left of his morale collapses. At this point, when he is feeling his most miserable and suggestibility is at a maximum, the therapist must offer him support and hope of recovery. He is told that he has the ability to re-create his life and to restore his self-respect, but only if he shuns the first drink. Always he will be only one drink away from ruin; he can never drink in the future; in this respect he is different from other men, and no compromise is possible. Either he gives up drink for ever and lives again, or his first drink is his last as a free man, and he sinks into the gutter and dies miserably.

It is important to give the first drink before nausea begins, for otherwise the conditioned aversion to alcohol will be weakened. A nurse should record the amount of alcohol given and vomited back. Usually four or five drinks of 1 oz (28 ml) each are given, ending with 8 oz (230 ml) of warm ale containing 60 mg of ipecacuanha, which helps to prolong the nausea. If vomiting does not occur within 15 minutes of taking the first drink, apomorphine 3 mg should be given intramuscularly. This will quickly produce results.

Nausea may persist for an hour or more after vomiting has ceased. The patient is left alone in bed for two hours, the bottles of alcohol placed in front of him. After this, if blood pressure and pulse are satisfactory, he gets up and is allowed to mix with the other patients. He usually prefers a light diet with plenty of fluids, but there is no objection to his taking the ordinary meals if he wishes. Activity is best restricted to watching television, reading or writing, or simply self-meditation. After the evening meal he returns to bed and prepares himself mentally for the next day's treatment.

Five or six treatments on successive days are given in all, but it is usually advisable to have one day of rest in the middle. Complications are rare, but emetine is a toxic drug and a careful watch should be kept for any sign of poisoning. Marked and persistent hypotension and tachycardia are indications that treatment should be stopped.

The essence of the treatment lies not so much in creating an aversion for alcohol, as in the indoctrination of the idea that the first drink will lead to rapid and uncontrollable relapse, whether taken now or twenty years hence. Compulsive drinkers have been known to relapse within twenty-four hours of a drink taken after ten years or more of abstinence; this is a fact that the patient must know and accept.

When aversion therapy has finished it is important to deal with the problems, often brought about by his drinking, which the patient may have to face on his discharge. It is also essential to enlist the full support of the family, and to make sure that they understand everything and do all they can to help. Underlying depression may now become more marked and may need treatment with one of the antidepressants, perhaps combined with a tranquilliser. But dependence on drugs, particularly barbiturates, should be avoided wherever possible.

Encouragement and supportive psychotherapy are essential and must be continued for at least two years after treatment, and preferably five years, if success is to be ensured. Any sign of relapse must be taken very seriously, and the patient should be admitted without delay for a second, perhaps shorter, course of aversion. Some patients, especially those under forty, seem to need repeated reinforcement; and we have found that one aversion treatment every two or three months, which can be given on an outpatient basis, may prevent relapse. Apomorphine is preferable to emetine in these conditions.

Apomorphine treatment. Apomorphine can be used in place of emetine to cause vomiting, and set up a conditioned aversion to alcohol. Apomorphine 3 mg is given intramuscularly, together with 1 oz of whisky or gin, in the way that has been described above. Vomiting starts about 5 to 10 minutes after the injection, but the unpleasant after-effects do not last very long, unless combined with ipecacuanha. This gives it an advantage over emetine for use with out-patients.

Dent, who in this country did so much work with alcoholics using apomorphine, believed that the drug worked not so much by setting up a temporary aversion as by reducing anxiety and craving (Dent, 1955).

He found that with milder cases it was sometimes possible to treat the patient on an out-patient basis, giving apomorphine by mouth and omitting the alcohol. The patient is provided with a supply of tablets of apomorphine 6 mg. The initial dose is one tablet, which is placed in the cheek and allowed to dissolve in the saliva, which is not swallowed for 10 minutes. If this does not cause any feeling of sickness, an hour later he takes two tablets, and so on, increasing the dose by one tablet every hour until eventually the dose is found which makes him sick. This has been as high as 200 mg, but generally very much less is needed, the average being around 50 mg. Once the vomiting dose has been found, the patient then takes three-quarters of this dose every two hours, apart from times of sleep, until the next day. On the second day the same process is gone through, starting with three-quarters of the vomiting dose found on the first day, and increasing until the new vomiting dose has been found. Three-quarters of the vomiting dose, as estimated on this second trial, is then taken for the rest of the second day and also every two hours during waking periods for a third day. If there is a big difference between the vomiting dose found on the first and the second day, a rise of more than half the original vomiting dose, treatment should be continued for an extra day, making four days in all.

The first day or two may be spent in bed, but on subsequent days the patient may be up and about, and may even attempt work, taking the sub-vomiting dose every two hours. During treatment, food may be taken as desired and soft drinks *ad lib*. When the patient sleeps during treatment the dosage is interrupted; but another dose will be taken immediately on waking, providing this is not earlier than two hours after the last dose. No alcohol may be taken after the first dose of apomorphine. Rather rarely patients may complain of swelling of the lining of the mouth and throat; treatment must then be discontinued, unless antihistamines can keep this in check.

This method is suitable for some patients who are very anxious to stop drinking, and it may be used with the first relapse into drinking in a patient who was previously treated by more drastic methods. More than one relapse may be treated in this way, but each time the vomiting dose of apomorphine must be found by trial afresh. The method is also suitable for patients who find it very important to remain at work, and it is reported that business men have been able to carry it out during a week-end.

Dent also used apomorphine by mouth during the day as a specific antidote for anxiety symptoms. No dangerous addiction to apomorphine can arise, as an increase in dosage leads to nausea and vomiting and the amount taken is self-limiting.

Disulfiram (Antabuse). Antabuse can be a most useful drug in the treatment of alcoholism, and it has been widely used since Jacobsen and Martensen-Larsen reported encouraging results in 1959. But like other methods it does not provide a cure, and the patient must take the drug regularly if it is to be effective. When a patient is on Antabuse, his reaction to alcohol may be violent and even fatal; and there must be careful selection of patients if these risks are to be avoided. Psychopathic personalities of both inadequate and aggressive types, with little or no ability to control sudden impulses, are not suitable. On the other hand, neurotic personalities with a strong desire to be helped often derive a feeling of security from taking Antabuse, knowing that any lapse will have devastating consequences. The drug is also useful after aversion therapy to help some patients through difficult times.

Antabuse works by inhibiting the enzyme responsible for breaking down acetaldehyde. The accumulation of this substance causes unpleasant symptoms to come on within 10 or 15 minutes of taking alcohol. Vasodilatation, hypotension and tachycardia make their effects felt, often to the point where the patient fears he is about to die. Nausea develops, and goes on to vomiting if much alcohol has been drunk. 'Hangover' effects may last for several hours. Toxic effects on the myocardium have been reported, and an ECG should generally be done before a patient is put on the drug; myocardial and hepatic diseases are contra-indications to Antabuse treatment.

This treatment can be given to out-patients, provided they are off alcohol and know the dangers of drinking. One gram (2 tablets) is taken each evening for three days, and then the dose is halved to 0·5 g daily. After a week it is advisable to make an alcohol test, partly to make sure that the dosage is adequate, but also to show the patient the consequences of drinking. Two ounces of whisky or gin, or its equivalent alcoholic content in beer, are given, and the patient must be watched closely for the next two hours. If the reaction is too severe, intravenous ascorbic acid 1 gram should be given immediately, followed by an intravenous anti-histamine, since part of the reaction is due to release of histamine.

If in such a test symptoms are alarming, the maintenance dose of Antabuse can be dropped to 0·25 g daily, but otherwise it should remain at 0·5 g. Antabuse is broken down slowly, and reactions to alcohol may occur for several days after stopping the drug.

Side effects of Antabuse are sometimes troublesome: acneiform eruptions, halitosis, gastro-intestinal disturbances, fatigue, headache, reduced sexual potency, and rarely psychotic episodes may occur. If symptoms of this kind are too severe, the drug should be stopped or replaced by calcium carbinide (Abstem).

Citrated calcium carbinide has recently been used in place of Antabuse. This drug also inhibits the breakdown of acetaldehyde, but after alcohol the reactions that occur are milder. As Glatt (1959) has pointed out, this may be a mixed blessing; for the reaction after a test dose of alcohol may be so mild as to be ineffective as a deterrent to drinking. The dosage is 50–100 mg daily, taken preferably in the morning or in two divided doses, since the drug is eliminated from the body in about twelve hours.

OTHER TREATMENTS

The success of any physical treatment of the compulsive alcoholic will depend on adequate follow-up and the application of all available methods to maintain teetotalism. In this, attention to social factors is supremely important. Alcoholics Anonymous* have an enormous fund of experience in this field and will give valuable assistance if contacted. In many parts of England there is a local branch. Here patients may meet others who can help to provide them with the right psychological environment. Cut off from his old boon-companions, the patient is likely to feel lonely and isolated, and he will derive comfort and strength from others who, like himself, have gone through the mill. These others will help to reinforce his resolution, rather than weaken it as his old companions would do, and will make no bones of telling him that a slip from teetotalism means relapse into all the old horrors. Old alcoholics usually fraternise well, though there may be more difficulties in this way in this country than in the USA. At many special clinics a group of ex-patients is formed, the members meeting once a month, and being prepared to help each other in emergencies when called on to do so. An element of religious conviction is a valuable aid to resolution, and plays a legitimate part at the meetings. Other voluntary bodies who cater for the needs of alcoholics are the Church Army, the Church of England Temperance Society, the Reginald Carter Foundation, the Joseph Rowntree Social Service Trust, and the Salvation Army.

* Address: Central Service Office, 11 Radcliffe Gardens, London, S.W.10, Telephone 01-352 9669

We cannot emphasise too much how important it is to assess each alcoholic individually and as fully as possible, and to adapt treatment to the needs of each case. It is true that the prognosis is better for patients of good personality, better for men than for women, for the married than for the single, better for those over forty, and for those with a strong incentive to recover. But this does not mean that the outlook is hopeless for patients who fall into other classes than these. Often when a patient is first seen only the bad points are noticed. No assessment should be made until a drunken patient has sobered up and the withdrawal symptoms have been dealt with. Large doses of vitamin C and the B complex should be given parenterally. Tranquillisers should cover the withdrawal period and prevent the onset of delirium tremens (see Chapter I), and antidepressant drugs should be given if there is evidence of depression. Loss of body weight should be corrected and a high protein high calorie diet should be given. Physical examination must be thorough, and should always include ECG and liver function examinations. Only when all this has been done is it right to proceed to the psychiatric assessment, and to decide what methods of treatment are to be used.

Some authorities maintain that many patients only drink to excess in phases of depression. It is true that one meets with cases like this, and there is certainly a relationship between suicide and alcoholism. Nevertheless, we have not been impressed by evidence that such a relationship is at all common. Many patients who give a history of this kind have been found on follow-up to have lost their tendencies to depression completely on giving up the drinking; and their depressive moods were simply hangover effects, reactive to their drinking habits rather than primary. Many true endogenous depressives avoid alcohol, as it only makes them feel more miserable. But patients with a reactive or endogenous depression do seem to obtain some relief from alcohol, especially if there is a good deal of underlying tension.

As the final word, it must be emphasised again that in this field, as elsewhere in psychiatry, it is supremely important to set one's therapeutic target at a practicable level. If one shoots too high, one will only fall short. The target must be judged individually in each case. In trying to reach it, more than one method may have to be used, together or at different stages, and the exploitation of anything at all promising should not be excluded simply because it fails to fit in with purely theoretical preconceptions.

CHAPTER ELEVEN

Insulin Sopor and Coma

Not long after insulin came to be generally used in medicine it was found that in small doses it could be used to improve appetite in cases of anorexia, and that there followed a general improvement in the physical and mental state. The clue was not followed up until Sakel (1938) came to use insulin hypoglycæmia to counter the symptoms of withdrawal in the treatment of morphine addiction. He found that he got the best results when a sufficient dosage of insulin was given to produce clinical hypoglycæmia, and that this phenomenon, hitherto considered dangerous, was readily controlled by the administration of sugar, when the patients were watched throughout. He was led to try its use in the treatment of schizophrenia, and the Vienna Clinic, which had seen the first introduction of the malarial treatment of general paralysis, provided him with the patients to experiment on. The idea seemed bizarre, but it was found to work. Once tried its results were, in individual patients, so surprisingly favourable that its use spread widely and quickly. In the international congress of 1938 reports were presented of its trial in most of the civilised countries of the world; nearly all of them were favourable. Its value as the best available treatment of early schizophrenia was generally accepted at the International Congress of Psychiatry in Paris in 1950.

This was also our view, until the advent of the phenothiazines in the 1950s. We always found that insulin coma, often combined with ECT, gave the best clinical results in treating schizophrenia. But it had to be used selectively and skilfully, and not just left to the young doctor in training. Differing doses, differing lengths of treatment, the use of a variety of ancillary treatments were all important, to get the greatest number of patients well. Even then, however, it is doubtful whether insulin coma therapy with all ancillary therapies succeeded in getting recoveries in much more than 60 per cent of patients; and relapses were far too common. The treatment by phenothiazines, given by mouth or in the form of long-acting intramuscular preparations, together with the continued use of ECT and a modified form of insulin sopor, is now for us the treatment of choice; and it brings about an 80 per cent remission rate in a much shorter time. Further-more the phenothiazines prevent the relapses which were so common after insulin was stopped.

However this book has always emphasised that, if there is a treat-ment that helps any single patient to a greater degree or in a different way than other treatments, then that treatment shall not be given up altogether. And every year, in recent years, cases still continue to occur where there is no sufficient response to drugs and ECT com-bined, or to ECT and narcosis (Chapter III) but who proceed to remit when the longer insulin coma treatment is used. As insulin coma is not used alone, it seems that the comas do not need to be so deep; no more than sopor is sometimes sufficient. The number of patients who need to be so treated may be no more than 10 or so a year even in a very busy hospital; but the method should still be used if less demanding treatments are not adequate, and chronicity is threatened. The occasional remissions so attained are impressive. Once the patient is out of the attack, all the other methods can be added to stabilise recovery. Insulin coma is no longer what it once was, the treatment *par excellence* of schizophrenia; but rightly used with other measures it can still save years of suffering in otherwise resistant patients.

We are, therefore, retaining this chapter in the present edition of the book, so that a guide is still available for those hospitals where the doctors are prepared to use *all* rational methods in the fight against chronicity.

As a general rule we believe it is wise to give most early schizo-phrenics the benefit of a full course of ECT while under the influence of the phenothiazines; and to make sure that the patient's weight is restored to normal with modified insulin treatment. ECT and narcosis may then be tried. Only if this proves insufficient is sopor or full coma treatment possibly required; and often additional light sopors will be sufficient. In cases of longer standing, thought unsuitable for insulin coma treatment because of the duration of the illness or because of splitting of thought and affect, the outlook has now improved to the point where they may now be accessible to insulin treatment in one form or another. For the phenothiazines can help to remedy some of the emotional splitting and personality disorganisation, while insulin benefits other aspects of the total illness.

Following improvement with insulin coma treatment, whether or not it has been combined with the other treatments recommended, it is still very important to keep the patient on maintenance doses of tranquillising drugs for at least two years, and better more, to try to prevent the tendency to relapse. Relapse was the bugbear in the days when insulin treatment was used alone; we now have a means of preventing or at least delaying it.

The Selection of Patients

If insulin treatment is to be used alone, the following are the points to be considered in selecting suitable patients. The matter is now a somewhat theoretical one, since by combining ECT, tranquillisers, narcosis and insulin sopors or light comas, a wider range of patients has become accessible to treatment.

The first point for consideration is the length of duration of the illness, and this does not mean of overt symptoms. The patient who has only recently come to show definite and unmistakable symptoms but has been known to have been gradually becoming queerer for several years is not generally a favourable case for treatment. The most favourable case would be the patient who had been well up to a few days or weeks of being seen, and he should be selected even if there is some lingering doubt of the true nature of the illness and probabilities only speak in favour of schizophrenia. An atypical onset should not be allowed to develop gradually over the course of months into an unmistakable clinical picture before treatment is begun. This position is likely to arise in atypical manic excitements, in obscure confusional states, and even in depressive states with a suggestion of catatonia, of hallucinations or other suggestive symptoms. In any case it must be remembered that schizophrenic psychoses greatly outnumber all others in persons under the age of 30. From the much greater success in the early case it follows that once treatment is decided on it should be begun at the earliest possible moment. Academic doubts about the certainty of the diagnosis should not be allowed to postpone treatment. Valuable time is sometimes wasted, perhaps because the personality is not yet disorganised and affective responses are lively. We have known months to be spent in procrastination, or in an extensive trial of ECT, while physicians talked of 'schizo-affective reactions'. Only when affective flattening was beginning to show was the time for insulin conceded to be ripe— when it was already too late to have its best effects.

The rapidity with which treatment can be inaugurated after the onset of the illness is by far the most important factor therapeutically. Patients treated in the first six months of their illness can be expected to do the best, and with every succeeding month the prognosis worsens. After a duration of two years the outlook is not so good; but even then patient's will be seen, in whom other factors are favourable, and who responds well to treatment.

Next in importance ranks the quality of the personality before the illness began. A frank, open and socially well-adjusted personality reacts better than one which has always been shy, shut off, awkward and autistic. There are probably a number of reasons for this. The autistic personality may not have always been so, but has become so as the result of an early and unrecognised schizophrenic process, which has perhaps become chronic, only to show a recent florid exacerbation. Further, restoration cannot at its optimum be to the same level in the defective as in the thoroughly normal personality. This is perhaps the principal factor that militates against the successful treatment of schizophrenia in the intellectually retarded.

The bodily physique has been found to be of importance, and the pyknic or athletic habitus is more favourable than the asthenic and the dysplastic. As, however, Polonio has found that pyknics do well either with or without treatment, which may be crucial for the hopes of a person of asthenic or dysplastic habitus, the latter should, if anything, be given priority. Freudenberg (1941) has found that an abundance of 'process symptoms', such as hallucinations, thought disorder, primary delusions, passivity feelings, etc., are unfavourable. A history of a previous attack with a full remission is, on the other hand, a favourable sign. It is also our impression that an atypical quality in the symptomatology, and loss of weight during the acute stages of the illness, are both signs of good omen.

There is an important class of patients of which special mention must be made. These are the involutional depressives with a marked paranoid colouring to their symptoms. Too often they are regarded as on a par with other involutional depressives, and receive only ECT. To the therapist's dismay, the affective symptoms recede under this treatment, leaving the patient still deluded, and, as time passes, more and more obviously paraphrenic. If insulin and ECT are combined in the early weeks of treatment, both types of symptoms, paranoid and depressive, will improve together, and better results will be obtained. A still further advance can be obtained, now that the phenothiazine and antidepressant drugs can be used to stabilise the clinical improvement which has been reached. However, this group of patients now generally does very well with ECT and the phenothiazines alone.

Favourable and unfavourable factors seem to act cumulatively, and very satisfactory results can be expected from the patient who shows all of the first and none of the second, whereas if the opposite is true treatment is hardly worth while. In patients who fall between these two groups the results obtained will also be intermediate; there will not be the same frequency of complete success as in the most favourable group, but considerable improvement, sufficient for social rehabilitation, will often be obtained even where a complete remission appears unattainable. It will be seen that the factors that favour a satisfactory response to insulin are also those clinically associated with a higher expectation of spontaneous remission; but this would be an inadequate argument in favour of a *laisser-faire* attitude. The tragedies of neglected insulin treatment in England have been a common-place to the psychiatrist of experience; we have as yet seen no tragedies from premature treatment skilfully applied.

The Risks of Treatment

The risks of insulin coma treatment are always worth while, if the treatment is needed to avoid the drift into chronicity, and even to speed up remission and avoid unnecessary deterioration. In skilled hands the mortality is very low. Mayer-Gross, an expert technician, had no deaths in 1000 cases treated. We had one avoidable death in several hundred patients treated since 1937. Maclay (1953) reported 44 deaths from insulin coma notified to the Board of Control from all mental hospitals in England and Wales, over a five and a half year period when practically every mental hospital in the country was using it.

Massed figures gathered earlier in the United States (Kinsey, 1941) gave a mortality of 90 deaths in 12,000 patients treated, of which about half were due to hypoglycæmic encephalopathy, which is thus seen to be the most serious risk of treatment; it is, on the other hand, an avoidable risk and is the rarer the more skilled the operator. In this series there were also 12 deaths from heart failure, 9 from aspiration pneumonia, 7 from pneumonia occurring otherwise, some of which were probably also avoidable. Earlier New York State hospital figures (Ross and Malzberg, 1939) show that there was a higher mortality rate in the untreated than in the treated patients. It may be that patients with better physique were selected for treatment, and if so that could partly explain the result. It is also true that the patient's bodily health rapidly deteriorates under an acute schizophrenic psychosis, thereby laying him open to a greater risk of tuberculosis and intercurrent disease than where the process is cut short by treatment. Twelve patients died of pulmonary tuberculosis in the control group, only one in the insulin treated group. A mortality of less than 1 per cent cannot be considered a reasonable bar to treatment in the average patient; and the risk of death or serious damage to bodily health can be neglected in all but the physically ill. Any advanced degree of cardiac disease is usually considered a contra-indication to treatment, as are also untreated Graves' disease, severe diabetes, and liver and kidney diseases causing marked impairment of function.

Risks should be balanced against possible gains. Careful trial with early interruption will show how the patient responds, and a therapist who is on the alert for signs of danger can often feel his way, even in the presence of such risks, with adequate safety. Treatment becomes more dangerous with increasing age; and over the age of 45 comas should be less deep and be combined with ECT. If the patient is able to stand up to treatment, it may well be successful.

It may be that after a prolonged series of deep comas patients can show a mild intellectual impairment on psychometric testing. It has not been shown that this change is permanent, and it is certainly less than that also seen in patients of all kinds treated by convulsion therapy, which is far from great or constant. The degree of impairment has been of practical importance in only a handful of patients reported in the literature, and is in any case not comparable with the disability caused by the disease itself. Mental impairment is of much greater importance after long irreversible coma, and a severe Korsakov picture can result from this. This improves somewhat as a rule, but usually leaves a greater or lesser degree of permanent impairment. Its occurrence is the principal reason why the deliberate production of irreversible comas, which often have an immediate curative effect on the schizophrenic process, has not been extensively tried as a method of treatment, and should remain exclusively in the hands of treatment experts of long experience. A minor but still important reason why treatment as early as possible is so desirable is that there is a lesser necessity for repeated deep comas, with the attendant risk of irreversible coma.

The Technique of Treatment

The following technique here described mostly arises from experience gained from 1937 onwards at the Maudsley Hospital in conjunction with Dr. Russell Fraser, and subsequently at Belmont

Hospital with Dr. Nellie Craske and at St. Thomas's Hospital where early cases can be admitted and treated under the conditions obtaining in a general hospital.

Lack of the best facilities should not prevent treatment altogether; and the dangers of treatment under adverse circumstances may have to be balanced against the dangers of delay. It is quite possible to carry out the insulin treatment of schizophrenia in a general ward, with the patient screened off during the coma period. Nevertheless, where schizophrenics are going to be treated in any number a special insulin treatment unit is very desirable. Excited patients cannot be easily handled in general wards, and even quietly behaved schizophrenics are likely to become noisy and difficult during hypoglycæmia. A fairly large room should be taken, in which all the patients it is proposed to treat at one time can be kept economically under observation: off this there should be one or two side-rooms available for the more restless and noisy. These rooms will be kept at a warm temperature, as patients perspire profusely and often throw off their bedclothes. One or two well-padded sides, which can easily be fitted to the bed of a restless patient, reduce the risk of falls and the need for restraint. They can be quietly and quickly removed before full awakening.

To staff the unit a well-trained team of nurses is required, of whom as many as possible should have both a general and a psychiatric training. Experience of medical and surgical emergencies is very valuable in the management of this complicated method of treatment. A sister should be in charge, and on duty during the treatment period every day. Changes in staff from day to day mean that minor alterations in the behaviour of individual patients during sopor and coma may be missed, to the danger of the patients: for behaviour varies widely from patient to patient while remaining very constant to the individual, and a nurse who knows the patient well can detect signs of danger that would not be at all noticeable to anyone else. Every effort should therefore be made to keep the team together, and avoid changes of more than one of the personnel at a time or at less than well-spaced intervals. The sister is of course the most important of all; and it will be her responsibility to assemble and maintain the equipment so that none is astray at an emergency.

The patients also should be kept together through the greater part of the day. Their food intake at every meal has to be carefully supervised, and they themselves must be kept under supervision to prevent the occurrence of after-shocks in the afternoon or evening. If they go out in the afternoon it should be in the company of a nurse supplied with glucose to give to any of them who may suddenly develop a recurrence of hypoglycæmic symptoms. With this social organisation, the patients have the advantage of being in a small treatment group in which staff are able to take a high degree of interest in the care and progress of each individual. They can also form relationships with one another. In the total treatment situation these factors play their part in the socialising of patients who are withdrawn, suspicious and afraid.

Apart from the usual ward apparatus such as intravenous syringes (1 to 20 ml), intravenous needles kept freshly sharpened and in perfect state, a variety of small basins, swabs, surgical spirit, etc., the following special equipment is required: blood-pressure apparatus, air-way, tongue-clips, mouth gag for use in the event of a fit, an emergency apparatus for giving oxygen, ampoules of noradrenaline, sodium amytal, atropine, hydrocortisone, nicotinic acid, vit. B₁, and luminal (all suitable for intravenous and intramuscular use). The means of cutting down on a vein should also be at hand.

On one or two small portable trays are placed the means of nasal interruption. The nasal tubes selected should be stiff and of fine bore, and should be discarded when they get soft from repeated boiling. On the same trays there will be lubricating oil, litmus paper and an aspiration syringe for sucking out a test sample of the stomach contents through the nasal tube. The container of 600 ml of 33 per cent sugared tea (6½ oz. sugar to the pint) is also on this tray. The tea should be prepared before treatment starts in the morning and kept till needed in bulk in a large jug containing sufficient for the needs of all patients. This reservoir of sugared tea must be kept warm, for instance in a large thermos jug, and from it the smaller receptacles for individual trays can be filled just before interruption.

Another special tray or trolley holds the equipment for an emergency intravenous interruption—one or two syringes each containing 20 ml of fresh sterile 33 per cent glucose solution and a sterilised bowl from which they may be rapidly refilled. Sealed bottles of 33 per cent glucose should also be at hand, and only opened before the injection starts. These should be ample amounts of 5 per cent glucose saline ready for emergency intravenous use. Sargant has adapted for use in insulin therapy a composite pressure apparatus which avoids the necessity of having to change syringes in giving large quantities of 33 per cent glucose or glucose salines intravenously, with the risk of losing one's place in the vein every time the change is made. From the illus-

tration it will be seen that it is a simple pressure bottle attached to a
syringe with a side-valve. The needle is inserted into the vein, and with
the first part of the withdrawal of the plunger, blood is sucked into
the syringe, thereby showing the needle is in position. Further with-

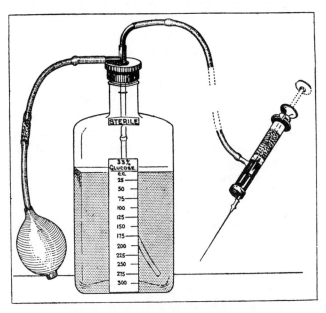

drawal of the plunger beyond the side-valve allows the 33 per cent
glucose solution in the pressure bottle to flow freely through the
syringe into the vein. Bottles of 5 per cent saline are kept in stock
which also fit the same screwcap of the apparatus. If after the 33 per
cent glucose has been given, a change to 5 per cent glucose in saline
is required, this is effected simply by unscrewing one bottle and screw-
ing on the other, pressure being re-established by more hand pumping.
Through all this, the doctor's attention can be concentrated on the
more important job of keeping the needle in place in the vein, a
ticklish matter if the patient is excited and restless, while the nurse
does the pumping and changes the bottles if necessary. Emergency
drugs such as hydrocortisone can be injected into the rubber connection between the bottle and the side-valve syringe without further
interference with the veins.

Three or four trays set ready with this apparatus and one left ready
overnight save time and prevent confusion in an emergency. The
greatest and most conscientious care should be taken by the nurse

preparing these trays to test and re-test the rubber tubing and glass connections. It should not burst apart when most urgently required.

For the avoidance of unnecessary risks, the closest attention to record keeping is required. The quality of the records will often distinguish a good clinic from a careless one. Four separate records may prove valuable. There should be a **temperature chart,** on which are entered the temperature, pulse and respiration rate daily at 6 a.m. and 9 p.m., the diet taken (as 'full', 'half', or 'excess'), any tube feed that may have had to be given, the daily insulin dose, duration of coma and time taken to awake after interruption. Any special complication is marked by an asterisk on the chart. The weight recorded weekly or bi-weekly is also noted. A space is left at the side of the chart for entering the average coma dose of insulin and the maximum safe period of coma for that particular patient, after these have been ascertained during the treatment.

A daily treatment chart is also kept. On it are shown half-hourly records of pulse and respiration rate during treatment, the amount of sweating, the amounts of insulin and glucose given each day, the time of onset of sopor and coma and the time taken to come round after interruption. Details of the patient's behaviour and neurological abnormalities in sopor and coma are also noted here.

In a conspicuous and convenient position in the ward there is a **treatment board.** On it are marked the times of onset of sopor and coma, the time when each patient is due to be interrupted, the time he is actually interrupted and the time of his awakening. It is filled in as these events occur by the doctor and nurses. The important data it provides can be read at a glance from any part of the ward, and help to prevent delays and omissions when emergencies engage the attention of the staff too exclusively to one patient. It is also useful for providing the data of the more detailed and permanent records.

Lastly, there should be an **insulin dosage book,** in which the next day's doses are entered at the end of each morning's work. It is for the information of the sister or nurse in charge when giving the insulin the next morning.

Great importance should be placed on giving a correctly balanced diet during treatment. If possible, measured normal meals should be prescribed and kept approximately to the same content each day. Excess of carbohydrates in the diet enhances the probability of after-shocks by increasing insulin sensitivity. The aim should be to have every patient on a constant diet, a regular daily routine and the same length of coma each morning. When the metabolism is kept steady in this way, it is rare to get sudden changes in the response to the morning insulin or the occurrence of after-shock. Furthermore, any ominous irregularity in behaviour is more likely to be noticed and reported. If the diet taken is inadequate tube-feeding must be resorted to. It must be remembered that a morning dose of insulin may still be in process of absorption for 18 hours after it has been injected.

Much of the treatment devolves on the nurse, and on her skill its success depends. Provided she is well chosen, the more responsibility she is given the better the standard of work she will attain. The sister and the senior nurses should be trained in all details of the technique, from the passing of the stomach-tube to the intravenous interruption, and they should be able to carry out these procedures with confidence. They learn to judge for themselves when the patient is going too deep, or showing abnormal symptoms, and to report to the doctor in time. In an emergency they are taught to act for themselves, and may have to do so if complications arise in several patients at a time and the doctor's whole attention has to be concentrated on only one. If the selected male and female nursing staff are trained to a high pitch of efficiency, a greater number of patients can be treated than if the doctor has to undertake every routine procedure himself. A doctor must always be on call, but it is not necessary with a trained staff for him to be in the insulin room except during the times of sopor and coma. If the nurses have been especially well selected and trained, they can even be left to handle the early stages of sopor and light coma, provided the doctor can get to the treatment ward within a minute of being summoned.

INDUCTION OF COMA

We usually give full treatment on five days a week. On the sixth half-doses of insulin are given, and the seventh is a rest day. If time is short, however, full treatment can be advantageously given on six days a week. The commencing dose of insulin is usually 20 units at 7 a.m. given intramuscularly, into the muscle and not into subcutaneous fat, by the nurse in charge, with the patient fasting from 8 p.m. the night before, and the dose is increased by this amount each day of full treatment until sopor occurs, when progression of doses may be slower. In some centres it is the practice to give a starting dose of 5 to 10 units a day for several days, in order to avoid the risks of insulin sensitivity.

When high doses of insulin have been reached without sopor, the jump may be 30 to 40 units or more each morning, instead of 20 units. It is well to divide big doses into two parts, injecting one at one site and the other at a second, in order to facilitate absorption.

When the doctor has gained experience and confidence, a much speedier method of induction may be used. Shurley and Bond (1948), after preliminary testing for insulin sensitivity, increase the dose by almost geometric progression. On successive days they give 50, 100, 200, 400, 600, 800, and even 1600 units. With this method, interruption is carried out at once when the patient is seen to be in sopor and before the onset of coma. **The next day a materially smaller dose is given.** By this means the minimum safe coma dose is rapidly established. In an acute illness it is certainly disadvantageous to waste weeks in an insulin-resistant patient, while he is gradually brought to coma dosage.

Once coma has been induced, the insulin dose should be adjusted until the minimum satisfactory coma dose has been found. **Neglect of this principle will lead to the occurrence of irreversible comas.** Insulin sensitivity frequently increases during treatment, and the regular daily dose may eventually be stabilised at well under half the amount that was necessary to produce the first coma. Furthermore, often enough the patient seems consciously to resist going into sopor or coma, and when he finally does so a much lower dose of insulin is needed to induce the same state on subsequent occasions. Sometimes sodium amytal 200 to 400 mg. has been given by mouth at 7 a.m. when the insulin is given. This may make the patient less restless and enable him to pass more smoothly into sopor. This dose of amytal is not enough to make the sleep induced by the drug indistinguishable from the hypoglycæmic phenomena. Sometimes very high doses of insulin fail to produce coma at all. Then the doses must be 'swung'. On one day 240 units should be given, and then in rotation 40, 120 and 240 units. In this way insulin sensitivity may often be increased to the point where a satisfactory coma is induced. Insulin resistance up to over 1000 units has, however, been reported, and the phenomena of insulin resistance in schizophrenia are little understood. Some patients, for instance, may go into coma with as little as 40 units or even less.

When the anxiety and fear of an unknown and threatening experience cause patients to resist the loss of consciousness, a trusted nurse or doctor standing quietly by the bed for a short time often enables this hurdle to be taken and a lower dose of insulin to be needed on subsequent occasions. A good atmosphere of confidence, expectation and security will also reduce the general dosage level in a unit.

Patients soon come to accept the daily unconsciousness and the sight of their friends' coma and interruption in a matter of fact way.

A method of lowering insulin resistance which may sometimes be used is to give several ECT during a pause in the course, and then recommence the insulin treatment. Stilbœstrol can also be helpful in some male patients, and is given in doses of 2 to 6 mg each morning before treatment. There are risks: sudden collapses have been seen, necessitating immediate intravenous glucose; and caution is necessary if the method is to be used. Freudenberg (1952) has observed that persistently high insulin requirements are associated with a relatively poor prognosis.

There is much confusion about the correct use of the word 'coma'. It is generally agreed that the length of time the patient is actually unconscious is the best index of the severity of a period of hypoglycæmia. Yet in papers on technique daily 'comas' of two and a half hours are recommended by some, while others advocate only three-quarters of an hour. These discrepancies are due to differences in the meaning given to the word coma. The criteria of coma given by Küppers (1937) have been adopted in our work. He differentiates the stages of loss of consciousness into sopor or pre-coma and true coma. Because of individual variations it is generally found that reflexes, motor phenomena, and most other physical signs cannot be used as criteria of onset of either of these stages, and reliance has to be placed on tests for the presence or absence of 'conscious' or purposive reactions.

The onset of **sopor** is usually indicated by the loss of a normal response to speech and impairment of orientation. But testing will still elicit some confused but purposive responses. There may be some difficulty in deciding the exact time of onset of sopor from earlier degrees of hypoglycæmia. This is not so important as to recognise when sopor deepens into coma. The onset of **coma** is distinguished by the loss of all purposive responses, simulating those of the conscious patient, even on careful testing. There should be no responses from visual, auditory or tactile stimuli. Painful stimuli may still produce some movements, but these are not directed towards the stimulus. Tests should include raising and dropping the patient's arm, trying to make his eyes follow a moving object, and giving a painful stimulus such as pressure on the supraorbital nerve. As coma supervenes the eyes may still remain open and some non-purposive movements persist, but the absence of purposive response can usually be demonstrated by testing. Some patients, while still in sopor and aware of the test stimuli, lose all initiative to respond. They must be distinguished from those in coma, and generally painful stimuli will reveal the difference.

THE SECOND PHASE

The second phase of treatment starts when the patient begins to go into sopor. The regulation of hypoglycæmia to achieve the maximum degree of safety is best done by concentrating on the duration of actual coma rather than of sopor. But very occasionally hypoglycæmia has become 'irreversible' when the patient is allowed to remain at the stage of apparent sopor for a very long time. As a precaution therefore, interruption is carried out after **an hour and a half** of sopor, if coma has not supervened.

When the patient has begun to go into coma, the length of the coma period allowed is increased gradually from five minutes on the first day to what proves to be the maximum safe duration for the individual. Using the criteria given above, the average daily period is half an hour, with considerable individual variations above and below this figure. The physician should not rely on rule of thumb, but should try to discover the safety limit for each patient. It is impossible to dogmatise about this. What, in duration and depth, is perfectly safe for a young man of thick-set physique may cause collapse in an asthenic young woman or an older person. The doctor may be warned that coma is getting too deep by the patient taking over twenty minutes to awake after the nasal feed. He should be guided by this, or interrupt when other signs of excessive depth occur. As the patient's physique improves with treatment, longer comas can be tolerated than initially; this will be indicated by changes in the depth of coma or alteration in waking time. Sometimes it may be desired to take the patient particularly deep. If this is done it is wise to interrupt immediately afterwards by the intravenous route, and not to wait a further twenty minutes or less for the patient to come round after a nasal interruption—unless after thorough testing this has been found to be safe. A particularly severe coma is also apt to cause an increased susceptibility to the next day's insulin and this must be remembered if deep comas are given. To prevent irreversible coma, a shorter coma is advised on the day following a deep coma, particularly if there have been signs of vascular shock or delayed awakening. For the general run of patients, it is best to give a maximum safe coma treatment, and to stick to it each day until recovery is manifest. Some patients, however, do well with submaximal comas, and others need dangerously deep comas to achieve results. This is why results vary from therapist to therapist, and success depends so much on his skill. With increasing depth of coma comes an added risk of irreversible coma, and great skill is needed to handle this emergency, but the risk must be faced if it is necessary to the patient's recovery.

Our remarks apply to comas occurring at the end of the third and the beginning of the fourth hours and are not applicable to those beginning in the fifth hour. Margins of safety must necessarily be lower in the latter. The insulin dosage should be so adjusted as to induce coma about three hours after injection.

SIGNS OF DANGER,
EXCESSIVE DEPTH AND EXHAUSTION

Signs of excessive depth call for interruption at any stage of coma. The peripheral circulation and blood pressure are valuable indicators of circulatory embarrassment, and repeated examination of the finger tips is advisable. When the blood pressure falls below 100 mm Hg or the peripheral circulation becomes poor, the coma should usually be interrupted. A falling blood pressure and a rising pulse or respiration rate should always be regarded as a danger sign, especially if combined with signs of failure of peripheral circulation. Interruption must be done in good time; the tube feed may be vomited or poorly absorbed, and when intravenous interruption is attempted the veins may be found to be collapsed and may occasionally have to be cut down on. In an emergency 33 per cent glucose can be given in amounts up to 50 ml into the vastus externus, and if given with hyalase the patient wakes unaware that he has had an injection. Its absorption needs an active circulation and it may not be sufficient in deep coma. It can, however, be given easily and quickly and will improve conditions for other measures to be taken. It may also be given by sternal puncture, if the equipment is available. Routine interruption by the intravenous instead of the nasal route diminishes the number of these emergencies; but with it, especially in women, veins may soon become thrombosed.

If pulse irregularities first appear during the later stages of coma and the pulse drops below 55, interruption is advisable. Earlier pulse irregularities before the onset of coma often subside with its onset, and should only require caution when they are frequent or persist for over half an hour. As a general rule, provided the blood pressure remains above 100, the pulse volume is good and the pulse rate between 70 and 100 per minute, these patients may be left for three-quarters of an hour before interruption. Some patients who start with extra-systoles in the initial stages of treatment lose them as treatment progresses.

Motor neurological signs are of little help in determining the onset of coma, but they are useful indications of its depth. In the earlier phase various types of movement may appear; they are clinically important only if they are excessive and produce exhaustion. Occasionally they may be the premonitory signs of an impending fit. The movements should not be allowed to continue for over an hour and a half or less if the patient is becoming exhausted by them. Premedication with Luminal 60 to 120 mg or Sodium Amytal 200 to 400 mg may help to diminish them or prevent their occurrence. If the jerking and movements are too great it is sometimes advisable to give intravenous Sodium Amytal 120 to 230 mg at the time to reduce them. The drowsiness induced by such a small dose of intravenous Amytal is easily distinguished from true coma and may enable the patient to pass through the restless phase into coma.

According to Mayer-Gross severe hyperkinetic conditions, restlessness and noisy excitement, can also be controlled by giving a part or the whole of the morning insulin dose intravenously. This brings on the deeper and quieter stages of coma more quickly. One has to learn by trial in each case how much of the total dose to give intramuscularly early on, and how much intravenously at a later stage in the day's treatment. As a general rule, however, intravenous is not to be preferred to intramuscular administration in the absence of any specific indication.

In the deeper stages of coma, waves of extensor tonus occur which are well seen in the arms as combined extension and pronation. They are really important, as they indicate that the safe limit of coma is being reached. But these movements are often precipitated or exaggerated by respiratory embarrassment or circulatory failure. If the air passages are freed by inserting a Hewitt's airway and the extensor tonus then subsides, coma may be allowed to continue. When these waves of extensor tonus are only spasmodic and the state of the circulation is satisfactory, coma may be continued for a further 15 minutes before interruption. But to be on the safe side it may be advisable to interrupt intravenously at the end of this time and not await the slower operation of a nasal feed. If the waves persist for longer than a minute, or the circulation is poor, immediate interruption should be done. Generalised tremor when the patient is not cold is another important sign of excessive depth and calls for early interruption. Interruption should be immediate if pulse and respiration rates fluctuate markedly, as this shows that medullary functions are being affected.

After going into coma sometimes the patient awakens spontaneously, generally after a period of severe spasmodic movements. If he is allowed to relapse into coma again after this should only be for half the normal length of coma, or even less, as this phenomenon may be the precursor of an irreversible coma. The condition of the reflexes is of little help in giving warning of excessive depth. **More important is any change from the usual neurological pattern seen during previous comas.** If unconsciousness seems deeper or the neurological pattern different from the usual for that particular patient, and the circulation is poor, interruption should be done as a precautionary measure. The doctor can then judge whether the particular change observed is actually a sign of danger in this case, and use the knowledge for the handling of subsequent comas. As has been emphasised, every patient is to some extent a law unto himself.

OTHER COMPLICATIONS

Epileptic fits occur early or late in the hypoglycæmic period. The early fit occurs 45 to 100 minutes after the start of treatment and before the onset of coma. It is generally easy to manage. Often after it is over the patient wakes up spontaneously and can drink his sugared tea, or glucose can be given nasally or intravenously if he remains confused. Fits occurring in late sopor or during coma are more dangerous and may be followed, especially in the case of those occurring in the later stages of coma, by delayed recovery or severe shock. Immediate intravenous interruption is necessary for these later fits. Sometimes absorption of sugar from the stomach **does not occur** for some hours afterwards, and therefore further intravenous glucose may be necessary in an hour's time, and even again later in the day. Fluids are valuable when signs of shock are present; up to 500 ml of 5 per cent glucose saline may be given after an initial 250 ml of 33 per cent glucose intravenously. Late fits in the stage of coma probably indicate excessive cerebral glycopenia, and that is why they should be dealt with efficiently and rapidly.

Some patients convulse easily and repeatedly under insulin. If for this or other reasons it is desired to obviate a fit, phenobarbitone 60 to 120 mg may be given each morning with the insulin, either by mouth, or as the soluble preparation by intramuscular injection. Alternatively Epanutin may be used in doses up to 300 mg in the day.

Respiratory complications occasionally arise from aspiration of saliva during coma, because of increase of salivation and diminution of protective reflexes. In the later stages of sopor and during coma the patient is best turned on his side to permit the saliva to drool out of the mouth. Respiratory stridor occurring in coma and not due to blocking of the air passages, nor relieved by passage of an airway, calls for immediate intravenous interruption as it may be a dangerous complication. The same is true of any sign of pulmonary œdema.

Vomiting after nasal interruption can often be dealt with by giving atropine 0·6 to 1·2 mg intramuscularly some minutes before the nasal feed. It is only a dangerous complication when it indicates a condition of vascular shock. If it does, the treatment of the shock will be required, i.e. intravenous glucose and, if necessary, saline. Some therapists give atropine 0·4 to 0·8 mg as a routine at the beginning of each day's treatment, in order to minimise vagotonic symptoms. They believe it conduces to a more comfortable management, both for the patient and the therapist. Mayer-Gross, however, prefers to give 0·6 mg of atropine sulphate as soon as the patient goes into coma.

Vomiting may spread round a small ward like an infection and can generally be dealt with by humour and firmness. There are patients who wake satisfactorily and eat breakfast but who are nauseated and uncomfortable until they eventually vomit; and this will occur day after day unless a little time is spent giving short and fairly light comas until the depth can be gradually increased.

INTERRUPTION

In the lightest stages of hypoglycæmia the patient can, as a rule, drink 600 ml of 33 per cent sugared tea (for preference flavoured with lemon) at the end of treatment. In sopor and coma the same amount has to be given by means of a nasal tube. When the tube has been passed, gastric juice should be withdrawn and tested for acidity with litmus paper before the sugar is poured down the tube. When the gastric juice is only weakly acid a teaspoonful of salt is added in case chloride deficiency is being caused by excessive sweating. When coma has been deep it is unwise to allow more than 20 minutes to elapse in waiting for the patient to come round before giving glucose intravenously. This time may have to be shortened if coma remains deep or other signs of danger are present. When a skilful technique in the preservation of the veins and the use of the pressure bottle has been acquired, therapy may be conducted on the basis of a routine intravenous interruption. Longer and deeper comas can then be given with greater safety. The state of the veins must be kept under observation and one or two unharmed veins should be always kept in reserve for use in emergency; if thrombosis has occurred in most of the conveniently placed veins a return to nasal interruptions is indicated. In interruption by the intravenous route 100 ml of 33 per cent glucose is generally sufficient, but up to 250 ml may be given if needed. The patient receives further sugar to drink when he awakes.

In deciding whether to use nasal or intravenous interruption as a routine, regard must be paid to other things besides the veins. Many patients intensely dislike the slow awakening after nasal interruption, during which the psychotic symptoms such as fear and suspicion may become more florid. Some therapists, on theoretical grounds, believe this stage is therapeutically valuable, and some try to make psychotherapeutic contact with the patient while it lasts. Our feeling is that humanitarian considerations weigh on the other side, and are points in favour of intravenous interruption and abbreviation of the wakening phase to a minimum. If confidence is established by using intravenous interruption for the first two or three awakenings, nasal interruption is then often accepted without comment.

Interruption of coma has recently been made much easier by the use of glucagon, a pancreatic hormone which rapidly increases blood sugar concentration; 1 mg (1 ml) given intramuscularly causes the patient to waken smoothly, as though from sleep, in 10 to 15 minutes. It is expensive and should not generally be used for routine interruption, but only on special occasions. Glucagon can also be most useful in treating late hypoglycæmia.

After the patient has come round he may be given a light breakfast. If glucagon has been given it is important then to provide a large carbohydrate meal without delay, otherwise hypoglycæmia will soon recur. Lunch should be given about 1 p.m., tea at 4.30, and another meal in the evening. The commonest time for after-shocks is about four hours after interruption. In the patient of asthenic build an after-shock may happen at any time, including the night, after treatment, even though he is taking a proper diet and did not go very deep during the treatment hours. They may come on rapidly without much sign of the usual march of events that precede the patient's sopor in treatment. If watched for and dealt with promptly they rarely cause much trouble, but they make the treatment more difficult. If the patient is liable to after-shocks, intravenous instead of intramuscular induction may help to avoid them. If the patient is not taking proper meals, additional glucose may be given prophylactically four hours after interruption or before the time an after-shock can be expected. But it has already been pointed out that too great a carbohydrate preponderance in the diet is undesirable. Regular balanced supervised meals at the right times and a correct morning dose of insulin are the best prevention of after-shocks.

IRREVERSIBLE COMA

This dangerous complication in which unconsciousness persists despite the giving of adequate intravenous glucose. It is most likely to occur in the first fortnight of coma treatment before the patient has become adapted. If this is remembered and special care is taken during this period, its occurrence will become rarer. It is also more likely to occur if insulin dosage has been stepped up steeply and has not been lowered as the patient starts having comas and insulin sensitivity increases.

In severe cases there are pronounced vascular shock, hypertonus, writhing movements, and the condition resembles one of anoxia. The milder cases may merely show delayed local recovery, such as mono-plegia or aphasia or a slight confusional state of short duration. The severe case may involve days of unconsciousness, but with skilful handling death should be avoided. The pathology of the condition is unknown; but treatment must be directed towards facilitating the entry of glucose into the brain cells, combating the alkalosis and anoxia, and restoration of the circulation to its maximal efficiency. We have seen great benefit from the giving of large amounts of intravenous salines in these cases. When the patient does not come round, as he should with the intravenous administration of 100 ml of 33 per cent glucose, this condition must be assumed to be present: and before the needle is withdrawn an additional 150 ml of 33 per cent glucose should be immediately given. If the patient still has not come round, 500 to 1000 ml of 5 per cent glucose in saline should be given *slowly* by the intravenous route. Hourly blood sugars should be commenced and the blood sugar level kept between 100 to 300 by further injections of 33 per cent glucose as required; 100 mg of hydrocortisone should be given intravenously and can be repeated if necessary in one to two hours.

If treatment has been prompt and efficient, the danger of acute collapse soon passes; but the patient may not recover consciousness for many hours or even days. Often absorption from the stomach starts again very slowly, and further intravenous glucose may have to be given later in the day, as insulin is still being absorbed from the morning injection. A stomach-tube should be passed when first aid measures have been completed, and four-hourly nasal feeds of glucose are given. If these are not being absorbed they are withdrawn every 4 hours and fresh glucose substituted until stomach absorption re-starts. Each time the previous feed is found unabsorbed, or has been vomited, 500 ml of 5 per cent glucose in saline should be given intra-venously. The blood sugar should be taken frequently during the day to make certain that hypoglycæmia has not recurred due to lack of stomach absorption and the persisting effects of the insulin. Kay (1961) gives two-hourly nasal feeds containing glucose 50 g, potassium chloride 2 g, sod. bic. 8 g, water 300 ml. When unconsciousness is prolonged and feeds are being absorbed, they should be based on citrated milk and adequate calories, water and carbohydrate. After the first day doses of penicillin should be given. In very severe cases in which it does not appear probable that the patient will come round for a long time, a vein should be cut down on and a continuous glucose saline drip started. Blood transfusions may be given alternat-ing with the saline drip. Eucortone has been recommended. Nicotinic acid 100 mg four-hourly and further injections of vitamin B₁ may also be given during the period of unconsciousness by the intravenous route via the continuous drip. The patient's strength must be main-tained by intravenous feeding till stomach absorption restarts. It is also important to maintain electrolyte balance.

With prompt treatment recovery from this condition generally takes place in the first 24 hours; but a period of unconsciousness lasting six days has been seen, when the doctor had failed to institute emergency measures immediately. After long periods of unconscious-ness very marked impairment of intellectual functions will be seen, but a surprising degree of recovery from this will occur in succeeding weeks and months. Following short-lived irreversible comas some dramatic improvements in schizophrenic symptomatology have been recorded. If, with effective measures, the patient has emerged rapidly from irreversible coma, the fact that the complication has occurred does not imply that treatment should be abandoned. It may be started again in three or four days' time, but thereafter the comas must be kept much shorter and less deep. On several occasions we have known treatment, started again under these circumstances, to proceed with-out further mischance to a successful conclusion.

Clinical Changes produced by Treatment

In patients who are going to react well to the treatment, it will generally be found that after the first few comas wakening from coma leads to an hour or two of a considerably improved mental state. Sometimes in the early case improvement occurs without the coma stage having been reached. The most prominent change is a great improvement in rapport and the affective attitude. For a time the patient regards the doctor and the nurses in a much warmer and more friendly manner, suspicion is for the moment in abeyance and there is often a considerable degree of insight into the delusions, feelings of unreality, etc. After this short interval, however, the patient sinks back into his old state, and remains in it for the rest of the day. Patients who are excited, agitated or panicky are often much improved in this respect for a longer period of time. As the days of treatment succeed one another the beneficial change lasts longer, and the state into which the patient relapses becomes less and less severe, until gradually the improvement is maximal. In the most fortunate patients this may occur with astonishing rapidity, less than a fortnight of intensive therapy sufficing to bring about what appears to be a complete remission.

In order to judge whether the maximum amount of benefit has been gained it is necessary to have a very thorough knowledge of the patient's symptoms and clinical state before beginning treatment. As improvement takes place delusions and other morbid ideas which have hitherto been concealed may be brought to the light of day and give a false impression to the naïve that the state is becoming more acute. A very careful clinical examination should be repeated when the termination of treatment is being considered; and treatment should not be stopped if there are any signs of activity of the disease, unless it is thought hopeless to proceed any further. By this it is not meant that the patient must have full insight into the symptoms of the past, but that there should not still be hallucinations occurring, or feelings of influence or passivity, etc. In any case it is well to give a further 10 to 20 comas after all acute symptoms have cleared.

Furthermore, it is probably desirable to continue a more modified form of insulin treatment until the patient has regained the physique that is normal and healthy for him. It is quite possible that relapse is more likely, even when there is complete restoration of mental normality, if the patient's normal state of bodily health has not been regained. Mental improvement and physical improvement often go side by side, but one may lag behind the other. If the patient regains his normal weight and physical state, and retains his mental symptoms quite unaltered, it is a bad sign, and it is usually not worth proceeding much further.

As has been observed by Polonio, there may be during treatment a change of physique in the somatotonic direction. More is attained by treatment in the asthenic than in the pyknic, though the latter has a better prognosis from the start. The importance of these aspects of physique has also been observed by Kallmann (1946) in his studies of twins. Large gains of weight of up to two stone under treatment are a most favourable omen. This has been confirmed in statistical studies.

The number of comas necessary is a matter of debate. Some experience indicates that the longer courses of treatment give the better results. Polonio found that restriction of the number of comas to 30 would diminish the proportion of successful results by 40 per cent. Mayer-Gross has expressed the opinion that little purpose is served by giving more than 60 comas; Freudenberg will give up to 80 comas in the difficult patient who has potentialities for recovery. In our experience 40 to 60 comas are sufficient for the great majority of patients. Maximal improvement is not always obtained before the end of treatment. In some cases recovery is not completed until two to four weeks after treatment has been finished.

Psychotherapy

It has now been shown that, if the patient can be maintained on phenothiazines by mouth or intramuscularly, the liability to relapse is much reduced. So, in order to maintain and stabilise the recovery, medication should continue for two to five years, or more, after the patient has recovered. We do not know just how long this time for continued drug administration should be. Some patients remain well while on phenothiazines, but relapse as soon as they are taken off them, for many years.

If the patient does relapse, full treatment will be re-instituted. Rarely, a second course of deep insulin may be used in a desperate case. ECT combined with drug therapy is valuable if there is relapse. When other measures fail, the possibility of leucotomy for the relapsing patient should not be forgotten.

Psychoanalysts have for long suffered under the criticism that their method of treatment was ineffective in the psychoses. Rosen some years ago (1947) claimed that he had obtained nearly a 100 per cent recovery rate by the intensive psychotherapy of schizophrenics along analytic lines. These results have never been confirmed by any independent worker. Nevertheless, there is a persisting tendency to suggest psychoanalysis or intensive psychotherapy for early cases of schizophrenia, without resort to physical treatment. As the early months of illness are the time when high rates of remission can be obtained, and the penalty of allowing chronicity to develop is paid by the patient by a lifetime in a mental hospital, it cannot be too forcibly emphasised that, until it is confirmed that psychotheraphy can produce in early cases results comparable with those produced by insulin or other physical treatments, such a suggestion is open to the strongest criticism.

If psychoanalysis is to be given as an experiment, it should at least be combined with the tranquillising drugs or insulin. Levy (1952) has claimed good results from narco-analytic exploration in the recovery stage after interruption in insulin therapy, together with group therapeutic discussions later in the day. Such an approach is moderate and may well be justified, but of course is not necessarily psychoanalytic. Even so much as this should be handled tentatively. We have seen many patients whose schizophrenic illness has become more acute with the emotional stirring up caused by psychoanalytic exploration. Milder psychotherapies on a more superficial level are better adapted to this psychosis.

If, in our view, the time has passed when one can legitimately treat an early and recoverable schizophrenia by non-physical methods alone, this is not to say that psychotherapy does not have a useful part to play, at least in those patients, and they are many, who have other problems besides those arising immediately from the illness itself. Vocational problems and home difficulties will need attention, and the attitude of the relatives to the patient and his oddities may require some guidance. Most of these problems will be best tackled during the stage of convalescence. Many patients make an uninterrupted recovery under tranquillisers, ECT or insulin treatment without any special psychotherapeutic handling whatever. The apparent psychological precipitants of a schizophrenic illness are frequently found, when the insight gained into the illness is fairly complete, to have been not part causes of the illness but the earliest signs of its onset. The type of psychotherapy most required with the schizophrenic patient is of a kind that might be found valuable after any grave physical illness. Once he is recovered the patient has to return to the outside world and try to manage his own affairs without the constant advice of the doctor; it will often help if the way is made a little smoother for him. While the disease is in active progress it is hopeless to try to influence the patient's ways of thinking; but it is not so hopeless when the fundamental thought disorder has been abolished, and there are only a few fragmentary delusional beliefs, suspicions or foci of apprehension which are left over as relics from the past.

In some of the most accessible patients attention to psychotherapeutic aspects, even during the acute stage of the illness, will be repaid. Environmental factors do play a part in the causation of the illness and enquiry along these lines may reveal modifiable factors. Gralnick (1946) and others lay great emphasis on the psychological value of the treatment situation. It is probably beneficial to get into contact with the patient during the best half hour or so of the day immediately on wakening after treatment, and to give him then the impression of friendly assistance, even though, as is probable, any influence one can exert on his morbid ideas is of the most trifling duration. As soon as he is well enough he should be kept fully occupied in the afternoon with occupation therapy, gardening, games, walks, visits to the cinema, and so on. The morale of the insulin ward, and the personal interest of the doctor in the lives and the feelings of his patients, are factors of great value. When recovery has occurred the possibilities of explanation and reassurance are much more favourable. The patient will probably have a very clear memory for a time of his many morbid experiences and will be anxious to get some explanation for them. Reassurance will also often be required on the subject of relapse. It should not be concealed from the patient that relapse may occur, but he should be told that the prospects of treatment need be no worse, should a relapse occur, than they have been with his first illness, and that if he only seeks advice in the early days of such a recurrence, they are bright indeed; he should, of course, on the other hand, be encouraged not to worry about himself, nor to keep forever a finger on the pulse of his mind.

Non-therapy

There is a school that takes an even wider departure from the usual medical attitude even than that adopted by psychoanalysts. Members of this and some kindred splinter groups maintain such tenets as the following:

1. There is no such thing as schizophrenia.

2. There is such a thing as schizophrenia, but it is not a mental illness.

3. Patients (wrongly so called) choose schizophrenia as a way of life.

4. This choice is made, not by the patients, but by hostile and hateful mothers and fathers and other family members.

5. Doctors, and especially psychiatrists, are involved and join in a conspiracy with the family against the schizophrenic.

6. It is really all a big mistake, because the family members are not communicating with one another but talking at cross purposes.

From the therapeutic point of view, the position is reached that, once the schizophrenic has chosen schizophrenia as his way of life, his choice should be respected. He should be understood, and permitted and helped to go his chosen way. Trying to return schizophrenics to 'normality' is merely bludgeoning them back into conformity with an artificial norm set by a profoundly abnormal and hurtful society.

This school is one whose very existence we deplore. There is, indeed, room in the field of abnormal psychology for studies along any number of lines, for every possible division and difference of views, and in fact for any imaginable hypothesis which is capable of scientific testing. But there is no room in medicine for the application of unsubstantiated hypotheses to the exclusion of successful methods of treatment. There is no room in psychiatry, as a caring profession, for an approach to the patient which is 'anti-iatric', which is permissive towards illness and the advance of pathological processes, and refuses to accept medical responsibilities. The observer, medically trained though he be, who works with patients in this way has to blind himself to the remediable sufferings of his protegés, and progressively divorces himself from realistic issues. The patient, permitted to have his delusions and hallucinations, drifts down hill. Eventually, when his best hopes of successful treatment have been lost through inaction, his choice of schizophrenia as a way of life takes him into a chronic ward for long-term care.

Follow-up

When recovery has occurred it is advisable to discharge the patient from hospital as rapidly as possible. A good measure of stability should, however, be obtained. Return to the normal environment, and an abbreviated recollection of the hospital atmosphere will aid the patient in the recovery of his self-confidence and powers of adaptation. Even if they have not been used during the insulin treatment, tranquillising drugs such as chlorpromazine should be given for two years or more to diminish the risk of relapse. During this time it is advisable to keep an eye on the patient in an out-patient clinic fairly regularly at three-monthly or six-monthly attendances. If there is the slightest sign of any relapse it should be promptly dealt with, and though a relapse may occur at any time up to many years later, it is most likely to occur fairly soon.

CHAPTER TWELVE

The Relation of Psychological to Somatic Treatment

In this book we have tried as far as possible to avoid theory and to deal in terms of empirically established facts, even if they were founded on clinical experience and not on the basis of planned experiment. If the reader has found the approach a mechanistic one, this will be because, in our view, both psychological and physical methods of treatment converge, and by different channels impinge upon the same processes, mechanisms and functions.

A purely mechanistic approach in psychiatry is not enough. It may be all right for the medical scientist who is engaged, in a spirit of scepticism, in organising a double-blind drug trial; but it does not provide the most favourable attitude for the therapist. The doctor who is trying to do his best for the single patient must have a philosophy, a treatment-faith, with which to work. It was, in fact, the faith that the shortest road to helping patients often lay in physical treatments that led to the experience out of which this book was created. This is not for every psychiatrist; but some kind of faith he must have, to keep going through many difficulties.

The patient must see that the doctor—the consultant—is determined to help him, and will not merely hand him over to a junior colleague when there is a disappointment; that he understands his suffering; that he will not bear down on him with drastic treatments (such as leucotomy) in conditions in which they would not have been offered to a member of his own family, or tolerated for himself; that he will do everything he can to help, will not give up, will be there to the end. The doctor's faith in his power to help is, of course, a strong and enduring suggestion that help will come, and a therapeutic weapon in its own right; but suggestion by itself is rarely enough, and nearly always fails. It needs the support of something more solid, more physical in fact. It is a terrible mistake to make false promises, hoping that suggestion will do the rest. It doesn't, and then the letdown is catastrophic. Never overstate what you believe you can do. Tell the truth. If you can't be sure of helping, say 'I will do everything to help you', but not 'I can help you'.

More than faith is needed to be effective. The faith that has nothing to back it is the weapon of the quack. The doctor's personality, and his faith in what he can do, will arouse the needed response in the patient, and will carry him on long enough for the effective means of treatment to take effect. We know now that we can help the anxiety neurotics, the depressives, the schizophrenics, even perhaps when the illness has been a long one and adjustments to illness have burdened the patient with habitual incapacities. But most of the patients with sex problems, most of the psychopaths and chronic hysterics, are still beyond our reach.

It is not easy to delimit the roles to be played by the psychological and the somatic approach to treatment. As we see it, it is not helpful to think of psychological events of any kind occurring without some physical or physiochemical change. On the other hand, any such change produces effects in the psychological field, which may be large enough to be observed. Such a view directs attention to the physical aspects of psychological changes as the point where a possible cause may be found, or, even if this is not so, where treatment may at times be most usefully applied. Looking at his problems from this angle, the clinician is encouraged to try lines of treatment which otherwise would not have occurred to him, sometimes with great success. But he is not obliged to make this his only point of view; and if he finds that nothing practical is to be gained from it, he should shift to another. It hardly needs saying that psychodynamic and social chains of cause and effect in the production of mental ill health can often be recognised in individual cases. Each of these in turn may prove the ones most easily influenced by the doctor's intervention; and as often as not he will have to apply his efforts along more than one line at the same time.

In recent years there has been a vast increase in the range and flexibility of the physical methods of treatment. Although psychological and social therapies have made no equivalent advance in methodology, they have benefited from the possibilities of wider application. The whole situation, in fact, has been turned topsy-turvy. In the neuroses, which at one time were considered to be territory reserved for individual psychotherapy, we have seen increasing room for physical methods of treatment, for group psychotherapy, and for a behaviour therapy based on learning and conditioning theory. In the graver psychiatric states, schizophrenia, depression, and the more recalcitrant and incapacitating forms of anxiety and obsessional neurosis, the first attack has had to be given over to the somatic methods, which in speed, convenience and certainty hold great advantages over all others. However, these methods have been so successful, that once they have played their part, re-training and rehabilitation techniques come into their own at a later stage.

Over the same period there has been a shift of emphasis in our conception of the pathogenesis of mental disorder. Symptoms which were once thought to be psychogenic have now been found to rest on a deeper physical deviation. Dynamic interpretations of the development of a mental illness can be misleading even when they are plausible. What appears to be the psychologically precipitating cause is not infrequently the first indication that an attack has started. Or it may be that the individual has been weakened emotionally or physiologically, so that trauma is operative for the first time. A careful examination of the earliest difficulties experienced by our patients before the gross onset of mental disorder will often show that they have only arisen because powers of adaptation were already in decline. The organic causation of apparently psychogenic symptoms is very easy to miss clinically. Bit by bit the syndromes of mental disturbance associated with disorders of electrolyte balance are becoming recognisable, though as yet we have little idea of their prevalence. We may be sure that at the present time we are calling neurotic, and struggling to treat by psychotherapy, a range of illnesses with physical components, whose nature is unrecognised and whose appropriate treatment is unguessed.

Psychogenetic interpretations do not lose their validity with the discovery of a physical ætiology; they merely lose in importance. Psychotherapists, however, have too often devoted the whole of their interest to the psychogenesis, and have too wholeheartedly linked with it their conception of the modifiability of the symptom. The discovery of a real or apparent psychogenesis may be an inadequate guide. The mechanisms by which symptoms develop are an attribute of the human make-up, and to show that they are at work is not to explain their appearance. It is not helpful for any medical purpose to find and demonstrate identical mechanisms in depressives, schizophrenics and neurotics. The pre-occupation with what is common to everyone has obscured the significance of individual and class differences, and has sometimes led the psychotherapist into an undue faith in his powers to make of any man what he will.

While it would seem that everyone is liable to neurotic symptoms if only the stress is sufficient, the degree of liability varies very widely from individual to individual; in some people such symptoms will show only when physical deterioration has taken place. If the previously stable patient is now showing a liability to psychogenic symptoms which was previously foreign to him, if there is evidence of a change of constitution, the suspicion arises that the alteration is based on a physical factor. Certain types of organic disorder seem to be particularly effective in producing neurotic symptoms, others much less so. Hysterical symptoms are common in disseminated sclerosis, rare in syringomyelia; they are common with lesions of the frontal and rare with lesions of the occipital cortex. Broadly speaking, interference with bodily well-being makes a man more, not less, liable to be disturbed by psychogenic stimuli. In the war neuroses, the psychological causes of anxiety and hysteria, till then relatively inoperative, began to have a greater effect when the man had lost severely in weight. The change in physique had altered his disposition and his ability to adapt. Head injuries illustrate the same phenomenon. Psychiatrists and neurologists are very apt to discover in the headaches of the post-concussive the operation of psychological factors, and to conclude therefore that the proper treatment is psychotherapeutic. The change that has escaped notice is that the psychogenic stimuli which now produce symptoms would not have been effective before the injury. The real disability is not a hysterical headache, but an increased susceptibility to hysteria; not the faints, attacks of giddiness or ill temper, which are so clearly due to the circumstances of the moment, but the raised autonomic lability.

Similar changes of disposition are also common in early senility and cerebral arteriosclerosis. Syndromes of this kind are seen more frequently than their causes can be elucidated. In persons showing acute anxiety states, it is sometimes found that the symptoms are in part due to a recent increase in a fluctuating susceptibility to anxiety. But their ætiology remains obscure, and so far it has only been possible to link the menopausal anxiety state with an œstrin deficiency, and the premenstrual tension state with water retention by the body and glandular disturbance.

Genuine psychogenic symptoms are, of course, quite likely to occur in the course of organic or endogenous psychoses. As a rule they are transitory, and can frequently be neglected once their nature is recognised. They represent mere superficial manifestations and have little relation to the main current of change. Remedial treatment of the underlying process takes precedence, as the ordinary methods of dealing directly with such symptoms leaves the patient open to their recurrence. Nevertheless it may be difficult, and accordingly important, to reach an explanation for them. They may be the only visible sign, at least upon superficial enquiry, of a basically physical disorder. If they are misconstrued, valuable time may be lost.

When we are dealing, not with a change of disposition which has been produced by some specific cause or causes, but with a developmental anomaly, there are likely to be serious difficulties in the way of treatment by either psychological or physical means. But this is no reason for despair. One of the outstanding qualities of the chronic neurotic is a lack of general drive; some psychopathic people have an excess of energy which may lead, after the building up of tension, to an explosive outburst. These seem to be primitive biological qualities that may have comparatively simple physical correlates. No very great degree of advance, for instance in endocrinology, may perhaps present us with the means of directly influencing them. Methods of increasing or diminishing the instincts of hunger or sex will overcome many neurotic symptoms. Modified insulin treatment, the antidepressant drugs (and large doses of chlorpromazine in anorexia nervosa) may all, in appropriate circumstances, start a patient eating in a few days, while months of analysis may be needed to achieve the same end by eliciting the psychological causes of a refusal to eat, or may totally fail to produce any worth while change. The operation of prefrontal leucotomy effectively alters the bodily and mental constitution; its disadvantages lie in the fact that it may do both more and less than we want. But the problems of psychotherapy of, for instance, an obsessional before and after leucotomy are quite different. A complicated psychological problem may sometimes be by-passed by a simpler and more direct physical approach. Psychotherapy would have a part to play in adapting the hypertensive patient to a necessary alteration in his mode of life. But if the hypertension is due to destruction by disease of one of his kidneys, while the other is still healthy, a surgical operation may render any re-adaptation superfluous. If there were a means of raising the intelligence of the defective, special education would no longer be needed. If we were provided with the chemical means of speeding the processes of maturation, the emotionally immature psychopaths who make up such a large part of the population in our penal institutions might become accessible to kinder methods of treatment. Until we have such effective means at our disposal, the various psychotherapies remain a necessity.

Although the possibilities of advance along these lines are important, they are still speculative. Physical treatment has established itself in the psychoses, and is becoming nearly as important in the neuroses. But the scope for psychotherapy remains enormous and will probably still expand. It will be long before constitutional peculiarities can be regulated or predetermined, and before the physical and somatopsychic aspects of hysteria, anxiety and other psychopathic behaviour problems are cleared up. There will never be a time when there are not people at odds with themselves or their circumstances, and in need of the help of the trained psychotherapist. In the meanwhile patients must be helped to the best of our ability along whatever lines lie open, regardless of personal predilections. Where we cannot alter the constitution we must try to vary the environment, or the manner in which the environment is dealt with by the individual. The patient can never show the clarity of insight and impartiality of judgment that the physician can, and is often unaware that his symptoms are being caused by factors that lie within his power to alter. In other cases the effective causes of the illness may be clear for all to see, but the co-operation of the physician may be needed for effective action to be taken.

A psychogenetic ætiology is not a *sine qua non* for successful psychotherapy. Even where the symptoms are springing from causes beyond our interference, and are themselves unalterable, much may be done to reduce their disabling effect. Psychotherapy does not consist merely of suggestion and re-education, but may involve a re-orientation of fundamental drives, and, when successful, bring about a far-reaching alteration of the patient's attitude to himself and to his environment. There are few patients who have found the best way of exploiting their positive advantages and of protecting themselves against their defects. Where some organic change has occurred, help in re-adaptation may be imperative. The patient who has undergone leucotomy is often much in need of psychotherapy, even though it be other than of an intensive or analytic kind.

To be effective psychotherapy, like other methods of treatment, must be realistic. It must set its goal within the compass of what is possible to the individual. Environmental circumstances are often very rigidly set and refractory to modification. What is possible for the intelligent may be out of the question for the dull. The mode of expression of temperamental tendencies may be alterable, while the tendencies themselves are beyond our reach. There is no evidence that psychotherapy will provide a personality with qualities it lacks, however frequently these qualities are shown by other persons. The best guide to a fair judgment of a man's capabilities is gained from his own past history, and not from a comparison of his present state with that of the 'normal' individual.

Furthermore, particular symptoms will be capable of treatment in certain settings, in others not. In certain settings they may demand treatment, in others not be worth bothering about. We have seen great pains taken to deal with the functional impotence of a middle-aged man, when it was merely the expression of a not very obvious depression. With attention to the underlying mood change the impotence could have been safely ignored. But in a young man whose marriage is being wrecked by a conditioned ejaculatio præcox, the emphasis might have to be the other way round, and treatment of the impotence regarded as the main method of attack on the associated depression as well.

All methods of treatment involve interfering at some point in the vicious circle that keeps a conditioned response or behaviour pattern alive. Deep psychotherapy may be no more effective than simpler methods, somatic or psychological. Even where the intervention is at a superficial level, it may succeed in abrogating symptoms that follow primitive physiological paths. A girl student, the patient of one of our colleagues, suffered from hyperhidrosis of the hands whenever she sat in the lecture room with men students. It was so excessive that she could not write or touch a book. This symptom was dealt with by a few hypnotic sessions, and deeper conflicts were left for the time being. She was an intelligent girl, and solved most of her problems for herself without help. But the more ingrained a behavioural pattern becomes, the more likely it is that a physical method of treatment will be required to unseat it. Leucotomy may be necessary after years of illness in the chronic anxiety neurotic; but that illness once began as a recent anxiety state, i.e. as a modifiable condition which could perhaps have been finally disposed of by such simple measures as exploration, psychotherapy and environmental readjustment, with or without the aid of drugs.

The type of psychotherapy chosen must be balanced against the patient's constitutional disposition. The hysteric often dislikes going over his past failures and seeing himself exposed as the sport of his own make-up; or, on the contrary, he may delight in confessions of his weakness but with iron-clad complacency defeat all attempts to alter his ways. Psychotherapeutic measures directed primarily towards increasing insight are likely to run up against the blank wall of obstinate self-deception. On the other hand, the hysteric is suggestible, and his suggestibility may be turned to account in procedures of another kind. The obsessional, intellectually over-scrupulous, will not accept the same crude suggestion and persuasion that are willingly absorbed by the hysteric; and though a more analytic approach will not make any difference to the given fact of his obsessional temperament, it will allow him to come to terms with himself, to adjust his life to his limitations, and to exploit his positive qualities, for instance, in types of work that appeal to his liking for detail and accuracy.

The main aim of a psychotherapeutic approach is to alter the attitude of the patient to himself and to his environment. But the aim of psychiatric therapy in the widest sense is to procure the optimal adjustment of the patient and his environment to one another. In the co-ordinated totality of treatment, therefore, psychotherapy has a defined but almost inevitable part. It should indeed precede, accompany and terminate physical therapy, not only in psychiatric but all medical and surgical disorders. Psychological and somatic methods are not mutually exclusive, but should be made complementary to one another. The 'bedside manner' and, for instance, the general medical handling of a case of gastric ulcer, involve the same psychological principles as the treatment of the neurotic individual. An interest in the personalities and lives of patients as human beings should be fostered in medical schools. To attend to the neurotic aspects of bodily disorders, which constantly face the physician and the surgeon, we do not need more psychiatrists. We need rather a wider diffusion of the psychiatric attitude and of psychiatric knowledge among the general medical public. Psychosomatic medicine will do itself no good if it takes yet more patients from a general medical attack. The failure to find a physical pathology for 'effort syndrome' switched all interest to the psychological side. But this in turn proved almost as barren of the possibility of therapeutic advance. Now, in a situation where premature theorising had got us nowhere, empiricism has come to the rescue. Patients of good personality who suffer from effort intolerance, palpitations, gastric upsets and phobic fears, are often greatly helped by the monoamine oxidase inhibitor drugs; and these drugs have been found surprisingly effective in a range of neurotic states that once could only be handled by purely psychotherapeutic methods.

The sociological approach in psychiatry is constantly changing our ideas of what we should call pathological. Important factors in the epidemiology of psychiatric illness are to be found in the social nexus. Many of the nervous complaints of ordinary people are evidence more of a sick state of society than of personal inadequacies. As the population pressure builds up, the decrease in privacy, the multiplying frequency of interpersonal contacts, the increasing tempo and noise and distraction, all tending in the direction of excessive nervous stimulation, are likely to bring about more psychiatric illness. On the other hand, to some extent society adjusts itself to the needs of the situation. Our society is more permissive than it used to be to deviants and rebels. And, for example, as homosexuality becomes a socially acceptable sexual orientation, the need for treatment can be expected to grow less; what we have long regarded as a medical problem may come, by society's self-adjustment, to be no problem at all.

Religious teaching and inspiration have transformed many neurotics and psychopaths from burdens on their families into benefactors of mankind. The drive that is provided by a faith or an idea may be contrasted with that given by nature to the hyperthymic pyknic. The one is well directed, but is liable to fail outside its own field; the other is capable of direction to almost any end, but is in danger of dissipation. A somatic approach is only capable of improving the instrument that is in our hands; psychotherapy may have something to say of the aim towards which it is directed. Both an efficient instrument and a worth-while aim are needed for a satisfactory life.

The main claim of the physical approach, that is the assumption that mental disorders are dependent on physiological changes, is that it is a useful working hypothesis. It has made great advances and looks like making more. It is in line with the main front of biological advance. It is here where psychiatry belongs. There is a tendency today to expand its field unduly, and for the psychiatrist to regard himself as a universal expert. Psychiatry is a young science, and in many fields where it is now being introduced it has more to learn than to teach. We should be more sure of the ground on which we daily tread before we venture too far afield. We are not the sole arbiters on the designing of a brave new world. It is our function as doctors to provide the health with which it may be fought for and enjoyed when won.

Bibliography

This bibliography is not a comprehensive one, but in addition to the references in the text, it includes a selection of some books and articles on physical treatment in psychiatry.

ADDERLEY, D. J., HAMILTON, M. (1953): "Use of succinylcholine in ECT. With particular reference to its effects on blood pressure." *British Medical Journal*, **i**, 195.

ALEXANDER, F., PORTIS, S. A. (1944): "Psychosomatic study of hypoglycaemic fatigue." *Psychosomatic Medicine*, **6**, 191.

ALEXANDER, L. (1953): *Treatment of Mental Disorders*. Philadelphia: Saunders.

ALEXANDER, L. (1956): "Therapeutic process in electroshock and the new therapies. Psychopathological considerations." *Journal of the American Medical Association*, **162**, 966.

ALEXANDER, S. P., BINDELGLAS, P. M. (1956): "Insulin coma therapy in patients resistant to chemotherapy." *Diseases of the Nervous System*, **17**, 220.

ALLEN, C., BROSTER, L. R. (1945): "A further case of paranoid psychosis successfully treated by adrenalectomy." *British Medical Journal*, **i**, 696.

ALPERS, B. J., HUGHES, J. (1942): "Changes in the brain after electrically induced convulsion in cats." *Archives of Neurology and Psychiatry*, **47**, 385.

ANGST, J. (1966): *Zur Atiologie und Nosologie endogener depressiver Psychosen*. Berlin, Springer.

BALLANTINE, H. T., CASSIDY, W. I., FLANAGAN, N. B., MARINO, R. (1967): "Stereotactic anterior cingulotomy for neuropsychiatric illness and intractable pain." *Journal of Neurosurgery*, **26**, 488.

BATT, J. C. (1943): "One hundred depressive psychoses treated with electrically induced convulsions." *Journal of Mental Science*, **89**, 289.

BAYLIS, M., CROWLEY, J., PREECE, J. M., SYLVESTER, P. E., MARKS, V. (1971): "Influence of folic acid on blood-phenytoin levels." *Lancet*, **i**, 62.

BEHRMAN, S. (1969): "Delayed phenytoin idiosyncrasy." *British Medical Journal*, **iv**, 496.

BENNETT, D. (1961): "Treatment of impotence with M.A.O.I." *Lancet*, **ii**, 1309.

BETTS, T. A., KALRA, P. L., COOPER, R., JEAVONS, P. M. (1968): "Epileptic fits as a probable side-effect of amitriptyline: report of 7 cases." *Lancet*, **i**, 390.

BEWLEY, T. H. (1967): "Drug addiction." *British Medical Journal*, **iii**, 603.

BEWLEY, T. H. (1968): "The diagnosis and management of heroin addiction." *Practitioner*, **200**, 215.

BIRLEY, J. L. T. (1964): "Modified frontal leucotomy: a review of 106 cases." *British Journal of Psychiatry*, **110**, 211.

BLAKEMORE C. B., ETTLINGER, G., FALCONER, M. A. (1966): "Cognitive abilities in relation to frequency of seizures and neuropathology of the temporal lobes in man." *Journal of Neurology, Neurosurgery and Psychiatry*, **29**, 268.

BLAKEMORE, C. B., FALCONER, M. A. (1967): "Long-term effects of anterior temporal lobectomy on certain cognitive functions." *Journal of Neurology, Neurosurgery and Psychiatry*, **30**, 364.

BLEULER, M. (1941): "Das Wesen der Schizophrenieremission nach Schock." Behandl Z. Neurol., **173**, 553.

BOND, E. D. (1954): "Results of psychiatric treatments with a control series. A 25-year study." *American Journal of Psychiatry*, **110**, 561.

BRADLEY, J. J. (1958): "Clinical observations on the action of gonadotrophin in adult male psychiatric patients." In *Psychoendocrinology*, Ch. 5. New York, Grune and Stratton.

BURKHARDT, G. (1890): "Uber Rindenexcisionem, als Beitrag zur operativen Therapie der Psychosen." *Allgemeine Zeitschrift für Psychiatrie*, **47**, 463.

BURT, C. G., GORDON, W. F., HOLT, N. F., HORDERN, A. (1962): "Amitryptyline in depressive states: a controlled trial." *Journal of Mental Science*, **108**, 711.

BUTTER, A. J. M. (1952): "Tridione compared with Malidone in the treatment of petit mal." *Journal of Neurology, Neurosurgery and Psychiatry*, **15**, 1.

CADE, J. F. J. (1949): "Lithium salts in the treatment of psychotic excitement. *Medical Journal of Australia*, **ii**, 349.

CAIRNS, H., DAVIDSON, M. A. (1951): "Hemispherectomy in the treatment of infantile hemiplegia." *Lancet*, **ii**, 411.

CAMERON, D. E., PANDE, S. K. (1958): "Treatment of the chronic paranoid schizophrenic patient." *Canadian Medical Association Journal*, **78**, 92.

CATZEL, P. (1966): *Paediatric Prescriber*, 3rd ed. Oxford, Blackwell.

CERLETTI, U., BINI, L. (1938): "L'elettroshock." *Archivio generale di neurologia, psichiatria e psicoanalisi*, **19**, 266.

CLEOBURY, J. F., SKINNER, G. R. B., THOULESS, M. E., WILDY, P. (1971): "Association between psychopathic disorder and serum antibody to herpes simplex virus (type 1)." *British Medical Journal*, **i**, 438.

CONNELL, P. H. (1958): *Amphetamine Psychosis*. London, Chapman and Hall.

CONNORS, C. K., KRAMER, R., ROTHSCHILD, G. H., SCHWARTZ, L., STONE, A. (1971): "Treatment of young delinquent boys with diphenylhydantoin sodium and methylphenidate." *Archives of General Psychiatry*, **24**, 156.

COPPEN, A. (1965): "Mineral metabolism in affective disorder." *British Journal of Psychiatry*, **111**, 1133.

COPPEN, A., SHAW, D. M. (1963): "Mineral metabolism in melancholia." *British Medical Journal*, **ii**, 1439.

COPPEN, A. et al. (1971): "Prophylactic lithium in affective disorders." *Lancet*, **ii**, 275.

DALLY, P. J. (1962): "Fatal reaction associated with tranylcypromine and methylamphetamine." *Lancet*, **i**, 1235.

DALLY, P. J. (1969): *Anorexia Nervosa*. London, Heinemann.

DALLY, P. J., OPPENHEIM, G. B., SARGANT, W. (1958): "Anorexia nervosa." *British Medical Journal*, **ii**, 633.

DALLY, P. J., SARGANT, W. (1960): "A new treatment of anorexia nervosa." *British Medical Journal*, **i**, 1770.

DALLOS, V., HEATHFIELD, K. (1969): "Iatrogenic epilepsy due to antidepressant drugs." *British Medical Journal*, **iv**, 80.

DALTON, K. (1959): "Menstruation and acute psychiatric illnesses." *British Medical Journal*, **i**, 148.

DALTON, K. (1960): "Menstruation and accidents." *British Medical Journal*, **ii**, 1425.

DALTON, K. (1961): "Menstruation and crime." *British Medical Journal*, **ii**, 1752.

DALTON, K. (1964): *The Premenstrual Syndrome*. London, Heinemann.

DEDICHEN, H. H. (1946): "A comparison of 1,459 shock-treated and 969 non-shock-treated psychoses in Norwegian hospitals." *Acta psychiatrica et neurologica*, supp. 37.

DE JONG, R. N. (1951): "Phenurone in the treatment of psychomotor attacks." *American Journal of Psychiatry*, **107**, 825.

DELAY, J. (1949): "Pharmacological explorations of the personality: narcoanalysis and methedrine shock." *Proceedings of the Royal Society of Medicine*, **42**, 491.

DELAY, J. (1950): *Méthodes biologiques en clinique psychiatrique*. Paris, Masson et Cie.

DELAY, J., DENIKER, P. (1952): "Le traitement des psychoses par une méthode neurolytique derivée de l'hibernothérapie." Congrès des médecins alienistes et neurolgistes. Luxembourg, July.

DELAY, J., DENIKER, P., TARDIEU, Y. (1953): "Hibernothérapie et cure de sommeil en thérapeutique psychiatrique et psychosomatique." *Presse médicale*, **61**, 1165.

DELAY, L., DENIKER, P., BUSSON, J. F., HAIM, A. (1959): "Le traitement de états dépressifs par les dérivés de l'acide isonicotinique: isoniazide et iproniazide." *Annales médico-psychologiques*, **i**, 125.

DELAY, J., DENIKER, P., ROPERT, R. (1956): "Four year's experience with chloropmazine in treatment of psychoses." *Presse médicale*, **64**, 493.

DELAY, J., DENIKER, P., ROPERT, R. (1960): "L'action du haloperidol dans les psychoses." Symposium Internat. sur le Haloperidol. *Acta medica*, Belgium, **21**.

DENT, J. Y. (1949): *British Journal of Addiction*, **46**, 20., (1953): *British Journal of Addiction*, **50**, 43.

DENT, J. Y. (1955): *Anxiety and its Treatment: With Special Reference to Alcoholism*, 3rd ed. London, Skeffington.

DEWHURST, K., BEARD, A. W. (1970): "Sudden religious conversions in temporal lobe epilepsy." *British Journal of Psychiatry*, **117**, 497.

DUSSIK, K. T. (1959): "The place of Sakel's insulin coma therapy in an active treatment unit of today." In *Insulin Treatment in Psychiatry*, ed. Rinkel, M. New York, Philosophical Library.

ELBANHAWY, A., SHELDON, P. W. E., PENNYBACKER, J. (1963): "On missing meningiomas." *Journal of Neurology, Neurosurgery and Psychiatry*, **26**, 462.

ELITHORN, A. (1959): "Prefrontal leucotomy and depression." *Proceedings of the Royal Society of Medicine*, **52**, 203.

ELITHORN, A., SLATER, E. (1956): "Prefrontal leucotomy. Views of patients and their relatives." *British Medical Journal*, **ii**, 739.

EMMINGHAUS, H. (1887): "Die Psychischen Störungen des Kindesalters." Addendum to Gerhardt's *Handbuch der Kinderkrankheiten*, Tübingen.

EVANS, V. L. (1945): "Electroconvulsive shock therapy and cardio-vascular disease." *Annals of Internal Medicine*, **22**, 692.

EY, H., FAURE, H. (1956): "Les diverses méthodes d'emploi de la chlorpromazine en thérapeutique psychiatrique et leurs indications." *Encéphale*, **45**, 361.

FABING, H. D. (1948): "Combined coramine-electroshock therapy in the treatment of psychotic excitement." *American Journal of Psychiatry*, **105**, 435.

FALCONER, M. A. (1953): "Discussion on the surgery of temporal lobe epilepsy: surgical and pathological aspects." *Proceedings of the Royal Society of Medicine*, **46**, 971.

FALCONER, M. A. (1954): "Clinical manifestations of temporal lobe epilepsy and their recognition in relation to surgical treatment." *British Medical Journal*, **ii**, 939.

FALCONER, M. A., TAYLOR, D. C. (1967): "Driving after temporal lobectomy for epilepsy." *British Medical Journal*, **i**, 266.

FALCONER, M. A., TAYLOR, D. C. (1968): "Surgical treatment of drug-resistant epilepsy due to mesial temporal sclerosis." *Archives of Neurology*, **19**, 353.

FIAMBERTI, A. M. (1948): "La leucotomia prefrontale transorbita: indicazioni e tecnica." *Archivio di psicologia, neurologia e psichiatria*, **9**, 444.

FIAMBERTI, A. M. (1952): "Acetylcholine in physiopathogenesis and therapy of schizophrenia." *International Congress on Psychiatry* (1950), **4**, 79.

FOLTZ, E. L. (1968): "Current status and use of rostral cingulotomy." *Southern Medical Journal*, **61**, 899.

FRANK, J. (1946): "Clinical survey, and results of 200 cases of prefrontal leucotomy." *Journal of Mental Science*, **92**, 497.

FRANK, J. (1946): "Discussion: prefrontal leucotomy with reference to indications and results." *Proceedings of the Royal Society of Medicine*, **39**, 455.

FRANK J. A. (1953): "A critical evaluation of carbon dioxide inhalation therapy in mental disorders." *American Journal of Psychiatry*, **110**, 93.

FRASER, R., SARGANT, W. (1938): "Diet in nervous and mental disorders." *Practitioner*, **140**, 515.

FRASER, R., SARGANT, W. (1940): "Some points in technique of insulin therapy of psychoses." *Journal of Mental Science*, **86**, 969.

FRASER, R., SMITH, P. H. (1941): "Simmonds' disease or panhypopituitarism (anterior): the clinical diagnosis by combined use of two objective tests." *Quarterly Journal of Medicine*, **10**, 297.

FREEMAN, W. (1949): "Transorbital leucotomy. The deep frontal cut." *Proceedings of the Royal Society of Medicine*, supp. **42**, 8.

FREEMAN, W. (1953): "Hazards of lobotomy. A study of 2,000 operations." *Journal of the American Medical Association*, **152**, 487.

FREEMAN, W. (1953): "Lobotomy and epilepsy. A study of 1,000 patients." *Journal of Neurology* (Minneapolis), **3**, 479.

FREEMAN, W. (1957): "Frontal lobotomy 1936–1956. A follow-up study of 3,000 patients from one to twenty years." *American Journal of Psychiatry*, **113**, 877.

FREEMAN, W., WATTS, J. W. (1946): "Prefrontal lobotomy: survey of 331 cases." *American Journal of the Medical Sciences*, **221**, 1.

FREEMAN, W., WATTS J. W. (1950): *Psychosurgery*, 2nd ed. (1st ed.

1942). Springfield, Ill., Thomas.

FREUDENBERG, R. (1941): "On the curability of mental diseases by 'shock' treatment." *Journal of Mental Science*, **87,** 529.

FREUDENBERG, R. (1947): "Ten years' experience of insulin therapy in schizophrenia." *Journal of Mental Science*, **93,** 9.

FREUDENBERG, R. K. (1952): "Observations on the relation between insulin coma dosage and prognosis in schizophrenia." *Journal of Mental Science*, **98,** 441.

FREYHAN, F. A. (1954): "Prefrontal lobotomy and transorbital leucotomy: a comparative study of 175 patients." *American Journal of Psychiatry*, **111,** 22.

FRIEDMAN, S., MOOORE, B. E., RANGER, C. O., RUSSMAN, C. (1951): "A progress study of lobotomised and control patients." *American Journal of Psychiatry*, **108,** 10.

FRISCH, E. P. (Ed.) (1966): "Chlormethiazole (Heminevrin)—a symposium." *Acta psychiatrica Scandinavica*, supp. **192,** 42.

FROLOV, Y. P. (1938): *Pavlov and His School*. London, Kegan Paul.

FROMMER, E. A. (1968): "Depressive illness in childhood." In *Recent Developments in Affective Disorders*, ed. Coppen, A. and Walk, A. *British Journal of Psychiatry*, Special Publication No. 2.

FROSTIG, J. P. (1940): "Clinical observations in insulin treatment of schizophrenia." *American Journal of Psychiatry*, **96,** 1167.

FULTON, J. F. (1949): *Functional Localisation in the Frontal Lobes and Cerebellum*. Oxford, Oxford University Press.

FULTON, J. F. (1952): "The Frontal Lobes and Human Behaviour." Sherrington Lecture II. Liverpool, University Press.

GATH, D. (1968): "A study of factors influencing referrals made by general practitioners to a child psychiatric department." *Journal of Child Psychology and Psychiatry and Allied Disciplines*, **9,** 213.

GATTOZZI, A. A. (1970): *Lithium in the Treatment of Mood Disorders*. National Institute of Mental Health, U.S.A.

GIBBERD, F. B., DUNNE, J. F., HANDLEY, A. J., HAZLEMAN, B. L. (1970): "Supervision of epileptic patients taking phenytoin." *British Medical Journal*, **i,** 147.

GIBBS, F. A., GIBBS, E. L., LENNOX, W. G. (1937): "Epilepsy: a paroxysmal cerebral dysrhythmia." *Brain*, **60,** 377.

GIBBS, E. L., GIBBS, F. A., FUSTER, B. (1948): "Psychomotor epilepsy." *Archives of Neurology and Psychiatry*, **60,** 331.

GANDER, D. R. (1965): "Treatment of depressive illnesses with combined antidepressants." *Lancet*, **ii,** 107.

GILLIES, H., HICKSON, B., MAYER-GROSS, W. (1952): "A follow-up study of 238 leucotomised patients." *British Medical Journal*, **i,** 527.

GJESSING, R. (1938): "Disturbance of somatic function in catatonic periodic courses and their compensation." *Journal of Mental Science*, **84,** 608; (1939): *Archiv für Psychiatrie und Nervenkrankheiten*, **109,** 525.

GLATT, M. M. (1959): Disulfiram and citrated carbimide in the treatment of alcoholism." *Journal of Mental Science*, **105,** 476.

GOLDIE, L., GREEN, J. M. (1959): "A study of the psychological factors in a case of sensory reflex epilepsy." *Brain*, **82,** 505.

GOLDMAN, D. (1960): "Pharmacological treatment of depression." *Diseases of the Nervous System*, supp. **21,** 74.

GOLLA, F. L. (1946): "Discussion: prefrontal leucotomy with

reference to indications and results." *Proceedings of the Royal Society of Medicine*, **39**, 443.

GOLLA, F. L., HODGE, R. S. (1949): "Hormone treatment of the sexual offender." *Lancet*, **i**, 1006.

GORDON, W. W. (1948): "Cerebral physiology and psychiatry." *Journal of Mental Science*, **94**, 118.

GORNALL, A. G., EGLITIS, B., MILLER, A., STOKES, A. B., DERVAN, J. G. (1953): "Metabolic observations in periodic catatonia." *American Journal of Psychiatry*, **109**, 584.

GOULD, J. (1954): "The use of vitamins in psychiatric practice." *Proceedings of the Royal Society of Medicine*, **47**, 215.

GRALNICK, A. (1945): "A 7-year survey of insulin treatment in schizophrenia." *American Journal of Psychiatry*, **101**, 449.

GRALNICK, A. (1946): "A 3-year survey of electroshock therapy." *American Journal of Psychiatry*, **102**, 583.

GRANT, R. H. E., STORES, O. P. R. (1970): "Folic acid in folate-deficient patients with epilepsy." *British Medical Journal*, **iv**, 644.

GREEN, J. R., DUISBERG, R. E. H., MCGRATH, W. B. (1951): "Focal epilepsy of psychomotor type." *Journal of Neurosurgery*, **8**, 157.

GREENBLATT, M. et al. (1953): "Five-year follow-up in one hundred cases of bilateral prefrontal lobotomy." *Journal of the American Medical Association*, **151**, 200.

GREENBLATT, M., SOLOMON, H. C. (1950): *Studies in Lobotomy*. New York, Grune and Stratton.

GREENBLATT, M., SOLOMON, H. C. (1952): "Survey of 9 years' lobotomy investigations." *American Journal of Psychiatry*, **109**, 267.

GRIFFITH, H., DAVIDSON, M. (1966): "Long-term changes in intellect and behaviour after hemispherectomy." *Journal of Neurology, Neurosurgery and Psychiatry*, **29**, 571.

GRINKER, R. R., SPIEGEL, J. P. (1945): *Men Under Stress*. Philadelphia, Blakiston.

GUEVVANT, J., ANDERSON, W. W., FISCHER, A., WEINSTEIN, M. R., JAROS, R. M., DESKINS, A. (1962): *Personality in Epilepsy*. Springfield, Ill.: Thomas.

GUTTMAN, E., MAYER-GROSS, W., SLATER, E. T. O. (1939): "Short distance prognosis of schizophrenia." *Journal of Neurology and Psychiatry*, **2**, 25.

GUTTMAN E., SARGANT, W. (1937): "Observations on benzendrine." *British Medical Journal*, **i**, 1013.

HAWKINS, J. R., TIBBETTS, R. W. (1956): "CO_2 inhalation therapy in neuroses. Controlled clinical trial." *Journal of Mental Science*, **102**, 52.

HERZBERG, B. N., JOHNSON, A. L., BROWN, S. (1970): Oral contraceptives and premenstrual depression. *Lancet*, **i**, 775.

HILL, D. (1944): "Cerebral dysrhythmia: its significance in aggressive behaviour." *Proceedings of the Royal Society of Medicine*, **37**, 317.

HILL, D. (1947): "Amphetamine in psychopathic states." *British Journal of Addiction*, **44**, 50.

HILL, D., FALCONER, M. A., PAMPIGLIONE, G. (1953): "Discussion on the surgery of temporal lobe epilepsy." *Proceedings of the Royal Society of Medicine*, **46**, 965.

HILL, D., WATTERSON, D. (1942): "Electroencephalographic studies of psychopathic personalities. *Journal of Neurology and Psychiatry*, **5**, 47.

HIMWICK, W. A. (1959): "Biochemical changes in the brain occurring during insulin hypoglycaemia." In *Insulin Treatment in Psychiatry*, ed. Rinkel and Himwich. New York, Philosophical Library.

H. M. BOARD OF CONTROL REPORT (1947): "Prefrontal leucotomy." London: H.M.S.O.

HOCH, P. H., POOL, J. L., RANSOHOFF, J., CATTELL, J. P., PENNES, H. H. (1955): "The psychosurgical treatment of pseudoneurotic schizophrenia." *American Journal of Psychiatry*, 111, 653.

HOLT, W. L., LANDAU, D., VERNON, T. (1950): "Insulin coma treatment of schizophrenia compared to electric coma treatment of patients on sub-shock insulin." *Journal of Nervous and Mental Disease*, 112, 357.

HOMBERGER, A. (1926): *Die Psychopathologie des Kindesalters*, Berlin, Springer.

HOUGHTON, A. W. J. (1971): "Convulsions precipitated by amitriptyline." *Lancet*, i, 138.

HORSLEY, J. S. (1943): *Narco-Analysis*. Oxford, Oxford University Press.

HUNTER BROWN, M., LIGHTHILL, J. A. (1968): "Selective anterior cingulotomy: a psychosurgical evaluation." *Journal of Neurosurgery*, 29, 513.

IBOR, J. LOPEZ (1952): "Indications respectives des méthodes de choc." *International Congress on Psychiatry* (1950), 4, 85.

"Insulin Shock Therapy." Study by the Temporary Commission on State Hospital Problems. New York, 1944.

JACKSON, H. (1954): "Leucotomy. A recent development." *Journal of Mental Science*, 100, 62.

JACOBSEN, E. (1952): "Deaths of alcoholic patients treated with Disulfiram in Denmark." *Quarterly Journal of Studies on Alcohol*, 13, 16.

JACOBSEN, E., MARTEN-LARSEN, O. (1949): "Treatment of alcoholism with tetraethylthiuram disulfide (Antabuse)." *Journal of the American Medical Association*, 139, 918.

JAMES, I. P. (1960): "Temporal lobectomy for psychomotor epilepsy." *Journal of Mental Science*, 106, 543.

JONES, G. N., MCGOWAN, P. K. (1949): "Leucotomy in periodic psychoses." *Journal of Mental Science*, 95, 101.

KALINOWSKY, L. B. (1958): "Appraisal of the 'tranquilizers' and their influence on other somatic treatments in psychiatry." *American Journal of Psychiatry*, 115, 194.

KALINOWSKY, L. B., HOCH, P. H. (1946): *Shock Treatments and other Somatic Procedures in Psychiatry*. London, Heinemann.

KALINOWSKY, L. B., HOCH, P. H. (1961): *Somatic Treatments in Psychiatry*. New York, Grune and Stratton.

KALINOWSKY, L. B., HIPPIUS, H. (1970): *Pharmacological, Convulsive and Other Somatic Treatments in Psychiatry*. New York, Grune and Stratton.

KALLMANN, F. J. (1946): "The genetic theory of schizophrenia." *American Journal of Psychiatry*, 103, 309.

KAY, W. W. (1961): "The treatment of prolonged insulin coma." *Journal of Mental Science*, 107, 194.

KEATING, L. E. (1961): "Epilepsy and behaviour disorder in schoolchildren." *Journal of Mental Science*, 107, 161.

KELLY, D. H. W. (1966): "Measurement of anxiety by forearm blood flow." *British Journal of Psychiatry*, **112**, 789.

KELLY, D. H. W., WALTER, C. J. S., SARGANT, W. (1966): "Modified leucotomy assessed by forearm blood flow and other measurements." *British Journal of Psychiatry*, **112**, 871.

KELLY, D. H. W., WALTER, C. J. S. (1968): "The relationship between clinical diagnosis and anxiety assessed by forearm blood flow and other measurements." *British Journal of Psychiatry*, **114**, 611.

KELLY, D. H. W., WALTER C. J. S., MITCHELL-HEGGS, N., SARGANT, W. (1972): "Modified leucotomy assessed clinically physiologically and psychologically at 6 weeks and 18 months." *British Journal of Psychiatry*. In press.

KELLY, D. H. W., SARGANT, W. (1965): "Present treatment of schizophrenia—a controlled follow-up study." *British Medical Journal*, **i**, 147.

KERSLEY, G. D., MANDEL, L., JEFFREY, M. R., DESMARAIS, N. H. L., BENE, E. (1950): "Insulin and ECT in the treatment of rheumatoid arthritis. Report on a pilot series of cases." *British Medical Journal*, **ii**, 855.

KERSLEY, G. D., MANDEL, L., TAYLOR, K. B., JEFFREY, M. R. (1951): "Spontaneous hypoglycaemia after insulin therapy." *British Medical Journal*, **ii**, 578.

KILOH, L. G., BALL, J. R. B. (1961): "Depression treated with imipramine: a follow-up study." *British Medical Journal*, **ii**, 168.

KINROSS-WRIGHT, V. (1955): "Chlorpromazine treatment of mental disorders." *American Journal of Psychiatry*, **111**, 907.

KINSEY, J. L. (1941): "Incidence and cause of death in shock therapy." *Archives of Neurology and Psychiatry*, **46**, 55.

KLÄSI, J. (1922): "Über die therapeutische Anwendung der 'Dauernarkose' mittels Somnifen bei Schizophrenen." *Zeitschrift für die gesamte Neurologie und Psychiatrie*, **74**, 557.

KLINE, N. S., SAUNDERS, J. C. (1958): "Psychic energizers." *Soc. Biol. Psychiat.* May.

KNIGHT, G. C. (1960): "330 cases of restricted orbital cortex undercutting." *Proceedings of the Royal Society for Medicine*, **53**, 728.

KNIGHT, G. C. (1965): "Stereotactic tractotomy in the surgical treatment of mental illness." *Journal of Neurology, Neurosurgery and Psychiatry*, **28**, 304.

KNIGHT, G. C. (1969): "Bifrontal stereotactic tractotomy: an atraumatic operation of value in the treatment of intractable psychoneurosis." *British Journal of Psychiatry*, **115**, 257.

KOLN, L. C., VOCEL, V. H. (1942): "The use of shock therapy in 305 mental hospitals." *American Journal of Psychiatry*, **99**, 90.

KORENYI, C., WHITTIER, J. R. (1967): "Drug treatment in Huntingdon's disease with special reference to fluphenazine." *Psychiatric Quarterly*, **41**, 203.

KUHN, R. (1963): "Über Kindliche Depressionen und ihre Behandlung." *Schweizéische medizinische Wochenschrift*, **93**, 86.

LABORIT, H., HUGUENARD, P. (1951): "L'Hibernation artificielle par Moyens Pharmacodynamics et Physique." *Presse médicale*, **59**, 1329.

LANGFELDT, E. (1937): "Prognosis in schizophrenia, and the factors influencing the course of the disease." *Acta psychiatrica et neurologica*, supp. **13**.

LE BEAU, J. (1948): "La résection bilatérale de certains aires corticales préfrontales (topectomy)." *Semaine des hôpitaux de Paris*, **60**, 1.

LE BEAU, J. (1954): "Anterior cingulectomy in man." *Journal of Neurosurgery*, **11**, 268.

LEES, F. (1967): "Alcohol and the nervous system." *Hospital Medicine*, **2**, 264.

LEFKOWITZ, M. M. (1969): "Effects of diphenylhydantoin on disruptive behaviour." *Archives of General Psychiatry*, **20**, 643.

LEMERE, F., VOEGTLIN, W. L. (1940): "Conditioned reflex therapy of alcohol addiction; specificity of conditioning against chronic alcoholism." *California and Western Medicine*, **53**, 268.

LEWIN W. (1961): "Observations on selective leucotomy." *Journal of Neurology, Neurosurgery and Psychiatry*, **24**, 37.

LEWIS, A., HOGHUGHI, M. (1969): "An evaluation of depression as a side effect of oral contraceptives." *British Journal of Psychiatry*, **115**, 697.

LEVY, S. (1952): "Narcosynthesis immediately following insulin shock." *American Journal of Psychiatry*, **108**, 611.

LIVINGSTONE, K. E. (1969): "The frontal lobes revisited." *Archives of Neurology*, **20**, 90.

LOEWENSTEIN, J. (1947): *Treatment of Impotence. With Special Reference to Mechanotherapy*. London, Hamilton.

LUESSENHOP, A. J., DE LA CRUZ, T. C., FENICHEL, G. M. (1970): "Disconnection of cerebral hemispheres for intractable seizures: results in infancy and childhood." *Journal of the American Medical Association*, **213**, 1630.

MCCLELLAN, J. H., SCHWARTZ, A. (1953): "The treatment of tuberculous patients with ECT." *American Journal of Psychiatry*, **109**, 899.

MACLAY, W. (1953): "Deaths due to treatment." *Proceedings of the Royal Society of Medicine*, **46**, 13.

MCKISSOCK, W. (1943): "Technique of prefrontal leucotomy." *Journal of Mental Science*, **89**, 194.

MCKISSOCK, W. (1951): "Rostral leucotomy." *Lancet*, **ii**, 91.

MCKISSOCK, W. (1959): "Discussion on psychosurgery." *Proceedings of the Royal Society of Medicine*, **53**, 206.

MCLARDY, T., MEYER, A. (1949): "Anatomical correlates of improvement after leucotomy." *Journal of Mental Science*, **95**, 182.

MALAMUD, N. (1948): "Fatalities resulting from treatment with sub-shock doses of insulin." *American Journal of Psychiatry*, **105**, 373.

MALLINSON, W. P. (1948): "Out-patient electro-convulsive therapy." *British Medical Journal*, **ii**, 641.

MALZBERG, B. (1943): "Outcome of electric shock therapy in New York State hospitals." *Psychiatric Quarterly*, **17**, 154.

MARTENSEN-LARSEN, O. (1953): "Five years' experience with disulfiram (Antabuse) in the treatment of alcoholics." *Quarterly Journal of Studies on Alcohol*, **14**, 406.

MAUDSLEY, H. (1867): *The Physiology and Pathology of the Mind*. London.

MAYER-GROSS, W. (1947): "Discussion: 10 years' experience of insulin treatment in schizophrenia." *Journal of Mental Science*, **93**, 25.

MAYER-GROSS, W. (1951): "Insulin coma therapy of schizophrenia." *Journal of Mental Science*, **97**, 132.

MEDUNA, L. J. (1950): *Carbon Dioxide Therapy*. Springfield, Ill., Thomas.

MEDUNA, L. J. (1952): "Clinical and biochemical indications of the convulsive and of the carbon dioxide treatments." *International Congress on Psychiatry* (1950), **4**, 135.

MEDUNA, L. J. (1958): *Carbon Dioxide Therapy*. Springfield, Ill., Thomas.

MERRITT, H. H., PUTNAM, T. J. (1938): "New series of anti-convulsant drugs tested by experiments on animals." *Archives of Neurology and Psychiatry*, **39**, 1003.

MERRITT, H. H., PUTNAM, T. J. (1945): "Experimental determination of anticonvulsive activity of chemical compounds." *Epilepsia*, **3**, 51.

METTLER, F. A. (Ed.) (1949): *Selective Partial Ablation of Frontal Cortex*. New York, Hoeber.

MEYER, A., BECK, E. (1945): "Neuropathological problems arising from prefrontal leucotomy." *Journal of Mental Science*, **9**, 411.

MYERSON, A., MYERSON, P. G. (1947): "Prefrontal lobotomy in the chronic depressive states of old age." *New England Journal of Medicine*, **237**, 511.

MIRA, E. (1939): "Psychiatric experience in Spanish war." *British Medical Journal*, **i**, 1217.

MITCHELL, W., FALCONER, M. A., HILL, D. (1954): "Epilepsy with fetishism relieved by temporal lobectory." *Lancet*, **ii**, 626.

MONIZ, E. (1936): *Tentatives opératoires dans le traitement de certaines psychoses*. Paris, Masson et Cie.

MONRO, A. B. (1950): "Electronarcosis in the treatment of schizophrenia." *Journal of Mental Science*, **106**, 254.

NEEL, J. V., SCHULL, W. J. (1968): "On some trends in understanding the genetics of man." *Perspectives in Biology and Medicine*, **11**, 565.

OLIVER, W. (1758): "Account of the effects of camphor in a case of insanity." *London Medical Journal*, **6**, 120.

PALMER, H. A. (1937): "The value of continuous narcosis in the treatment of mental disorder." *Journal of Mental Science*, **83**, 636.

PALMER, H. A. (1945): "Abreactive techniques: ether." *Journal of the Royal Army Medical Corps*, **84**, 86.

PAPEZ, J. W. (1937): "A proposed mechanism of emotion." *Archives of Neurology and Psychiatry*, **38**, 725.

PARE, C. M. B., REES, L., SAINSBURY, M. J. (1962): "Differentiation of two genetically specific types of depression by the response to antidepressants." *Lancet*, **ii**, 1340.

PARSONAGE, M. J., NORRIS, J. W. (1967): "Use of diazepam in treatment of severe convulsive status epilepticus." *British Medical Journal*, **iii**, 85.

PAVLOV, I. P. (1941): "Conditioned reflexes and psychiatry." In *Lectures on Conditioned Reflexes*, vol. 2. Translated and edited by Horsley Gantt. London, Lawrence and Wishart.

PENFIELD, W., ERICKSON, T. C. (1941): *Epilepsy and Cerebral Localisation*. London, Baillière, Tindall and Cox.

PENFIELD, W., FLANIGIN, H. (1950): "Surgical therapy of temporal lobe seizures." *Archives of Neurology and Psychiatry*, **64**, 491.

PEOPLES, S. A., GUTTMANN, E. (1936): "Hypertension produced with benzedrine: its psychological accompaniments." *Lancet*, **i**, 1107.

Perris, C. (Ed.) (1964): "A study of bipolar (manic-depressive) and unipolar recurrent depressive psychoses." *Acta psychiatrica et neurologica scandinavica*, supp. **194**.

Pippard, J. (1955): "Rostral leucotomy." *Journal of Mental Science*, **101**, 756.

Pippard, J. (1955): "Personality changes after rostral leucotomy." *Journal of Mental Science*, **101**, 774.

Pippard, J. (1955): "Second leucotomies." *Journal of Mental Science*, **101**, 788.

Pippard, J. (1962): "Leucotomy in Britain today." *Journal of Mental Science*, **108**, 249.

Polatin, P., Hoch, P. (1945): "Electroshock therapy in pregnant mental patients." *New York State Journal of Medicine*, **45**, 1562.

Polatin, P., Spotnitz, H. (1946): "Effects of combined ambulatory insulin and electroshock therapy in the treatment of schizophrenia." *New York State Journal of Medicine*, **46**, 2648.

Polatin, P., Spotnitz, H., Weisel, B. (1940): "Ambulatory insulin treatment of mental disorders." *New York State Journal of Medicine*, **40**, 843.

Polonio, P. (1951): "L'insuline et l'insuline-cardiazol dans les maladies mentales." *Anais portugueses de psiquiatria*, **3**, 87.

Polonio, P. (1952): "L'insuline et l'insuline-cardiazol dans les maladies mentales." *International Congress on Psychiatry* (1950), **4**, 184.

Polonio, P., Slater, E. (1954): "A prognostic study of insulin treatment in schizophrenia." *Journal of Mental Science*, **100**, 442.

Pool, J. L. (1949): "Topectomy." *Proceedings of the Royal Society of Medicine*, supp. **42**, 1.

Pool, J. L. (1951): "Topectomy, 1946–1951. Report on 106 consecutive non-project topectomy operations." *Transactions of the College of Physicians of Philadelphia*, **19**, 49.

Poppen, J. L. (1948): "Technique of prefrontal lobotomy." *Journal of Neurosurgery*, **5**, 514.

Powell, L. W. *et al.* (1958): "Acute meprobamate poisoning." *New England Medical Journal*, **259**, 716.

Prinzmetal, A., Bloomberg, W. (1935): "Use of benzedrine for from treatment of narcolepsy." *Journal of the American Medical Association*, **105**, 2051.

Rees, L. (1949): "Electronarcosis in treatment of schizophrenia." *Journal of Mental Science*, **95**, 625.

Rees, L. (1950): "Insulin therapy." In *Recent Progress in Psychiatry*, **2**, 635. London, Churchill.

Rees, L. (1952): "A comparative study of the value of insulin coma, electronarcosis, electroshock and leucotomy in treatment of schizophrenia." *International Congress on Psychiatry* (1950), **4**, 303.

Report of Advisory Committee on the Health and Welfare of Handicapped Persons (1967): *People with Epilepsy*. London, H.M.S.O.

Rice, D. (1956): "The use of lithium salts in the treatment of manic states." *Journal of Mental Science*, **102**, 604.

Richens, A., Rowe, D. J. F. (1970): "Disturbance of calcium metabolism by anticonvulsant drugs." *British Medical Journal*, **iv**, 73.

ROHDE, P., SARGANT, W. (1961): "Treatment of schizophrenia in general hospitals." *British Medical Journal*, **ii**, 67.

ROSEN, J. N. (1947): "The treatment of schizophrenia psychosis by direct analytic therapy." *Psychiatric Quarterly*, **21**, 3.

ROSS, J. R., MALZBERG, B. (1939): "A review of the results of the pharmacological shock therapy and metrazol convulsive therapy in New York State." *American Journal of Psychiatry*, **96**, 297.

ROSS, T. A. (1937): *The Common Neuroses: Their Treatment by Psychotherapy*. London, Wood.

ROTH, M. (1956): "Affective disorders arising in the senium." *Journal of Mental Science*, **102**, 141.

ROWNTREE, D. W., KAY, W. W. (1952): "Clinical, biochemical and physiological studies in cases of recurrent schizophrenia." *Journal of Mental Science*, **98**, 100.

RYLANDER, G. (1948): "Personality analyses before and after prefrontal lobotomy." *Proceedings. Association for Research in Nervous and Mental Disease*, **27**, 691.

RYLE, A., POND, D. A., HAMILTON, M. (1965): "The prevalence and patterns of psychological disturbance in children of primary age." *Journal of Child Psychology and Psychiatry and Allied Disciplines*, **6**, 101.

SAKEL, M. (1938): "The pharmacological shock treatment of schizophrenia." *Nervous and Mental Diseases Monograph Series*, no. 62. New York, Nervous and Mental Disease Publ. Co.

SAKEL, M. (1952): "Insulinotherapy and shock therapies." *International Congress on Psychiatry* (1950), **4**, 163.

SANDISON, R. A., SPENCER, A. M., WHITELAW, J. D. A. (1954): "The therapeutic value of lysergic acid diethylamide (LSD 25) in mental illness." *Journal of Mental Science*, **100**, 491.

SANDS, D. E. (1946): "Electric convulsion therapy in 301 patients in a general hospital." *British Medical Journal*, **ii**, 289.

SARGANT, W. (1942): "Physical treatment of acute war neuroses: some clinical observations." *British Medical Journal*, **ii**, 574.

SARGANT, W. (1943): "Physical treatment of acute psychiatric states." *War Medicine*, **4**, 577.

SARGANT, W. (1946): "Discussion: prefrontal leucotomy with reference to indications and results." *Proceedings of the Royal Society of Medicine*, **39**, 458.

SARGANT, W. (1947): "Discussion: 10 years' experience of insulin therapy in schizophrenia." *Journal of Mental Science*, **93**, 22.

SARGANT, W. (1948): "Some observations on abreaction with drugs." *Digest of Neurology and Psychiatry*, **16**, 193.

SARGANT, W. (1949): "Some cultural group abreactive techniques and their relation to modern treatments." *Proceedings of the Royal Society of Medicine*, **42**, 367.

SARGANT, W. (1951a): "The mechanism of conversion." *British Medical Journal*, **ii**, 311.

SARGANT, W. (1951b): "Leucotomy in psychosomatic disorders." *Lancet*, **ii**, 87.

SARGANT, W. (1952): "Indications and mechanism of abreaction and its relation to the shock therapies." *International Congress on Psychiatry* (1950), **4**, 192.

SARGANT, W. (1952): "Anxiety states and their treatment by

intravenous acetylcholine." *Proceedings of the Royal Society of Medicine*, **45**, 515.

SARGANT, W. (1953): "Ten years' clinical experience of modified leucotomy operations." *British Medical Journal*, **ii**, 800.

SARGANT, W. (1957): "Aim and method in treatment: twenty years of American and British psychiatry." *Journal of Mental Science*, **103**, 699.

SARGANT, W. (1957): *Battle for the Mind*. London, Heinemann; New York, Doubleday.

SARGANT, W. (1958): "Sedatives and tranquillizers." *British Medical Journal*, **ii**, 1031.

SARGANT, W. (1960): "Some newer drugs in the treatment of depression and their relation to other somatic treatments." *Psychosomatics*, **1**, no. 1.

SARGANT, W. (1961): "Drugs in the treatment of depression." *British Medical Journal*, **i**, 225.

SARGANT, W. (1961): "The physical treatments of depression: their indications and proper use." *Journal of Neuropsychiatry, Supplement No. 1*, **2**.

SARGANT, W. (1961): "The treatment prognosis for functional psychosis in Great Britain." *American Journal of Psychiatry*, **117**, 29.

SARGANT, W. (1962): "The present indications for leucotomy." *Lancet*, **i**, 1197.

SARGANT, W. (1963): "Combining the antidepressant drugs." *Lancet*, **ii**, 634; *British Medical Journal*, **ii**, 806.

SARGANT, W., CRASKE, N. (1941): "Modified insulin therapy in war neuroses." *Lancet*, **ii**, 212.

SARGANT, W., DALLY, P. J. (1962): "Treatment of anxiety states by antidepressant drugs." *British Medical Journal*, **i**, 6.

SARGANT, W., SHORVON, H. J. (1945): "Acute war neuroses: special reference to Pavlov's experimental observations and mechanism of abreaction." *Archives of Neurology and Psychiatry*, **54**, 231.

SARGANT, W., SLATER, E. (1940): "Acute war neuroses." *Lancet*, **ii**, 1.

SARGANT, W., SLATER, E. (1950): "Treatment of obsessional neurosis." *Proceedings of the Royal Society of Medicine*, **43**, 1007.

SARGANT, W., SLATER, E. (1951): "Physical methods of treatment in psychiatry." *British Medical Journal*, **i**, 1315.

SARGANT, W., SLATER, E. (1952): "Influence of the 1939–45 war on British psychiatry." *International Congress on Psychiatry* (1950), **6**, 180.

SARGANT, W., WALTER, C. J. S., WRIGHT, N. (1966): "New treatment of some chronic tension states." *British Medical Journal*, **i**, 322.

SCHOU, M. (1960): "Lithium in psychiatric therapy." *Psychopharmacologia*, **1**, 65.

SCOVILLE, W. B. (1960): "Late results of orbital undercutting." *American Journal of Psychiatry*, **117**, 525.

SCOVILLE, W. B., WILK, E. K., PEPE, A. J. (1951): "Selective cortical undercutting." *American Journal of Psychiatry*, **107**, 730.

SEAGER, C. P., BIRD, R. L. (1962): "Imipramine with electrical treatment in depression: a controlled trial." *Journal of Mental Science*, **108**, 704.

SEIGNOT, M. (1961): "Un cas de maladie de tic de Gilles de la

Tourette guéri par le R.1625 (haliperidol)." *Annales médico-psychologiques*, **119**, 578.

SHEPHERD, M., OPPENHEIM, A. N., MITCHELL, S. (1966): "Childhood behaviour disorders and the child guidance clinic: an epidemiological study." *Journal of Child Psychology and Psychiatry and Allied Disciplines*, **7**, 39.

SERAFETINIDES, E. A., FALCONER, M. A. (1962): "The effects of temporal lobectomy in epileptic patients with psychosis." *Journal of Mental Science*, **108**, 584.

SHORVON, H. J. (1946): "The depersonalisation syndrome." *Proceedings of the Royal Society of Medicine*, **39**, 779.

SHORVON, H. J. (1947a): "Prefrontal leucotomy and the depersonalisation syndrome." *Lancet*, **ii**, 714.

SHORVON, H. J. (1947b): "Benzedrine in psychopathy and behaviour disorders." *British Journal of Addiction*, **44**, 58.

SHORVON, H. J. (1953): "Abreaction." *Proceedings of the Royal Society of Medicine*, **46**, 158.

SHORVON, H. J., RICHARDSON, J. S. (1949): "Sudden obesity and psychological trauma." *British Medical Journal*, **ii**, 951.

SHORVON, H. J., ROOK, A. J., WILKINSON, D. S. (1950): Psychological treatment in skin disorders with special reference to abreactive techniques." *British Medical Journal*, **ii**, 1300.

SHORVON, H. J., SARGANT, W. (1957): "Excitatory abreaction: special reference to its mechanism and the use of ether." *Journal of Mental Science*, **93**, 709.

SHURLEY, J. T., BOND, E. D. (1948): "Insulin shock therapy in schizophrenia." *Veterans Administration Medical Bulletin*, **10**, 501.

SILFENOS, P. E. (1952): "A case of anorexia nervosa treated successfully by lobotomy." *American Journal of Psychiatry*, **109**, 356.

SIMON, J. L., TAUBE, H. (1946): "A preliminary study of the use of methedrine in psychiatric diagnosis." *Journal of Nervous and Mental Disease*, **104**, 593.

SLATER, E., BEARD, A. W., GLITHERO, E. (1963): "The schizophrenia-like psychoses of epilepsy." *British Journal of Psychiatry*, **109**, 95.

SLATER, P., SARGANT, W., GLEN, M. (1942): "Influence of Sodium Amytal on intelligence test scores." *Lancet*, **i**, 676.

SMITH, A. D. M. (1960): "Megaloblastic madness." *British Medical Journal*, **ii**, 1840.

SNAITH, R. P., MEHTA, S., RABY, A. H. (1970): "Serum folate and vitamin B_{12} in epileptics with and without mental illness." *British Journal of Psychiatry*, **116**, 179.

SPIEGEL, E. A., WYCIS, H. T. (1951): "Stereoencephalotomy." *Journal of Neurophysiology*, **8**, 452.

SPIEGEL, E. A., WYCIS, H. T. (1952): *Stereoencephalotomy.* New York, Grune and Stratton.

SPIEGEL, E. A., WYCIS, H. T., FREED, H., ORCHINIK, C. W. (1956): "A follow-up study of patients treated by thalamotomy and by combined frontal and thalamic lesions." *Journal of Nervous and Mental Disease*, **124**, 399.

STANLEY, W. J., FLEMING, H. (1962): "A clinical comparison of phenelzine and electro-convulsive therapy in the treatment of depressive illness." *Journal of Mental Science*, **108**, 708.

STENGEL, E. (1950): "A follow-up investigation of 330 cases treated by prefrontal leucotomy." *Journal of Mental Science*, **96**, 633.

STEVENS, D. A., BOYDSTUN, J. A., DYKMAN, R. A., PETERS, J. E., SINTON, D. W. (1967): "Presumed minimal brain dysfunction in children." *Archives of General Psychiatry*, **16**, 281.

STEVENSON, G. H., MCCAUSLAND, A. (1953): Prefrontal lobotomy for the attempted prevention of recurring manic depressive illness. *American Journal of Psychiatry*, **109**, 662.

STRÖM-OLSEN, R., CARLISLE, S. (1971): "Bifrontal stereotactic tractotomy: a follow-up of its effects on 210 patients." *British Journal of Psychiatry*, **118**, 141.

SYDENSTRICKER, V. P., CLECKLEY, H. M. (1941): "Effect of nicotinic acid in stupor, lethargy and various other psychiatric disorders." *American Journal of Psychiatry*, **98**, 83.

TAYLOR, D. C., FALCONER, M. A. (1968): "Clinical, socio-economic and psychological changes after temporal lobectomy for epilepsy." *British Journal of Psychiatry*, **114**, 1247.

THORPE, F. T. (1958): "An evaluation of prefrontal leucotomy in the affective disorders of old age: a follow-up study." *Journal of Mental Science*, **104**, 403.

TODD, J., COLLINS, A. D., MARTIN, F. F. R., DEWHURST, K. E. (1962): "Mental symptoms due to insulincomata. Report on two cases." *British Medical Journal*, **ii**, 828.

TOOTH, G. C., NEWTON, M. P. (1961): *Leucotomy in England and Wales 1942–1954*. London, H.M.S.O.

TOW, P. M. (1955): "Personality changes following frontal leucotomy." London, Oxford.

TOW, P. M., LEWIN, W. (1953): "Orbital leucotomy." *Lancet*, **ii**, 644.

TOWER, D. B. (1957): In *Modern Trends in Neurology* (2nd series), ed. Williams, D. London, Butterworths.

WALSH, P. J. F. (1962): "Korsakov's psychosis precipitated by convulsive seizures in chronic alcoholics." *Journal of Mental Science*, **108**, 560.

WALTER, C. J. S., MITCHELL-HEGGS, N., SARGANT, W. (1972a): "Modified narcosis, ECT and antidepressant drugs: a review of technique and immediate outcome of 679 courses of combined treatment in 484 patients." *British Journal of Psychiatry*. In press.

WALTER, C. J. S., MITCHELL-HEGGS, N., SARGANT, W. (1972b): "Treatment with modified narcosis: a retrospective controlled follow-up study of 106 patients." *British Journal of Psychiatry*. In press.

WEBB, H. E., LASCELLES, R. G. (1962): "Treatment of facial and head pain associated with depression." *Lancet*, **i**, 355.

WEIR MITCHELL, S. (1885): *Fat and Blood*, 4th ed. Philadelphia: Lippincott.

WEISS, G., WERRY, J., MINDE, K., DOUGLAS, V., SYKES, D. (1968): "The effects of dextroamphetamine and chlorpromazine on behaviour and intellectual functioning." *Journal of Child Psychology, Psychiatry and Allied Disciplines*, **9**, 145.

WEST, E. D., DALLY, P. J. (1959): "Effects of iproniazid in depressive syndromes." *British Medical Journal*, **i**, 1491.

WILCOX, P. H. (1960): "Drugs and electroshock treatment." *Progress in Neurology and Psychiatry*, **15**, 535.

WILCOX, P. H. (1958): "Abreaction produced by low non-convulsive electrostimulation." *Diseases of the Nervous System*, **19**, 87.

WILL, O. A., DUVAL, A. N. (1947): "Use of electroshock therapy in

psychiatric illness complicated by pulmonary tuberculosis."
Journal of Nervous and Mental Diseases, **105,** 637.

WILL, O. A., REHFELDT, F. C., NEUMANN, F. C. (1948): "A fatality
in electroshock therapy." *Journal of Nervous and Mental Disease*,
107, 105.

WILLIAMS, D. (1941): "The significance of an abnormal EEG."
Journal of Neurology and Psychiatry, **4,** 257.

Witts Committee on the Safety of Drugs. Ministry of Health Report,
February 1964.

WORSTER-DROUGHT, C. (1970): "Epileptic death due to suffocation
during sleep." *Lancet*, **ii,** 876.

YOUNG, C. J. (1949): "Leucocyte counts in prevention of drug
agranulocytosis." *British Medical Journal*, **ii,** 261.

ZIEGLER, L. H. (1943): "Bilateral prefrontal lobotomy: survey."
American Journal of Psychiatry, **100,** 178.

Index